GREEK MYTHS

Robert Graves

GREEK MYTHS

Illustrated Edition

CASSELL

Cassell Publishers Limited
Wellington House, 125 Strand
London WC2R OBB

Originally published in two volumes
by Penguin Books in 1955
Hardback edition first published
by Cassell & Co Ltd in 1958
This condensed and illustrated edition
first published 1981
Reprinted 1985, 1992, 1993, 1995

This condensation of *Greek Myths* is the work of John Buchanan-Brown

ISBN 0 304 30720 3

Typesetting by D. P. Media Limited, Hitchin, Hertfordshire

Printed by Canale S.p.A., Turin, Italy

frontispiece: *Statue of Zeus (Vatican Museum)*
opposite: *Battle of the Centaurs and Lapiths (Vatican Museum)*

CONTENTS

ACKNOWLEDGEMENTS

The publishers are grateful to the undermentioned for permission to reproduce the illustrations appearing on the following pages:

Sonia Halliday: 25, 30 top, 59, 118 top, 123

Michael Holford: 18 top, 19, 26, 30 bottom, 36, 38, 42, 54 top, 55, 69, 74 bottom, 79, 106, 107, 128 bottom, 138 bottom, 147, 151, 156, 158, 160 left, 178, 179, 187, 210

The Mansell Collection: 5, 13, 27 bottom, 47, 58, 64, 78 top, 104, 112, 115 bottom, 134, 160 right, 164 top, 192, 194, 198

Photoresources: 51 top, 63, 74 top, 86, 87 bottom, 91, 101, 115 top, 131, 162, 203 bottom, 206

Scala: 2, 50, 54 bottom, 146, 202, 207

Rev. Professor Raymond V. Schoder, S. J.: 18 bottom, 22, 43, 51 bottom, 71, 87 top, 93, 98, 99, 118 bottom, 136, 143, 150, 164 bottom, 168, 170, 171, 174, 175, 182, 183, 203 top

Ronald Sheridan: 11, 23, 27 top, 31, 34, 66, 78 bottom, 88, 96, 110, 114, 126, 128 top, 138 top, 154, 190, 214

Weidenfeld & Nicolson: 16, 17

1

IN THE BEGINNING

The Pelasgian Creation Myth

IN THE BEGINNING, EURYNOME, the Goddess of All Things, rose naked from Chaos, but found nothing substantial for her feet to rest upon, and therefore divided the seas from the sky, dancing lonely upon its waves. She danced towards the south, and the wind set in motion behind her seemed something new and apart with which to begin a work of creation. Wheeling about, she caught hold of this north wind, rubbed it between her hands, and behold! the great serpent Ophion. Eurynome danced to warm herself, wildly and more wildly, until Ophion, grown lustful, coiled about those divine limbs and was moved to couple with her. So Eurynome was got with child.

Next, she assumed the form of a dove, brooding on the waves and, in due process of time, laid the Universal Egg. At her bidding, Ophion coiled seven times about this egg, until it hatched and split in two. Out tumbled all things that exist, her children: sun, moon, planets, stars, the earth with its mountains and rivers, its trees, herbs, and living creatures.

Next, the goddess created the seven planetary powers, setting a Titaness and a Titan over each. But the first man was Pelasgus, ancestor of the Pelasgians; he sprang from the soil of Arcadia, followed by certain others, whom he taught to make huts and feed upon acorns, and sew pig-skin tunics such as poor folk once wore in Euboea and Phocis.

The Homeric and Orphic Creation Myths

Some say that all gods and all living creatures originated in the stream of Oceanus which girdles the world, and that Tethys was the mother of all his children.

But the Orphics say that black-winged Night, a goddess of whom even Zeus stands in awe, was courted by the Wind and laid a silver egg in the womb of Darkness; and that Eros was hatched from this egg and set the Universe in motion. Eros was double-sexed and golden-winged and, having four heads, sometimes roared like a bull or a lion, sometimes hissed like a serpent or bleated like a ram. Night lived in a cave with him, displaying herself in triad: Night, Order, and Justice. Before this cave sat the inescapable mother Rhea, playing on a brazen drum, and compelling man's attention to the oracles of the goddess. Eros created earth, sky, and moon, but the triple-goddess ruled the universe, until her sceptre passed to Uranus.

Marble statue of the Cycladic Mother Goddess (National Archaeological Museum, Athens)

The Olympian Creation Myth

At the beginning of all things Mother Earth emerged from Chaos and bore her son Uranus as she slept. Gazing down fondly at her from the mountains, he showered fertile rain upon her secret clefts, and she bore grass, flowers, and trees, with the beasts and birds proper to each. This same rain made the rivers flow, so that lakes and seas came into being.

Her first children of semi-human form were the hundred-handed giants Briareus, Gyges, and Cottus. Next appeared the three wild, one-eyed Cyclopes, builders of gigantic walls and master-smiths, whose sons Odysseus encountered in Sicily. Their names were Brontes, Steropes, and Arges, and their ghosts have dwelt in the volcano Aetna since Apollo killed them in revenge for the death of Asclepius.

The Five Ages of Man

Some say that Earth bore men spontaneously, as the best of her fruits. These were the so-called golden race, subjects of Cronus, who lived without cares or labour, eating only acorns, wild fruit, and honey that dripped from the trees, drinking the milk of sheep and goats, never growing old, dancing, and laughing much; death, to them, was no more terrible than sleep. They are all gone now, but their spirits survive as genii of happy rustic retreats, givers of good fortune, and upholders of justice.

Next came a silver race, eaters of bread, likewise divinely created. The men were utterly subject to their mothers and dared not disobey them, although they might live to be a hundred years old. They were quarrelsome and ignorant, and never sacrificed to the gods but, at least, did not make war on one another. Zeus destroyed them all.

Next came a brazen race, who fell like fruits from the ash-trees, and were armed with brazen weapons. They ate flesh as well as bread, and delighted in war, being insolent and pitiless men. Black Death has seized them all.

The fourth race of men was brazen too, but nobler and more generous, being begotten by the gods on mortal mothers. They fought gloriously in the siege of Thebes, the expedition of the Argonauts, and the Trojan War. These became heroes, and dwell in the Elysian Fields.

The fifth race is the present race of iron, unworthy descendants of the fourth. They are degenerate, cruel, unjust, malicious, libidinous, unfilial, treacherous.

The Castration of Uranus

Uranus fathered the Titans upon Mother Earth, after he had thrown his rebellious sons, the Cyclopes, into Tartarus, a gloomy place in the Underworld which lies as far distant from the earth as the earth does from the sky; it would take a falling anvil nine days to reach its bottom. In revenge, Mother Earth persuaded the Titans to attack their father; and they did so, led by Cronus, the youngest of the seven, whom she armed with a flint sickle. They surprised Uranus as he slept, and it was with the flint sickle that the merciless Cronus castrated him, grasping his genitals with the left hand (which has ever since been the hand of ill-omen) and afterwards throwing them, and the sickle too, into the sea by Cape Drepanuum. But drops of blood flowing from the wound fell upon Mother Earth, and she bore the Three Erinnyes, furies who avenge crimes of parricide and perjury – by name Alecto, Tisiphone, and Megaera.

The Titans then released the Cyclopes from Tartarus, and awarded the sovereignty of the earth to Cronus.

However, no sooner did Cronus find himself in supreme command than he confined the Cyclopes to Tartarus again together with the Hundred-handed Ones and, taking his sister Rhea to wife, ruled in Elis.

The Dethronement of Cronus

Cronus married his sister Rhea, to whom the oak is sacred. But it was prophesied by Mother Earth, and by his dying father Uranus, that one of his own sons would dethrone him. Every year, therefore, he swallowed the children whom Rhea bore him: first Hestia, then Demeter and Hera, then Hades, then Poseidon.

Rhea was enraged. She bore Zeus, her third son, at dead of night on Mount Lycaeum in Arcadia, where no creature casts a shadow and, having bathed him in the River Neda, gave him to Mother Earth; by whom he was carried to Lyctos in Crete, and hidden in the cave of Dicte on the Aegean Hill. Mother Earth left him there to be nursed by the Ash-nymph Adrasteia and her sister Io, both daughters of Melisseus, and by the Goat-nymph Amaltheia. His food was honey, and he drank Amaltheia's milk, with Goat-Pan, his foster-brother.

Around the infant Zeus's golden cradle, which was hung upon a tree (so that Cronus might find him neither in heaven, nor on earth, nor in the sea) stood the armed Curetes, Rhea's sons. They clashed their spears against their shields, and shouted to drown the noise of his wailing, lest Cronus might hear it from far off. For Rhea had wrapped a stone in swaddling clothes, which she gave to Cronus on Mount Thaumasium in Arcadia; he swallowed it, believing that he was swallowing the infant Zeus.

Curetes clanging armour
to drown the cries of the
infant Zeus. A terracotta
relief (British Museum)

Zeus grew to manhood among the shepherds of Ida, occupying
another cave; then sought out Metis the Titaness, who lived beside
the Ocean stream. On her advice he visited his mother Rhea, and
asked to be made Cronus's cup-bearer. Rhea readily assisted him in
his task of vengeance; she provided the emetic potion, which Metis
had told him to mix with Cronus's honeyed drink. Cronus, having
drunk deep, vomited up first the stone, and then Zeus's elder
brothers and sisters. They sprang out unhurt and, in gratitude, asked
him to lead them in a war against the Titans, who chose the gigantic
Atlas as their leader; for Cronus was now past his prime.

The war lasted ten years but, at last, Mother Earth prophesied
victory to her grandson Zeus, if he took as allies those whom Cronus
had confined in Tartarus; so he came secretly to Campe, the old
gaoleress of Tartarus, killed her, took her keys and, having released
the Cyclopes and the Hundred-handed Ones, strengthened them
with divine food and drink. The Cyclopes thereupon gave Zeus the
thunderbolt as a weapon of offence; and Hades, a helmet of darkness;
and Poseidon, a trident. After the three brothers had held a council of
war, Hades entered unseen into Cronus's presence, to steal his

weapons; and while Poseidon threatened him with the trident and thus diverted his attention, Zeus struck down with the thunderbolt. The three Hundred-handed Ones now took up rocks and pelted the remaining Titans, and a sudden shout from Goat-Pan put them to flight. The gods rushed in pursuit. Cronus, and all the defeated Titans, except Atlas, were confined in Tartarus and guarded there by the Hundred-handed Ones. Atlas, as their war-leader, was awarded an exemplary punishment, being ordered to carry the sky on his shoulders.

The Birth of Athene

Athene's own priests tell the following story of her birth. Zeus lusted after Metis the Titaness, who turned into many shapes to escape him until she was caught at last and got with child. An oracle of Mother Earth then declared that this would be a girl-child and that, if Metis conceived again, she would bear a son who was fated to depose Zeus, just as Zeus had deposed Cronus, and Cronus had deposed Uranus. Therefore, having coaxed Metis to a couch with honeyed words, Zeus suddenly opened his mouth and swallowed her, and that was the end of Metis, though he claimed afterwards that she gave him counsel from inside his belly. In due process of time, he was seized by a raging headache as he walked by the shores of Lake Triton, so that his skull seemed about to burst, and he howled for rage until the whole firmament echoed. Up ran Hermes, who at once divined the cause of Zeus's discomfort. He persuaded Hephaestus to fetch his wedge and beetle and make a breach in Zeus's skull, from which Athene sprang, fully armed, with a mighty shout.

The Fates

There are three conjoined Fates, robed in white, whom Erebus begot on Night: by name Clotho, Lachesis, and Atropos. Of these, Atropos is the smallest in stature, but the most terrible.

Zeus, who weighs the lives of men and informs the Fates of his decisions can, it is said, change his mind and intervene to save whom he pleases, when the thread of life, spun on Clotho's spindle, and measured by the rod of Lachesis, is about to be snipped by Atropos's shears.

Others hold, on the contrary, that Zeus himself is subject to the Fates, as the Pythian priestess once confessed in an oracle; because they are not his children, but parthenogenous daughters of the Great Goddess Necessity, against whom not even the gods contend, and who is called 'The Strong Fate'.

The Birth of Aphrodite

Aphrodite, Goddess of Desire, rose naked from the foam of the sea and, riding on a scallop shell, stepped ashore first on the island of Cythera; but finding this only a small island, passed on to the

Peloponnese, and eventually took up residence at Paphos, in Cyprus, still the principal seat of her worship. Grass and flowers sprang from the soil wherever she trod. At Paphos, the Seasons, daughters of Themis, hastened to clothe and adorn her. She takes the air accompanied by doves and sparrows.

Hera and Her Children

Hera, daughter of Cronus and Rhea, having been born on the island of Samos or, some say, at Argos, was brought up in Arcadia by Temenus, son of Pelasgus. The Seasons were her nurses. After banishing their father Cronus, Hera's twin-brother Zeus sought her out at Cnossus in Crete or, some say, on Mount Thornax in Argolis, where he courted her, at first unsuccessfully. She took pity on him only when he adopted the disguise of a bedraggled cuckoo, and tenderly warmed him in her bosom. There he resumed his true shape and ravished her, so that she was shamed into marrying him.

All the gods brought gifts to the wedding; notably Mother Earth gave Hera a tree with golden apples, which was later guarded by the Hesperides in Hera's orchard on Mount Atlas. She and Zeus spent their wedding night on Samos, and it lasted three hundred years.

To Hera and Zeus were born the deities Ares, Hephaestus, and Hebe, though some say that Hephaestus was her parthenogenous child – a wonder which Zeus would not believe until he had imprisoned her in a mechanical chair with arms that folded about the sitter, thus forcing her to swear by the River Styx that she did not lie.

Zeus and Hera

Only Zeus, the Father of Heaven, might wield the thunderbolt; and it was with the threat of its fatal flash that he controlled his quarrelsome and rebellious family of Mount Olympus. He also ordered the heavenly bodies, made laws, enforced oaths, and pronounced oracles. When his mother Rhea, foreseeing what trouble his lust would cause, forbade him to marry, he angrily threatened to violate her. Though she at once turned into a menacing serpent, this did not daunt Zeus, who become a male serpent and twining about her in an indissoluble knot, made good his threat. It was then that he began his long series of adventures in love. He fathered the Seasons and the Three Fates on Themis; the Charites on Eurynome; the Three Muses on Mnemosyne, with whom he lay for nine nights; and, some say, Persephone, the Queen of the Underworld, whom his brother Hades forcibly married, on the nymph Styx. Thus he lacked no power either above or below earth; and his wife Hera was equal to him in one thing alone: that she could still bestow the gift of prophecy on any man or beast she pleased.

A time came when Zeus's pride and petulance became so intolerable that Hera, Poseidon, Apollo, and all the other Olympians, except Hestia, surrounded him suddenly as he lay asleep on his

*The birth of Aphrodite
(Museo delle Terme,
Rome)*

couch and bound him with rawhide thongs, knotted into a hundred knots, so that he could not move. He threatened them with instant death, but they had placed his thunderbolt out of reach and laughed insultingly at him. While they were celebrating their victory, and jealously discussing who was to be his successor, Thetis the Nereid, foreseeing a civil war on Olympus, hurried in search of the hundred-handed Briareus, who swiftly untied the thongs, using every hand at once, and released his master. Because it was Hera who had led the conspiracy against him, Zeus hung her up from the sky with a golden bracelet about either wrist and an anvil fastened to either ankle. The other deities were vexed beyond words, but dared attempt no rescue for all her piteous cries. In the end Zeus undertook to free her if they swore never more to rebel against him; and this each in turn grudgingly did. Zeus punished Poseidon and Apollo by sending them as bond-servants to King Laomedon, for whom they built the city of Troy; but he pardoned the others as having acted under duress.

Births of Hermes, Apollo, Artemis and Dionysus
Amorous Zeus lay with numerous nymphs descended from the Titans or the gods and, after the creation of man, with mortal women too; no less than four great Olympian deities were born to him out of wedlock. First, he begat Hermes on Maia, daughter of Atlas, who bore him in a cave on Mount Cyllene in Arcadia. Next, he begat Apollo and Artemis on Leto, daughter of the Titans Coeus and Phoebe, transforming himself and her into quails when they coupled;

but jealous Hera sent the serpent Python to pursue Leto all over the world, and decreed that she should not be delivered in any place where the sun shone. Carried on the wings of the South Wind, Leto at last came to Ortygia, close to Delos, where she bore Artemis, who was no sooner born than she helped her mother across the narrow straits, and there, between an olive-tree and a date-palm growing on the north side of Delian Mount Cynthus, delivered her of Apollo on the ninth day of labour. Delos, hitherto a floating island, became immovably fixed in the sea and by decree no one was allowed either to be born or to die there: sick folk and pregnant women were ferried over to Ortygia instead.

Dionysus springing from the thigh of Zeus (Vatican Museum)

Finally, Zeus, disguised as a mortal, had a secret love affair with Semele ('moon'), daughter of King Cadmus of Thebes, and jealous Hera, disguising herself as an old neighbour, advised Semele, then already six months with child, to make her mysterious lover a request: that he would no longer deceive her, but reveal himself in his true nature and form. How, otherwise, could she know that he was not a monster? Semele followed this advice and, when Zeus refused her plea, denied him further access to her bed. Then, in anger, he appeared as thunder and lightning, and she was consumed. But Hermes saved her six-months' son; sewed him up inside Zeus's thigh, to mature there for three months longer; and, in due course of time, delivered him. Thus Dionysus is called 'twice-born', or 'the child of the double door'.

The Birth of Eros

Some argue that Eros, hatched from the world-egg, was the first of the gods since, without him, none of the rest could have been born. Others hold that he was Aphrodite's son by Hermes, or by Ares, or by her own father, Zeus; or the son of Iris by the West Wind. He was a wild boy, who showed no respect for age or station but flew about on golden wings, shooting barbed arrows at random or wantonly setting hearts on fire with his dreadful torches.

above: *The birth of Athene. Detail of a vase (British Museum)*

opposite: *Eros (British Museum)*

right: *Zeus and Hera (Archaeological Museum, Palermo, Sicily)*

2

THE OLYMPIANS

Poseidon's Nature and Deeds

WHEN ZEUS, POSEIDON, and Hades, after deposing their father Cronus, shook lots in a helmet, for the lordship of the sky, sea, and murky underworld, leaving the earth common to all, Zeus won the sky, Hades the underworld, and Poseidon the sea. Poseidon, who is equal to his brother Zeus in dignity, though not in power, and of a surly, quarrelsome nature, at once set about building his under-water palace off Aegze in Euboea. In its spacious stables he keeps white chariot horses and a golden chariot, at the approach of which storms instantly cease.

Needing a wife who would be at home in the sea-depths, he courted Thetis the Nereid; but when it was prophesied by Themis that any son born to Thetis would be greater than his father, he allowed her to marry a mortal named Peleus. Amphitrite, whom he next approached, fled to the Atlas Mountains to escape him; but he sent messengers after her, among them one Delphinus, who pleaded Poseidon's cause so winningly that she yielded. Poseidon set Delphinus's image among the stars as a constellation, the Dolphin.

Amphitrite bore Poseidon three children: Triton, Rhode, and Benthesicyme; but he caused her almost as much jealousy as Zeus did Hera by his love affairs with goddesses, nymphs, and mortals.

Poseidon is greedy of earthly kingdoms, and once claimed possession of Attica by thrusting his trident into the acropolis at Athens, where a well of sea-water immediately gushed out and is still to be seen. Later, during the reign of Cecrops, Athene came and took possession in a gentler manner, by planting the first olive-tree beside the well. Poseidon, in a fury, challenged her to single combat, but Zeus interposed and ordered them to submit the dispute to arbitration. Zeus himself expressed no opinion, but while all the other gods supported Poseidon, all the goddesses supported Athene. Thus, by a majority of one, the court ruled that Athene had the better right to the land, because she had given it the better gift.

Poseidon also disputed Troezen with Athene; and on this occasion

Zeus issued an order for the city to be shared equally between them. Next, he tried unsuccessfully to claim Aegina from Zeus, and Naxos from Dionysus; and in a claim for Corinth with Helius received the Isthmus only, while Helius was awarded the Acropolis. In fury, he tried to seize Argolis from Hera, refusing to appear before his Olympian peers who, he said, were prejudiced against him. Zeus, therefore, referred the matter to the River-gods Inachus, Cephissus, and Asterion, who judged in Hera's favour.

Poseidon boasts of having created the horse, though some say that, when he was newly born, Rhea gave one to Cronus to eat; and of having invented the bridle, though Athene had done so before him; but his claim to have instituted horse-racing is not disputed. Certainly, horses are sacred to him, perhaps because of his amorous pursuit of Demeter. It is said that, wearied and disheartened by her search for her daughter, Persephone, and disinclined for passionate dalliance she transformed herself into a mare. She did not, however, deceive Poseidon, who transformed himself into a stallion and covered her, from which outrageous union sprang the nymph Despoena and the wild horse Arion.

Hermes's Nature and Deeds

When Hermes was born on Mount Cyllene his mother Maia laid him in swaddling bands on a winnowing fan, but he grew with astonishing quickness into a little boy, and as soon as her back was turned, slipped off and went looking for adventure. Arrived at Pieria, where Apollo was tending a fine herd of cows, he decided to steal them. But, fearing to be betrayed by their tracks, he quickly made shoes from the bark of a fallen oak and tied them to the feet of the cows, which he then drove off by night. Apollo discovered the loss, but Hermes's trick deceived him, and he was forced to offer a reward for the apprehension of the thief. Silenus and his satyrs spread out in different directions to track him down, but without success until a party of them passed through Arcadia, and heard the muffled sound of music. The nymph Cyllene, from the mouth of a cave, told them that a most gifted child, to whom she was acting as nurse, had constructed an ingenious musical toy from the shell of a tortoise and some cow-gut, with which he had lulled his mother to sleep.

'And from whom did he get the cow-gut?' asked the alert satyrs, noticing two hides stretched outside the cave. 'Do you charge the poor child with theft?' asked Cyllene. Harsh words were exchanged.

At that moment Apollo came up, and entering the cave, he awakened Maia and told her severely that Hermes must restore the stolen cows. Maia pointed to the child, still wrapped in his swaddling bands and feigning sleep. 'What an absurd charge!' she cried. But Apollo had already recognized the hides. He picked up Hermes, carried him to Olympus, and there formally accused him of theft, offering the hides as evidence. Zeus, loth to believe that his own

*Poseidon. Detail from a
bronze statue (National
Archaeological Museum,
Athens)*

The Rhodes Aphrodite (Rhodes Museum)

new-born son was a thief, encouraged him to plead not guilty, but Apollo would not be put off and Hermes, at last, confessed.

'Very well, come with me,' he said, 'and you may have your herd. I slaughtered only two, and those I cut up into twelve equal portions as a sacrifice to the twelve gods.'

'*Twelve* gods?' asked Apollo. 'Who is the twelfth?'

'Your servant, sir,' replied Hermes modestly. 'I ate no more than my share, though I was very hungry, and duly burned the rest.'

Now, this was the first flesh-sacrifice ever made.

The two gods returned to Mount Cyllene, where Hermes retrieved something that he had hidden underneath a sheepskin.

'What have you there?' asked Apollo.

In answer, Hermes showed his newly-invented tortoise-shell lyre, and played such a ravishing tune on it with the plectrum he had also invented that he was forgiven at once. He led Apollo to Pylus, and there gave him the remainder of the cattle, which he had hidden in a cave.

'A bargain!' cried Apollo. 'You keep the cows, and I take the lyre.'

'Agreed,' said Hermes, and they shook hands on it.

While the hungry cows were grazing, Hermes cut reeds, made them into a shepherd's pipe, and played another tune. Apollo, again delighted, cried: 'A bargain! If you give me that pipe, I will give you this golden staff with which I herd my cattle; in future you shall be the god of all herdsmen and shepherds.'

'My pipe is worth more than your staff,' replied Hermes. 'But I will make the exchange, if you teach me augury too.'

'I cannot do that,' Apollo said, 'but if you go to my old nurses, the Thriae, they will teach you.'

They again shook hands and Apollo, taking the child back to Olympus, told Zeus all that had happened. Zeus could not help being amused. 'You seem to be a very ingenious, eloquent, and persuasive godling,' he said.

'Then make me your herald, Father,' Hermes answered, 'and I will be responsible for the safety of all divine property, and never tell lies, though I cannot promise always to tell the whole truth.'

'That would not be expected of you,' said Zeus, with a smile. 'But your duties would include the making of treaties, the promotion of commerce, and the maintenance of free rights of way for travellers on any road in the world.' Zeus gave him a herald's staff which everyone was ordered to respect; a round hat against the rain, and winged golden sandals which carried him about with the swiftness of wind.

Afterwards, the Thriae showed Hermes how to foretell the future from the dance of pebbles in a basin of water; and he himself invented both the game of knuckle-bones and the art of divining by them. Hades also engaged him as his herald, to summon the dying gently and eloquently, by laying the golden staff upon their eyes.

He then assisted the Three Fates in the composition of the Alphabet, invented astronomy, the musical scale, the arts of boxing and gymnastics, weights and measures and the cultivation of the olive-tree.

Hermes had numerous sons, including Echion the Argonauts' herald; Autolycus the thief; and Daphnis the inventor of bucolic poetry.

Aphrodite's Nature and Deeds

Aphrodite could seldom be persuaded to lend the other goddesses her magic girdle which made everyone fall in love with its wearer; for she was jealous of her position. Zeus had given her in marriage to Hephaestus, the lame Smith-god; but the true father of the three children with whom she presented him – Phobus, Deimus, and Harmonia – was Ares, the God of War. Hephaestus knew nothing of the deception until, one night, the lovers stayed too long together in bed at Ares's Thracian palace; then Helius, as he rose, saw them and told Hephaestus.

Hephaestus angrily retired to his forge, and hammered out a bronze hunting-net, as fine as gossamer but quite unbreakable, which he secretly attached to the posts and sides of his marriage-bed. He told Aphrodite: 'Dear wife, I am taking a short holiday on Lemnos, my favourite island.' Aphrodite did not offer to accompany him and, when he was out of sight, sent hurriedly for Ares. The two went merrily to bed but, at dawn, found themselves entangled in the net, naked and unable to escape. Hephaestus surprised them there, and summoned all the gods to witness his dishonour. He then announced that he would not release his wife until the marriage-gifts which he had paid Zeus, were restored to him.

Marble statue of Aphrodite (Soli, Cyprus)

Up ran the gods, but the goddesses, from a sense of delicacy, stayed in their houses. Apollo, nudging Hermes, asked: 'You would not mind being in Ares's position, would you, net and all?'

Hermes swore that he would not, were there three times as many nets, and all the goddesses looking on. At this, both gods laughed uproariously, but Zeus was so disgusted that he refused to hand back the marriage-gifts, or to interfere. Poseidon pretended to sympathize with Hephaestus. 'Since Zeus refuses to help,' he said, 'I will undertake that Ares, as a fee for his release, pays the equivalent of the marriage-gifts in question.'

'That is all very well,' Hephaestus replied gloomily. 'But if Ares defaults, you will have to take his place under the net.'

'I cannot think that Ares will default,' Poseidon said nobly. 'But if he should do so, I am ready to pay the debt and marry Aphrodite myself.'

So Ares was set at liberty, and returned to Thrace; and Aphrodite went to Paphos, where she renewed her virginity in the sea.

Flattered by Hermes's frank confession of his love for her, Aphrodite presently spent a night with him, the fruit of which was Hermaphroditus, a double-sexed being; and, equally pleased by Poseidon's intervention on her behalf, she bore him two sons, Rhodis and Herophilus. Later, Aphrodite yielded to Dionysus, and bore him Priapus; an ugly child with enormous genitals. He is a gardener and carries a pruning-knife.

Though Zeus never lay with his adopted daughter Aphrodite, the magic of her girdle put him under constant temptation, and at last he decided to humiliate her by making her fall desperately in love with a mortal. This was the handsome Anchises, King of the Dardanians, a grandson of Ilus and, one night, when he was asleep in his herdsman's hut on Trojan Mount Ida, Aphrodite visited him in the guise of a Phrygian princess, and lay with him. When they parted at dawn, she revealed her identity, and made him promise not to tell anyone that she had slept with him. Anchises was horrified to learn that he had uncovered the nakedness of a goddess, and begged her to spare his life. She assured him that he had nothing to fear, and that their son, Aeneas, would be famous.

above: *The Ptoan Apollo. Detail (National Museum of Athens)*

opposite: *The Piombino Apollo (Louvre)*

right: *The 'Todi' Ares. Detail of bronze statue (Vatican Museum)*

One day, the wife of King Cinyras the Cyprian foolishly boasted that her daughter Smyrna was more beautiful even than Aphrodite. The goddess avenged this insult by making Smyrna fall in love with her father and climb into his bed one dark night, when her nurse had made him too drunk to realize what he was doing. Later, Cinyras discovered that he was both the father and grandfather of Smyrna's unborn child, and wild with wrath, seized a sword. Aphrodite hurriedly changed Smyrna into a myrrh-tree, which the descending sword split in halves. Out tumbled the infant Adonis. Aphrodite concealed Adonis in a chest, which she entrusted to Persephone, Queen of the Dead.

Persephone had the curiosity to open the chest, and found Adonis. He was so lovely that she lifted him out and brought him up in her own palace. The news reached Aphrodite, who at once visited Tartarus to claim Adonis; and when Persephone would not assent, having by now made him her lover, she appealed to Zeus. Zeus, well aware that Aphrodite also wanted to lie with Adonis, refused to judge so unsavoury a dispute; and transferred it to a lower court, presided over by the Muse Calliope. Calliope's verdict was that Persephone and Aphrodite had equal claims on Adonis, but that he should be allowed a brief annual holiday from the amorous demands of both. She therefore divided the year into three equal parts, of which he was to spend one with Persephone, one with Aphrodite, and the third by himself.

Aphrodite did not play fair: by wearing her magic girdle all the time, she persuaded Adonis to give her his own share of the year, grudge the share due to Persephone, and disobey the court-order.

Persephone, justly aggrieved, went to Thrace, where she told her benefactor Ares that Aphrodite now preferred Adonis to himself. Ares grew jealous and, disguised as a wild boar, rushed at Adonis who was out hunting on Mount Lebanon, and gored him to death before Aphrodite's eyes. Anemones sprang from his blood, and his soul descended to Tartarus. Aphrodite went tearfully to Zeus, and pleaded that Adonis should not have to spend more than the gloomier half of the year with Persephone, but might be her companion for the summer months. This Zeus magnanimously granted.

Ares's Nature and Deeds

Thracian Ares loves battle for its own sake, and his sister Eris is always stirring up occasions for war. Like her, he never favours one city or party more than another, delighting in the slaughter of men and the sacking of towns. All his fellow-immortals hate him, except Eris, and Aphrodite, and greedy Hades who welcomes the fighting-men slain in cruel wars.

Ares has not been consistently victorious. Athene has twice worsted him in battle; and once, the gigantic sons of Aloeus conquered and kept him imprisoned in a brazen vessel until he was released by

Hermes; and, on another occasion, Heracles sent him running. He professes too deep a contempt for litigation ever to appear in court as a plaintiff, and has only once done so as a defendant: that was when charged with the murder of Poseidon's son Halirrhothius. He pleaded justification, claiming to have saved his daughter Alcippe from being violated. Since no one else had witnessed the incident, the court acquitted him. This was the first judgement ever pronounced in a murder trial; and the hill on which the proceedings took place became known as the Areiopagus.

Hestia's Nature and Deeds

It is Hestia's glory that, alone of the great Olympians, she never takes part in wars or disputes. Like Artemis and Athene, moreover, she has always resisted every amorous invitation offered her; for, after the dethronement of Cronus, when Poseidon and Apollo came forward as rival suitors, she swore by Zeus's head to remain a virgin for ever. At that, Zeus gratefully awarded her the first victim of every public sacrifice, because she had preserved the peace of Olympus.

She was the Goddess of the Hearth and in every private house and city hall protected suppliants who fled to her for protection. Universal reverence was paid Hestia, not only as the mildest, most upright and most charitable of all the Olympians, but as having invented the art of building houses; and her fire was so sacred that, if ever a hearth went cold, either by accident or in token of mourning, it was kindled afresh with the aid of a fire-wheel.

Apollo's Nature and Deeds

Apollo was Zeus's son by Leto. Themis fed him on nectar and ambrosia, and when he was four days old he called for bow and arrows, made straight for Mount Parnassus, where the serpent Python, his mother's enemy, was lurking. Severely wounded with arrows, Python fled to the Oracle of Mother Earth at Delphi, but Apollo dared follow him into the shrine, and there despatched him beside the sacred chasm.

Mother Earth reported this outrage to Zeus, who not only ordered Apollo to visit Tempe for purification, but instituted the Pythian Games in honour of Python. Quite unabashed, Apollo disregarded Zeus's command to visit Tempe. Instead, he went to Aigialaea accompanied by Artemis; and then, disliking the place, to Tarrha in Crete, where King Carmanor performed the ceremony.

On his return to Greece, Apollo sought out Pan, and, having coaxed him to reveal the art of prophecy, seized the Delphic Oracle. Leto, on hearing the news, came with Artemis to Delphi, where she turned aside to perform some private rite in a sacred grove. The giant Tityus interrupted her devotions, and was trying to violate her, when Apollo and Artemis, hearing screams, ran up and killed him with a volley of arrows — a vengeance which Zeus, Tityus's father, was

right: *Artemis of Ephesus Detail of statue (Town Hall, Ephesus)*

right: *Hephaestus in his smithy. Amphora (British Museum)*

opposite: *Athene with her chariot (Acropolis Museum, Athens)*

pleased to consider a pious one. In Tartarus, Tityus was stretched out for torment, his arms and legs securely pegged to the ground, while two vultures ate his liver.

Next, Apollo killed the satyr Marsyas. This was how it came about. One day, Athene made a double-flute from stag's bones, and played on it at a banquet of the gods. She could not understand, at first, why Hera and Aphrodite were laughing silently behind their hands, although her music seemed to delight the other deities; she therefore went away by herself into a Phrygian wood, took up the flute again beside a stream, and watched her image in the water, as she played. Realizing at once how ludicrous those swollen cheeks made her look, she threw down the flute, and laid a curse on anyone who picked it up.

Marsyas stumbled upon the flute, which he had no sooner put to his lips than it played of itself, inspired by the memory of Athene's music; and he went about Phrygia delighting the ignorant peasants. They cried out that Apollo himself could not have made better music, even on his lyre, and Marsyas was foolish enough not to contradict them. This of course, provoked the anger of Apollo, who invited him to a contest, the winner of which should inflict whatever punishment he pleased on the loser.

The contest proved an equal one, until Apollo cried out to Marsyas: 'I challenge you to do with your instrument as much as I can do with mine. Turn it upside down, and both play and sing at the same time.'

This, with the flute, was manifestly impossible, and Marsyas failed to meet the challenge. Then Apollo took a most cruel revenge on Marsyas, flaying him alive and nailing his skin to a pine near the source of the river which now bears his name.

Afterwards, Apollo won a second musical contest, at which King Midas presided. This time he beat Pan, becoming the acknowledged god of Music. Another of his duties was once to guard the herds and flocks of the gods, but he later delegated this task to Hermes.

Though Apollo refuses to bind himself in marriage, he has got many nymphs and mortal women with child; among them, Phthia, and Thalia the Muse, and Coronis, and Aria, and Cyrene. He also seduced the nymph Dryope, but was not invariably successful in love. On one occasion he tried to steal Marpessa from Idas, but she remained true to her husband. On another, he pursued Daphne, the mountain nymph, a priestess of Mother Earth, daughter of the river Peneius in Thessaly; but when he overtook her, she cried out to Mother Earth who, in the nick of time, spirited her away to Crete, where she became known as Pasiphaë. Mother Earth left a laurel-tree in her place, and from its leaves Apollo made a wreath to console himself.

There was also the case of the beautiful youth Hyacinthus, a Spartan prince, with whom not only the poet Thamyris fell in love – the first man who ever wooed one of his own sex – but Apollo himself, the first god to do so. But the West Wind had also taken a fancy to Hyacinthus, and became insanely jealous of Apollo, who was one day teaching the boy how to hurl a discus, when the West Wind caught it in mid-air, dashed it against Hyacinthus's skull, and killed him. From his blood sprang the hyacinth flower, on which his initial letters are still to be traced.

Apollo earned Zeus's anger only once after the famous conspiracy to dethrone him. This was when his son Asclepius, the physician, had the temerity to resurrect a dead man, and thus rob Hades of a subject; Hades naturally lodged a complaint on Olympus, Zeus killed Asclepius with a thunderbolt, and Apollo in revenge killed the Cyclopes. Zeus was enraged at the loss of his armourers, and would have banished Apollo to Tartarus for ever, had not Leto pleaded for his forgiveness. The sentence was reduced to one year's hard labour, which Apollo was to serve in the sheep-folds of King Admetus of Therae. Obeying Leto's advice, Apollo not only carried out the sentence humbly, but conferred great benefits on Admetus.

Artemis's Nature and Deeds

Artemis, Apollo's sister, goes armed with bow and arrows and, like him, has the power both to send plagues or sudden death among mortals, and to heal them. She is the protectress of little children, and of all sucking animals, but she also loves the chase.

One day, while still a child, her father Zeus asked her what presents she would like. Artemis answered: 'Pray give me eternal virginity; as many names as my brother Apollo; a bow and arrows like his; the office of bringing light; a hunting tunic reaching to my knees; sixty ocean nymphs, as my maids of honour; twenty river nymphs to take care of my buskins and feed my hounds; all the mountains in the world; and, lastly, any city you care to choose for me, but one will be enough, because I intend to live on mountains most of the time. Unfortunately, since my mother Leto bore me without pains, the Fates have made me patroness of childbirth.'

Zeus smiled proudly, saying: 'You shall have all this, and more besides: not one, but thirty cities, and a share in many others, and I appoint you guardian of their roads and harbours.'

Artemis thanked him and went first to Mount Leucus in Crete, and next to the Ocean stream, where she chose nymphs for her attendants. She then visited the Cyclopes on the Island of Lipara. Brontes, who had been instructed to make whatever she wanted, took her on his knee; but, disliking his endearments, she tore a handful of hair from his chest, where a bald patch remained to the day of his death. The nymphs were terrified at the wild appearance of the Cyclopes, and well they might be, for whenever a little girl is disobedient her mother threatens her with Brontes, Arges, or Steropes. But Artemis boldly told them to make her a silver bow, with a quiverful of arrows, in return for which they should eat the first prey she brought down.

Persephone fleeing from Hades (Acropolis Museum, Athens)

With these weapons she went to Arcadia, where Pan gave her three lop-eared hounds, two parti-coloured and one spotted, together capable of dragging live lions back to their kennels; and seven swift hounds from Sparta.

Once the River-god Alpheius, son of Thetis, dared fall in love with Artemis and pursue her across Greece; but she came to Letrini in Elis, where she daubed her face, and those of all her nymphs, with white mud, so that she became indistinguishable from the rest of the company. Alpheius was forced to retire, pursued by mocking laughter.

Artemis requires the same perfect chastity from her companions as she practises herself. When Zeus had seduced one of them, Callisto, daughter of Lycaon, Artemis noticed that she was with child. Changing her into a bear, she shouted to the pack, and Callisto would have been hunted to death had she not been caught up to Heaven by Zeus who, later, set her image among the stars. Callisto's child, Arcas, was saved, and became the ancestor of the Arcadians.

On another occasion, Actaeon happened to see Artemis bathing in a stream not far off, and stayed to watch. Lest he should afterwards dare boast to his companions that she had displayed herself naked in his presence, she changed him into a stag and, with his own pack of fifty hounds, tore him to pieces.

Hephaestus's Nature and Deeds

Hephaestus, the ugly and ill-tempered Smith-god, was so weakly at birth that his disgusted mother, Hera, dropped him from the height of Olympus, to rid herself of the embarrassment. He survived this misadventure, however, without bodily damage, because he fell into the sea, where Thetis and Eurynome were at hand to rescue him. These gentle goddesses kept him with them in an underwater grotto, where he set up his first smithy and rewarded their kindness by making them all sorts of ornamental and useful objects.

When nine years had passed, Hera met Thetis, wearing a brooch of his workmanship, and asked: 'Where in the world did you find that wonderful jewel?'

Thetis hesitated, but Hera forced the truth from her. At once she fetched Hephaestus back to Olympus, where she set him up in a far finer smithy, made much of him, and arranged that he should marry Aphrodite.

Hephaestus became so far reconciled with Hera that he dared reproach Zeus himself for hanging her by the wrists from Heaven when she rebelled against him. But angry Zeus only heaved him down from Olympus a second time. He was a whole day falling. On striking the earth of the island of Lemnos, he broke both legs and, though immortal, had little life left in his body when the islanders found him. Afterwards pardoned and restored to Olympus, he could walk only with golden leg-supports.

Demeter's Nature and Deeds

Though the priestesses of Demeter, goddess of the cornfield, initiate brides and bridegrooms into the secrets of the couch, she has no husband of her own. While still young and gay, she bore Core and the lusty Iacchus to Zeus, her brother, out of wedlock. She also bore Plutus to the Titan Iasius, with whom she fell in love at the wedding of Cadmus and Harmonia. Inflamed by the nectar, the lovers slipped out and lay together openly in a thrice-ploughed field. On their return, Zeus, guessing what they had been at, and enraged that Iasius should have dared to touch Demeter, struck him dead with a thunderbolt.

Demeter herself has a gentle soul, and Erysichthon, son of Tropias, was one of the few men with whom she ever dealt harshly. Erysichthon dared invade a grove which the Pelasgians had planted for her at Dotium, and began cutting down the sacred trees, to provide timber for his new banqueting hall. Demeter assumed the form of Nicippe, priestess of the grove, and mildly ordered Erysichthon to desist. Only when he threatened her with his axe did she reveal herself in splendour and condemned him to suffer perpetual hunger. He grew hungrier and thinner the more he ate, until his parents could no longer afford to keep him supplied with food, and he became a beggar in the streets, eating filth.

Hades fell in love with Core, and went to ask Zeus's leave to marry her. Zeus feared to offend his eldest brother by a refusal, but knew that Demeter would not forgive him if Core were committed to Tartarus; he therefore answered that he could neither give nor withhold his consent. This emboldened Hades to abduct the girl, as she was picking flowers in a meadow. (It may have been anywhere in the widely separated regions which Demeter visited in her wandering search for Core, but her own priests say that it was at Eleusis.) She sought Core for nine days and nights, neither eating nor drinking, and calling fruitlessly all the while. The only news she could get came from old Hecate, who early one morning had heard Core crying 'A rape! A rape!' but, on hurrying to the rescue, found no sign of her.

On the tenth day, Demeter came in disguise to Eleusis, where King Celeus and his wife Metaneira entertained her; and she was invited to remain as wet-nurse to Demophoön, the newly-born prince. Their lame daughter Iambe tried to console Demeter and the dry-nurse, old Baubo, persuaded her to drink barley-water by a jest: she groaned as if in travail and, unexpectedly, produced from beneath her skirt Demeter's own son Iacchus, who leaped into his mother's arms and kissed her.

'Oh, how greedily you drink!' cried Abas, an elder son of Celeus's: Demeter metamorphosed him into a lizard. Somewhat ashamed of herself, Demeter now decided to do Celeus a service, by making Demophoön immortal. That night she held him over the fire, to burn away his mortality. Metaneira happened to enter the hall and broke

Persephone holding a pomegranate. Terracotta (British Museum)

the spell; so Demophoön died. 'Mine is an unlucky house!' Celius complained. 'Dry your tears,' said Demeter. 'You still have three sons on whom I intend to confer such great gifts that you will forget your double loss.'

For Triptolemus, who herded his father's cattle, had recognized Demeter and given her the news she needed: ten days before this his brothers Eumolpus, a shepherd, and Eubuleus, a swineherd, had been out in the fields, when the earth suddenly gaped open, engulfing Eubuleus's swine before his very eyes; then a chariot drawn by black horses appeared, and dashed down the chasm. The chariot-driver's face was invisible, but his right arm was tightly clasped around a shrieking girl.

Demeter summoned Hecate. Together they approached Helius, who sees everything, and forced him to admit that Hades had been the villain. Demeter was so angry that she continued to wander about the earth, forbidding the trees to yield fruit and the herbs to grow. Zeus sent her first a message by Iris and then a deputation of the Olympian gods, with conciliatory gifts, begging her to be reconciled to his will. But she would not return to Olympus, and swore that the earth must remain barren until Core had been restored.

Only one course of action remained for Zeus. He sent Hermes with a message to Hades: 'If you do not restore Core, we are all undone!' and with another to Demeter: 'You may have your daughter again, on the single condition that she has not yet tasted the food of the dead.'

Because Core had refused to eat so much as a crust of bread ever since her abduction, Hades was obliged to cloak his vexation, telling her mildly: 'My child, you seem to be unhappy here, and your mother weeps for you. I have therefore decided to send you home.'

Core's tears ceased to flow, but, just as she was setting off for Eleusis, one of Hades's gardeners, Ascalaphus, began to cry: 'Having seen the Lady Core pick a pomegranate and eat seven seeds, I am ready to bear witness that she has tasted the food of the dead!'

At Eleusis, Demeter joyfully embraced Core; but, on hearing about the pomegranate, grew more dejected than ever, and said again: 'I will neither return to Olympus, nor remove my curse from the land.' Zeus then persuaded Rhea to plead with her; and a compromise was at last reached. Core should spend three months of the year in Hades's company, as Queen of Tartarus, with the title of Persephone, and the remaining nine in Demeter's.

Demeter finally consented to return home. Before leaving Eleusis, she instructed Triptolemus, Eumolpus, and Celeus (together with Diocles, King of Pherae, who had been assiduously searching for Core all this while) in her worship and mysteries. Triptolemus she supplied with seed-corn, a wooden plough, and a chariot drawn by serpents; and sent him all over the world to teach mankind the art of agriculture. But she punished Ascalaphus for his tale-bearing.

Athene's Nature and Deeds

Athene invented the flute, the trumpet, the earthenware pot, the plough, the rake, the ox-yoke, the horse-bridle, the chariot, and the ship. She first taught the science of numbers, and all women's arts. Although a goddess of war, she gets no pleasure from battle, but rather from settling disputes, and upholding the law by pacific means. She bears no arms in time of peace and, if ever she needs any, will usually borrow a set from Zeus. Her mercy is great: when the judges' votes are equal she always gives a casting vote to liberate the accused. Yet in battle she never loses, even against Ares himself, being better grounded in tactics and strategy, and wise captains always approach her for advice.

Many gods, Titans, and giants would gladly have married Athene, but she has repulsed all advances. Once, not wishing to borrow arms from Zeus, she asked Hephaestus to make her a set of her own. Hephaestus refused payment, saying that he would undertake the work for love. When, missing the implication of these words, she entered the smithy to watch him, he suddenly turned about and tried to outrage her. Hephaestus was the victim of a malicious joke: Poseidon informed him that Athene was on her way with Zeus's consent, expecting to have violent love made to her. As she tore herself away, Hephaestus ejaculated against her thigh. She wiped off the seed with a handful of wool, which she threw away in disgust; it fell to the ground near Athens and accidentally fertilized Mother Earth. Revolted at the prospect of bearing a child which Hephaestus had tried to father on Athene, Mother Earth declared that she would accept no responsibility for it.

'Very well,' said Athene, 'I will take care of it myself.' So she took charge of the infant, called him Erichthonius and, not wishing Poseidon to laugh at the success of his joke, hid him in a sacred basket; this she gave to Aglauros, eldest daughter of the Athenian King Cecrops, with orders to guard it carefully.

Cecrops, a son of Mother Earth, was the first king to recognize paternity. He also instituted monogamy, divided Attica into twelve communities, built temples to Athene, and abolished certain bloody sacrifices in favour of sober barley-cake offerings. His wife was named Agraulos; and his three daughters, Aglauros, Herse, and Pandrosos. One evening when the girls had returned from a festival, carrying Athene's sacred baskets on their heads, Hermes bribed Aglauros to give him access to Herse, with whom he had fallen violently in love. Aglauros kept Hermes's gold, but did nothing to earn it, because Athene had made her jealous of Herse's good fortune; so Hermes turned Aglauros to stone, and had his will of Herse. After Herse had borne Hermes two sons, Cephalus and Ceryx, she and Pandrosos and their mother Agraulos were curious enough to peep beneath the lid of the basket which Aglauros had carried. Seeing a child with a serpent's tail for legs, they screamed in fear and leaped from the Acropolis.

Pan and his pipes. Bronze statuette (British Museum)

Athene was so grieved that she let fall the enormous rock which she had been carrying to the Acropolis as an additional fortification, and it became Mount Lycabettus. As for the crow that had brought her the news, she changed its colour from white to black, and forbade all crows ever again to visit the Acropolis. Erichthonius then took refuge in Athene's aegis, where she reared him so tenderly that some mistook her for his mother. His image was set among the stars as the constellation Auriga, since he had introduced the four-horse chariot.

Athene, though as modest as Artemis, is far more generous. When Teiresias, one day, was accidentally surprised in a bath, she laid her hands over his eyes and blinded him, but gave him inward sight by way of a compensation.

Pan's Nature and Deeds

Some say that Hermes fathered Pan on Dryope, daughter of Dryops, or on the nymph Oeneis. He is said to have been so ugly at birth that his mother ran away from him in fear, and Hermes carried him up to Olympus for the gods' amusement: but Pan was Zeus's foster-brother, and therefore far older than Hermes. Still others make him the son of Cronus and Rhea; or of Zeus by Hybris, which is the least improbable account.

He lived in Arcadia, where he guarded flocks, herds, and bee-hives, took part in the revels of the mountain-nymphs, and helped hunters to find their quarry. He was, on the whole, easy-going and lazy, loving nothing better than his afternoon sleep, and revenged himself on those who disturbed him with a sudden loud shout which made the hair bristle on their heads.

Pan seduced several nymphs, such as Echo, and Eupheme, nurse of the Muses, who bore him Crotus, the Bowman in the Zodiac. Once he tried to violate the chaste Pitys, who escaped him only by being metamorphosed into a fir-tree, a branch of which he afterwards wore as a chaplet. On another occasion he pursued the chaste Syrinx to the River Ladon, where she became a reed; there, since he could not distinguish her from among all the rest, he cut several reeds at random, and made them into a Pan-pipe. His greatest success in love was the seduction of Selene, which he accomplished by disguising his hairy black goatishness with well-washed white fleeces. Not realizing who he was, Selene consented to ride on his back, and let him do as he pleased with her.

The Olympian gods, while despising Pan, exploited his powers. Apollo wheedled the art of prophecy from him, and Hermes copied his pipe, claimed it as his own invention, and sold it to Apollo.

Pan is the only god who has died. To one Thamus, a sailor in a ship bound for Italy, a divine voice shouted across the sea: 'Thamus, when you reach Palodes, proclaim that the great god Pan is dead!', which Thamus did; and the news was greeted from the shore with groans.

Dionysus's Nature and Deeds

At Hera's orders the Titans seized Zeus's newly-born son Dionysus and tore him into shreds. These they boiled in a cauldron, but he was rescued and reconstituted by his grandmother Rhea. Persephone, now entrusted with his charge by Zeus, brought him to King Athamas of Orchomenus and his wife Ino, whom she persuaded to rear the child in the women's quarters, disguised as a girl. But Hera could not be deceived, and punished the royal pair with madness.

Then Hermes temporarily transformed Dionysus into a kid or a ram, and presented him to the nymphs Macris, Nysa, Erato, Bromie, and Bacche, of Mount Nysa. They tended Dionysus, for which ser-vice Zeus subsequently placed their images among the stars, as the Hyades. On Mount Nysa Dionysus invented wine, for which he is chiefly celebrated.

When he grew to manhood Hera recognized him as Zeus's son, and drove him mad also. He went wandering all over the world, accompanied by his tutor Silenus and a wild army of Satyrs and Maenads, whose weapons were the ivy-twined staff tipped with a pine-cone, called the *thyrsus*, and swords and serpents and bullroarers. He sailed to Egypt, bringing the vine with him; and at Pharos King Proteus received him hospitably.

Among the Libyans of the Nile Delta, opposite Pharos, were certain Amazon queens whom Dionysus invited to march with him against the Titans. Dionysus's defeat of the Titans and restoration of King Ammon was the earliest of his many military successes. He then turned east and made for India and conquered the whole country, which he taught the art of viniculture, also giving it laws and founding great cities. On his return he was opposed by the Amazons, a horde of whom he chased as far as Ephesus. Others fled to Samos, and Dionysus followed them in boats, killing many.

Next, Dionysus returned to Europe by way of Phrygia, where his grandmother Rhea purified him of the many murders he had committed during his madness, and initiated him into her Mysteries. He then invaded Thrace; but no sooner had his people landed at the mouth of the river Strymon than Lycurgus, King of the Edonians, captured the entire army, except Dionysus himself, who plunged into the sea and took refuge in Thetis's grotto. Rhea helped the prisoners to escape, and drove Lycurgus mad: he struck his own son Dryas dead with an axe, in the belief that he was cutting down a vine, and the whole land of Thrace grew barren in horror of his crime. When Dionysus announced that this barrenness would continue unless Lycurgus were put to death, the Edonians led him to Mount Pangaeum, where wild horses pulled his body apart.

Dionysus met with no further opposition in Thrace, but travelled on to Thebes, and invited the women to join his revels on Mount Cithaeron. Pentheus, King of Thebes, disliking Dionysus's dissolute appearance, arrested him, together with all his Maenads, but went mad and, instead of shackling Dionysus, shackled a bull. The Maenads escaped again, and went raging out upon the mountain. Pentheus attempted to stop them; but, inflamed by wine and religious ecstasy, they rent him limb from limb. His mother Agave led the riot, and it was she who wrenched off his head.

At Orchomenus the three daughters of Minyas, by name Alcithoë, Leucippe, and Arsippe, refused to join in the revels, though Dionysus himself invited them, appearing in the form of a girl. He then changed his shape, becoming successively a lion, a bull, and a panther, and drove them insane. Leucippe offered her own son Hippasus as sacrifice, and the three sisters, having torn him to pieces and devoured him, skimmed the mountains in a frenzy until at last Hermes changed them into birds.

When all Boeotia had acknowledged Dionysus's divinity, he made a tour of the Aegean Islands, spreading joy and terror wherever he went. Arriving at Icaria, he found that his ship was unseaworthy, and hired another from certain Tyrrhenian sailors who claimed to be bound for Naxos. But they proved to be pirates and, unaware of his godhead, steered for Asia to sell him as a slave. Dionysus made a vine grow from the deck and enfold the mast, while ivy twined about the rigging; he also turned the oars into serpents, and became a lion himself, filling the vessel with phantom beasts and the sound of flutes, so that the terrified pirates leaped overboard and became dolphins.

It was at Naxos that Dionysus met the lovely Ariadne whom Theseus had deserted, and married her without delay. She bore him Oenopion, Thoas, Staphylus, Latromis, Euanthes, and Tauropolus. Later, he placed her bridal chaplet among the stars.

From Naxos he came to Argos and punished Perseus, who at first opposed him and killed many of his followers, by inflicting a madness on the Argive women. Perseus hastily admitted his error, and appeased Dionysus by building a temple in his honour.

Finally, having established his worship throughout the world, Dionysus ascended to Heaven, and now sits at the right hand of Zeus as one of the Twelve Great Ones.

The Gods of the Underworld

When ghosts descend to Tartarus, each is supplied by pious relatives with a coin laid under the tongue of its corpse. They are thus able to pay Charon, the miser who ferries them in a crazy boat across the Styx. Penniless ghosts must wait for ever on the near bank; unless they have evaded Hermes, their conductor, and crept down by a back entrance. A three-headed dog named Cerberus guards the opposite shore of Styx.

The first region of Tartarus contains the cheerless Asphodel Fields, where souls of heroes stray without purpose among the throngs of less distinguished dead that twitter like bats. Their one delight is in libations of blood poured to them by the living: when they drink they feel themselves almost men again. Beyond these meadows lie Erebus and the palace of Hades and Persephone. Close by, newly arrived ghosts are daily judged by Minos, Rhadamanthys, and Aeacus at a place where three roads meet. As each verdict is given the ghosts are directed along one of the three roads: that leading back to the Asphodel Meadows, if they are neither virtuous nor evil; that leading to the punishment-field of Tartarus, if they are evil; that leading to the orchards of Elysium, if they are virtuous.

Elysium, ruled over by Cronus, lies near Hades's dominions, but forms no part of them; it is a happy land of perpetual day, without cold or snow, where games, music, and revels never cease, and where the inhabitants may elect to be reborn on earth whenever they please. Near by are the Fortunate Islands, reserved for those who have been three times born, and three times attained Elysium.

Hades seldom visits the upper air, except on business or when he is overcome by sudden lust. Once he dazzled the Nymph Minthe with the splendour of his golden chariot and its four black horses, and would have seduced her without difficulty had not Queen Persephone

Hades and Persephone in the Underworld. Detail of an Apulian amphora (British Museum)

metamorphosed Minthe into sweet-smelling mint. He willingly allows none of his subjects to escape, and few who visit Tartarus return alive to describe it.

Hades never knows what is happening in the world above, or in Olympus, except for fragmentary information which comes to him when mortals strike their hands upon the earth and invoke him with oaths and curses. His most prized possession is the helmet of invisibility, given him as a mark of gratitude by the Cyclopes when he consented to release them at Zeus's order. All the riches of gems and precious metals hidden beneath the earth are his, but he owns no property above ground, except for certain gloomy temples in Greece.

Queen Persephone, however, can be both gracious and merciful. She is faithful to Hades, but has had no children by him and prefers the company of Hecate, goddess of witches, to his.

Tisiphone, Alecto, and Megaera, the Erinnyes or Furies, live in Erebus, and are older than Zeus or any of the other Olympians. Their task is to hear complaints brought by mortals against the insolence of the young to the aged, of children to parents, of hosts to guests, and of householders or city councils to suppliants – and to punish such crimes by hounding the culprits relentlessly. These Erinnyes are crones, with snakes for hair, dog's heads, coal-black bodies, bat's wings, and bloodshot eyes. In their hands they carry brass-studded scourges, and their victims die in torment. It is unwise to mention them by name in conversation; hence they are usually styled the Eumenides, which means 'The Kindly Ones' – as Hades is styled Pluton, or Pluto, 'The Rich One'.

Tyche and Nemesis

Tyche is a daughter of Zeus, to whom he has given power to decide what the fortune of this or that mortal shall be. On some she heaps gifts from a horn of plenty, others she deprives of all that they have. Tyche is altogether irresponsible in her awards, and runs about juggling with a ball to exemplify the uncertainty of chance. But if it ever happens that a man, whom she has favoured, boasts of his abundant riches and neither sacrifices a part of them to the gods, nor alleviates the poverty of his fellow-citizens, then the ancient goddess Nemesis steps in to humiliate him. Nemesis carries an apple-bough in one hand, and a wheel in the other, and wears a silver crown adorned with stags; the scourge hangs at her girdle.

Coin of Dionysus (Archaeological Museum, Syracuse, Sicily)

3

OF HEROES, GODS AND MEN

Orpheus

ORPHEUS, SON OF THE Thracian King Oeagrus and the Muse Calliope, was the most famous poet and musician who ever lived. Apollo presented him with a lyre, and the muses taught him its use, so that he not only enchanted wild beasts, but made the trees and rocks move from their places to follow the sound of his music.

After a visit to Egypt, Orpheus joined the Argonauts, with whom he sailed to Colchis, his music helping them to overcome many difficulties – and, on his return, married Eurydice, and settled among the savage Cicones of Thrace.

One day, near Tempe, in the valley of the river Peneius, Eurydice met Aristaeus, who tried to force her. She trod on a serpent as she fled, and died of its bite; but Orpheus boldly descended into Tartarus, hoping to fetch her back. On his arrival, he not only charmed the ferryman Charon, the Dog Cerberus, and the three Judges of the Dead with his plaintive music, but temporarily suspended the tortures of the damned; and so far soothed the savage heart of Hades that he won leave to restore Eurydice to the upper world. Hades made a single condition: that Orpheus might not look behind him until she was safely back under the light of the sun. Eurydice followed Orpheus up through the dark passage, guided by the sounds of his lyre, and it was only when he reached the sunlight again that he turned to see whether she were still behind him, and so lost her for ever.

When Dionysus invaded Thrace, Orpheus neglected to honour him, but taught other sacred mysteries and preached the evil of sacrificial murder to the men of Thrace. In vexation, Dionysus set the Maenads upon him at Deium in Macedonia. First waiting until their husbands had entered Apollo's temple, where Orpheus served as priest, they seized the weapons stacked outside, burst in, murdered their husbands, and tore Orpheus limb from limb. His head they threw into the river Hebrus, but it floated, still singing, down to the sea, and was carried to the island of Lesbos.

Tearfully, the Muses collected his limbs and buried them at Leibethra, at the foot of Mount Olympus, where the nightingales now sing sweeter than anywhere else in the world. As for Orpheus's head: after being attacked by a jealous Lemnian serpent (which Apollo at once changed into a stone) it was laid to rest in a cave at Antissa, sacred to Dionysus. There it prophesied day and night until Apollo, finding that his oracles at Delphi, Gryneium, and Clarus were deserted, came and stood over the head, crying: 'Cease from interference in my business'. Thereupon the head fell silent. Orpheus's lyre had likewise drifted to Lesbos and been laid up in a temple of Apollo, at whose intercession, and that of the Muses, the lyre was placed in heaven as a constellation.

Ganymedes

Ganymedes, the son of King Tros who gave his name to Troy, was the most beautiful youth alive and therefore chosen by the gods to be Zeus's cup-bearer. It is said that Zeus, desiring Ganymedes also as his bedfellow, disguised himself in eagle's feathers and abducted him from the Trojan plain.

Afterwards, on Zeus's behalf, Hermes presented Tros with a golden vine, the work of Hephaestus, and two fine horses, in compensation for his loss, assuring him at the same time that Ganymedes had become immortal, exempt from the miseries of old age, and was now smiling, golden bowl in hand, as he dispensed bright nectar to the Father of Heaven.

The Giants' Revolt

Enraged because Zeus had confined their brothers, the Titans, in Tartarus, certain tall and terrible giants plotted an assault on Heaven. They had been born from Mother Earth at Thracian Phlegra, twenty-four in number.

Without warning, they seized rocks and fire-brands and hurled them upwards from their mountain tops, so that the Olympians were hard pressed. Hera prophesied that the giants could never be killed by any god, but only by a single, lion-skinned mortal; and that even he could do nothing unless the enemy were anticipated in their search for a certain herb of invulnerability, which grew in a secret place on earth. Zeus at once took counsel with Athene; sent her off to warn Heracles, the lion-skinned mortal; and forbade Eos, Selene, and Helius to shine for a while. Under the light of the stars, Zeus groped about, found the herb, and brought it safely to Heaven.

The Olympians could now join battle with the giants. Heracles let loose his first arrow against Alcyoneus, the enemy's leader. He fell, but sprang up again revived, because this was his native soil of Phlegra. 'Quick!' cried Athene. 'Drag him away to another country!' Heracles caught Alcyoneus and dragged him over the Thracian border, where he despatched him with a club.

Then Porphyrion leaped into Heaven from the great pyramid of rocks which the giants had piled up, and none of the gods stood his ground. He made for Hera, whom he tried to strangle; but, wounded in the liver by an arrow from Eros's bow, he turned from anger to lust. Zeus, seeing that his wife was about to be outraged, felled Porphyrion with a thunderbolt. Up he sprang again, but Heracles, returning in the nick of time, mortally wounded him with an arrow. Meanwhile, Ephialtes had beaten Ares to his knees; however, Apollo shot the wretch in the left eye and Heracles planted another arrow in the right. Thus died Ephialtes.

Now, whenever a god wounded a giant, it was Heracles who had to deal the death blow. The peace-loving goddesses Hestia and Demeter took no part in the conflict, but stood dismayed, wringing their hands.

Discouraged, the remaining giants fled back to earth, pursued by the Olympians. Athene threw a vast missile at Enceladus, which crushed him flat and became the island of Sicily. And Poseidon broke off part of Cos with his trident and threw it at Polybutes; this became the nearby islet of Nisyros, beneath which he lies buried.

The remaining giants made a last stand at Bathos, near Arcadian Trapezus. Hermes, borrowing Hades's helmet of invisibility, struck down Hippolytus, and Artemis pierced Gration with an arrow; while the Fates' pestles broke the heads of Agrius and Thoas. Ares, with his spear, and Zeus, with his thunderbolt, now accounted for the rest, though Heracles was called upon to despatch each giant as he fell.

Typhon

In revenge for the destruction of the giants, Mother Earth lay with Tartarus, and presently brought forth her youngest child, Typhon: the largest monster ever born. From the thighs downward he was coiled serpents, and his arms, which reached a hundred leagues in either direction, had countless serpents' heads instead of hands. His brutish ass-head touched the stars, his vast wings darkened the sun, fire flashed from his eyes, and flaming rocks hurtled from his mouth. When he came rushing towards Olympus, the gods fled in terror to Egypt, where they disguised themselves as animals.

Athene alone stood her ground, and taunted Zeus with cowardice until, resuming his true form, he let fly a thunderbolt at Typhon, and followed this up with a sweep of the same flint sickle that had served to castrate his father Uranus. Typhon fled to Mount Casius, and there the two grappled. Typhon twined his myriad coils about Zeus, disarmed him of his sickle and, after severing the sinews of his hands and feet with it, dragged him into the Corycian Cave. Zeus now could not move a finger, and Typhon had hidden the sinews in a bear-skin, over which Delphyne, a serpent-tailed sister-monster, stood guard.

Zeus's defeat spread dismay among the gods, but Hermes and Pan went secretly to the cave, where Pan frightened Delphyne with a

The three-headed monster Typhon. A sculpture from Naxos (Acropolis Museum, Athens)

sudden shout, while Hermes abstracted the sinews and replaced them on Zeus's limbs.

Zeus returned to Olympus and, mounted upon a chariot drawn by winged horses, once more pursued Typhon with thunderbolts. Typhon reached Mount Haemus in Thrace and, picking up whole mountains, hurled them at Zeus, who interposed his thunderbolts, so that they rebounded on the monster, wounding him frightfully. He fled towards Sicily, where Zeus ended the running fight by hurling Mount Aetna upon him, and fire belches from its cone to this day.

Deucalion's Flood

Deucalion's Flood, so called to distinguish it from the Ogygian and other floods, was caused by Zeus's anger against the impious sons of Lycaon, the son of Pelasgus. News of their crimes reached Olympus, and Zeus himself visited them, disguised as a poor traveller. They had the effrontery to set umble soup before him, mixing the guts of their brother Nyctimus with the umbles of sheep and goats that it contained. Zeus was undeceived and, thrusting away the table changed all of them except Nyctimus, whom he restored to life, into wolves.

On his return to Olympus, Zeus in disgust let loose a great flood on the earth, meaning to wipe out the whole race of man; but Deucalion, King of Phthia, warned by his father Prometheus the Titan, built an ark, victualled it, and went aboard with his wife Pyrrha. Then the South Wind blew, the rain fell, and the rivers roared down to the sea which, rising with astonishing speed, washed away every city of the coast and plain; until the entire world was flooded, but for a few mountain peaks, and all mortal creatures seemed to have been lost, except Deucalion and Pyrrha. The ark floated about for nine days until, at last, the waters subsided, and it came to rest on Mount Parnassus.

Disembarking, they offered a sacrifice to Father Zeus, and went down to pray at the shrine of Themis, beside the river Cephissus. They pleaded humbly that mankind should be renewed, and Zeus, hearing their voices from afar, sent Hermes to assure them that whatever request they might make would be granted forthwith. Themis appeared in person, saying: 'Shroud your heads, and throw the bones of your mother behind you!' Since Deucalion and Pyrrha had different mothers, both now deceased, they decided that the Titaness meant Mother Earth, whose bones were the rocks lying on the river bank. Therefore, stooping with shrouded heads, they picked up rocks and threw them over their shoulders; these became either men or women, according as Deucalion or Pyrrha had handled them.

However, as it proved, Deucalion and Pyrrha were not the sole survivors of the Flood, for Megarus, a son of Zeus, had been roused from his couch by the scream of cranes that summoned him to the peak of Mount Gerania, which remained above water. Similarly, the inhabitants of Parnassus were awakened by the howling of wolves and followed them to the mountain top. They named their new city Lycorea, after the wolves. Thus the flood proved of little avail, for some of the Parnassians migrated to Arcadia, and revived Lycaon's abominations.

This Deucalion was the brother of Cretan Ariadne and the father of Orestheus, King of the Ozolian Locrians, in whose time a white bitch littered a stick, which Orestheus planted, and which grew into a vine. Another of his sons, Amphictyon, entertained Dionysus, and was the first man to mix wine with water. But his eldest and most famous son was Hellen, father of all Greeks.

Atlas and Prometheus
Prometheus, the creator of mankind, whom some include among the seven Titans, was the son either of the Titan Eurymedon, or of Iapetus by the nymph Clymene; and his brothers were Epimetheus, Atlas, and Menoetius.

Atlas and Menoetius joined Cronus and the Titans in their unsuccessful war against the Olympian gods. Zeus killed Menoetius with a thunderbolt, but spared Atlas, whom he condemned to support Heaven on his shoulders for all eternity.

Atlas was the father of the Pleiades, the Hyades, and the Hesperides; and has held up the Heavens ever since, except when Heracles temporarily relieved him of the task. Some say that Perseus petrified Atlas into Mount Atlas by showing him the Gorgon's head.

Prometheus, being wiser than Atlas, foresaw the issue of the rebellion against Cronus, and therefore preferred to fight on Zeus's side, persuading Epimetheus to do the same. He was, indeed, the wisest of his race, and Athene taught him architecture, astronomy, mathematics, navigation, medicine, metallurgy, and other useful arts, which he passed on to mankind. But Zeus, who had decided to extirpate the whole race of man, and spared them only at Prometheus's urgent plea, grew angry at their increasing powers and talents.

One day, when a dispute took place at Sicyon, as to which portions of a sacrificial bull should be offered to the gods, and which should be reserved for men, Prometheus was invited to act as arbiter. He therefore flayed and jointed a bull, and sewed its hide to form two open-mouthed bags, filling these with what he had cut up. One bag contained all the flesh, but this he concealed beneath the stomach, and the other contained the bones, hidden beneath a rich layer of fat. When he offered Zeus the choice of either, Zeus chose the bag containing the bones and fat (still the divine portion); but punished Prometheus by withholding fire from mankind.

Prometheus at once went to Athene, with a plea for a backstairs admittance to Olympus, and this she granted. On his arrival, he lighted a torch at the fiery chariot of the Sun and presently broke from it a fragment of glowing charcoal, which he thrust into the pithy hollow of a giant fennel-stalk. Then, extinguishing his torch, he stole away undiscovered, and gave fire to mankind.

Zeus swore revenge. He ordered Hephaestus to make a clay woman, and the four Winds to breathe life into her, and all the goddesses to adorn her. This woman, Pandora, the most beautiful ever created, Zeus sent as a gift to Epimetheus, but Epimetheus, having been warned by his brother to accept no gift from Zeus, respectfully excused himself. Now angrier even than before, Zeus had Prometheus chained naked to a pillar in the Caucasian mountains, where a greedy vulture tore at his liver all day, and there was no end to the pain, because every night his liver grew whole again.

But Zeus excused his savagery by circulating a falsehood: Athene, he said, had invited Prometheus to Olympus for a secret love affair.

Epimetheus, alarmed by his brother's fate, hastened to marry Pandora, whom Zeus had made as foolish, mischievous, and idle as she was beautiful. Presently she opened a jar, which Prometheus had warned Epimetheus to keep closed, and in which he had been at pains to imprison all the Spites that might plague mankind: such as Old Age, Labour, Sickness, Insanity, Vice and Passion. Out these flew in a cloud, stung Epimetheus and Pandora and then attacked the race of mortals. Delusive Hope, however, whom Prometheus had also shut in the jar, discouraged them by her lies from a general suicide.

Eos

At the close of every night, Eos, a daughter of the Titans Hyperion and Theia, rises from her couch in the east, mounts her chariot and

above: *Ganymedes and Zeus (Hermitage Museum, Leningrad)*

opposite: *Hermes, Eurydice and Orpheus in the Underworld (Louvre)*

right: *Apollo and Artemis in the battle of the gods and giants (Archaeological Museum, Delphi)*

rides to Olympus, where she announces the approach of her brother Helius. When Helius appears, she accompanies him on his travels until she announces their safe arrival on the western shores of Ocean.

Aphrodite was once vexed to find Ares in Eos's bed, and cursed her with a constant longing for young mortals, whom thereupon she secretly and shamefacedly began to seduce. First, Orion; next, Cephalus; then Cleitus; though she was married to Astraeus, who came of Titan stock.

Lastly, Eos carried off Ganymedes and Tithonus, sons of Tros. When Zeus robbed her of Ganymedes she begged him to grant Tithonus immortality, and to this he assented. But she forgot to ask also for perpetual youth, and Tithonus became daily older, his voice grew shrill, and, when Eos tired of nursing him, he turned into a cicada.

Orion

Orion, a hunter of Boeotian Hyria, and the handsomest man alive, was the son of Poseidon and Euryale. Coming one day to Hyria in Chios, he fell in love with Merope, daughter of Dionysus's son Oenopion. Oenopion had promised Merope to Orion in marriage, if he would free the island from the dangerous wild beasts that infested it; and this he set himself to do. But when the task was at last accomplished, and he claimed her as his wife, Oenopion brought him rumours of lions, bears, and wolves still lurking in the hills, and refused to give her up.

One night Orion, in disgust, drank a skinful of Oenopion's wine, which so inflamed him that he broke into Merope's bedroom, and forced her to lie with him. When dawn came, Oenopion invoked his father, Dionysus, who sent satyrs to ply Orion with still more wine, until he fell fast asleep; whereupon Oenopion put out both his eyes and flung him on the seashore. An oracle announced that the blind man would regain his sight, if he travelled to the east and turned his eye-sockets towards Helius at the point where he first rises from Ocean. Orion at once rowed out to sea in a small boat and, following the sound of a Cyclops's hammer, reached Lemnos. There he entered the smithy of Hephaestus, snatched up an apprentice named Cedalion, and carried him off on his shoulders as a guide. Cedalion led Orion over land and sea, until he came to the farthest Ocean, where Eos fell in love with him, and her brother Helius restored his sight.

After visiting Delos in Eos's company, Orion returned to avenge himself on Oenopion, whom he could not, however, find anywhere in Chios, because he was hiding in an underground chamber made for him by Hephaestus. Sailing on to Crete, where he thought that Oenopion might have fled for protection to his grandfather Minos, Orion met Artemis, who shared his love of the chase. She soon persuaded him to forget his vengeance and, instead, come hunting with her.

Now, Apollo was aware that Orion had not refused Eos's invitation to her couch in the holy island of Delos. Fearing that his sister Artemis might prove as susceptible as Eos, Apollo went to Mother Earth and, repeating Orion's boast that he would rid the whole earth of wild beasts and monsters, arranged for a monstrous scorpion to pursue him. Orion attacked the scorpion, but, finding that its armour was proof against any mortal weapon, dived into the sea and swam away in the direction of Delos where, he hoped, Eos would protect him. Apollo then called to Artemis: 'Do you see that black object bobbing about in the sea, far away, close to Ortygia? It is the head of a villain called Candaon, who has just seduced Opis, one of your Hyperborean priestesses. I challenge you to transfix it with an arrow!' Now, Candaon was Orion's Boeotian nickname, though Artemis did not know this. She took careful aim, let fly, and, swimming out to retrieve her quarry, found that she had shot Orion through the head. In great grief she implored Apollo's son Asclepius to revive him, and he consented; but was destroyed by Zeus's thunderbolt before he could accomplish his task. Artemis then set Orion's image among the stars, eternally pursued by the Scorpion; his ghost had already descended to the Asphodel Fields.

Helius

Helius is a brother of Selene and Eos. Roused by the crowing of the cock, and heralded by Eos, he drives his four-horse chariot daily across the Heavens from a palace in the far east, near Colchis, to an equally magnificent far-western palace, where his horses pasture in the Islands of the Blessed. He sails home along the Ocean stream, which flows around the world, embarking his chariot and team on a golden ferry-boat.

Helius can see everything that happens on earth, but is not particularly observant – once he even failed to notice the robbery of his sacred cattle by Odysseus's companions. Rhodes is his freehold. It happened that, when Zeus was allotting islands and cities to the various gods, he forgot to include Helius among these, and 'Alas!' he said, 'now I shall have to begin all over again.'

'No, Sire,' replied Helius politely, 'today I noticed signs of a new island emerging from the sea, to the south of Asia Minor. I shall be well content with that.'

Zeus called the Fate Lachesis to witness that any such new island should belong to Helius; and, when Rhodes had risen well above the waves, Helius claimed it and begot seven sons and a daughter there on the Nymph Rhode. Some say that Rhodes had existed before this time, and was re-emerging from the great flood which Zeus sent. The Telchines were its aboriginal inhabitants and Poseidon fell in love with one of them, the nymph Halia, on whom he begot Rhode. The Telchines, foreseeing the flood, sailed away in all directions, and abandoned their claims on Rhodes. Rhode was thus left the sole

above: *Helius riding across the sky in his chariot.*
Detail from a two-handled bowl (British Museum)

opposite above: *Pandora. Vase (British Museum)*

opposite below: *Atlas watching the vulture*
attacking the chained Prometheus. From a
black-figured vase (Vatican Museum)

heiress, and her seven sons by Helius ruled in the island after its re-emergence. They became famous astronomers, and when one of them, by name Actis, was banished for fratricide, he fled to Egypt. There he founded the city of Heliopolis, and first taught the Egyptians astrology, inspired by his father Helius. The Rhodians built the Colossus, seventy cubits high, in his honour.

One morning Helius yielded to his son Phaëthon who had been constantly plaguing him for permission to drive the sun-chariot. Phaëthon wished to show his sisters Prote and Glymene what a fine fellow he was: and his fond mother Rhode encouraged him. But, not being strong enough to check the career of the white horses, Phaëthon drove them first so high above the earth that everyone shivered, and then so near the earth that he scorched the fields. Zeus, in a fit of rage, killed him with a thunderbolt, and he fell into the river Po. His grieving sisters were changed into poplar trees on its banks.

Tereus

Tereus, a son of Ares, ruled over the Thracians then occupying Phocian Daulis and, having acted as mediator in a boundary dispute for Pandion, King of Athens and father of the twins Butes and Erechtheus, married their sister Procne, who bore him a son, Itys.

Unfortunately Tereus had fallen in love with Pandion's younger sister Philomela. A year later, concealing Procne in a rustic cabin near his palace at Daulis, he reported her death to Pandion, who offered him Philomela in Procne's place. When Philomela reached the palace, Tereus forced her to lie with him. Procne soon heard the news, but Tereus cut out her tongue and confined her to the slaves' quarters, where she could communicate with Philomela only by weaving a secret message into the pattern of a bridal robe – 'Procne is among the slaves.'

Meanwhile, an oracle had warned Tereus that Itys would die by the hand of a blood relative and, suspecting his brother Dryas of a murderous plot to seize the throne, struck him down unexpectedly with an axe. The same day, Philomela read the message woven into the robe. She hurried to the slaves' quarters, and released Procne.

'Oh, to be revenged on Tereus, who pretended that you were dead, and seduced me!' wailed Philomela, aghast.

Procne, being tongueless, could not reply, but flew out and, seizing her son Itys, killed him, gutted him, and then boiled him in a copper cauldron for Tereus to eat on his return.

When Tereus realized what flesh he had been tasting, he grasped the axe with which he had killed Dryas and pursued the sisters as they fled from the palace. He soon overtook them and was on the point of committing a double murder when the gods changed all three into birds; Procne became a swallow; Philomela, a nightingale; Tereus, a hoopoe.

Boreas

Oreithyia, daughter of Erechtheus, King of Athens, and his wife Praxithea, was one day whirling in a dance beside the river Ilissus, when Boreas, son of Astraeus and Eos, and brother of the South and West Winds, carried her off. Wrapped in a mantle of dark clouds, he ravished her.

Boreas had long loved Oreithyia and repeatedly sued for her hand, but Erechtheus put him off until at length, complaining that he had wasted too much time in words, he resorted to his natural violence.

He took her to the city of the Thracian Cicones, where she became his wife, and bore him twin sons, Calais and Zetes, who grew wings when they reached manhood; also two daughters, namely Chione and Cleopatra.

Once, disguising himself as a dark-maned stallion, he covered twelve of the three thousand mares belonging to Erichthonius, son of Dardanus, which used to graze in the water-meadows beside the river Scamander. Twelve fillies were born from this union; they could race over ripe ears of standing corn without bending them, or over the crests of waves.

The Athenians regard Boreas as their brother-in-law and, having once successfully invoked him to destroy King Xerxes's fleet, they built him a fine temple on the banks of the river Ilissus.

Io

Io, daughter of the River-god Inachus, was a priestess of Argive Hera. Zeus, over whom Iynx, daughter of Pan and Echo, had cast a spell, fell in love with Io, and when Hera charged him with infidelity and turned Iynx into a wryneck as a punishment, lied: 'I have never touched Io.' He then turned her into a white cow, which Hera claimed as hers and handed over for safe keeping to Argus Panoptes, ordering him: 'Tether this beast secretly to an olive-tree at Nemea.' But Zeus sent Hermes to fetch her back, and himself led the way to Nemea dressed in woodpecker disguise. Hermes, though the cleverest of thieves, knew that he could not steal Io without being detected by one of Argus's hundred eyes; he therefore charmed him asleep by playing the flute, crushed him with a boulder, cut off his head, and released Io. Hera, having placed Argus's eyes in the tail of a peacock, as a constant reminder of his foul murder, set a gadfly to sting Io and chase her all over the world.

Io first went to Dodona, and presently reached the sea called the Ionian after her, but there turned back and travelled north to Mount Haemus and then, by way of the Danube's delta, coursed sun-wise around the Black Sea, crossing the Crimean Bosphorus, and following the River Hybristes to its source in the Caucasus, where Prometheus still languished on his rock. She regained Europe by way of Colchis, the land of the Chalybes, and the Thracian Bosphorus; then away she galloped through Asia Minor to Tarsus and Joppa,

Helius, the sun-god. A silver-gilt disc (British Museum)

thence to Media, Bactria, and India and, passing south-westward through Arabia, across the Indian Bosphorus, reached Ethiopia. Thence she travelled down from the sources of the Nile, where the pygmies make perpetual war with the cranes, and found rest at last in Egypt. There Zeus restored her to human form and, having married Telegonus, she gave birth to Epaphus – her son by Zeus, who had *touched* her to some purpose – and founded the worship of Isis, as she called Demeter. Epaphus, who was rumoured to be the divine bull Apis, reigned over Egypt, and had a daughter, Libya, the mother by Poseidon of Agenor and Belus.

Europe and Cadmus

Agenor, Libya's son by Poseidon and twin to Belus, left Egypt to settle in the Land of Canaan, where he married Telephassa, who bore him Cadmus, Phoenix, Cilix, Thasus, Phineus, and one daughter, Europe.

Zeus, falling in love with Europe, sent Hermes to drive Agenor's cattle down to the seashore at Tyre, where she and her companions used to walk. He himself joined the herd, disguised as a snow-white bull. Europe was struck by his beauty and, on finding him gentle as a lamb, mastered her fear and began to play with him; in the end, she climbed upon his shoulders, and let him amble down with her to the edge of the sea. Suddenly he swam away, while she looked back in terror at the receding land. Wading ashore near Cretan Gortyna, Zeus became an eagle and ravished Europe. She bore him three sons: Minos, Rhadamanthys, and Sarpedon.

Agenor sent his sons in search of their sister, forbidding them to return without her. They set sail at once but, having no notion where the bull had gone, each steered a different course. Phoenix travelled westward to what is now Carthage; Cilix went to the Land of the Hypachaeans, which took his name, Cilicia; and Phineus to Thynia, a peninsula separating the Sea of Marmara from the Black Sea. Thasus and his followers, first making for Olympia, then set off to colonize the island of Thasos and work its rich gold mines.

Cadmus sailed with Telephassa to Rhodes, where he dedicated a brazen cauldron to Athene of Lindus, and built Poseidon's temple. They next touched at Thera, and built a similar temple, finally reaching the land of the Thracian Edonians. Here Telephassa died and Cadmus and his companions proceeded on foot to the Delphic Oracle. When he asked where Europe might be found, the Pythoness advised him to give up his search and, instead, follow a cow and build a city wherever she should sink down for weariness.

Departing, Cadmus came upon some cowherds in the service of King Pelagon, who sold him a cow. He drove her eastward through Boeotia, never allowing her to pause until, at last, she sank down where the city of Thebes now stands, and here he erected an image of Athene.

Europe and the Bull.
Metope (Seljuk Museum,
Konya, Turkey)

Cadmus, warning his companions that the cow must be sacrificed to Athene without delay, sent them to fetch lustral water from the Castalian Spring, but did not know that it was guarded by a great serpent. This serpent killed most of Cadmus's men, and he took vengeance by crushing its head with a rock. No sooner had he offered Athene the sacrifice, than she appeared, ordering him to sow the serpent's teeth in the soil. When he obeyed her, armed Sown Men at once sprang up. Cadmus tossed a stone among them and they began to brawl, each accusing the other of having thrown it, and fought so fiercely that only five survived: Echion, Udaeus, Chthonius, Hyperenor, and Pelorus, who offered Cadmus their services.

Cadmus and Harmonia
When Cadmus had served eight years in bondage to expiate the murder of the Castalian serpent, Athene secured him the land of Boeotia. With the help of his Sown Men, he built the Theban acropolis, named 'The Cadmea' in his own honour and, after being initiated into the mysteries which Zeus had taught Iasion, married Harmonia, the daughter of Aphrodite and Ares.

This was the first mortal wedding ever attended by the Olympians. Twelve golden thrones were set up for them in Cadmus's house, and they all brought gifts. Aphrodite presented Harmonia with the famous golden necklace made by Hephaestus which conferred irresistible beauty on its wearer. Athene gave her a golden robe, which similarly conferred divine dignity on its wearer, and Hermes a lyre. Cadmus's own present to Harmonia was another rich robe; and Electra, Iasion's mother, taught her the rites of the Great Goddess; while Demeter assured her a prosperous barley harvest by lying with Iasion in a thrice-ploughed field during the celebrations.

In his old age, Cadmus resigned the Theban throne in favour of his grandson Pentheus, whom his daughter Agave had borne to Echion, and lived quietly in the city. But when Pentheus was done to death by his mother, Dionysus foretold that Cadmus and Harmonia would rule over barbarian hordes. These same barbarians, he said, would sack many Greek cities until, at last, they plundered a temple of Apollo, whereupon they would suffer just punishment; but Ares would turn Cadmus and Harmonia into serpents and they would live happily for all time in the Islands of the Blessed.

Cadmus and Harmonia therefore emigrated to the land of the Encheleans who, when attacked by the Illyrians, chose them as their rulers. Agave was now married to Lycotherses, King of Illyria, but on hearing that her parents commanded the Enchelean forces, she murdered Lycotherses too, and gave the kingdom to Cadmus. In their old age, when the prophecy had been wholly fulfilled, Cadmus and Harmonia duly became blue-spotted black serpents, and were sent by Zeus to the Islands of the Blessed.

Belus and the Danaids

King Belus, who ruled at Chemmis in the Thebaid, was the son of Libya by Poseidon, and twin-brother of Agenor. His wife Anchinoë, daughter of Nilus, bore him the twins Aegyptus and Danaus, and a third son, Cepheus. Aegyptus was given Arabia as his kingdom; but also subdued the country of the Melampodes, and named it Egypt after himself. Fifty sons were born to him of various mothers: Danaus, sent to rule Libya, had fifty daughters, called the Danaids, also born of various mothers.

On Belus's death, the twins quarrelled over their inheritance, and as a conciliatory gesture Aegyptus proposed a mass-marriage between the fifty princes and the fifty princesses. Danaus would not consent and, when an oracle confirmed his fears that Aegyptus had it in his mind to kill all the Danaids, prepared to flee from Libya.

With Athene's assistance, he built a ship for himself and his daughters and they sailed towards Greece together, by way of Rhodes. There Danaus dedicated an image to Athene in a temple raised for her by the Danaids.

From Rhodes they sailed to the Peloponnese and landed near

Lerna, where Danaus announced that he was divinely chosen to become King of Argos. Gelanor the Argive king, would doubtless have kept the throne, despite Danaus's declaration that Athene was supporting him, had not a wolf come boldly down from the hills, attacked a herd of cattle grazing near the city walls, and killed the leading bull. This was read as an omen that Danaus would take the throne by violence if he were opposed, and therefore persuaded Gelanor to resign it peacefully.

Danaus, convinced that the wolf had been Apollo in disguise, dedicated the famous shrine to Wolfish Apollo at Argos, and became so powerful a ruler that all the Pelasgians of Greece called themselves Danaans. He also built the citadel of Argos, and his daughters brought the Mysteries of Demeter from Egypt, and taught these to the Pelasgian women.

Danaus had found Argolis suffering from a prolonged drought, since Poseidon had dried up all the rivers and streams. He sent his daughters in search of water, with orders to placate Poseidon. One of them, by name Amymone, while chasing a deer in the forest, happened to disturb a sleeping satyr. He sprang up and tried to ravish her; but Poseidon, whom she invoked, hurled his trident at the satyr. The fleeing satyr dodged, the trident stuck quivering in a rock, and Poseidon himself lay with Amymone, who was glad that she could carry out her father's instructions so pleasantly. On learning her errand, Poseidon told her to pull his trident from the rock. When she did so, three streams of water jetted up from the three tine-holes. This spring, now named Amymone, is the source of the river Lerna, which never fails, even at the height of summer.

Aegyptus now sent his sons to Argos, forbidding them to return until they had punished Danaus and his whole family. On their arrival, they begged Danaus to reverse his former decision and let them marry his daughters – intending, however, to murder them on the wedding night. When he still refused, they laid siege to Argos. Now, the Argive citadel was waterless at the time in question. Seeing that thirst would soon force him to capitulate, Danaus promised to do what the sons of Aegyptus asked, as soon as they raised the siege.

A mass-marriage was arranged, and Danaus paired off the couples; but during the wedding-feast he secretly doled out sharp pins which his daughters were to conceal in their hair; and at midnight each stabbed her husband through the heart. There was only one survivor: on Artemis's advice, Hypermnestra saved the life of Lynceus, because he had spared her maidenhead, and helped him in his flight. At dawn, Danaus learned of Hypermnestra's disobedience, and she was tried for her life; but acquitted by the Argive judges.

The murdered men's heads were buried at Lerna, and their bodies given full funeral honours below the walls of Argos; but, although Athene and Hermes purified the Danaids in the Lernaean Lake with

Zeus's permission, the Judges of the Dead have condemned them to the endless task of carrying water in jars perforated like sieves.

Lynceus and Hypermnestra were reunited, and Danaus, deciding to marry off the other daughters before noon on the day of their purification, called for suitors. He proposed a marriage race, the winner to have first choice of a wife, and the others the next choices, in their order of finishing the race. Since he could not find enough men who would risk their lives by marrying murderesses, only a few ran; but when the wedding night passed without disaster to the new bridegrooms, more suitors appeared, and another race was run on the following day. Lynceus later killed Danaus, and reigned in his stead. Meanwhile, Aegyptus had come to Greece, but when he learned of his sons' fate, fled to Aroe, where he died, and was buried at Patrae, in a sanctuary of Serapis.

Leda

Some say that when Zeus fell in love with Nemesis, she fled from him into the water and became a fish; he pursued her as a beaver. She leaped ashore, and transformed herself into this wild beast or that, but could not shake Zeus off, because he borrowed the form of even fiercer and swifter beasts. At last she took to the air as a wild goose; he became a swan, and trod her triumphantly at Rhamnus in Attica. Nemesis came to Sparta, where Leda, wife of King Tyndareus, presently found a hyacinth-coloured egg lying in a marsh, which she brought home and hid in a chest: from it Helen of Troy was hatched.

The most usual account, however, is that it was Leda herself with whom Zeus companied in the form of a swan beside the river Eurotas; that she laid an egg from which were hatched Helen, Castor, and Polydeuces; and that she was consequently deified as the goddess Nemesis. Now, Leda's husband Tyndareus had also lain with her the same night and, though some hold that all these three were Zeus's children – and Clytaemnestra too, who had been hatched, with Helen, from a second egg – others record that Helen alone was a daughter of Zeus, and that Castor and Polydeuces were Tyndareus's sons; others again, that Castor and Clytaemnestra were children of Tyndareus, while Helen and Polydeuces were children of Zeus.

Ixion

Ixion, a son of Phlegyas, the Lapith king, agreed to marry Dia, daughter of Eioneus. Inviting Eioneus to a banquet, he laid a pitfall in front of the palace, with a great charcoal fire underneath, into which the unsuspecting Eioneus fell and was burned. Zeus, having behaved equally ill himself when in love, not only purified Ixion but brought him to eat at his table.

Ixion was ungrateful, and planned to seduce Hera: Zeus, however, reading Ixion's intentions, shaped a cloud into a false Hera with whom Ixion, being far too gone in drink to notice the deception, duly

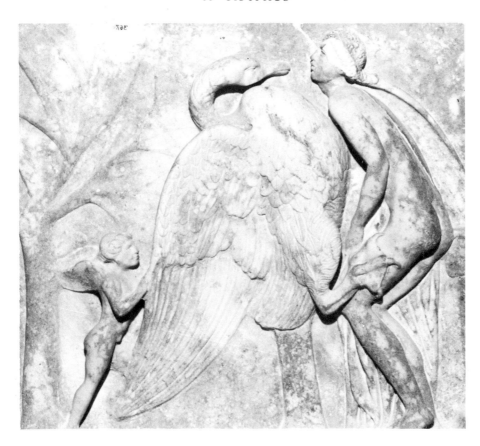

Leda and the Swan
(Heraklion Museum,
Crete)

took his pleasure. He was surprised in the act by Zeus, who ordered
Hermes to scourge him mercilessly and then bind him to a fiery wheel
which rolled without cease through the sky.

The false Hera bore Ixion the outcast child Centaurus who, when
he grew to manhood, is said to have sired horse-centaurs on Magnesian mares, of whom the most celebrated was the learned Cheiron.

Sisyphus

Sisyphus, son of Aeolus, married Atlas's daughter Merope, the
Pleiad, who bore him Glaucus, Ornytion, and Sinon, and owned a
fine herd of cattle on the Isthmus of Corinth.

Near him lived Autolycus, son of Chione, whose twin-brother
Philammon was begotten by Apollo, though Autolycus himself
claimed Hermes as his father.

Now, Autolycus was a past master in theft, Hermes having given
him the power of metamorphosing whatever beasts he stole. Thus,
although Sisyphus noticed that his own herds grew steadily smaller,
while those of Autolycus increased, he was unable at first to convict
him of theft; and therefore, one day, engraved the inside of all his
cattle's hooves with the monogram SS. That night Autolycus helped

*Sisyphus in Hades.
Black-figured Attic vase*

himself as usual, and at dawn hoof-prints along the road provided Sisyphus with sufficient evidence to summon neighbours in witness of the theft. He visited Autolycus's stable, recognized his stolen beasts by their marked hooves and, leaving his witnesses to remonstrate with the thief, hurried around the house and, while the argument was in progess outside, seduced Autolycus's daughter Anticleia. She bore him Odysseus, the manner of whose conception is enough to account for his habitual cunning.

Sisyphus founded Ephyra, afterwards known as Corinth, and peopled it with men sprung from mushrooms.

After Zeus's abduction of Aegina, her father the River-god Asopus came to Corinth in search of her. Sisyphus knew well what had happened to Aegina but would not reveal anything unless Asopus undertook to supply the citadel of Corinth with a perennial spring. Asopus accordingly made the spring Peirene rise: then Sisyphus told him all he knew.

Zeus, who had narrowly escaped Asopus's vengeance, ordered his brother Hades to fetch Sisyphus down to Tartarus and punish him everlastingly for his betrayal of divine secrets. Yet Sisyphus would not be daunted: he cunningly put Hades himself in handcuffs by persuading him to demonstrate their use, and then quickly locking them. Thus Hades was kept a prisoner in Sisyphus's house for some days, until at last Ares, whose interests were threatened, came hurrying up, set him free, and delivered Sisyphus into his clutches.

Sisyphus, however, kept another trick in reserve. Before descending to Tartarus, he instructed his wife Merope not to bury him; and, on reaching the Palace of Hades went straight to Persephone, and told her that, as an unburied person, he had no right to be there but should have been left on the far side of the river Styx. 'Let me return to the upper world,' he pleaded, 'arrange for my burial, and avenge the neglect shown me. My presence here is most irregular. I will be back within three days.' Persephone was deceived and granted his request; but as soon as Sisyphus found himself once again under the light of the sun, he repudiated his promise to Persephone. Finally, Hermes was called upon to hale him back by force.

Sisyphus was now given an exemplary punishment. The Judges of the Dead showed him a huge block of stone – identical in size with that into which Zeus had turned himself when fleeing from Asopus – and ordered him to roll it up the brow of the hill and topple it down the farther slope. He has never yet succeeded in doing so. As soon as he has almost reached the summit, he is forced back by the weight of the shameless stone, which bounces to the very bottom once more; where he wearily retrieves it and must begin all over again, though sweat bathes his limbs, and a cloud of dust rises above his head.

Merope, ashamed to find herself the only Pleiad with a husband in the Underworld – and a criminal too – deserted her six starry sisters in the night sky and has never been seen since.

Alcestis

Alcestis, the most beautiful of Pelias's daughters, was asked in marriage by many kings and princes. Not wishing to endanger his political position by refusing any of them, and yet clearly unable to satisfy more than one, Pelias let it be known that he would marry Alcestis to the man who could yoke a wild boar and a lion to his chariot and drive them around the race-course. At this, Admetus King of Pherae summoned Apollo, whom Zeus had bound to him for one year as a herdsman, and asked: 'Have I treated you with the respect due to your godhead?' 'You have indeed,' Apollo assented. 'Then,' pleaded Admetus, 'pray help me to win Alcestis, by enabling me to fulfil Pelias's conditions.' 'I shall be pleased to do so,' replied Apollo. Heracles lent him a hand and presently Admetus was driving his chariot around the race-course drawn by this savage team.

It is not known why Admetus omitted the customary sacrifice to Artemis before marrying Alcestis, but the goddess was quick enough to punish him. When he entered the bridal chamber that night, he recoiled in horror. No lovely naked bride awaited him, but a tangled knot of hissing serpents. Admetus ran shouting for Apollo, who kindly intervened with Artemis on his behalf. The neglected sacrifice having been offered at once, all was well, Apollo even obtaining Artemis's promise that, when Admetus's death came, he should be spared on condition that a member of his family died voluntarily for love of him.

This fatal day came sooner than Admetus expected. Hermes flew into the palace one morning and summoned him to Tartarus. General consternation prevailed; Admetus ran in haste to his old parents, and begged each of them in turn to surrender him the butt-end of existence. Both roundly refused, saying that he should be content with his appointed lot, like everyone else.

Then, for love of Admetus, Alcestis took poison and her ghost descended to Tartarus; but Heracles arrived unexpectedly with a new wild-olive club, and rescued her.

Athamas

Athamas the Aeolian, brother of Sisyphus and Salmoneus, ruled over Boeotia. At Hera's command, he married Nephele, a phantom whom Zeus created in her likeness when he wished to deceive Ixion the Lapith, and who was now wandering disconsolately about the halls of Olympus. She bore Athamas two sons: Phrixus and Leucon, and a daughter, Helle. But Athamas resented the disdain in which Nephele held him and, falling in love with Ino, daughter of Cadmus, brought her secretly to his palace at the foot of Mount Laphystium, where he begot Learchus and Melicertes on her.

Learning about her rival from the palace servants, Nephele returned in fury to Olympus, complaining to Hera that she had been insulted. Hera took her part, and vowed: 'My eternal vengeance shall fall upon Athamas and his House!'

Nephele thereupon went back to Mount Laphystium, where she publicly reported Hera's vow, and demanded that Athamas should die. But the men of Boeotia, who feared Athamas more than Hera, would not listen to Nephele; and the women of Boeotia were devoted to Ino, who now persuaded them to parch the seed-corn, without their husbands' knowledge, so that the harvest would fail. Ino foresaw that when the grain was due to sprout, but no blade appeared, Athamas would send to ask the Delphic Oracle what was amiss. She had already bribed Athamas's messengers to bring back a false reply: that the land would regain its fertility only if Nephele's son Phrixus were sacrificed to Zeus on Mount Laphystium.

Bronze statuette of Hermes with a ram (National Archaeological Museum, Athens)

This Phrixus was a handsome young man, with whom his aunt Biadice, Cretheus's wife, had fallen in love, and whom, when he rebuffed her advances, she accused of trying to ravish her. The men of Boeotia, believing Biadice's story, applauded Apollo's wise choice of a sin-offering and demanded that Phrixus should die; whereupon Athamas, loudly weeping, led Phrixus to the mountain top. He was on the point of cutting his throat when Heracles, who happened to be in the neighbourhood, came running up and wrested the sacrificial flint from his hand. 'My father Zeus,' Heracles exclaimed, 'loathes human sacrifices!' Nevertheless, Phrixus would have perished despite this plea, had not a winged golden ram, supplied by Hermes at Hera's order – or, some say, by Zeus himself – suddenly flown down to the rescue from Olympus.

'Climb on my back!' cried the ram, and Phrixus obeyed.

'Take me too!' pleaded Helle. 'Do not leave me to the mercy of my father.'

So Phrixus pulled her up behind him, and the ram flew eastwards, making for the land of Colchis, where Helius stables his horses. Before long, Helle felt giddy and lost her hold; she fell into the straits between Europe and Asia, now called the Hellespont in her honour; but Phrixus reached Colchis safely, and there sacrificed the ram to Zeus the Deliverer. Its golden fleece became famous a generation later when the Argonauts came in search of it.

Overawed by the miracle of Mount Laphystium, Athamas's messengers confessed that they had been bribed by Ino to bring back a false reply from Delphi; and presently all her wiles, and Biadice's, came to light. Nephele thereupon again demanded that Athamas should die, and the sacrificial fillet, which Phrixus had worn, was placed on his head; only Heracles's renewed intervention saved him from death.

But Hera was incensed with Athamas and drove him mad, not only on Nephele's account, but because he had connived at Ino's harbouring of the infant Dionysus, Zeus's bastard by her sister Semele, who was living in the palace disguised as a girl. Seizing his bow,

Athamas suddenly yelled: 'Look, a white stag! Stand back while I shoot!' So saying, he transfixed Learchus with an arrow, and proceeded to tear his still-quivering body into pieces.

Ino snatched up Melicertes, her younger son, and fled; but would hardly have escaped Athamas's vengeance, had not the infant Dionysus temporarily blinded him, so that he began to flog a she-goat in mistake for her. Ino ran to the Molurian Rock, where she leaped into the sea and was drowned – this rock afterwards became a place of ill-repute, because the savage Sciron used to hurl strangers from it. But Zeus, remembering Ino's kindness to Dionysus, would not send her ghost down to Tartarus and deified her instead as the Goddess Leucothea. He also deified her son Melicertes as the God Palaemon, and sent him to the Isthmus of Corinth riding on dolphin-back; the Isthmian Games, founded in his honour by Sisyphus, were celebrated there every fourth year.

Athamas, now banished from Boeotia, and childless because his remaining son, Leucon, had sickened and died, enquired from the Delphic Oracle where he should settle, and was told: 'Wherever wild beasts entertain you to dinner.' Wandering aimlessly northward, without food or drink, he came on a wolf-pack devouring a flock of sheep in a desolate Thessalian plain. The wolves fled at his approach, and he and his starving companions ate what mutton had been left. Then he recalled the oracle and, having adopted Haliartus and Coronea, his Corinthian grand-nephews, founded a city which he called Alos, from his wanderings, or from his serving-maid Alos; and the country was called Athamania; afterwards he married Themisto and raised a new family.

The Mares of Glaucus

Glaucus, son of Sisyphus and Merope, and father of Bellerophon, lived at Potniae near Thebes where, scorning the power of Aphrodite, he refused to let his mares breed. He hoped by this means to make them more spirited than other contestants in the chariot races which were his chief interest. But Aphrodite was vexed; and complained to Zeus that he had gone so far as to feed the mares on human flesh. When Zeus permitted her to take what action she pleased against Glaucus, she led the mares out by night to drink from a well sacred to herself, and graze on a herb called hippomanes which grew at its lip. This she did just before Jason celebrated the funeral games of Pelias on the seashore at Iolcus; and no sooner had Glaucus yoked the mares to his chariot pole than they bolted, overthrew the chariot, dragged him along the ground, entangled in the reins, for the whole length of the stadium, and then ate him alive.

Glaucus's ghost, called the Taraxippus, or Horse-scarer, then haunted the Isthmus of Corinth, where his father Sisyphus first taught him the charioteer's art, and delighted in scaring the horses at the Isthmian Games, thus causing many deaths.

Perseus

Abas, King of Argolis and grandson of Danaus, married Aglaia, to whose twin sons, Proetus and Acrisius, he bequeathed his kingdom, bidding them rule alternately. Their quarrel, which began in the womb, became more bitter than ever when Proetus lay with Acrisius's daughter Danaë, and barely escaped alive. Since Acrisius now refused to give up the throne at the end of his term, Proetus fled to the court of Iobates, King of Lycia, whose daughter Anteia he married; returning presently at the head of a Lycian army. A bloody battle was fought, but since neither side gained the advantage, Proetus and Acrisius reluctantly agreed to divide the kingdom between them. Acrisius's share was to be Argos and its environs; Proetus's was to be Tiryns, the Heraeum, Midea, and the coast of Argolis.

Acrisius, who was married to Aganippe, had no sons, but only this one daughter Danaë whom Proetus had seduced; and, when he asked an oracle how to procure a male heir, was told: 'You will have no sons, and your grandson must kill you.' To forestall this fate, Acrisius imprisoned Danaë in a dungeon with brazen doors, guarded by savage dogs; but, despite these precautions, Zeus came upon her in a shower of gold, and she bore him a son named Perseus. When Acrisius learned of Danaë's condition, he would not believe that Zeus was the father, and suspected his brother Proetus but, not daring to kill his own daughter, locked her and the infant Perseus in a wooden ark, which he cast into the sea. This ark was washed towards the island of Seriphos, where a fisherman named Dictys hauled it ashore, and found both Danaë and Perseus still alive. He took them at once to his brother, King Polydectes, who reared Perseus in his own house.

Some years passed and Perseus, grown to manhood, defended Danaë against Polydectes who had tried to force marriage upon her. Polydectes then assembled his friends and, pretending that he was about to sue for the hand of Hippodameia, daughter of Pelops, asked them to contribute one horse apiece as his love-gift.

'Alas,' answered Perseus, 'I possess no horse, nor any gold to buy one. But if you intend to marry Hippodameia, and not my mother, I will contrive to win whatever gift you name.' He added rashly: 'Even the Gorgon Medusa's head, if need be.'

'That would indeed please me more than any horse in the world,' replied Polydectes at once. Now, the Gorgon Medusa had serpents for hair, huge teeth, protruding tongue, and altogether so ugly a face that all who gazed at it were petrified with fright.

Athene overheard the conversation and, being a sworn enemy of Medusa's, accompanied Perseus on his adventure. First she led him to the city of Deicterion in Samos, where images of all the three Gorgons are displayed, thus enabling him to distinguish Medusa from her immortal sisters Stheno and Euryale; then she warned him never to look at Medusa directly, but only at her reflection, and presented him with a brightly-polished shield.

Medusa. Detail from a vase (British Museum)

Hermes also helped Perseus, giving him an adamantine sickle with which to cut off Medusa's head. But Perseus still needed a pair of winged sandals, a magic wallet to contain the decapitated head, and the dark helmet of invisibility which belonged to Hades. All these things were in the care of the Stygian Nymphs, from whom Perseus had to fetch them; but their whereabouts were known only to the Gorgons' sisters, the three swan-like Graeae, who had a single eye and tooth among the three of them. Perseus accordingly sought out the Graeae on their thrones at the foot of Mount Atlas. Creeping up behind them, he snatched the eye and tooth, as they were being passed from one sister to another, and would not return either until he had been told where the Stygian Nymphs lived.

Perseus then collected the sandals, wallet, and helmet from the nymphs, and flew westwards to the Land of the Hyperboreans, where he found the Gorgons asleep, among rain-worn shapes of men and wild beasts petrified by Medusa. He fixed his eyes on the reflection in the shield, Athene guided his hand, and he cut off Medusa's head with one stroke of the sickle; whereupon, to his surprise, the winged horse Pegasus, and the warrior Chrysaor grasping a golden falchion, sprang fully-grown from her dead body.

Hurriedly thrusting the head into his wallet, he took flight; and though Stheno and Euryale, awakened by their new nephews, rose to pursue him, the helmet made Perseus invisible, and he escaped safely southward.

At sunset, Perseus alighted near the palace of the Titan Atlas to whom, as a punishment for his inhospitality, he showed the Gorgon's head and thus transformed him into a mountain; and on the following day turned eastward and flew across the Libyan desert, Hermes helping him to carry the weighty head. By the way he dropped the Graeae's eye and tooth into Lake Triton; and some drops of Gorgon blood fell on the desert sand, where they bred a swarm of venomous serpents.

Perseus paused for refreshment at Chemmis in Egypt, and then flew on. As he rounded the coast of Philistia he caught sight of a naked woman chained to a sea-cliff, and instantly fell in love with her. This was Andromeda, daughter of Cepheus, the Ethiopian King of Joppa, and Cassiopeia. Cassiopeia had boasted that both she and her daughter were more beautiful than the Nereids, who complained of this insult to their protector Poseidon. Poseidon sent a flood and a female sea-monster to devastate Philistia; and when Cepheus consulted the Oracle of Ammon, he was told that his only hope of deliverance lay in sacrificing Andromeda to the monster. His subjects had therefore obliged him to chain her to a rock, naked except for certain jewels, and leave her to be devoured.

As Perseus flew towards Andromeda, he saw Cepheus and Cassiopeia watching anxiously from the shore near by, and alighted beside them. On condition that, if he rescued her, she should be his wife and return to Greece with him, Perseus took to the air again, grasped his sickle and, diving from above, beheaded the approaching monster.

Cepheus and Cassiopeia grudgingly welcomed him as their son-in-law and, on Andromeda's insistence, the wedding took place at once; but the festivities were rudely interrupted when Agenor, King Belus's twin brother, entered at the head of an armed party, claiming Andromeda for himself. He was doubtless summoned by Cassiopeia, since she and Cepheus at once broke faith with Perseus, pleading that the promise of Andromeda's hand had been forced from them by circumstances, and that Agenor's claim was the prior one.

'Perseus must die!' cried Cassiopeia fiercely.

In the ensuing fight, Perseus struck down many of his opponents but, being greatly outnumbered, was forced to snatch the Gorgon's head and turn the remaining two hundred of them to stone. Poseidon set the images of Cepheus and Cassiopeia among the stars; but Athene afterwards placed Andromeda's image in a more honourable constellation, because she had insisted on marrying Perseus, despite her parents' ill faith.

Perseus returned hurriedly to Seriphos, taking Andromeda with him, and found that Danaë and Dictys, threatened by the violence of Polydectes, had taken refuge in a temple. He therefore went straight to the palace where Polydectes was banqueting and announced that he had brought the promised love-gift. Greeted by a storm of insults, he displayed the Gorgon's head and turned them all to stone. He then gave the head to Athene, who fixed it on her aegis; and Hermes returned the sandals, wallet, and helmet to the guardianship of the Stygian nymphs.

After raising Dictys to the throne of Seriphos, Perseus set sail for Argos. Acrisius, hearing of his approach, fled to Pelasgian Larissa; but Perseus happened to be invited there for the funeral games and competed in the fivefold contest. When it came to the discus-throw, his discus, carried out of its path by the wind and the will of the Gods, struck Acrisius's foot and killed him. Greatly grieved, Perseus buried his grandfather in the temple of Athene which crowned the local acropolis and then, being ashamed to reign in Argos, went to Tiryns, where Proetus had been succeeded by his son Megapenthes, and arranged to exchange kingdoms with him.

Zeus with a thunderbolt. Bronze miniature (National Archaeological Museum, Athens)

The Rival Twins

WHEN the male line of Polycaon's House had died out after five generations, the Messenians invited Perieres, the son of Aeolus, to be their king, and he married Perseus's daughter Gorgophone. She survived him and was the first widow to remarry, her new husband being Oebalus the Spartan. Hitherto it had been customary for women to commit suicide on the death of their husbands.

Aphareus and Leucippus were Gorgophone's sons by Perieres, whereas Tyndareus and Icarius were her sons by Oebalus. Tyndareus succeeded his father on the throne of Sparta, Icarius acting as his co-king; but Hippocoön and his twelve sons expelled both of them. Taking refuge with King Thestius in Aetolia, Tyndareus married his daughter Leda, who bore him Castor and Clytaemnestra, at the same time bearing Helen and Polydeuces to Zeus. Later, having adopted Polydeuces, Tyndareus regained the Spartan throne.

Meanwhile, his half-brother Aphareus had succeeded Perieres on the throne of Messene, where Leucippus acted as his co-king and enjoyed the lesser powers. Aphareus took to wife his half-sister Arene, who bore him Idas and Lynceus; though Idas was, in truth, Poseidon's son. Now, Leucippus's daughters, the Leucippides, namely Phoebe, a priestess of Athene, and Hilaeria, a priestess of Artemis, were betrothed to their cousins, Idas and Lynceus; but Castor and Polydeuces, who are commonly known as the Dioscuri, carried them off, and had two sons by them; which occasioned a bitter rivalry between the two sets of twins.

The Dioscuri, who were never separated from one another in any adventure, became the pride of Sparta. Castor was famous as a soldier and tamer of horses, Polydeuces as the best boxer of his day; both won prizes at the Olympic Games. Their cousins and rivals were no less devoted to each other; Idas had greater strength than Lynceus, but Lynceus such sharp eyes that he could see in the dark or divine the whereabouts of buried treasure.

Now, Evenus, a son of Ares, had married Alcippe, by whom he became the father of Marpessa. In an attempt to keep her a virgin, he invited each of her suitors in turn to run a chariot race with him; the victor would win Marpessa, the vanquished would forfeit his head. Soon many heads were nailed to the walls of Evenus's house and Apollo, falling in love with Marpessa, expressed his disgust of so barbarous a custom; and said that he would soon end it by challenging Evenus to a race. But Idas had also set his heart on Marpessa, and begged a winged chariot from his father Poseidon. Before Apollo could act, he had driven to Aetolia, and carried Marpessa away from the midst of a band of dancers. Evenus gave chase, but could not overtake Idas, and felt such mortification that, after killing his horses, he drowned himself in the river Lycormas, ever since called the Evenus.

When Idas reached Messene, Apollo tried to take Marpessa from them. They fought a duel, but Zeus parted them, and ruled that Marpessa herself should decide whom she preferred to marry. Fearing that Apollo would cast her off when she grew old, as he had done with many another of his loves, she chose Idas for her husband.

Idas and Lynceus were among the Calydonian hunters, and sailed in the *Argo* to Colchis. One day, after the death of Aphareus, they and the Dioscuri patched up their quarrel sufficiently to join forces in a cattle-raid on Arcadia. The raid proved successful, and Idas was chosen by lot to divide the booty among the four of them. He therefore quartered a cow, and ruled that half the spoil should go to the man who ate his share first, the remainder to the next quickest. Almost before the others had settled themselves to begin the contest, Idas bolted his own share and then helped Lynceus to bolt his; soon down went the last gobbet, and he and Lynceus drove the cattle away towards Messene. The Dioscuri remained, until Polydeuces, the slower of the two, had finished eating; whereupon they marched against Messene, and protested to the citizens that Lynceus had forfeited his share by accepting help from Idas, and that Idas had forfeited his by not waiting until all the contestants were ready. Idas and Lynceus happened to be away on Mount Taygetus, sacrificing to Poseidon; so the Dioscuri seized the disputed cattle, and other plunder as well, and then hid inside a hollow oak to await their rival's return. But Lynceus had caught sight of them from the summit of Taygetus; and Idas, hurrying down the mountain slope, hurled his spear at the tree and transfixed Castor. When Polydeuces rushed out to avenge his brother, Idas tore the carved headstone from Aphareus's tomb, and threw it at him. Although badly crushed,

Polydeuces contrived to kill Lynceus with his spear; and at this point Zeus intervened on behalf of his son, striking Idas dead with a thunderbolt.

After setting up a trophy beside the Spartan race-course to celebrate his victory over Lynceus, Polydeuces prayed to Zeus: 'Father, let me not outlive my dear brother!' Since, however, it was fated that only one of Leda's sons should die, and since Castor's father Tyndareus had been a mortal, Polydeuces, as the son of Zeus, was duly carried up to Heaven. Yet he refused immortality unless Castor might share it, and Zeus therefore allowed them both to spend their days alternately in the upper air, and under the earth at Therapne. In further reward of their brotherly love, he set their images among the stars as the Twins.

Poseidon made Castor and Polydeuces the saviours of shipwrecked sailors, and granted them power to send favourable winds; in response to a sacrifice of white lambs offered on the prow of any ship, they would come hastening through the sky, followed by a train of sparrows. They presided at the Spartan Games, and because they invented the war-dance and war-like music were the patrons of all bards who sang of ancient battles.

Bellerophon

Bellerophon, son of Glaucus and grandson of Sisyphus, left Corinth under a cloud, having first killed one Bellerus and then his own brother. He fled as a suppliant to Proetus, King of Tiryns; but (so ill luck would have it) Anteia, Proetus's wife, fell in love with him at sight. When he rejected her advances, she accused him of having tried to seduce her, and Proetus believed the story. Yet he dared not risk the Furies' vengeance by the murder of a suppliant, and therefore sent him to Anteia's father Iobates, King of Lycia, carrying a sealed letter, which read: 'Pray remove the bearer from this world; he has tried to violate my wife, your daughter.'

Iobates, equally loth to ill-treat a royal guest, asked Bellerophon to do him the service of destroying the Chimaera, a fire-breathing she-monster with lion's head, goat's body, and serpent's tail. Before setting about this task, Bellerophon consulted the' seer Polyeidus, and was advised to catch and tame the winged horse Pegasus.

Bellerophon found Pegasus drinking at Peirene, on the Acropolis of Corinth, and threw over his head a golden bridle, Athene's timely present. Bellerophon then overcame the Chimaera by flying above her on Pegasus's back, riddling her with arrows, and then thrusting between her jaws a lump of lead fixed to the point of his spear. The Chimaera's fiery breath melted the lead, which trickled down her throat, searing her vitals.

Iobates, however, far from rewarding Bellerophon, sent him at once against the warlike Solymians and their allies, the Amazons; both of whom he conquered by soaring above them, well out of

Perseus cutting off Medusa's head (Archaeological Museum, Palermo, Sicily)

Perseus with Medusa's head. Detail from a red-figured water jug (British Museum)

bowshot, and dropping large boulders on their heads. Next, he beat off a band of Carian pirates; but when Iobates showed no gratitude even then but, on the contrary, sent the palace guards to ambush him on his return Bellerophon prayed that, while he advanced on foot, Poseidon would flood the Xanthian Plain behind him. Poseidon heard his prayer, and sent great waves rolling slowly forward and, because no man could persuade him to retire, the Xanthian women hoisted their skirts to the waist and came rushing towards him. Bellerophon's modesty was such that he turned tail and ran; and the waves retreated with him.

Convinced now that Proetus must have been mistaken about the attempt on Anteia's virtue, Iobates produced the letter, and demanded an exact account of the affair. On learning the truth, he implored Bellerophon's forgiveness, gave him his daughter Philonoë in marriage, and made him heir to the Lycian throne.

Bellerophon, at the height of his fortune, presumptuously undertook a flight to Olympus, as though he were an immortal; but Zeus sent a gadfly, which stung Pegasus under the tail, making him rear and fling his rider ingloriously to earth. Bellerophon, who had fallen into a thorn-bush, wandered about the earth, lame, blind, lonely and accursed, always avoiding the paths of men, until death overtook him.

The Calydonian Boar

Oeneus, King of Calydon in Aetolia, married Althaea. She first bore him Toxeus, and then Meleager, said to have been, in reality, her son by Ares. When Meleager was seven days old, the Fates announced that he could live only so long as a certain brand on the hearth remained unburned. Althaea at once snatched the brand from the fire, extinguished it with a pitcherful of water, and then hid it in a chest.

Meleager grew up to be the best javelin-thrower in Greece. He might still be alive but for Oeneus who forgot to include Artemis in his yearly sacrifices to the gods. Artemis, informed of this, sent a huge boar to ravage Calydon; but Oeneus despatched heralds, inviting all the bravest fighters of Greece to hunt the boar, and promising that whoever killed it should have its pelt and tusks.

Many answered the call, among them the chaste, swift-footed Atalanta, only daughter of Iasus and Clymene. Iasus had wished for a male heir and Atalanta's birth disappointed him so cruelly that he exposed her on the Parthenian Hill near Calydon, where she was suckled by a bear which Artemis sent to her aid. Atalanta grew to womanhood among a clan of hunters who found and reared her, but remained a virgin, and always carried arms.

Oeneus entertained the huntsmen royally; and though Ancaeus and Cepheus at first refused to hunt in company with a woman, Meleager declared that unless they withdrew their objection he would cancel the chase altogether. The truth was that Meleager now felt a sudden love for Atalanta and wished to ingratiate himself with her. His uncles, Althaea's brothers, took an immediate dislike to the girl, convinced that her presence could lead only to mischief. Thus the chase began under bad auspices; Artemis had seen to this.

The first blood shed was human: two Centaurs, Hylaeus and Rhaecus, who had joined the chase, decided to ravish Atalanta, each in turn assisting the other. But as soon as they ran towards her, she shot them both down.

Presently the boar came bounding out, killed two of the hunters, hamstrung another, and drove young Nestor up a tree. Jason and several others flung ill-aimed javelins, Iphicles alone contriving to graze its shoulder. Then Telamon and Peleus went in boldly with boar-spears; but Telamon tripped and, while Peleus was pulling him to his feet, the boar saw them and charged. Atalanta let fly a timely arrow, which sank in behind the ear, and sent it scurrying off. Ancaeus swung his battle-axe at the boar as it charged, but was not quick enough; the next instant he lay castrated and disembowelled. In his excitement, Peleus killed Eurytion with a javelin aimed at the boar, which Amphiaraus had succeeded in blinding. Next, it rushed at Theseus, whose javelin flew wide; but Meleager also flung and transfixed its right flank, and then, as the boar whirled around in pain, drove his hunting-spear deep to the heart.

The boar fell dead at last.

At once, Meleager flayed it, and presented the pelt to Atalanta, saying: 'You drew first blood, and had we left the beast alone, it would soon have succumbed to your arrow.'

His uncles were deeply offended. The eldest, Plexippus, argued that Meleager had won the pelt himself and that, on his refusal, it should have gone to the most honourable person present – namely himself, as Oeneus's brother-in-law. Plexippus's younger brother supported him with the contention that Iphicles, not Atalanta, had drawn first blood. Meleager, in a lover's rage, killed them both.

Althaea, as she watched the dead bodies being carried home, set a curse upon Meleager; which prevented him from defending Calydon when his two surviving uncles declared war on the city. At last his wife Cleopatra persuaded him to take up arms, and he killed both these uncles, whereupon the Furies instructed Althaea to take the unburned brand from the chest and cast it on the fire. Meleager felt a sudden scorching of his inwards, and the enemy overcame him with ease. Althaea and Cleopatra hanged themselves, and Artemis turned all but two of Meleager's shrieking sisters into guinea-hens.

Delighted by Atalanta's success, Iasus recognized her at last as his daughter; but when she arrived at the palace his first words were: 'My child, prepare to take a husband!' – a disagreeable announcement, since the Delphic Oracle had warned her against marriage. She answered: 'Father, I consent on one condition. Any suitor for my hand must either beat me in a foot race, or else let me kill him.' 'So be it,' said Iasus.

Many unfortunate princes lost their lives in consequence, because she was the swiftest mortal alive; but Melanion, a son of Amphidamas the Arcadian, invoked Aphrodite's assistance. She gave him three golden apples, saying: 'Delay Atalanta by letting these fall, one after the other, in the course of the race.' The stratagem was successful. Atalanta stooped to pick up each apple in turn and reaching the winning-post just behind Melanion.

The marriage took place, but the Oracle's warning was justified because, one day, as they passed by a precinct of Zeus, Melanion persuaded Atalanta to come inside and lie with him there. Vexed that his precinct had been defiled, Zeus changed them both into lions: for lions do not mate with lions, but only with leopards, and they were thus prevented from ever again enjoying each other. This was Aphrodite's punishment, first for Atalanta's obstinacy in remaining a virgin, and then for her lack of gratitude in the matter of the golden apples.

Midas

Midas, son of the Great Goddess of Ida by a satyr, was a pleasure-loving King of Macedonian Bromium, where he ruled over the Brigians and planted his celebrated rose gardens. In his infancy, a procession of ants was observed carrying grains of wheat up the side of his cradle and placing them between his lips as he slept – a prodigy which the soothsayers read as an omen of the great wealth that would accrue to him.

One day, the debauched old satyr Silenus, Dionysus's former pedagogue, happened to straggle from the main body of the riotous Dionysian army as it marched out of Thrace into Boeotia, and was found sleeping off his drunken fit in the gardens. The gardeners bound him with garlands of flowers and led him before Midas, to whom he told wonderful tales. Midas, enchanted by Silenus's fictions, entertained him for five days and nights, and then ordered a guide to escort him to Dionysus's headquarters.

Dionysus, who had been anxious on Silenus's account, sent to ask how Midas wished to be rewarded. He replied without hesitation: 'Pray grant that all I touch be turned into gold.' However, not only stones, flowers, and the furnishing of his house turned to gold, but the food he ate and the water he drank. Midas soon begged to be released from his wish, because he was fast dying of hunger and thirst; whereupon Dionysus told him to visit the source of the river Pactolus, near Mount Tmolus, and there wash himself. He obeyed, and was at once freed from the golden touch, but the sands of the river Pactolus are bright with gold to this day.

Midas, having thus entered Asia, was adopted by the childless Phrygian King Gordius. While only a poor peasant, Gordius had

above: *Pegasus and Bellerophon with the Chimera*
(British Museum)

opposite above: *The Dioscuri: Castor and*
Polydeuces. Amphora by Exekias (Vatican Museum)

opposite below: *Pegasus (British Museum)*

been surprised one day to see a royal eagle perch on the pole of his ox-cart. He drove the team towards Phrygian Telmissus, where there was a reliable oracle; but at the gate of the city he met a young prophetess who, when she saw the eagle still perched on the pole, insisted on his offering immediate sacrifices to Zeus the King. 'Let me come with you, peasant,' she said, 'to make sure that you choose the correct victims.' 'By all means,' replied Gordius. 'You appear to be a wise and considerate young woman. Are you prepared to marry me?' 'As soon as the sacrifices have been offered,' she answered.

Meanwhile, the King of Phrygia had died suddenly, without issue, and an oracle announced: 'Phrygians, your new king is approaching with his bride, seated in an ox-cart!'

When the ox-cart entered the market place of Telmissus, Gordius was unanimously acclaimed king. In gratitude, he dedicated the cart to Zeus, together with its yoke, which he had knotted to the pole in a peculiar manner. An oracle then declared that whoever discovered how to untie the knot would become the lord of all Asia. Yoke and pole were consequently laid up in the Acropolis at Gordium where the priests of Zeus guarded them jealously for centuries – until Alexander the Macedonian cut the knot with his sword. After Gordius's death, Midas succeeded to the throne, promoted the worship of Dionysus, and founded the city of Ancyra.

Midas attended the famous musical contest between Apollo and Marsyas, umpired by the River-god Tmolus. Tmolus awarded the prize to Apollo who, when Midas dissented from the verdict, punished him with a pair of ass's ears. For a long time, Midas managed to conceal these under a Phrygian cap; but his barber, made aware of the deformity, found it impossible to keep the shameful secret close, as Midas had enjoined him to do on pain of death. He therefore dug a hole in the river-bank and, first making sure that nobody was about, whispered into it: 'King Midas has ass's ears!' Then he filled up the hole, and went away, at peace with himself until a reed sprouted from the bank and whispered the secret to all who passed. When Midas learned that his disgrace had become public knowledge, he condemned the barber to death, drank bull's blood, and perished miserably.

Narcissus

Narcissus was a Thespian, the son of the blue Nymph Leiriope, whom the River-god Cephisus had once ravished. The seer Teiresias told Leiriope, the first person ever to consult him: 'Narcissus will live to a ripe old age, provided that he never knows himself.' Anyone might excusably have fallen in love with Narcissus, even as a child, and when he reached the age of sixteen, his path was strewn with heartlessly rejected lovers of both sexes; for he had a stubborn pride in his own beauty.

Among these was the nymph Echo, who could no longer use her

voice, except in foolish repetition of another's: a punishment for having kept Hera entertained with long stories while Zeus's concubines made good their escape. One day when Narcissus went out to net stags, Echo stealthily followed him, longing to address him, but unable to speak first. At last Narcissus, finding that he had strayed from his companions, shouted: 'Is anyone here?'

'Here!' Echo answered, which surprised Narcissus, since no one was in sight.

'Come!'

'Come!'

'Why do you avoid me?'

'Why do you avoid me?'

'Let us come together here!'

'Let us come together here!' repeated Echo, and joyfully rushed from her hiding place to embrace Narcissus. Yet he shook her off roughly, and ran away. 'I will die before you ever lie with me!' he cried.

'Lie with me!' Echo pleaded.

But Narcissus had gone, and she spent the rest of her life pining away for love and mortification, until only her voice remained.

One day, Narcissus sent a sword to Ameinius, his most insistent suitor. Ameinius killed himself on Narcissus's threshold, calling on the gods to avenge his death. Artemis heard the plea. At Donacon in Thespia, Narcissus came upon a spring, clear as silver, and as he cast himself down, exhausted, on the grassy verge to slake his thirst, he fell in love with his reflection, gazing enraptured into the pool. How could he endure both to possess and yet not to possess?

Echo, although she had not forgiven Narcissus, grieved with him; she sympathetically echoed 'Alas! Alas!' as he plunged a dagger in his breast, and also the final 'Ah, youth, beloved in vain, farewell!' as he expired. His blood soaked the earth, and up sprang the white narcissus flower with its red corolla.

Arion

Arion of Lesbos, a son of Poseidon and the Nymph Oneaea, was a master of the lyre. One day his patron Periander, tyrant of Corinth, reluctantly gave him permission to visit Taenarus in Sicily to compete in a musical festival. Arion won the prize, and so many rich gifts that these excited the greed of the sailors engaged to bring him back to Corinth.

'We much regret, Arion, that you will have to die,' remarked the captain of the ship.

'What crime have I committed?' asked Arion.

'You are too rich,' replied the captain.

'Spare my life, and I will give you all my prizes,' Arion pleaded.

'You would only retract your promise on reaching Corinth,' said the captain, 'and so would I, in your place. A forced gift is no gift.'

'Very well,' cried Arion resignedly. 'But pray allow me to sing a last song.'

When the captain gave his permission, Arion, dressed in his finest robe, mounted on the prow, where he invoked the gods with impassioned strains, and then leaped overboard. The ship sailed on.

However, his song had attracted a school of music-loving dolphins, one of which took Arion on his back, and that evening he overtook the ship and reached the port of Corinth several days before it cast anchor there. Periander was overjoyed at his miraculous escape, and when the ship docked, sent for the captain and crew, whom he asked with pretended anxiety for news of Arion.

'He has been delayed at Taenarus,' the captain answered, 'by the lavish hospitality of the inhabitants.'

Periander made them all swear that this was the truth, and then suddenly confronted them with Arion. Unable to deny their guilt, they were executed on the spot. Apollo later set the images of Arion and his lyre among the stars.

4

MINOS AND THESEUS

Minos and His Brothers

WHEN ZEUS LEFT EUROPE, after having fathered Minos, Rhadamanthys, and Sarpedon on her in Crete, she married Asterius, the reigning king. This marriage proving childless, Asterius adopted Minos, Rhadamanthys, and Sarpedon, and made them his heirs. But when the brothers grew to manhood, they quarrelled for the love of a beautiful boy named Miletus, begotten by Apollo on the Nymph Areia. Miletus having decided that he liked Sarpedon best, was driven from Crete by Minos, and sailed with a large fleet to Caria in Asia Minor, where he founded the city and kingdom of Miletus.

After Asterius's death, Minos claimed the Cretan throne and, in proof of his right to reign, boasted that the gods would answer whatever prayer he offered. First dedicating an altar to Poseidon, and making all preparations for a sacrifice, he then prayed that a bull might emerge from the sea. At once, a dazzlingly-white bull swam ashore, but Minos was so struck by its beauty that he sent it to join his own herds, and slaughtered another instead. Minos's claim to the throne was accepted by every Cretan, except Sarpedon who, still grieving for Miletus, declared that it had been Asterius's intention to divide the kingdom equally between his three heirs; and, indeed, Minos himself had already divided the island into three parts, and chosen a capital for each.

Expelled from Crete by Minos, Sarpedon fled to Cilicia in Asia Minor, where he allied himself with Cilix against the Milyans, conquered them, and became their king. Zeus granted him the privilege of living for three generations; and when he finally died, the Milyan kingdom was called Lycia, after his successor Lycus.

Meanwhile, Minos had married Pasiphaë, a daughter of Helius and the nymph Crete, but Poseidon, to avenge the affront offered him by Minos, made Pasiphaë fall in love with the white bull which had been withheld from sacrifice. She confided her unnatural passion to Daedalus, the famous Athenian craftsman, who now lived in exile at Cnossus. Daedalus promised to help her, and built a hollow wooden cow, which he set on wheels concealed in its hooves, and pushed into the meadow near Gortys, where Poseidon's bull was grazing. Then, having shown Pasiphaë how to open the folding doors in the cow's back, and slip inside with her legs thrust down into its hindquarters, he discreetly retired. Soon the white bull ambled up and mounted the cow, so that Pasiphaë had all her desire, and later gave birth to the Minotaur, a monster with a bull's head and a human body.

Minos consulted an oracle to know how he might best avoid scandal and conceal Pasiphaë's disgrace. The response was: 'Instruct Daedalus to build you a retreat at Cnossus!' This Daedalus did, and Minos spent the remainder of his life in the inextricable maze called the Labyrinth, at the very heart of which he concealed Pasiphaë and the Minotaur.

Rhadamanthys, wiser than Sarpedon, remained in Crete; he lived at peace with Minos, and was awarded a third part of Asterius's dominions. Renowned as a just and upright law-giver, inexorable in his punishment of evildoers, he legislated both for the Cretans and for the islanders of Asia Minor. Every ninth year, he would visit Zeus's cave and bring back a new set of laws, a custom afterwards followed by his brother Minos. He bequeathed land in Crete to his son Gortys, after whom the Cretan city was named. Rhadamanthys also bequeathed land in Asia Minor to his son Erythrus; and the island of Chios to Oenopion, the son of Ariadne, whom Dionysus first taught how to make wine; and Lemnos to Thoas, another of Ariadne's sons.

Rhadamanthys eventually fled to Boeotia because he had killed a kinsman, and lived there in exile at Ocaleae, where he married Alcmene, Heracles's mother, after the death of Amphitryon. But some say that Alcmene was married to Rhadamanthys in the Elysian Fields, after her death. For Zeus had appointed him one of the three Judges of the Dead; his colleagues were Minos and Aeacus, and he resided in the Elysian Fields.

Scylla and Nisus

Minos was the first king to control the Mediterranean Sea, which he cleared of pirates, and in Crete ruled over ninety cities. When the Athenians had murdered his son Androgeus, he decided to take vengeance on them, and sailed around the Aegean collecting ships and armed levies. Some islanders agreed to help him, some refused. Meanwhile, Minos was harrying the Isthmus of Corinth. He laid siege to Nisa, afterwards called Megara, ruled by Nisus the Egyptian, who had a daughter named Scylla. A tower stood in the city, and Scylla used to spend much time at its top. Here she climbed daily when the war began, to watch the fighting.

The siege of Nisa was protracted, and Scylla soon came to know the name of every Cretan warrior. Struck by the beauty of Minos, she fell perversely in love with him.

One night Scylla crept into her father's chamber, and cut off the famous bright lock on which his life and throne depended; then, taking from him the keys of the city gate, she opened it, and stole out. She made straight for Minos's tent, and offered him the lock of hair in exchange for his love. That same night, having entered the city and sacked it, he duly lay with Scylla; but would not take her to Crete, because he loathed the crime of parricide. Scylla, however, swam after his ship, and clung to the stern until her father Nisus's soul in the form of a sea-eagle swooped down upon her with talons and hooked beak. The terrified Scylla let go and was drowned; her soul flew off as a ciris-bird.

This war dragged on until Minos, finding that he could not subdue Athens, prayed Zeus to avenge Androgeus's death; and the whole of Greece was consequently afflicted with earthquakes and famine. The kings of the various city states assembled at Delphi to consult the Oracle, and were instructed to make Aeacus offer up prayers on their behalf. When this had been done, the earthquakes everywhere ceased, except in Attica.

The Athenians thereupon sought to redeem themselves from the curse by sacrificing to Persephone the daughters of Hyacinthus on the grave of the Cyclops Geraestus. These girls had come to Athens from Sparta. Yet the earthquakes continued and, when the Athenians again consulted the Delphic Oracle, they were told to give Minos whatever satisfaction he might ask; which proved to be a tribute of seven youths and seven maidens, sent every nine years to Crete as a prey for the Minotaur.

Daedalus and Talos

The parentage of Daedalus is disputed. His mother is named Alcippe by some; by others, Merope; by still others, Iphinoë; and all give him a different father, though it is generally agreed that he belonged to the royal house of Athens. He was a wonderful smith, having been instructed in his art by Athene herself.

One of his apprentices, Talos the son of his sister Polycaste, had already surpassed him in craftsmanship while only twelve years old. Talos happened one day to pick up the jawbone of a serpent and, finding that he could use it to cut a stick in half, copied it in iron and thereby invented the saw. This, and other inventions of his secured him a great reputation at Athens, and Daedalus, who himself claimed to have forged the first saw, soon grew unbearably jealous. Leading Talos up to the roof of Athene's temple on the Acropolis, he suddenly toppled him over the edge. Yet, for all his jealousy, he would have done Talos no harm had he not suspected him of incestuous relations with his mother Polycaste. Daedalus then hurried down to the foot of the Acropolis, and thrust Talos's corpse into a bag, proposing to bury

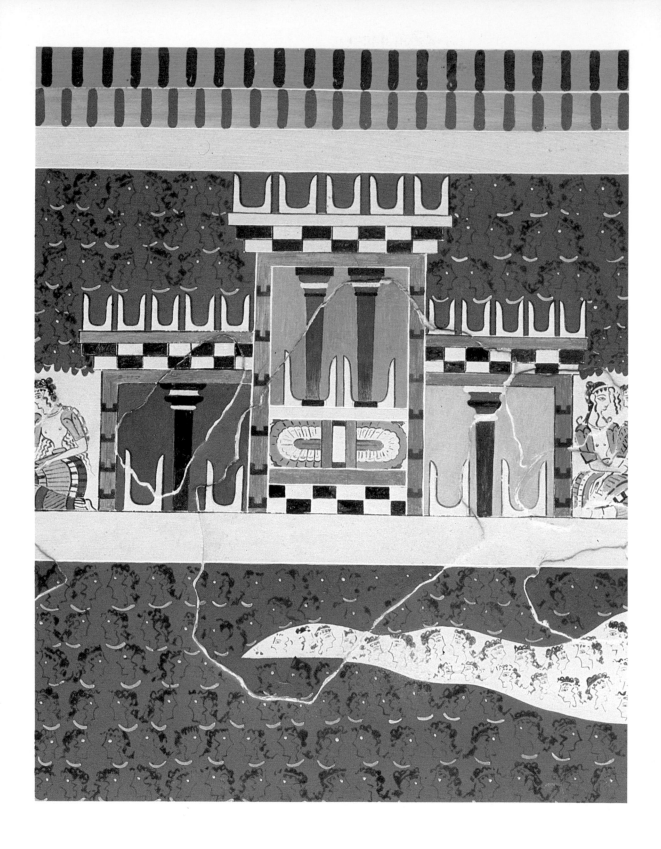

Fresco showing a contemporary view of the Palace of Cnossus (The Minoan Royal Palace, Knossos, Crete)

Coin showing Scylla (Pennisi Collection, Acireale, Sicily)

Relief of a bull's head (The Minoan Royal Palace, Knossos, Crete)

A bronze miniature of Icarus about to fly (British Museum)

it secretly. But his crime did not escape detection, whereupon the Areiopagus banished him for murder.

Now, Talos was also the name of Minos's bull-headed bronze servant, given him by Zeus to guard Crete. He was forged by Hephaestus in Sardinia, and had a single vein which ran from his neck down to his ankles, where it was stoppered by a bronze pin. It was his task to run thrice daily around the island of Crete and throw rocks at any foreign ship; and also to go thrice yearly, at a more leisurely pace, through the villages of Crete, displaying Minos's laws inscribed on brazen tablets. In the end, Medea killed Talos by pulling out the pin and letting his life-blood escape.

Daedalus took refuge in one of the Attic demes, whose people are named Daedalids after him; and then in Cretan Cnossus, where King Minos delighted to welcome so skilled a craftsman. He lived there for some time, at peace and in high favour, until Minos, learning that he had helped Pasiphaë to couple with Poseidon's white bull, locked him up for a while in the Labyrinth, together with his son Icarus, but Pasiphaë freed them both.

It was not easy, however, to escape from Crete, since Minos kept all his ships under military guard, and now offered a large reward for his apprehension. But Daedalus made a pair of wings for himself, and another for Icarus, the quill feathers of which were threaded together, but the smaller ones held in place by wax. Having tied on Icarus's pair for him, he said with tears in his eyes 'My son, be warned! Neither soar too high, lest the sun melt the wax; nor swoop too low, lest the feathers be wetted by the sea.' Then he slipped his arms into his own pair of wings and they flew off. 'Follow me closely,' he cried, 'do not set your own course!'

As they sped away from the island in a north-easterly direction, flapping their wings, the fishermen, shepherds, and ploughmen who gazed upward mistook them for gods.

They had left Naxos, Delos, and Paros behind them on the left hand, and were leaving Lebynthos and Calymne behind on the right, when Icarus disobeyed his father's instructions and began soaring towards the sun, rejoiced by the lift of his great sweeping wings. Presently, when Daedalus looked over his shoulder, he could no longer see Icarus; but scattered feathers floated on the waves below. The heat of the sun had melted the wax, and Icarus had fallen into the sea and drowned. Daedalus circled around, until the corpse rose to the surface, and then carried it to the near-by island now called Icaria, where he buried it. This island has now given its name to the surrounding sea.

Daedalus flew westward until, alighting at Cumae near Naples, he dedicated his wings to Apollo there, and built him a golden-roofed temple. Afterwards, he visited Camicus in Sicily, where he was hospitably received by King Cocalus, and lived among the Sicilians, enjoying great fame and erecting many fine buildings.

Meanwhile, Minos had raised a fleet, and set out in search of Daedalus. He brought with him a Triton shell, and wherever he went promised to reward anyone who could pass a linen thread through it: a problem which, he knew, Daedalus alone would be able to solve. Arrived at Camicus, he offered the shell to Cocalus, who undertook to have it threaded; and, sure enough, Daedalus found out how to do this. Fastening a gossamer thread to an ant, he bored a hole at the point of the shell and lured the ant up the spirals by smearing honey on the edges of the hole. Then he tied the linen thread to the other end of the gossamer and drew that through as well. Cocalus returned the threaded shell, claiming the reward, and Minos, assured that he had at last found Daedalus's hiding-place, demanded his surrender. But Cocalus's daughters were loth to lose Daedalus, who made them such beautiful toys, and with his help they concocted a plot. Daedalus led a pipe through the roof of the bathroom, down which they poured boiling water upon Minos, while he luxuriated in a warm bath. Cocalus returned the corpse to the Cretans, saying that Minos had stumbled over a rug and fallen into a cauldron of boiling water.

Minos's followers buried him with great pomp, and Zeus made him a judge of the dead in Tartarus, with his brother Rhadamanthys and his enemy Aeacus as colleagues. But Daedalus left Sicily to join Iolaus, the nephew and charioteer of Tirynthian Heracles, who led a body of Athenians and Thespians to Sardinia. Many of his works survived in Sardinia; they were called Daedaleia.

The Birth of Theseus
Aegeus's first wife was Melite, daughter of Hoples; and his second, Chalciope, daughter of Rhexenor; but neither bore him any children. Ascribing this, and the misfortunes of his sisters Procne and Philomela, to Aphrodite's anger, he introduced her worship into Athens, and then went to consult the Delphic Oracle. The Oracle warned him not to untie the mouth of his bulging wine-skin until he reached the highest point of Athens, lest he die one day of grief, a response which Aegeus could not interpret.

On his way home he called at Corinth; and here Medea made him swear a solemn oath that he would shelter her from all enemies if she ever sought refuge at Athens, and undertook in return to procure him a son by magic. Next, he visited Troezen, where his old comrades Pittheus and Troezen, sons of Pelops, had recently come from Pisa to share a kingdom with King Aetius.

Now, while Pittheus was still living at Pisa, Bellerophon had asked to marry his daughter Aethra, but had been sent away to Caria in disgrace before the marriage could be celebrated; though still contracted to Bellerophon, she had little hope of his return. Pittheus, therefore, grieving at her enforced virginity, and influenced by the spell which Medea was casting on all of them from afar, made Aegeus drunk, and sent him to bed with Aethra. Later in the same night, Poseidon also enjoyed her. Poseidon, however, generously conceded to Aegeus the paternity of any child born to Aethra in the course of the next four months.

Aegeus, when he awoke and found himself in Aethra's bed, told her that if a son were born to them he must not be exposed or sent away, but secretly reared in Troezen. Then he sailed back to Athens, to celebrate the All-Athenian Festival, after hiding his sword and his sandals under a hollow rock, known as the Altar of Strong Zeus, which stood on the road from Troezen to Hermium. If, when the boy grew up, he could move this rock and recover the tokens, he was to be sent with them to Athens. Meanwhile, Aethra must keep silence, lest Aegeus's nephews, the fifty children of Pallas, plotted against her life. The sword was an heirloom from Cecrops.

At a place called Genethlium, on the way from the city to the harbour of Troezen, Aethra gave birth to a boy. He was brought up in Troezen, where his guardian Pittheus discreetly spread the rumour that Poseidon had been his father; and one Connidas acted as his pedagogue.

One day Heracles, dining at Troezen with Pittheus, removed his lion-skin and threw it over a stool. When the palace children came in, they screamed and fled, all except seven-year-old Theseus, who ran to snatch an axe from the woodpile, and returned boldly, prepared to attack a real lion.

At the age of sixteen years he visited Delphi, and offered his first manly hair-clippings to Apollo. He shaved, however, only the forepart of his head, like the Arabians and Mysians, or like the war-like Abantes of Euboea, who thereby deny their enemies any advantage in close combat. This kind of tonsure, and the precinct where he performed the ceremony, were both later called Thesean. He was now a strong, intelligent and prudent youth; and Aethra, leading him to the rock underneath which Aegeus had hidden the sword and sandals, told him the story of his birth. He had no difficulty in moving the rock, and recovered the tokens. Yet, despite Pittheus's warnings and his mother's entreaties, he would not visit Athens by the safe sea route, but insisted on travelling overland; impelled by a desire to emulate the feats of his cousin-german Heracles, whom he greatly admired.

The Labours of Theseus
Theseus set out to free the bandit-ridden coast road which led from Troezen to Athens. He would pick no quarrels but take vengeance on all who dared molest him, making the punishment fit the crime, as was Heracles's way. At Epidaurus, Periphetes the cripple waylaid him. Periphetes, whom some call Poseidon's son, and others the son of Hephaestus and Anticleia, owned a huge brazen club, with which he used to kill wayfarers; hence his nickname Corunetes, or

'cudgel-man' Theseus wrenched the club from his hands and battered him to death. Delighted with its size and weight, he proudly carried it about ever afterwards; and though he himself had been able to parry its murderous swing, in his hands it never failed to kill.

At the narrowest point of the Isthmus, where both the Corinthian and Saronic Gulfs are visible, lived Sinis, the son of Polypemon. He had been nicknamed Pityocamptes, or 'pine-bender', because he was strong enough to bend down the tops of pine-trees until they touched the earth, and would often ask innocent passers-by to help him with this task, but then suddenly release his hold. As the tree sprang upright again, they were hurled high into the air, and killed by the fall. Or he would bend down the tops of two neighbouring trees until they met, and tie one of his victim's arms to each, so that he was torn asunder when the trees were released.

Theseus wrestled with Sinis, overpowered him, and served him as he had served others. At this, a beautiful girl ran to hide herself in a thicket of rushes and wild asparagus. He followed her and, after a long search, found her invoking the plants, promising never to burn or destroy them if they hid her safely. When Theseus swore not to do her any violence, she consented to emerge, and proved to be Sinis's daughter Perigune. Perigune fell in love with Theseus at sight, forgiving the murder of her hateful father and, in due course, bore him a son, Melanippus.

Next, at Crommyum, he hunted and destroyed a fierce and monstrous wild sow, which had killed so many Crommyonians that they no longer dared plough their fields. Then, following the coast road, Theseus came to the precipitous cliffs rising sheer from the sea, which had become a stronghold of the bandit Sciron. Sciron used to seat himself upon a rock and force passing travellers to wash his feet: when they stooped to the task he would kick them over the cliff into the sea, where a giant turtle swam about, waiting to devour them. Theseus, refusing to wash Sciron's feet, lifted him from the rock and flung him into the sea.

Continuing his journey to Athens, Theseus met Cercyon the Arcadian. He would challenge passers-by to wrestle with him and then crush them to death in his powerful embrace; but Theseus lifted him up by the knees and, to the delight of Demeter, who witnessed the struggle, dashed him headlong to the ground. Cercyon's death was instantaneous. Theseus did not trust to strength so much as skill, for he had invented the art of wrestling, the principles of which were not hitherto understood.

On reaching Attic Corydallus, Theseus slew Sinis's father Polypemon, surnamed Procrustes, who lived beside the road and had two beds in his house, one small, the other large. Offering a night's lodging to travellers, he would lay the short men on the large bed, and rack them out to fit it; but the tall men on the small bed, sawing off as much of their legs as projected beyond it. Some say, however, that he used only one bed, and lengthened or shortened his lodgers according to its measure. In either case, Theseus served him as he had served others.

Theseus and Medea

Arrived in Attica, Theseus was met beside the river Cephissus by the sons of Phytalus, who purified him from the blood he had spilled, but especially from that of Sinis, a maternal kinsman of his. Afterwards, the Phytalids welcomed Theseus as their guest, which was the first true hospitality he had received since leaving Troezen. Dressed in a long garment that reached to his feet and with his hair neatly plaited, he entered Athens. As he passed the nearly-completed temple of Apollo the Dolphin, a group of masons working on the roof mistook him for a girl, and impertinently asked why he was allowed to wander about unescorted. Disdaining to reply, Theseus unyoked the oxen from the masons' cart and tossed one of them into the air, high above the temple roof.

Now, while Theseus was growing up in Troezen, Aegeus had kept his promise to Medea. He gave her shelter in Athens when she fled from Corinth in the celebrated chariot drawn by winged serpents, and married her, rightly confident that her spells would enable him to beget an heir; for he did not yet know that Aethra had borne him Theseus. Medea, however, recognized Theseus as soon as he arrived in the city, and grew jealous on behalf of Medus, her son by Aegeus. She therefore persuaded Aegeus that Theseus came as a spy or an assassin, and had him invited to a feast at the Dolphin Temple; Aegeus, who used the temple as his residence, was then to offer him a cup of wine already prepared by her. This cup contained wolfsbane, a poison which she had brought from Bithynian Acherusia. Some say that when the roast beef was served Theseus drew his sword, as if to carve, and thus attracted his father's attention. Others that he had unsuspectingly raised the cup to his lips before Aegeus noticed the Erechtheid serpents carved on the ivory sword-hilt and dashed the poison to the floor.

Theseus with the bandit Sciron, whose feet he refused to wash. Red-figured drinking vessel (Antikenabteilung, Charlottenburg, Berlin)

Then followed the greatest rejoicing that Athens had ever known. Aegeus embraced Theseus, summoned a public assembly, and acknowledged him as his son. He lighted fires on every altar and heaped the gods' images with gifts; hecatombs of garlanded oxen were sacrificed and, throughout the palace and the city, nobles and commoners feasted together, and sang of Theseus's glorious deeds that already outnumbered the years of his life.

Theseus then went in vengeful pursuit of Medea, who eluded him by casting a magic cloud about herself; and presumably left Athens with Medus, and an escort which Aegeus generously provided.

Pallas and his fifty sons, who even before this had declared that Aegeus was not a true Erechtheid and thus had no right to the throne, broke into open revolt when this footloose stranger threatened to balk their hopes of ever ruling Athens. They divided their forces: Pallas with twenty-five of his sons and numerous retainers marched against the city from the direction of Sphettus, while the other twenty-five lay in ambush at Gargettus. But Theseus, informed of their plans by a herald named Leos, sprang the ambush and destroyed the entire force. Pallas thereupon sued for peace.

Theseus in Crete

It is a matter of dispute whether Medea persuaded Aegeus to send Theseus against Poseidon's ferocious white bull, or whether it was after her expulsion from Athens that he undertook the destruction of this fire-breathing monster, hoping thereby to ingratiate himself further with the Athenians. Brought by Heracles from Crete, let loose on the plain of Argos, and driven thence across the Isthmus to Marathon, the bull had killed men by the hundred between the cities of Probalinthus and Tricorynthus. Yet Theseus boldly seized those murderous horns and dragged the bull in triumph through the streets of Athens, and up the steep slope of the Acropolis, where he sacrificed it to Athene, or to Apollo.

In requital for the murder of Androgeus, Minos had given orders that the Athenians should send seven youths and seven maidens every ninth year to the Cretan Labyrinth, where the Minotaur waited to devour them. This Minotaur, whose name was Asterius, was the bull-headed monster which Pasiphaë had borne to the white bull. Soon after Theseus's arrival at Athens the tribute fell due for the third time, and he so deeply pitied those parents whose children were liable to be chosen by lot, that he offered himself as one of the victims, despite Aegeus's earnest attempts at dissuasion.

On the two previous occasions, the ship which conveyed the fourteen victims had carried black sails, but Theseus was confident that the gods were on his side, and Aegeus therefore gave him a white sail to hoist on return, in signal of success.

When the lots had been cast at the Law Courts, Theseus led his companions to the Dolphin Temple where, on their behalf, he offered Apollo a branch of consecrated olive, bound with white wool. The fourteen mothers brought provisions for the voyage, and told their children fables and heroic tales to hearten them. Theseus, however, replaced two of the maiden victims with a pair of effeminate youths, possessed of unusual courage and presence of mind. These he commanded to take warm baths, avoid the rays of the sun, perfume their hair and bodies with unguent oils, and practise how to talk, gesture, and walk like women. He was thus able to deceive Minos by passing them off as maidens.

The Delphic Oracle had advised Theseus to take Aphrodite for his guide and companion on the voyage. He therefore sacrificed to her on the strand; and lo! the victim, a she-goat, became a he-goat in its death-throes. This prodigy won Aphrodite her title of Epitragia.

Theseus sailed on the sixth day of Munychion [April]. Every year on this date the Athenians would send virgins to the Dolphin Temple in propitiation of Apollo, because Theseus had omitted to do so before taking his leave. The god's displeasure was shown in a storm, which forced him to take shelter at Delphi and there offer belated sacrifices.

When the ship reached Crete some days afterwards, Minos rode down to the harbour to count the victims. Falling in love with one of the Athenian maidens, he would have ravished her then and there, had Theseus not protested that it was his duty as Poseidon's son to defend virgins against outrage by tyrants. Minos, laughing lewdly, replied that Poseidon had never been known to show delicate respect for any virgins who took his fancy.

'Ha!' he cried, 'prove yourself a son of Poseidon, by retrieving this bauble for me!' So saying, he flung his golden signet ring into the sea.

'First prove that you are a son of Zeus!' retorted Theseus.

This Minos did. His prayer: 'Father Zeus, hear me!' was at once answered by lightning and a clap of thunder. Without more ado, Theseus dived into the sea, where a large school of dolphins escorted him honourably down to the palace of the Nereids. Some say that

Thetis the Nereid then gave him the jewelled crown, her wedding gift from Aphrodite, which Ariadne afterwards wore; others, that Amphitrite the Sea-goddess did so herself, and that she sent the Nereids swimming in every direction to find the golden ring. At all events, when Theseus emerged from the sea, he was carrying both the ring and the crown.

Aphrodite had indeed accompanied Theseus: for not only did two of the Athenian maidens invite the chivalrous Theseus to their couches, and were not spurned, but Minos's own daughter Ariadne fell in love with him at first sight. 'I will help you to kill my half-brother, the Minotaur,' she secretly promised him, 'if I may return to Athens with you as your wife.' This offer Theseus gladly accepted, and swore to marry her. Now, before Daedalus left Crete, he had given Ariadne a magic ball of thread, and instructed her how to enter and leave the labyrinth. She must open the entrance door and tie the loose end of the thread to the lintel; the ball would then roll along, diminishing as it went and making, with devious turns and twists, for the innermost recess where the Minotaur was lodged. This ball Ariadne gave to Theseus, and instructed him to follow it until he reached the sleeping monster, whom he must seize by the hair and sacrifice to Poseidon. He could then find his way back by rolling up the thread into a ball again.

That same night Theseus did as he was told; but whether he killed the Minotaur with a sword given him by Ariadne, or with his bare hands, or with his celebrated club, is much disputed. A sculptured frieze at Amyclae shows the Minotaur bound and led in triumph by Theseus to Athens; but this is not the generally accepted story.

When Theseus emerged from the Labyrinth, spotted with blood, Ariadne embraced him passionately, and guided the whole Athenian party to the harbour. For, in the meantime, the two effeminate-looking youths had killed the guards of the women's quarters, and released the maiden victims. They all stole aboard their ship, and rowed hastily away. But although Theseus had first stove in the hulls of several Cretan ships, to prevent pursuit, the alarm sounded and he was forced to fight a sea-battle in the harbour, before escaping, fortunately without loss, under cover of darkness.

Some days later, after disembarking on the island then named Dia, but later known as Naxos, Theseus left Ariadne asleep on the shore, and sailed away. Why he did so must remain a mystery. Some say that he deserted her in favour of a new mistress, Aegle, daughter of Panopeus; others that, while wind-bound on Dia, he reflected on the scandal which Ariadne's arrival at Athens would cause. Others again, that Dionysus, appearing to Theseus in a dream, threateningly demanded Ariadne for himself, and that, when Theseus awoke to see Dionysus's fleet bearing down on Dia, he weighed anchor in sudden terror; Dionysus having cast a spell which made him forget his promise to Ariadne and even her very existence.

The Minotaur (National Archaeological Museum, Athens)

Whatever the truth of the matter may be, Dionysus's priests at Athens affirm that when Ariadne found herself alone on the deserted shore, she broke into bitter laments, remembering how she had trembled while Theseus set out to kill her monstrous half-brother; how she had offered silent vows for his success; and how, through love of him, she had deserted her parents and motherland. She now invoked the whole universe for vengeance, and Father Zeus nodded assent. Then, gently and sweetly, Dionysus with his merry train of satyrs and maenads came to Ariadne's rescue. He married her without delay, setting Thetis's crown upon her head, and she bore him many children. Of these only Thoas and Oenopion are sometimes called Theseus's sons. The crown, which Dionysus later set among the stars as the Corona Borealis, was made by Hephaestus of fiery gold and red Indian gems, set in the shape of roses.

To resume the history of Theseus: from Naxos he sailed to Delos, and there sacrificed to Apollo, celebrating athletic games in his honour. It was then that he introduced the novel custom of crowning the victor with palm-leaves, and placing a palm-stem in his right hand. He also prudently dedicated to the god a small wooden image of Aphrodite, the work of Daedalus, which Ariadne had brought from Crete and left aboard his ship – it might have been the subject of cynical comment by the Athenians.

Ariadne was soon revenged on Theseus. Whether in grief for her loss, or in joy at the sight of the Attic coast, from which he had been kept by prolonged winds, he forgot his promise to hoist the white sail. Aegeus, who stood watching for him on the Acropolis, where the Temple of the Wingless Victory was to stand, sighted the black sail, swooned, and fell headlong to his death into the valley below. But some say that he deliberately cast himself into the sea, which was thenceforth named the Aegean.

Theseus was not informed of this sorrowful accident until he had completed the sacrifices vowed to the gods for his safe return; he then buried Aegeus, and honoured him with a hero-shrine.

The Federalization of Attica

When Theseus succeeded his father Aegeus on the throne of Athens, he reinforced his sovereignty by executing nearly all his opponents, except Pallas and the remainder of his fifty sons. Some years later he killed these too as a precautionary measure and was purified of their blood at Troezen, where his son Hippolytus now reigned as king, and spent a whole year there. On his return, he suspected a half-brother, also named Pallas, of disaffection, and banished him at once; Pallas then founded Pallantium in Arcadia.

Theseus proved to be a law-abiding ruler, and initiated the policy of federalization, which was the basis of Athens' later well-being. Hitherto, Attica had been divided into twelve communities, each managing its own affairs without consulting the Athenian king, except in time of emergency. The Eleusinians had even declared war on Erechtheus, and other internecine quarrels abounded. If these communities were to relinquish their independence, Theseus must approach each clan and family in turn; which he did. He found the yeomen and serfs ready to obey him, and persuaded most of the large landowners to agree with his scheme by promising to abolish the monarchy and substitute democracy for it, though remaining commander-in-chief and supreme judge. Those who remained unconvinced by the arguments he used respected his strength at least.

Theseus was thus empowered to dissolve all local governments, after summoning their delegates to Athens, where he provided these with a common Council Hall and Law Court. But he forbore to interfere with the laws of private property. Next, he united the suburbs with the city proper which, until then, had consisted of the Acropolis and its immediate Southern dependencies, including the ancient Temples of Olympian Zeus, Pythian Apollo, Mother Earth, Dionysus of the Marshes, and the Aqueduct of Nine Springs.

He named the sixteenth day of Hecatomboeon [July] 'Federation Day', and made it a public festival in honour of Athene, when a bloodless sacrifice was also offered to Peace. By renaming the Athenian Games celebrated on this day 'All-Athenian', he opened it to the

Theseus and Antiope
(Archaeological Museum,
Chalcis)

whole of Attica; and also introduced the worship of Federal Aphrodite and of Persuasion. Then, resigning the throne, as he had promised, he gave Attica its new constitution, and under the best of auspices: for the Delphic Oracle prophesied that Athens would now ride the stormy seas as safely as a pig's bladder.

To enlarge the city still further, Theseus invited all worthy strangers to become his fellow-citizens. His heralds, who went throughout Greece, used a formula, namely: 'Come hither, all ye people!' Great crowds thereupon flocked into Athens, and he divided the population of Attica into three classes: the Eupatrids, or

A Centaur biting a Lapith (Archaeological Museum, Olympia)

'those who deserve well of their fatherland'; the Georges, or 'farmers'; and the Demiurges, or 'artificers'. The Eupatrids took charge of religious affairs, supplied magistrates, interpreted the laws, embodying the highest dignity of all; the Georges tilled the soil and were the backbone of the state; the Demiurges, by far the most numerous class, furnished such various artificers as soothsayers, surgeons, heralds, carpenters, sculptors, and confectioners. Thus Theseus became the first king to found a commonwealth, which is why Homer, in the *Catalogue of Ships*, styles only the Athenians a sovereign people.

Theseus, the first Athenian king to mint money, stamped his coins with the image of a bull. His coinage caused the standard of value to be quoted in terms of 'ten oxen', or 'one hundred oxen', for a considerable time. In emulation of Heracles, who had appointed his father Zeus patron of the Olympic Games, Theseus now appointed his father Poseidon patron of the Isthmian Games. Next, Theseus made good the Athenian claim to the sovereignty of Megara and then, having summoned Peloponnesian delegates to the Isthmus, prevailed upon them to settle a long-standing frontier dispute with their Ionian neighbours. At a place agreed by both parties, he raised the celebrated column marked on its eastern side: 'This is not the Peloponnese, but Ionia!', and on the western: 'This is not Ionia, but the Peloponnese!' He also won Corinthian assent to the Athenians' taking the place of honour at the Isthmian Games.

Theseus and the Amazons
Some say that Theseus took part in Heracles's successful expedition against the Amazons, and received as his share of the booty their queen Antiope, also called Melanippe; but that this was not so unhappy a fate for her as many thought, because she had betrayed the city of Themiscyra on the river Thermodon to him, in proof of the passion he had already kindled in her heart.

Others say that Theseus visited their country some years later, in the company of Peirithous and his comrades; and that the Amazons, delighted at the arrival of so many handsome warriors, offered them no violence. Antiope came to greet Theseus with gifts, but she had hardly climbed aboard his ship, before he weighed anchor and abducted her.

Antiope's sister Oreithyia, mistaken by some for Hippolyte whose girdle Heracles won, swore vengeance on Theseus. She concluded an alliance with the Scythians, and led a large force of Amazons across the ice of the Cimmerian Bosphorus, then crossed the Danube and passed through Thrace, Thessaly, and Boeotia. At Athens she encamped on the Areiopagus and there sacrificed to Ares; an event from which, some say, the hill won its name; but first she ordered a detachment to invade Laconia and discourage the Peloponnese from reinforcing Theseus by way of the Isthmus.

Bull-leaping (The Minoan Royal Palace, Knossos, Crete)

The Athenian forces were already marshalled, but neither side cared to begin hostilities. At last, on the advice of an oracle, Theseus sacrificed to Phobus, son of Ares, and offered battle on the seventh day of Boedromion, the date on which the Boedromia was celebrated at Athens; though some say the festival had already been founded in honour of the victory which Xuthus won over Eumolpus in the reign of Erechtheus. The Amazons' battle-front stretched between what was later called the Amazonium and the Pnyx Hill near Chrysa. Theseus's right wing moved down from the Museum and fell upon their left wing, but was routed and forced to retire as far as the Temple of the Furies. The Athenian left wing, however, charged from the Palladium, Mount Ardettus and the Lyceum, and drove the Amazon right wing back to their camp, inflicting heavy casualties.

Some say that the Amazons offered peace terms only after four months of hard fighting; the armistice, sworn near the sanctuary of Theseus, was later commemorated in the Amazonian sacrifice on the eve of his festival. But others say that Oreithyia with a few followers escaped to Megara, where she died of grief and despair; and that the remaining Amazons, driven from Attica by the victorious Theseus, settled in Scythia.

This, at any rate, was the first time that the Athenians repulsed foreign invaders. Some of the Amazons left wounded on the field of battle were sent to Chalcis to be cured, and Molpadia is buried near the temple of Mother Earth. Others lie in Amazonium.

The truth about Antiope seems to be that she survived the battle, and that Theseus was eventually compelled to kill her, as the Delphic Oracle had foretold, when he entered into an alliance with King Deucalion the Cretan, and married his sister Phaedra. The jealous Antiope, who was not his legal wife, interrupted the wedding festivities by bursting in, fully armed, and threatening to massacre the guests. Theseus and his companions hastily closed the doors, and despatched her in a grim combat, though she had borne him Hippolytus, and never lain with another man.

Phaedra and Hippolytus

After marrying Phaedra, Theseus sent his bastard son Hippolytus to Pittheus, who adopted him as heir to the throne of Troezen. Thus Hippolytus had no cause to dispute the right of his legitimate brothers Acamas and Demophoön, Phaedra's sons, to reign over Athens.

Hippolytus, who had inherited his mother Antiope's exclusive devotion to chaste Artemis, raised a new temple to the goddess at Troezen, not far from the theatre. Thereupon Aphrodite, determined to punish him for what she took as an insult to herself, saw to it that when he attended the Eleusinian Mysteries, Phaedra should fall passionately in love with him.

Since at that time Theseus was away in Thessaly with Peirithous, Phaedra followed Hippolytus to Troezen. There she built the Temple of Peeping Aphrodite to overlook the gymnasium, and would daily watch unobserved while he kept himself fit by running, leaping, and wrestling, stark naked. An ancient myrtle-tree stood in the Temple enclosure; Phaedra would jab at its leaves, in frustrated passion, with a jewelled hair-pin. When, later, Hippolytus attended the All-Athenian Festival and lodged in Theseus's palace, she used the Temple of Aphrodite on the Acropolis for the same purpose.

Phaedra disclosed her incestuous desire to no one, but ate little, slept badly, and grew so weak that her old nurse guessed the truth at last, and officiously implored her to send Hippolytus a letter. This Phaedra did: confessing her love, and saying that she was now converted by it to the cult of Artemis, whose two wooden images, brought from Crete, she had just rededicated to the goddess. Would he not come hunting one day? 'We women of the Cretan Royal House,' she wrote, 'are doubtless fated to be dishonoured in love: witness my grandmother Europe, my mother Pasiphaë, and lastly my own sister Ariadne! Ah, wretched Ariadne, deserted by your father, the faithless Theseus, who has since murdered your own royal mother – why have the Furies not punished you for showing such unfilial indifference to her fate? – and must one day murder me! I count on you to revenge yourself on him by paying homage to Aphrodite in my company. Could we not go away and live together, for a while at least, and make a hunting expedition the excuse? Meanwhile, none can suspect our true feelings for each other. Already we are lodged under the same roof, and our affection will be regarded as innocent, and even praiseworthy.'

Hippolytus burned this letter in horror, and came to Phaedra's chamber, loud with reproaches; but she tore her clothes, threw open the chamber doors, and cried out: 'Help, help! I am ravished!' Then she hanged herself from the lintel, and left a note accusing him of monstrous crimes.

Theseus, on receiving the note, cursed Hippolytus, and gave orders that he must quit Athens at once, never to return. Later he remembered the three wishes granted him by his father Poseidon, and prayed earnestly that Hippolytus might die that very day. 'Father,' he pleaded, 'send a beast across Hippolytus's path, as he makes for Troezen!'

Hippolytus had set out from Athens at full speed. As he drove along the narrow part of the Isthmus a huge wave, which overtopped even the Molurian Rock, rolled roaring shoreward; and from its crest sprang a great dog-seal bellowing and spouting water. Hippolytus's four horses swerved towards the cliff, mad with terror, but being an expert charioteer he restrained them from plunging over the edge. The beast then galloped menacingly behind the chariot, and he failed to keep his team on a straight course. Not far from the sanctuary of Saronian Artemis stood a wild olive, and it was on a branch of this tree that a loop of Hippolytus's reins caught. His chariot was flung sideways against a pile of rocks and broken into pieces. Hippolytus, entangled in the reins, and thrown first against the tree-trunk, and then against the rocks, was dragged to death by his horses, while the pursuer vanished.

The Athenians raised a barrow in Hippolytus's memory close to the Temple of Themis, because his death had been brought about by curses. Some say that Theseus, accused of his murder, was found guilty, ostracized, and banished to Scyros, where he ended his life in shame and grief. But his downfall is more generally believed to have been caused by an attempted rape of Persephone.

Hippolytus's ghost descended to Tartarus, and Artemis, in high indignation, begged Asclepius to revive his corpse. Asclepius opened the doors of his ivory medicine cabinet and took out the herb with which Cretan Glaucus had been revived. With it he thrice touched Hippolytus's breast, repeating certain charms, and at the third touch the dead man raised his head from the ground. But Hades

A red-figured Attic case depicting Theseus carrying off Helen (Antikensammlung, Munich)

and the Three Fates, scandalized by this breach of privilege, persuaded Zeus to kill Asclepius with a thunderbolt.

Lapiths and Centaurs

Some say that Peirithous the Lapith was the son of Ixion and Dia, daughter of Elioneus; others, that he was the son of Zeus who, disguised as a stallion, coursed around Dia before seducing her.

Almost incredible reports of Theseus's strength and valour had reached Peirithous, who ruled over the Magnetes, at the mouth of the river Peneus; and one day he resolved to test them by raiding Attica and driving away a herd of cattle that were grazing at Marathon. When Theseus at once went in pursuit, Peirithous boldly turned about to face him; but each was filled with such admiration for the other's nobility of appearance that the cattle were fogotten, and they swore an oath of everlasting friendship.

Peirithous married Hippodameia, daughter of Butes, and invited all the Olympians to his wedding, except Ares and Eris; he remembered the mischief which Eris had caused at the marriage of Peleus and Thetis. Since more feasters came to Peirithous's palace than it could contain, his cousins the Centaurs, together with Nestor, Caeneus, and other Thessalian princes, were seated at tables in a vast, tree-shaded cave near by.

The Centaurs, however, were unused to wine and, when they smelled its fragrance, pushed away the sour milk which was set before them, and ran to fill their silver horns from the wine-skins. In their ignorance they swilled the strong liquor unmixed with water, becoming so drunk that when the bride was escorted into the cavern to greet them, Eurytion leaped from his stool, overturned the table, and dragged her away by the hair. At once the other Centaurs followed his disgraceful example, lecherously straddling the nearest women and boys.

Peirithous and his paranymph Theseus sprang to Hippodameia's rescue, cut off Eurytion's ears and nose and, with the help of the Lapiths, threw him out of the cavern. The ensuing fight, in the course of which Caeneus the Lapith was killed, lasted until nightfall; and thus began the long feud between the Centaurs and their Lapith neighbours, engineered by Ares and Eris in revenge for the slight offered them.

On this occasion the Centaurs suffered a serious reverse, and Theseus drove them from their ancient hunting grounds on Mount Pelion to the land of the Aethices near Mount Pindus. But it was not an easy task to subdue the Centaurs, who now, rallying their forces, invaded Lapith territory. They surprised and slaughtered the main Lapith army, and when the survivors fled to Pholoë in Elis, the vengeful Centaurs expelled them and converted Pholoë into a bandit stronghold of their own. Finally the Lapiths settled in Malea.

Theseus in Tartarus

After Hippodameia's death Peirithous persuaded Theseus, whose wife Phaedra had recently hanged herself, to visit Sparta in his company and carry away Helen, a sister of Castor and Polydeuces, the Dioscuri, with whom they were both ambitious to be connected by marriage. They swore to stand by each other in this perilous enterprise; to draw lots for Helen when they had won her; and then to carry off another of Zeus's daughters for the loser, whatever the danger might be.

This decided, they led an army into Lacedaemon; then, riding ahead of the main body, seized Helen while she was offering a sacrifice in the Temple of Upright Artemis at Sparta, and galloped away with her. They soon outdistanced their pursuers, shaking them off at Tegea where, as had been agreed, lots were drawn for Helen; and Theseus proved the winner. He foresaw, however, that the Athenians would by no means approve his having thus picked a quarrel with the redoubtable Dioscuri, and therefore sent Helen, who was not yet nubile, to the Attic village of Aphidnae, where he charged his friend Aphidnus to guard her with the greatest attention and secrecy. Aethra, Theseus's mother, accompanied Helen and cared well for her.

left: *The deeds of Theseus. Vase (British Museum)*

left: *Theseus and the Minotaur. Detail from a black-figured vase (British Museum)*

opposite: *Amazons on horseback. Silver panel with gold sections (British Museum)*

Some years passed and, when Helen was old enough for Theseus to marry her, Peirithous reminded him of their pact. Together they consulted an oracle of Zeus, and his ironical response was: 'Why not visit Tartarus and demand Persephone, the wife of Hades, as a bride for Peirithous? She is the noblest of my daughters.' Theseus was outraged when Peirithous, who took this suggestion seriously, held him to his oath; but he dared not refuse to go, and presently they descended, sword in hand, to Tartarus, and were soon knocking at the gates of Hades's palace. Hades listened calmly to their impudent request and, feigning hospitality, invited them to be seated. Unsuspectingly they took the settee he offered, which proved to be the Chair of Forgetfulness and at once became part of their flesh, so that they could not rise again without self-mutilation. Coiled serpents hissed all about them, and they were well lashed by the Furies and mauled by Cerberus's teeth, while Hades looked on, smiling grimly.

Thus they remained in torment for four full years, until Heracles, coming at Eurystheus's command to fetch up Cerberus, recognized them as they mutely stretched out their hands, pleading for his help. Persephone received Heracles like a brother, graciously permitting him to release the evil-doers and take them back to the upper air, if he could. Heracles thereupon grasped Theseus by both hands and heaved with gigantic strength until, with a rending noise, he was torn free; but a great part of his flesh remained sticking to the rock, which is why Theseus's Athenian descendants were all so absurdly small-buttocked. Next, he seized hold of Peirithous's hands, but the earth quaked warningly, and he desisted; Peirithous had, after all, been the leading spirit in this blasphemous enterprise.

The Death of Theseus
During Theseus's absence in Tartarus the Dioscuri assembled an army of Laconians and Arcadians, marched against Athens, and demanded the return of Helen. When the Athenians denied that they were sheltering her, or had the least notion where she might be, the Dioscuri proceeded to ravage Attica, until the inhabitants of Deceleia, who disapproved of Theseus's conduct, guided them to Aphidnae, where they found and rescued their sister. The Dioscuri then razed Aphidnae to the ground; but the Deceleians became immune from all Spartan taxes and entitled to seats of honour at Spartan festivals – their lands alone were spared in the Peloponnesian War, when the invading Spartans laid Attica waste.

Now, Peteos son of Orneus and grandson of Erechtheus had been banished by Aegeus, and the Dioscuri, to spite Theseus, brought back his son Menestheus from exile, and made him regent of Athens. This Menestheus was the first demagogue. During Theseus's absence in Tartarus he ingratiated himself with the people by reminding the nobles of the power which they had forfeited through Federalization, and by telling the poor that they were being robbed of country and religion, and had become subject to an adventurer of obscure origin – who, however, had now vacated the throne and was rumoured dead.

When Aphidnae fell, and Athens was in danger, Menestheus persuaded the people to welcome the Dioscuri into the city as their benefactors and deliverers. They did indeed behave most correctly, and asked only to be admitted to the Eleusinian Mysteries, as Heracles had been. This request was granted, and the Dioscuri became honorary citizens of Athens. Aphidnus was their adoptive father, as Pylius had been Heracles's on a similar occasion. Divine honours were thereafter paid them at the rising of their constellation, in gratitude for the clemency which they had shown to the common people; and they cheerfully brought Helen back to Sparta, with Theseus's mother Aethra and a sister of Peirithous as her bond-woman. Some say that they found Helen still a virgin; others, that Theseus had got her with child and that at Argos, on the way home, she gave birth to a girl, Iphigeneia, and dedicated a sanctuary to Artemis in gratitude for her safe delivery.

Theseus, who returned from Tartarus soon afterwards, at once raised an altar to Heracles the Saviour, and reconsecrated to him all but four of his temples and groves. However, he had been greatly weakened by his tortures, and found Athens so sadly corrupted by faction and sedition, that he was no longer able to maintain order. First smuggling his children out of the city to Euboea, where Elpenor son of Chalcodon sheltered them and then, solemnly cursing the people of Athens from Mount Gargettus, he sailed for Crete, where Deucalion had promised to shelter him.

A storm blew the ship off her course, and his first landfall was the island of Scyros, near Euboea, where King Lycomedes, though a close friend of Menestheus, received him with all the splendour due to his fame and lineage. Theseus, who had inherited an estate on Scyros, asked permission to settle there. But Lycomedes had long regarded this estate as his own and, under the pretence of showing Theseus its boundaries, inveigled him to the top of a high cliff, pushed him over, and then gave out that he had fallen accidentally while taking a drunken, post-prandial stroll.

Menestheus, now left in undisturbed possession of the throne, was among Helen's suitors, and led the Athenian forces to Troy, where he won great fame as a strategist but was killed in battle. The sons of Theseus succeeded him.

Theseus was a skilled lyre-player and has now become joint-patron with Heracles and Hermes of every gymnasium and wrestling school in Greece. His resemblance to Heracles is proverbial. He took part in the Calydonian Hunt; avenged the champions who fell at Thebes; and only failed to be one of the Argonauts through being detained in Tartarus when they sailed for Colchis.

Ill-treated slaves and labourers, whose ancestors looked to him for

Battle of the Centaurs and the Lapiths (British Museum)

protection against their oppressors, used to seek refuge in his sanctuary, where sacrifices were offered to him on the eighth day of every month. This day may have been chosen because he first arrived at Athens from Troezen on the eighth of Hecatomboeon, and returned from Crete on the eighth day of Pyanepsion. Or perhaps because he was a son of Poseidon: for Poseidon's feasts are also observed on that day of the month, since eight, being the first cube of an even number, represents Poseidon's unshakable power.

5

THEBES AND MYCENAE

Oedipus

LAIUS, SON OF LABDACUS, married Iocaste, and ruled over Thebes. Grieved by his prolonged childlessness, he secretly consulted the Delphic Oracle, which informed him that this was a blessing, because any child born to Iocaste would become his murderer. He therefore put Iocaste away, without offering any reason for his decision, which caused her such vexation that, having made him drunk, she inveigled him into her arms again as soon as night fell. When, nine months later, Iocaste was brought to bed of a son, Laius snatched him from the nurse's arms, pierced his feet with a nail and, binding them together, exposed him on Mount Cithaeron.

Yet the Fates had ruled that this boy should reach a green old age. A Corinthian shepherd found him, named him Oedipus because his feet were deformed by the nail-wound, and brought him to Corinth. Here King Polybus was reigning at the time, and being childless, was pleased to rear Oedipus as his own son.

One day, taunted by a Corinthian youth with not in the least resembling his supposed parents, Oedipus went to ask the Delphic Oracle what future lay in store for him. 'Away, wretch!' the Pythoness cried in disgust. 'You will kill your father and marry your mother!'

Since Oedipus loved Polybus and Periboa, his queen, he at once decided against returning to Corinth. But in the narrow defile between Delphi and Daulis he happened to meet Laius, who ordered him roughly to step off the road and make way for his betters. Laius was in a chariot and Oedipus on foot. Oedipus retorted that he acknowledged no betters except the gods and his own parents.

'So much the worse for you!' cried Laius, and ordered his charioteer Polyphontes to drive on. One of the wheels bruised Oedipus's foot and, transported by rage, he killed Polyphontes with his spear. Then, flinging Laius on the road entangled in the reins, and whipping up the team, he made them drag him to death. It was left to the king of Plataeae to bury both corpses.

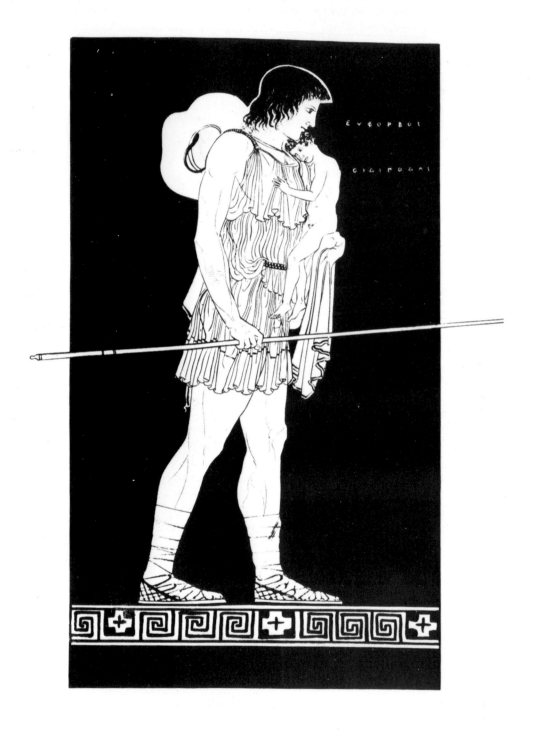

Oedipus as an infant

Laius had been on his way to ask the Oracle how he might rid Thebes of the Sphinx. This monster, with her woman's head, lion's body, serpent's tail, and eagle's wings, had flown to Thebes from the uttermost part of Ethiopia. Hera had recently sent her to punish Thebes for Laius's abduction of the boy Chrysippus. Settling close to the city, the Sphinx now asked every Theban wayfarer a riddle taught her by the Three Muses: 'What being, with only one voice, has sometimes two feet, sometimes three, sometimes four, and is weakest when it has the most?' Those who could not solve the riddle she throttled and devoured on the spot.

Oedipus, approaching Thebes, guessed the answer. 'Man,' he replied, 'because he crawls on all fours as an infant, stands firmly on his two feet in his youth, and leans upon a staff in his old age.' The mortified Sphinx leaped from Mount Phicium and dashed herself to pieces in the valley below. At this the grateful Thebans acclaimed Oedipus king, and he married Iocaste, unaware that she was his mother.

Plague then descended upon Thebes, and the Delphic Oracle, when consulted once more, replied: 'Expel the murderer of Laius!' Oedipus, not knowing whom he had met in the defile, pronounced a curse on Laius's murderer and sentenced him to exile.

Blind Teiresias, the most renowned seer in Greece at this time, now demanded an audience with Oedipus. Some say that once, on Mount Cyllene, Teiresias had seen two serpents in the act of coupling. When both attacked him, he struck at them with his staff, killing the female. Immediately he was turned into a woman, and became a celebrated harlot; but seven years later he happened to see the same sight again at the same spot, and this time regained his manhood by killing the male serpent.

Once Hera began reproaching Zeus for his numerous infidelities. He defended them by arguing that, at any rate, when he did share her couch, she had the more enjoyable time by far, deriving infinitely greater pleasure from the sexual act than he.

'What nonsense!' cried Hera.

Teiresias, summoned to settle the dispute from his personal experience, answered:

> 'If the parts of love-pleasure be counted as ten,
>   Thrice three go to women, one only to men.'

Hera was so exasperated by Zeus's triumphant grin that she blinded Teiresias; but Zeus compensated him with inward sight, and a life extended to seven generations.

Teiresias now appeared at Oedipus's court, and revealed to Oedipus the will of the gods: that plague would cease only if a Sown Man died for the sake of the city. Iocaste's father Menoeceus, one of those who had risen out of the earth when Cadmus sowed the serpent's teeth, at once leaped from the walls.

Oedipus and the Sphinx (National Archaeological Museum, Athens)

Oedipus being questioned by the Sphinx. An Attic vase (Vatican Museum)

opposite: *The Sphinx (Archaeological Museum, Delphi)*

Teiresias then announced further: 'The plague will now cease. Yet the gods had another in mind, for he has killed his father and married his mother. Know, Queen Iocaste, that it is your husband Oedipus!'

At first, none would believe Teiresias, but his words were soon confirmed by a letter from Periboea at Corinth. She wrote that the sudden death of King Polybus now allowed her to reveal the circumstances of Oedipus's adoption. Iocaste then hanged herself for shame and grief, while Oedipus blinded himself with a pin taken from her garments.

Some say that Iocaste's brother Creon expelled Oedipus, who, after wandering for many years through country after country, guided by his faithful daughter Antigone, finally came to Colonus in Attica. Here the Erinnyes, who have a grove there, hounded him to death, and Theseus buried his body in the precinct of the Solemn Ones at Athens, lamenting by Antigone's side.

The Seven Against Thebes

So many princes visited Argos in the hope of marrying either Aegeia, or Deipyla, the daughters of King Adrastus, that, fearing to make powerful enemies if he singled out any two of them as his sons-in-law, he consulted the Delphic Oracle. Apollo's response was: 'Yoke to a two-wheeled chariot the boar and lion which fight in your palace.'

Among the less fortunate of these suitors were Polyneices and Tydeus. Polyneices and his twin Eteocles had been elected co-kings of Thebes after the banishment of Oedipus, their father. They agreed to reign for alternate years, but Eteocles, to whom the first term fell, would not relinquish the throne at the end of the year, pleading the evil disposition shown by Polyneices, and banished him from the city. Tydeus, son of Oeneus of Calydon, had killed his brother Melanippus when out hunting; though he claimed that this was an accident, it had been prophesied that Melanippus would kill him, and the Calydonians therefore suspected him of having tried to forestall his fate, and he was also banished.

Now, the emblem of Thebes is a lion, and the emblem of Calydon, a boar; and the two fugitive suitors displayed these devices on their shields. Adrastus, mindful of the prophecy, therefore married Aegia to Polyneices, and Deipyla to Tydeus, with a promise to restore both princes to their kingdoms; but said that he would first march against Thebes, which lay nearer.

Adrastus mustered his Argive chieftains, bidding them arm themselves and set out eastward. Of these champions, Amphiaraus, foreseeing that all except Adrastus would die fighting against Thebes, at first refused to go.

Now Adrastus's sister Eriphyle was married to Amphiaraus. Tydeus therefore called Polyneices and said: 'Eriphyle fears that she is losing her looks; if you were to offer her the magic necklace which was Aphrodite's wedding gift to your ancestress Harmonia, Cadmus's wife, she would soon compel Amphiaraus to come with us.'

This was discreetly done, and the expedition set out, their march taking them through Nemea, where Lycurgus was king. When they asked leave to water their troops in his country, Lycurgus consented, and his bond-woman Hypsipyle guided them to the nearest spring. Hypsipyle was acting as nursemaid to Lycurgus's son Opheltes. She set the boy down for a moment while she guided the Argive army to the drinking pool, whereupon a serpent writhed around his limbs and bit him to death. Adrastus and his men returned from the spring too late to do more than kill the serpent and bury the boy. When Amphiaraus warned them that this was an ominous sign, they instituted the Nemean Games in the boy's honour.

Arrived at Cithaeron, Adrastus sent Tydeus as his herald to the Thebans, with a demand that Eteocles should resign the throne in favour of Polyneices. When this was refused, Tydeus challenged their chieftains to single combat, one after another, and emerged victorious from every encounter; soon, no more Thebans dared come forward. The Argives then approached the city walls, and each of the champions took up his station facing one of the seven gates.

Teiresias the seer, whom Eteocles consulted, prophesied that the Thebans would be victorious only if a prince of the royal house freely offered himself as a sacrifice to Ares; whereupon Menoeceus, the son of Creon, killed himself before the gates. Teiresias's prophecy was fulfilled: the Thebans were, indeed, defeated in a skirmish and withdrew into the city; but no sooner had Capaneus set a scaling-ladder against the wall and begun to mount it, than Zeus struck him dead with a thunderbolt. At this, the Thebans took courage, and made a furious sally, killing three more of the seven champions.

Polyneices, to save further slaughter, offered to decide the succession of the throne by single combat with Eteocles. Eteocles accepted the challenge and each mortally wounded the other. Creon, their uncle, then took command and routed the dismayed Argives. Amphiaraus fled in his chariot along the banks of the river Ismenus, and was on the point of being thrust between the shoulders by a Theban pursuer, when Zeus cleft the earth with a thunderbolt and he vanished from sight, chariot and all, and now reigns alive among the dead.

Seeing that the day was lost, Adrastus escaped; but when, later, he heard that Creon would not permit his dead enemies to be buried, visited Athens as a suppliant and persuaded Theseus to march against Thebes and punish Creon's impiety. Theseus took the city in a surprise attack, imprisoned Creon, and gave the dead champions' corpses to their kinsfolk.

Now, before Theseus's arrival at Thebes, Antigone, sister of Eteocles and Polyneices, had disobeyed Creon's orders by secretly building a pyre and laying Polyneices's corpse upon it. Creon noticed

*The Seven against Thebes.
Part of the Thracian
Panagyurishté Treasure
(Plovdiv Museum,
Bulgaria)*

*Apollo in his temple at
Delphi. Detail of vase
(Allard Pierson Museum,
Amsterdam)*

and, going to investigate, surprised Antigone in her act of disobedience. He summoned his son Haemon, to whom Antigone had been affianced, and ordered him to bury her alive in Polyneices's tomb. Haemon feigned readiness to do as he was told but, instead, married Antigone secretly, and sent her away to live among his shepherds. She bore him a son who, many years later, came to Thebes, and took part in certain funeral games; but Creon, who was still King of Thebes, guessed his identity by the serpent mark on his body, borne by all descendants of Cadmus, and sentenced him to death. Heracles interceded for his life, but Creon proved obdurate; whereupon Haemon killed both Antigone and himself.

The Epigoni

The sons of the seven champions who had fallen at Thebes swore to avenge their fathers. They are known as the Epigoni. The Delphic Oracle promised them victory if Alcmaeon, son of Amphiaraus, took command. But he felt no desire to attack Thebes, and hotly disputed the propriety of the campaign with his brother Amphilochus. When they could not agree whether to make war or no, the decision was referred to their mother Eriphyle. Recognizing the situation as a familiar one, Thersander, the son of Polyneices, followed his father's example: he bribed Eriphyle with the magic robe which Athene had given his ancestress Harmonia at the same time as Aphrodite had given her the magic necklace. Eriphyle decided for war, and Alcmaeon reluctantly assumed command.

In a battle fought before the walls of Thebes, the Epigoni lost Aegialeus, son of Adrastus, and Teiresias the seer then warned the Thebans that their city would be sacked. The walls, he announced, were fated to stand only so long as one of the original seven champions remained alive, and Adrastus, now the sole survivor, would die of grief when he heard of Aegialeus's death. Consequently, the Thebans' wisest course was to flee that very night. Teiresias added that whether they took his advice or no made no odds to him; he was destined to die as soon as Thebes fell into Argive hands. Under cover of darkness, therefore, the Thebans escaped northward with their wives, children, weapons, and a few belongings, and when they had travelled far enough, called a halt and founded the city of Hestiaea. At dawn, Teiresias, who went with them, paused to drink at the spring of Tilphussa, and suddenly expired.

That same day, which was the very day on which Adrastus heard of Aegialeus's death and died of grief, the Argives, finding Thebes evacuated, broke in, razed the walls, and collected the booty. They sent the best of it to Apollo at Delphi, including Teiresias's daughter Manto, who had stayed behind; and she became his Pythoness.

Nor was this the end of the matter. Thersander happened to boast in Alcmaeon's hearing that most of the credit for the Argive victory was due to himself: he bribed Eriphyle, just as his father Polyneices did before him, to give the order to march. Alcmaeon thus learned for the first time that Eriphyle's vanity had caused his father's death, and might well have caused his own. He consulted the Delphic Oracle, and Apollo replied that she deserved death. Alcmaeon mistook this for a dispensation to matricide and, on his return, he duly killed Eriphyle, but, as she lay dying, Eriphyle cursed Alcmaeon: 'Lands of all the world: deny shelter to my murderer!' The avenging Erinnyes thereupon pursued him and drove him mad.

Alcmaeon fled first to Thesprotia and then to Psophis, where King Phegeus purified him for Apollo's sake. Phegeus married him to his daughter Arsinoë, to whom Alcmaeon gave the necklace and the robe, which he had brought in his baggage. But the Erinnyes, disregarding this purification, continued to plague him, and the land of Psophis grew barren on his account. The Delphic Oracle then advised Alcmaeon to approach the River-god Achelous, by whom he was once more purified; he married Achelous's daughter Callirrhoë, and settled on land recently formed by the silt of the river, which had not been included in Eriphyle's ban. There he lived at peace for a while.

A year later, Callirrhoë, fearing that she might lose her beauty, refused Alcmaeon admittance to her couch unless he gave her the celebrated robe and necklace. For love of Callirrhoë, he dared revisit Psophis, where he deceived Phegeus: making no mention of his marriage to Callirrhoë, he invented a prediction of the Delphic Oracle, to the effect that he would never be rid of the Erinnyes until he had dedicated both robe and necklace to Apollo's shrine. Phegeus thereupon made Arsinoë surrender them, which she was glad to do, believing that Alcmaeon would return to her as soon as the Erinnyes left him. But one of Alcmaeon's servants blabbed the truth and Phegeus grew so angry that he ordered his sons to kill Alcmaeon when he left the palace. Arsinoë witnessed the murder and, unaware of Alcmaeon's double-dealing, loudly upbraided her father and brothers. Phegeus begged her to be silent and listen; but Arsinoë stopped her ears and wished violent death upon him and her brothers before the next new moon. In retaliation, Phegeus locked her in a chest and presented her as a slave to the King of Nemea; at the same time telling his sons: 'Take this robe and this necklace to Delphic Apollo. He will see to it that they cause no further mischief.'

Meanwhile, Callirrhoë, informed of what had happened at Psophis, prayed that her infant sons by Alcmaeon might become full-grown men in a day, and avenge his murder. Zeus heard her plea, and her sons went to Nemea, where, they knew, the sons of Phegeus had broken their return journey from Delphi in the hope of persuading Arsinoë to retract her curse. But she would not listen to them either; and Callirrhoë's sons not only surprised and killed them but, hastening towards Psophis, killed Phegeus too, before the next moon appeared in the sky. Since no king or river-god in Greece would consent to purify them of their crimes, they travelled westward to Epirus, and colonized Acarnania, which was named after the elder of the two, Acarnan.

Tantalus

The parentage and origin of Tantalus are disputed. His mother was Pluto, a daughter of Cronus and Rhea or, some say, of Oceanus and Tethys; and his father either Zeus, or Tmolus, the oak-chapleted deity of Mount Tmolus who, with his wife Omphale, ruled over the kingdom of Lydia and had judged the contest between Pan and Apollo.

By his wife Euryanassa, daughter of the River-god Pactolus, Tantalus became the father of Pelops, Niobe, and Broteas. Yet some call Pelops a bastard, or the son of Atlas and the nymph Linos.

Tantalus was the intimate friend of Zeus, who admitted him to Olympian banquets of nectar and ambrosia until, good fortune turning his head, he betrayed Zeus's secrets and stole the divine food to share among his mortal friends. Before this crime could be discovered, he committed a worse. Having called the Olympians to a banquet on Mount Sipylus, Tantalus found that the food in his larder was insufficient for the company and, either to test Zeus's omniscience, or merely to demonstrate his good will, cut up his son Pelops, and added the pieces to the stew prepared for them, as the sons of Lycaon had done with their brother Nyctimus when they entertained Zeus in Arcadia. None of the gods failed to notice what was on their trenchers, or to recoil in horror, except Demeter who, being dazed by her loss of Persephone, ate the flesh from the left shoulder.

For these two crimes Tantalus was punished with the ruin of his kingdom and, after his death by Zeus's own hand, with eternal torment in the company of Ixion, Sisyphus, Tityus, the Danaids, and others. Now he hangs, perennially consumed by thirst and hunger, from the bough of a fruit-tree which leans over a marshy lake. Its waves lap against his waist, and sometimes reach his chin, yet whenever he bends down to drink, they slip away, and nothing remains but the black mud at his feet; or, if he ever succeeds in scooping up a handful of water, it slips through his fingers before he can do more than wet his cracked lips, leaving him thirstier than ever. The tree is laden with pears, shining apples, sweet figs, ripe olives and pomegranates, which dangle against his shoulders; but whenever he reaches for the luscious fruit, a gust of wind whirls them out of his reach.

Moreover, an enormous stone, a crag from Mount Sipylus, overhangs the tree and eternally threatens to crush Tantalus's skull. This is his punishment for a third crime: namely theft, aggravated by perjury. One day, while Zeus was still an infant in Crete, being suckled by the she-goat Amaltheia, Hephaestus had made Rhea a golden mastiff to watch over him; which subsequently became the guardian of his temple at Dicte. But Pandareus, son of Merops, a native of Miletus, dared to steal the mastiff, and brought it to Tantalus for safe keeping on Mount Sipylus. After the hue and cry had died down, Pandareus asked Tantalus to return it to him, but Tantalus swore by Zeus that he had neither seen nor heard of a golden dog. This oath coming to Zeus's ears, Hermes was given orders to investigate the matter; and although Tantalus continued to perjure himself, Hermes recovered the dog by force or by stratagem, and Zeus crushed Tantalus under a crag of Mount Sipylus.

After punishing Tantalus, Zeus was pleased to revive Pelops; and therefore ordered Hermes to collect his limbs and boil them again in the same cauldron, on which he laid a spell. The Fate Clotho then rearticulated them; Demeter gave him a solid ivory shoulder in place of the one she had picked clean; and Rhea breathed life into him; while Goat-Pan danced for joy.

Pelops emerged from the magic cauldron clothed in such radiant beauty that Poseidon fell in love with him on the spot, and carried him off to Olympus in a chariot drawn by golden horses. There he appointed him his cup-bearer and bed-fellow; as Zeus later appointed Ganymedes, and fed him on ambrosia. Pelops first noticed that his left shoulder was of ivory when he bared his breast in mourning for his sister Niobe. All true descendants of Pelops are marked in this way and, after his death, the ivory shoulder-blade was laid up at Pisa.

Tantalus's ugly son Broteas carved the oldest image of the Mother of the Gods, which still stands on the Coddinian Crag, to the north of Mount Siplyus. He was a famous hunter, but refused to honour Artemis, who drove him mad; crying aloud that no flame could burn him, he threw himself upon a lighted pyre and let the flames consume him.

Pelops and Oenomaus

Pelops inherited the Paphlagonian throne from his father Tantalus, and for a while resided at Enete, on the shores of the Black Sea, whence he also ruled over the Lydians and Phrygians. But he was expelled from Paphlagonia by the barbarians, and retired to Lydian Mount Sipylus, his ancestral seat. When Ilus, King of Troy, would not let him live in peace even there, but ordered him to move on, Pelops brought his fabulous treasures across the Aegean Sea. He was resolved to make a new home for himself and his great horde of followers, but first to sue for the hand of Hippodameia, daughter of King Oenomaus, the Arcadian, who ruled over Pisa and Elis.

Whether he had been warned by an oracle that his son-in-law would kill him, or whether he had himself fallen in love with Hippodameia, is disputed; but Oenomaus devised a new way to prevent her from ever getting married. He challenged each of Hippodameia's suitors in turn to a chariot race, and laid out a long course from Pisa, which lies beside the river Alpheius, opposite Olympia, to

Bronze statue of a charioteer (Archaeological Museum, Delphi)

Poseidon's altar on the Isthmus of Corinth. Oenomaus insisted that Hippodameia must ride beside each suitor, thus distracting his attention from the team – but allowed him a start of half an hour or so, while he himself sacrificed a ram on the altar of Warlike Zeus at Olympia. Both chariots would then race towards the Isthmus and the suitor, if overtaken, must die; but should he win the race, Hippodameia would be his, and Oenomaus must die. Since, however, the wind-begotten mares, Psylla and Harpinna, which Ares had given him, were immeasurably the best in Greece, being swifter even than the North Wind; and since his chariot, skilfully driven by Myrtilus, was especially designed for racing, he had never yet failed to overtake his rival and transfix him with his spear, another gift from Ares.

Myrtilus, Oenomaus's charioteer, was the son of Hermes by Theobule. He too had fallen in love with Hippodameia, but dared not enter the contest. Meanwhile, the Olympians had decided to intervene and put an end to the slaughter, because Oenomaus was boasting that he would one day build a temple of skulls: as Evenus, Diomedes, and Antaeus had done. When therefore Pelops, landing in Elis, begged his lover Poseidon, whom he invoked with a sacrifice on the seashore, either to give him the swiftest chariot in the world for his courtship of Hippodameia, or to stay the rush of Oenomaus's brazen spear, Poseidon was delighted to be of assistance. Pelops soon found himself the owner of a winged golden chariot, which could race over the sea without wetting the axles, and was drawn by a team of tireless, winged, immortal horses.

Having visited Mount Sipylus and dedicated to Temnian Aphrodite an image made of green myrtle-wood, Pelops tested his chariot by driving it across the Aegean Sea. Almost before he had time to glance about him, he had reached Lesbos, where his charioteer Cillus died because of the swiftness of the flight. Pelops spent the night in Lesbos and, in a dream, saw Cillus's ghost lamenting his fate, and pleading for heroic honours. At dawn, he burned his body, heaped a barrow over the ashes, and founded the sanctuary of Cillaean Apollo close by. Then he set out again, driving the chariot himself.

On coming to Pisa, Pelops was alarmed to see the row of heads nailed above the palace gates, and began to regret his ambition. He therefore promised Myrtilus, if he betrayed his master, half the kingdom and the privilege of spending the bridal night with Hippodameia when she had been won.

Before entering the race Pelops sacrificed to Cydonian Athene. Some say that Cillus's ghost appeared and undertook to help him; others, that Sphaerus was his charioteer; but it is more generally believed that he drove his own team, Hippodameia standing beside him.

Meanwhile, Hippodameia had fallen in love with Pelops and, far from hindering his progress, had herself offered to reward Myrtilus generously, if her father's course could by some means be checked. Myrtilus therefore removed the lynch-pins from the axles of Oenomaus's chariot, and replaced them with others made of wax. As the chariots reached the neck of the Isthmus and Oenomaus, in hot pursuit, was poising his spear, about to transfix Pelops's back, the wheels of his chariot flew off, he fell entangled in the wreckage and was dragged to death. His ghost later haunted the Horse-scarer at Olympia. But Oenomaus, before he died, laid a curse on Myrtilus, praying that he might perish at the hands of Pelops.

Pelops, Hippodameia, and Myrtilus then set out for an evening drive across the sea. 'Alas!' cried Hippodameia, 'I have drunk nothing all day; thirst parches me.' The sun was setting and Pelops called a halt at the desert island of Helene, which lies not far from the island of Euboea, and went up the strand in search of water. When he returned with his helmet filled, Hippodameia ran weeping towards him and complained that Myrtilus had tried to ravish her. Pelops sternly rebuked Myrtilus, and struck him in the face, but he protested indignantly: 'This is the bridal night, on which you swore that I should enjoy Hippodameia. Will you break your oath?' Pelops made no reply, but took the reins from Myrtilus and drove on. As they approached Cape Geraestus Pelops dealt Myrtilus a sudden kick, which sent him flying head-long into the sea; and Myrtilus, as he sank, laid a curse on Pelops and all his house.

Hermes set Myrtilus's image among the stars as the constellation of the Charioteer; but his corpse was washed ashore on the coast of Euboea and buried in Arcadian Pheneus, behind the temple of Hermes.

Pelops drove on, until he reached the western stream of Oceanus, where he was cleansed of blood guilt by Hephaestus; afterwards he came back to Pisa, and succeeded to the throne of Oenomaus. He soon subjugated nearly the whole of what was then known as Apia, or Pelasgiotis, and renamed it the Peloponnese, meaning 'the island of Pelops', after himself. His courage, wisdom, wealth, and numerous children, earned him the envy and veneration of all Greece.

To atone for the murder of Myrtilus, who was Hermes's son, Pelops built the first temple of Hermes in the Peloponnese; he also tried to appease Myrtilus's ghost by building a cenotaph for him in the hippodrome at Olympia, and paying him heroic honours. Some say that Oenomaus was not the true Horse-scarer: it was the ghost of Myrtilus.

Over the tomb of Hippodameia's unsuccessful suitors, on the farther side of the river Alpheius, Pelops raised a tall barrow, paying them heroic honours too; and about a furlong away stood the sanctuary of Artemis Cordax, so called because Pelops's followers there celebrated his victories by dancing the Rope Dance, which they had brought from Lydia.

Atreus and Thyestes

Eurystheus's father, Sthenelus, having banished Amphitryon, and seized the throne of Mycenae, sent for Atreus and Thyestes, his brothers-in-law, and installed them at near-by Midea. A few years later, when Sthenelus and Eurystheus were both dead, an oracle advised the Mycenaeans to choose a prince of the Pelopid house to rule over them. They thereupon summoned Atreus and Thyestes from Midea and debated which of these two (who were fated to be always at odds) should be crowned king.

Now, Atreus had once vowed to sacrifice the finest of his flocks to Artemis; and Hermes, anxious to avenge the death of Myrtilus on the Pelopids, consulted his old friend Goat-Pan, who made a horned lamb with a golden fleece appear among the Acarnanian flock which Pelops had left to his sons Atreus and Thyestes. He foresaw that Atreus would claim it as his own and, from his reluctance to give Artemis the honours due to her, would become involved in fratricidal war with Thyestes. Atreus kept his vow, in part at least, by sacrificing the lamb's flesh; but he stuffed and mounted the fleece and locked it in a chest. He grew so proud of his life-like treasure that he could not refrain from boasting about it in the market place, and the jealous Thyestes, for whom Atreus's newly-married wife Aerope had conceived a passion, agreed to be her lover if she gave him the lamb. For Artemis had laid a curse upon it, and this was her doing.

In the debate Atreus claimed the throne of Mycenae by right of primogeniture, and also as possessor of the lamb. Thyestes asked him: 'Do you then publicly declare that its owner should be king?' 'I do,' Atreus replied. 'And I concur,' said Thyestes, smiling grimly. A

Helius (National Archaeological Museum, Athens)

herald then summoned the people of Mycenae to acclaim their new king, but Thyestes unexpectedly rose to upbraid Atreus as a vainglorious boaster, and led the magistrates to his home, where he displayed the lamb, justified his claim to its ownership, and was pronounced the rightful king of Mycenae.

Zeus, however, favoured Atreus, and sent Hermes to him, saying: 'Call Thyestes, and ask him whether, if the sun goes backward on the dial, he will resign his claim to the throne in your favour?' Atreus did as he was told, and Thyestes agreed to abdicate should such a portent occur. Thereupon Zeus reversed the laws of Nature. Helius, already in mid-career, wrested his chariot about and turned his horses' heads towards the dawn. The seven Pleiades, and all the other stars, retraced their courses; and that evening, for the first and last time, the sun set in the east. Thyestes's deceit and greed being thus plainly attested, Atreus succeeded to the throne of Mycenae, and banished him.

When, later, Atreus discovered that Thyestes had committed adultery with Aerope, he could hardly contain his rage. Nevertheless, for a while he feigned forgiveness.

Atreus now sent a herald to lure Thyestes back to Mycenae, with the offer of an amnesty and a half-share in the kingdom; but, as soon as Thyestes accepted this, slaughtered Aglaus, Orchomenus, and Callileon, Thyestes's three sons by one of the Naiads, on the very altar of Zeus where they had taken refuge; and then sought out and killed the infant Pleisthenes the Second, and Tantalus the Second, his twin. He hacked them all limb from limb, and set chosen morsels of their flesh, boiled in a cauldron, before Thyestes, to welcome him on his return. When Thyestes had eaten heartily, Atreus sent in their bloody heads and feet and hands, laid out on another dish, to show him what was now inside his belly. Thyestes fell back, vomiting, and laid an ineluctable curse upon the seed of Atreus.

Exiled once more, Thyestes fled first to King Thesprotus at Sicyon, where his own daughter Pelopia was a priestess. For, desiring revenge at whatever cost, he had consulted the Delphic Oracle and been advised to beget a son on his own daughter. Thyestes found Pelopia sacrificing by night to Athene Colocasia and, being loth to profane the rites, concealed himself in a near-by grove. Presently Pelopia, who was leading the solemn dance, slipped in a pool of blood that had flowed from the throat of a black ewe, the victim, and stained her tunic. She ran at once to the temple fish-pond, removed her tunic and was washing out the stain, when Thyestes sprang from the grove and ravished her. Pelopia did not recognize him, because he was wearing a mask, but contrived to steal his sword; and Thyestes, finding the scabbard empty and fearing detection, escaped to Lydia, the land of his fathers.

Meanwhile, fearing the consequences of his crime, Atreus consulted the Delphic Oracle, and was told: 'Recall Thyestes from Sicyon!'

He reached Sicyon too late to meet Thyestes and, falling in love with Pelopia, whom he assumed to be King Thesprotus's daughter, asked leave to make her his third wife; having by this time executed Aerope. Thesprotus did not undeceive Atreus, and the wedding took place at once. In due course she bore the son begotten on her by Thyestes, whom she exposed on a mountain; but goatherds rescued him and gave him to a she-goat for suckling – hence his name, Aegisthus, or 'goat-strength'. Atreus believed that Thyestes had fled from Sicyon at news of his approach; that the child was his own; and that Pelopia had been affected by the temporary madness which sometimes overtakes women after childbirth. He therefore recovered Aegisthus from the goatherds and reared him as his heir.

A succession of bad harvests then plagued Mycenae, and Atreus sent his sons, Agamemnon and Menelaus, to Delphi for news of Thyestes, whom they met by chance on his return from a further visit to the Oracle. They haled him back to Mycenae, where Atreus, having thrown him into prison, ordered Aegisthus, then seven years of age, to kill him as he slept.

Thyestes awoke suddenly to find Aegisthus standing over him, sword in hand; he quickly rolled sideways and escaped death. Then he rose, disarmed the boy with a shrewd kick at his wrist, and sprang to recover the sword. But it was his own, lost years before in Sicyon! He seized Aegisthus by the shoulder and cried: 'Tell me instantly how this came into your possession?' Aegisthus stammered: 'Alas, my mother Pelopia gave it me.' 'I will spare your life, boy,' said Thyestes, 'if you carry out the three orders I now give you.' 'I am your servant in all things,' wept Aegisthus, who had expected no mercy. 'My first order is to bring your mother here,' Thyestes told him.

Aegisthus thereupon brought Pelopia to the dungeon and, recognizing Thyestes, she wept on his neck, called him her dearest father, and commiserated with his sufferings. 'How did you come by this sword, daughter?' Thyestes asked. 'I took it from the scabbard of an unknown stranger who ravished me one night at Sicyon,' she replied. 'It is mine,' said Thyestes. Pelopia, stricken with horror, seized the sword, and plunged it into her breast. Aegisthus stood aghast, not understanding what had been said. 'Now take this sword to Atreus,' was Thyestes's second order, 'and tell him that you have carried out your commission. Then return!' Dumbly Aegisthus took the bloody thing to Atreus, who went joyfully down to the seashore, where he offered a sacrifice of thanksgiving to Zeus, convinced that he was rid of Thyestes at last.

When Aegisthus returned to the dungeon, Thyestes revealed himself as his father, and issued his third order: 'Kill Atreus, my son Aegisthus, and this time do not falter!' Aegisthus did as he was told, and Thyestes reigned once more in Mycenae.

Another golden-fleeced horned lamb then appeared among Thyestes's flocks and grew to be a ram and, afterwards, every new Pelopid

Menelaus (Museo delle Terme, Rome)

Agamemnon. Detail of vase (British Museum)

king was thus divinely confirmed in possession of his golden sceptre; these rams grazed at ease in a paddock enclosed by unscalable walls.

Agamemnon and Clytaemnestra

When Aegisthus killed Atreus, his sons, Agamemnon and Menelaus, were still infants. Snatching them up, one under each arm, their nurse fled with them to Polypheides, king of Sicyon, at whose instance they were subsequently entrusted to Oeneus the Aetolian. After they had spent some years at Oeneus's court, King Tyndareus of Sparta restored their fortunes. Marching against Mycenae, he exacted an oath from Thyestes that he would bequeath the sceptre to Agamemnon, as Atreus's heir, and go into exile, never to return. Thyestes thereupon departed to Cythera, while Aegisthus, fearing Agamemnon's vengeance, fled to King Cylarabes, son of King Sthenelus the Argive.

Agamemnon first made war against Tantalus, King of Pisa, killed him in battle and forcibly married his widow Clytaemnestra, whom Leda had borne to King Tyndareus of Sparta. The Dioscuri, Clytaemnestra's brothers, thereupon marched on Mycenae; but Agamemnon had already gone to his benefactor Tyndareus, who forgave him and let him keep Clytaemnestra. After the death of the Dioscuri, Menelaus married their sister Helen, and Tyndareus abdicated in his favour. Clytaemnestra bore Agamemnon one son, Orestes, and three daughters: Electra, Iphigeneia, and Chrysothemis.

When Paris, the son of King Priam of Troy, abducted Helen and thus provoked the Trojan War, both Agamemnon and Menelaus were absent from home for ten years; but Aegisthus did not join their expedition, preferring to stay behind at Argos and seek revenge on the House of Atreus.

Now, Nauplius, the husband of Clymene, having failed to obtain requital from Agamemnon and the other Greek leaders for the stoning of his son Palamedes, had sailed away from Troy and coasted around Attica and the Peloponnese, inciting the lonely wives of his enemies to adultery. Aegisthus, therefore, when he heard that Clytaemnestra was among those most eager to be convinced by Nauplius, planned not only to become her lover, but to kill Agamemnon, with her assistance, as soon as the Trojan War ended.

Hermes, sent to Aegisthus by Omniscient Zeus, warned him to abandon this project, on the ground that when Orestes had grown to manhood, he would be bound to avenge his father. However, Hermes failed to deter Aegisthus. At first, Clytaemnestra rejected his advances, because Agamemnon, apprised of Nauplius's visit to Mycenae, had instructed his court bard to keep close watch on her and report to him, in writing, the least sign of infidelity. But Aegisthus seized the old minstrel and marooned him without food on a lonely island, where birds of prey were soon picking his bones. Clytaemnestra then yielded to Aegisthus's embraces, and he celebrated his unhoped-for success with burnt offerings to Aphrodite, and gifts of tapestries and gold to Artemis, who was nursing a grudge against the House of Atreus.

Clytaemnestra had small cause to love Agamemnon: after killing her former husband Tantalus, and the new-born child at her breast, he had married her by force, and then gone away to a war which promised never to end; he had also sanctioned the sacrifice of Iphigencia at Aulis, and was said to be bringing back Priam's daughter Cassandra, the prophetess, as his wife in all but name. It is true that Cassandra had borne Agamemnon twin sons: Teledamus and Pelops, but he does not seem to have intended any insult to Clytaemnestra. Her informant had been Nauplius's surviving son Oeax who, in vengeance for his brother's death, was maliciously provoking her to do murder.

Clytaemnestra therefore conspired with Aegisthus to kill both Agamemnon and Cassandra. Fearing, however, that they might arrive unexpectedly, she wrote Agamemnon a letter asking him to light a beacon on Mount Ida when Troy fell; and herself arranged for a chain of fires to relay his signal to Argolis. A watchman was also stationed on the roof of the palace at Mycenae, gazing towards Mount Arachne. At last, one dark night, he saw the distant beacon blaze and ran to wake Clytaemnestra. Aegisthus thereupon posted one of his own men in a watch-tower near the sea, promising him two gold talents for the first news of Agamemnon's landing.

No sooner had Agamemnon disembarked, than he bent down to kiss the soil, weeping for joy. Meanwhile the watchman hurried to Mycenae to collect his fee, and Aegisthus chose twenty of the boldest warriors, posted them in ambush inside the palace, ordered a great banquet and then, mounting his chariot, rode down to welcome Agamemnon.

Clytaemnestra greeted her travel-worn husband with every appearance of delight, unrolled a purple carpet for him, and led him to the bath-house; but Cassandra remained outside the palace, caught in a prophetic trance, refusing to enter, and crying that she smelt blood, and that the curse of Thyestes was heavy upon the dining-hall. When Agamemnon had washed himself and set one foot out of the bath, Clytaemnestra came forward, as if to wrap a towel about him, but instead threw over his head a garment of net. Entangled in this, like a fish, Agamemnon perished at the hands of Aegisthus, who struck him twice with a two-edged sword. He fell back, into the silver-sided bath, where Clytaemnestra avenged her wrongs by beheading him with an axe. She then ran out to kill Cassandra with the same weapon, not troubling first to close her husband's eyelids or mouth; but wiped off on his hair the blood which had splashed her, to signify that he had brought about his own death.

A fierce battle was now raging in the palace, between Agamemnon's bodyguard and Aegisthus's supporters, but Aegisthus won the day. Outside, Cassandra's head rolled to the ground, and Aegisthus also had the satisfaction of killing her twin sons by Agamemnon; yet he failed to do away with another of Agamemnon's bastards, by name Halesus, who contrived to make his escape and, after long wandering in exile, founded the Italian city of Falerii.

The Vengeance of Orestes

Orestes was reared by his loving grand-parents Tyndareus and Leda and, as a boy, accompanied Clytaemnestra and Iphigeneia to Aulis. On the evening of the murder, Orestes, then ten years of age, was rescued by his sister Electra who, aided by her father's ancient tutor, wrapped him in a robe embroidered with wild beasts, which she herself had woven, and smuggled him out of the city.

After hiding for a while among the shepherds of the river Tanus, which divides Argolis from Laconia, the tutor made his way with Orestes to the court of Strophius, a firm ally of the House of Atreus, who ruled over Crisa, at the foot of Mount Parnassus. At Crisa, Orestes found an adventurous playmate, namely Strophius's son Pylades, who was somewhat younger than himself, and their friendship was destined to become proverbial. From the old tutor he learned with grief that Agamemnon's body had been flung out of the house and hastily buried by Clytaemnestra, without either libations or myrtle-boughs; and that the people of Mycenae had been forbidden to attend the funeral.

Aegisthus reigned at Mycenae for seven years, yet he was little more than a slave to Clytaemnestra, the true ruler of Mycenae, and he lived in abject fear of vengeance. Even while surrounded by a trusty foreign bodyguard, he never passed a single night in sound sleep, and had offered a handsome reward for Orestes's assassination.

Electra had been betrothed to her cousin Castor of Sparta, before his death and demi-deification. Though the leading princes of Greece

The gold mask of
Agamemnon (National
Archaeological Museum,
Athens)

now contended for her hand, Aegisthus feared that she might bear a son to avenge Agamemnon, and therefore announced that no suitor could be accepted. He would gladly have destroyed Electra, who showed him implacable hatred, lest she lay secretly with one of the Palace officers and bore him a bastard; but Clytaemnestra, feeling no qualms about her part in Agamemnon's murder, and scrupulous not to incur the displeasure of the gods, forbade him to do so. She allowed him, however, to marry Electra to a Mycenaean peasant who, being afraid of Orestes and also chaste by nature, never consummated their unequal union.

Thus, neglected by Clytaemnestra, who had now borne Aegisthus three children, by name Erigone, Aletes, and the second Helen, Electra lived in disgraceful poverty, and was kept under constant close supervision. In the end it was decided that, unless she would accept her fate, as her sister Chrysothemis had done, and refrain from publicly calling Aegisthus and Clytaemnestra 'murderous adulterers', she would be banished to some distant city and there confined in a dungeon where the light of the sun never penetrated. Yet Electra despised Chrysothemis for her subservience and disloyalty to their dead father, and secretly sent frequent reminders to Orestes of the vengeance required from him.

Orestes, now grown to manhood, visited the Delphic Oracle, to enquire whether or not he should destroy his father's murderers. Apollo's answer, authorized by Zeus, was that if he neglected to avenge Agamemnon he would become an outcast from society, debarred from entering any shrine or temple, and afflicted with a leprosy that ate into his flesh, making it sprout white mould. He was recommended to pour libations beside Agamemnon's tomb, lay a ringlet of his hair upon it and, unaided by any company of spearmen, craftily exact the due punishment from the murderers. At the same time the Pythoness observed that the Erinnyes would not readily forgive a matricide, and therefore, on behalf of Apollo, she gave Orestes a bow of horn, with which to repel their attacks, should they become insupportable. After fulfilling his orders, he must come again to Delphi, where Apollo would protect him.

In the eighth year Orestes secretly returned to Mycenae, by way of Athens, determined to destroy both Aegisthus and his own mother.

One morning, with Pylades at his side, he visited Agamemnon's tomb and there, cutting off a lock of his hair, he invoked Infernal Hermes, patron of fatherhood. When a group of slave-women approached, dirty and dishevelled for the purposes of mourning, he took shelter in a near-by thicket to watch them. Now, on the previous night, Clytaemnestra had dreamed that she gave birth to a serpent, which she wrapped in swaddling clothes and suckled. Suddenly she screamed in her sleep, and alarmed the whole Palace by crying that the serpent had drawn blood from her breast, as well as milk. The opinion of the sooth-sayers whom she consulted was that she had incurred the anger of the dead; and those mourning slave-women consequently came on her behalf to pour libations upon Agamemnon's tomb, in the hope of appeasing his ghost. Electra, who was one of the party, poured the libations in her own name, not her mother's; offered prayers to Agamemnon for vengeance, instead of pardon; and bade Hermes summon Mother Earth and the gods of the Underworld to hear her plea. Noticing a ringlet of fair hair upon the tomb, she decided that it could belong only to Orestes: both because it closely resembled her own in colour and texture, and because no one else would have dared to make such an offering.

Torn between hope and doubt, she was measuring her feet against Orestes's foot-prints in the clay beside the tomb, and finding a family resemblance, when he emerged from his hiding-place, showed her that the ringlet was his own, and produced the robe in which he had escaped from Mycenae.

Electra welcomed him with delight, and together they invoked their ancestor, Father Zeus, whom they reminded that Agamemnon had always paid him great honour and that, were the House of Atreus to die out, no one would be left in Mycenae to offer him the customary hecatombs: for Aegisthus worshipped other deities.

When the slave-women told Orestes of Clytaemnestra's dream, he recognized the serpent as himself, and declared that he would indeed play the cunning serpent and draw blood from her false body. Then he instructed Electra to enter the Palace and tell Clytaemnestra nothing about their meeting; he and Pylades would follow, after an interval, and beg hospitality at the gate, as strangers and suppliants, pretending to be Phocians and using the Parnassian dialect. If the porter refused them admittance, Aegisthus's inhospitality would outrage the city; if he granted it, they would not fail to take vengeance.

Presently Orestes knocked at the Palace gate, and asked for the master or mistress of the house. Clytaemnestra herself came out, but did not recognize Orestes. He pretended to be an Aeolian from Daulis, bearing sad news from one Strophius, whom he had met by chance on the road to Argos: namely, that her son Orestes was dead, and that his ashes were being kept in a brazen urn. Strophius wished to know whether he should send these back to Mycenae, or bury them at Crisa.

Clytaemnestra at once welcomed Orestes inside and, concealing her joy from the servants, sent his old nurse, Geilissa, to fetch Aegisthus from a near-by temple. But Geilissa saw through Orestes's disguise and, altering the message, told Aegisthus to rejoice because he could now safely come alone and weaponless to greet the bearers of glad tidings: his enemy was dead.

Unsuspectingly, Aegisthus entered the Palace where, to create a further distraction, Pylades had just arrived, carrying a brazen urn. He told Clytaemnestra that it held Orestes's ashes, which Strophius

Orestes and Electra (National Museum, Naples)

had now decided to send to Mycenae. This seeming confirmation of the first message put Aegisthus completely off his guard; thus Orestes had no difficulty in drawing his sword and cutting him down. Clytaemnestra then recognized her son, and tried to soften his heart by baring her breast, and appealing to his filial duty; Orestes, however, beheaded her with a single stroke of the same sword, and she fell beside the body of her paramour. Standing over the corpses, he addressed the Palace servants, holding aloft the still blood-stained net in which Agamemnon had died, eloquently exculpating himself for the murder of Clytaemnestra by this reminder of her treachery, and adding that Aegisthus had suffered the sentence prescribed by law for adulterers.

Not content with killing Aegisthus and Clytaemnestra, Orestes next disposed of the second Helen, their daughter; and Pylades beat off the sons of Nauplius, who had come to Aegisthus's rescue.

The Trial of Orestes
The Mycenaeans who had supported Orestes in his unheard-of action would not allow the bodies of Clytaemnestra and Aegisthus to lie within their city, but buried them at some distance beyond the walls. That night, Orestes and Pylades stood guard at Clytaemnestra's tomb, lest anyone should dare rob it; but, during their vigil, the serpent-haired, dog-headed, bat-winged Erinnyes appeared, swinging their scourges. Driven to distraction by these fierce attacks, against which Apollo's bow of horn was of little avail, Orestes fell prostrate on a couch, where he lay for six days, his head wrapped in a cloak – refusing either to eat or to wash.

Old Tyndareus now arrived from Sparta, and brought a charge of matricide against Orestes, summoning the Mycenaean chieftains to judge his case. He decreed that, pending the trial, none should speak either to Orestes or Electra, and that both should be denied shelter, fire, and water. Thus Orestes was prevented even from washing his blood-stained hands.

Meanwhile, Menelaus, laden with treasure, landed at Nauplia, where a fisherman told him that Aegisthus and Clytaemnestra had been murdered. He sent Helen ahead to confirm the news at Mycenae; but by night, lest the kinsmen of those who had perished at Troy should stone her. Helen, feeling ashamed to mourn in public for her sister Clytaemnestra, since she herself had caused even more bloodshed by her infidelities, asked Electra, who was now nursing the afflicted Orestes: 'Pray, niece, take offerings of my hair and lay them on Clytaemnestra's tomb, after pouring libations to her ghost.' Electra, when she saw that Helen had been prevented by vanity from cutting off more than the very tips of her hair, refused to do so. 'Send your daughter Hermione instead,' was her curt advice. Helen thereupon summoned Hermione from the palace.

Menelaus then entered the palace, where he was greeted by his foster-father Tyndareus, clad in deep mourning, and warned not to set foot on Spartan soil until he had punished his criminal nephew and niece. Tyndareus held that Orestes should have contented himself with allowing his fellow-citizens to banish Clytaemnestra. If they had demanded her death he should have interceded on her behalf. As matters now stood, they must be persuaded, willy-nilly, that not only Orestes, but Electra who had spurred him on, should be stoned to death as matricides.

Fearing to offend Tyndareus, Menelaus secured the desired verdict. But at the eloquent plea of Orestes himself, who was present in court and had the support of Pylades, the judges commuted the sentence to one of suicide. Pylades then led Orestes away, nobly refusing to desert either him or Electra, to whom he was betrothed; and proposed that, since all three must die, they should first punish Menelaus's cowardice and disloyalty by killing Helen, the originator of every misfortune that had befallen them. While, therefore, Electra waited outside the walls to intercept Hermione on her return from Clytaemnestra's tomb and hold her as a hostage for Menelaus's good behaviour, Orestes and Pylades entered the palace, with swords hidden beneath their cloaks, and took refuge at the central altar, as though they were suppliants. Helen, who sat near by, was deceived by their lamentations, and approached to welcome them. Whereupon both drew their swords and, while Pylades chased away Helen's Phrygian slaves, Orestes attempted to murder her. But Apollo, at Zeus's command, rapt her in a cloud to Olympus, where she became an immortal; joining her brothers, the Dioscuri, as a guardian of sailors in distress.

Meanwhile, Electra had secured Hermione, led her into the palace, and barred the gates. Menelaus, seeing his daughter threatened, ordered an immediate rescue. His men burst open the gates, and

A silver plate of Athene (Antikenabteilung, Charlottenburg, Berlin)

Orestes was just about to set the palace alight, kill Hermione, and die himself either by sword or fire, when Apollo providentially appeared, wrenched the torch from his hand, and drove back Menelaus's warriors. Apollo commanded Menelaus to take another wife, betroth Hermione to Orestes, and return to rule over Sparta; Clytaemnestra's murder need no longer concern him, now that the gods had intervened.

Orestes then set out for Delphi, still pursued by the Erinnyes. The Pythian Priestess was terrified to see him crouched as a suppliant on the marble navel-stone – stained by the blood from his unwashed hands – and the hideous troop of black Erinnyes sleeping beside him. Apollo, however, reassured her by promising to act as advocate for Orestes, whom he ordered to face his ordeal with courage. After a period of exile, he must make his way to Athens, and there embrace the ancient image of Athene who, as the Dioscuri had already prophesied, would shield him with her Gorgon-faced aegis, and annul the curse. While the Erinnyes were still fast asleep, Orestes escaped under the guidance of Hermes.

Orestes's exile lasted for one year: he wandered far, over land and sea, pursued by the tireless Erinnyes and constantly purified both with the blood of pigs and with running water; yet these rites never served to keep his tormentors at bay for more than an hour or two, and he soon lost his wits.

When a year had passed, Orestes visited Athens, which was then governed by his kinsman Pandion. He went at once to Athene's temple on the Acropolis, sat down, and embraced her image. The Black Erinnyes soon arrived, out of breath, having lost track of him while he crossed the Isthmus. Though at his first arrival none wished to receive him, as being hated by the gods, presently some were emboldened to invite him into their houses, where he sat at a separate table and drank from a separate wine cup.

The Erinnyes, who had already begun to accuse him to the Athenians, were soon joined by Tyndareus with his grand-daughter Erigone, daughter of Aegisthus and Clytaemnestra. But Athene hurried to Athens and, swearing-in the noblest citizens as judges, summoned the Areopagus to try what was then only the second case of homicide to come before it.

In due course the trial took place, Apollo appearing as counsel for the defence, and the eldest of the Erinnyes as public prosecutrix. In an elaborate speech, Apollo denied the importance of motherhood, asserting that a woman was no more than the inert furrow in which the husbandman cast his seed; and that Orestes had been abundantly justified in his act, the father being the one parent worthy of the name. When the voting proved equal, Athene confessed herself wholly on the father's side, and gave her casting vote in favour of Orestes. Thus honourably acquitted, he returned in joy to Argolis, swearing to be a faithful ally to Athens so long as he lived. The

Erinnyes, however, loudly lamented this subversal of the ancient law by upstart gods; and Erigone hanged herself for mortification.

The Pacification of the Erinnyes

In gratitude for his acquittal, Orestes dedicated an altar to Warlike Athene; but the Erinnyes threatened, if the judgement were not reversed, to let fall a drop of their own hearts' blood which would bring barrenness upon the soil, blight the crops, and destroy all the offspring of Athens. Athene nevertheless soothed their anger by flattery: acknowledging them to be far wiser than herself, she suggested that they should take up residence in a grotto at Athens, where they would gather such throngs of worshippers as they could never hope to find elsewhere. If they accepted this invitation she would decree that no house where worship was withheld from them might prosper; but they, in return, must undertake to invoke fair winds for her ships, fertility for her land, and fruitful marriages for her people – also rooting out the impious, so that she might see fit to grant Athens victory in war. The Erinnyes, after a short deliberation, graciously agreed to these proposals.

With expressions of gratitude, good wishes, and charms against withering winds, drought, blight, and sedition, the Erinnyes – henceforth addressed as the Solemn Ones – bade farewell to Athene, and were conducted by her people in a torchlight procession to the entrance of a deep grotto at the south-eastern angle of the Areopagus. Appropriate sacrifices were there offered to them, and they descended into the grotto, which now became both an oracular shrine and, like the Sanctuary of Theseus, a place of refuge for suppliants.

Yet only three of the Erinnyes had accepted Athene's generous offer; the remainder continued to pursue Orestes; and some people go so far as to deny that the Solemn Ones were ever Erinnyes. The name 'Eumenides' was first given to the Erinnyes by Orestes, in the following year, after his daring adventure in the Tauric Chersonese, when he finally succeeded in appeasing their fury at Carneia with the holocaust of a black sheep.

Iphigeneia Among the Taurians

Still pursued by such of the Erinnyes as had turned deaf ears to Athene's eloquent speeches, Orestes went in despair to Delphi, where he threw himself on the temple floor and threatened to take his own life unless Apollo saved him from their scourgings. In reply, the Pythian priestess ordered him to sail up the Bosphorus and northward across the Black Sea; his woes would end only when he had seized an ancient wooden image of Artemis from her temple in the Tauric Chersonese, and brought it to Athens.

Now, the king of the Taurians was the fleet-footed Thoas, a son of Dionysus and Ariadne, and father of Hypsipyle; and his people, so called because Osiris once yoked bulls (*tauroi*) and ploughed their

*Orestes slaying Aegisthus
(National Archaeological
Museum, Athens)*

*Orestes and
Clytaemnestra. Amphora
(British Museum)*

land, came of Scythian stock. They lived by rapine, and whenever one of their warriors took a prisoner, he beheaded him, carried the head home, and there impaled it on a tall stake above the chimney, so that his household might live under the dead man's protection. Moreover, every sailor who had been shipwrecked, or driven into their port by rough weather, was publicly sacrificed to Taurian Artemis. When they had performed certain preparatory rites, they felled him with a club and nailed his severed head to a cross; after which the body was either buried, or tossed into the sea from the precipice crowned by Artemis's temple. But any princely stranger who fell into their hands was killed with a sword by the goddess's virgin-priestess; and she threw his corpse into the sacred fire, welling up from Tartarus, which burns in the divine precinct. The ancient image of the goddess, which Orestes was ordered to seize, had fallen here from Heaven. This temple was supported by vast columns, and approached by forty steps, its altar of white marble permanently stained with blood.

Now, Iphigeneia had been rescued from sacrifice at Aulis by Artemis, wrapped in a cloud, and wafted to the Tauric Chersonese, where she was at once appointed Chief Priestess and granted the sole right of handling the sacred image. The Taurians thereafter addressed her as Artemis. Iphigeneia loathed human sacrifice, but piously obeyed the goddess.

Orestes and Pylades knew nothing of all this; they still believed that Iphigeneia had died under the sacrificial knife at Aulis. Nevertheless, they hastened to the land of the Taurians in a fifty-oared ship which, on arrival, they left at anchor, guarded by their oarsmen, while they hid in a sea-cave. It was their intention to approach the temple at nightfall, but they were surprised beforehand by some credulous herdsmen who, assuming them to be the Dioscuri, or some other pair of immortals, fell down and adored them. At this juncture Orestes went mad once more, bellowing like a calf and howling like a dog; he mistook a herd of calves for Erinnyes, and rushed from the cave, sword in hand, to slaughter them. The disillusioned herdsmen thereupon overpowered the two friends who, at Thoas's orders, were marched off to the temple for immediate sacrifice.

During the preliminary rites Orestes conversed in Greek with Iphigeneia; soon they joyfully discovered each other's identity, and on learning the nature of his mission, she began to lift down the image for him to carry away. Thoas, however, suddenly appeared, impatient at the slow progress of the sacrifice, and the resourceful Iphigeneia pretended to be soothing the image. She explained to Thoas that the goddess had averted her gaze from the victims whom he had sent, because one was a matricide, and the other was abetting him: both were quite unfit for sacrifice. She must take them, together with the image, which their presence had polluted, to be cleansed in the sea, and offer the goddess a torchlight sacrifice of young lambs.

Meanwhile, Thoas was to purify the temple with a torch, cover his head when the strangers emerged, and order everyone to remain at home and thus avoid pollution.

Thoas, wholly deceived, began to purify the temple. Presently Iphigeneia, Orestes, and Pylades conveyed the image down to the shore by torchlight but, instead of bathing it in the sea, hastily carried it aboard their ship. The Taurian temple-servants, who had come with them, now suspected treachery and showed fight. They were subdued in a hard struggle, after which Orestes's oarsmen rowed the ship away. A sudden gale, however, sprang up, driving her back towards the rocky shore, and all would have perished, had not Poseidon calmed the sea at Athene's request; with a favouring breeze, they made the Island of Sminthos.

This was the home of Chryses, the priest of Apollo, and his grandson of the same name, whose mother Chryseis now proposed to surrender the fugitives to Thoas. For, although some hold that Athene had visited Thoas, who was manning a fleet to sail in pursuit, and cajoled him so successfully that he even consented to repatriate Iphigeneia's Greek slave-women, it is certain that he came to Sminthos with murderous intentions. Then Chryses the Elder, learning the identity of his guests, revealed to Chryses the Younger that he was not, as Chryseis had always pretended, Apollo's son, but Agamemnon's, and therefore half-brother to Orestes and Iphigeneia. At this, Chryses and Orestes rushed shoulder to shoulder against Thoas, whom they succeeded in killing; and Orestes, taking up the image, sailed safely home to Mycenae, where the Erinnyes at last abandoned their chase.

The Reign of Orestes

Aegisthus's son Aletes now usurped the kingdom of Mycenae, believing that Orestes and Pylades had been sacrificed on the altar of Tauric Artemis. But Electra, doubting its truth, went to consult the Delphic Oracle. Iphigeneia had just arrived at Delphi, and was pointed out to Electra as Orestes's murderess. Revengefully she seized a firebrand from the altar and, not recognizing Iphigeneia after the lapse of years, was about to blind her with it, when Orestes himself entered and explained all. The reunited children of Agamemnon then went joyfully back to Mycenae, where Orestes ended the feud between the House of Atreus and House of Thyestes, by killing Aletes; whose sister Erigone, it is said, would also have perished by his hand, had not Artemis snatched her away to Attica.

Some say that Iphigeneia died either at Brauron, or at Megara, where she now has a sanctuary; others, that Artemis immortalized her as the Younger Hecate. Electra, married to Pylades, bore him Medon and Strophius the Second; she lies buried at Mycenae. Orestes married his cousin Hermione: by her he fathered Tisamenus, his heir and successor; and by Erigone his second wife, Penthilus.

When Menelaus died, the Spartans invited Orestes to become their king, preferring him, as a grandson of Tyndareus, to Nicostratus and Megapenthes, begotten by Menelaus on a slave-girl. Orestes who, with the help of troops furnished by his Phocian allies, had already added a large part of Arcadia to his Mycenaean domains, now made himself master of Argos as well; for King Cylarabes, grandson of Capaneus, left no issue. He also subdued Achaea but, in obedience to the Delphic Oracle, finally emigrated from Mycenae to Arcadia where, at the age of seventy, he died of a snake bite at Oresteium, or Orestia, the town which he had founded during his exile.

Orestes was buried at Tegea, but in the reign of Anaxandrides, co-king with Aristo, and the only Laconian who ever had two wives and occupied two houses at the same time, the Spartans, in despair because they had hitherto lost every battle fought with the Tegeans, sent to Delphi for advice, and were instructed to possess themselves of Orestes's bones. Since the whereabouts of these were unknown, they sent Lichas, one of Sparta's benefactors, to ask for further enlightenment. He was given the following response in hexameters:

> Level and smooth the plain of Arcadian Tegea. Go thou
> Where two winds are ever, by strong necessity, blowing;
> Where stroke rings upon stroke, where evil lies upon evil;
> There all-teeming earth doth enclose the prince whom thou seekest.
> Bring thou him to thy house, and thus be Tegea's master!

Because of a temporary truce between the two states, Lichas had no difficulty in visiting Tegea; where he came upon a smith forging a sword of iron, instead of bronze, and gazed open-mouthed at the novel sight. 'Does this work surprise you?' cried the jovial smith. 'Well, I have something here to surprise you even more! It is a coffin, seven cubits long, containing a corpse of the same length, which I found beneath the smithy floor while I was digging yonder well.'

Lichas guessed that the winds mentioned in the verses must be those raised by the smith's bellows; the strokes those of his hammer; and the evil lying upon evil, his hammer-head beating out the iron sword – for the Iron Age brought in cruel days. He at once returned with the news to Sparta, where the judges, at his own suggestion, pretended to condemn him for a crime of violence; then, fleeing to Tegea as if from execution, he persuaded the smith to hide him in the smithy. At midnight, he stole the bones out of the coffin and hurried back to Sparta, where he re-interred them near the sanctuary of the Fates. Spartan armies ever after were victorious over the Tegeans.

Tisamenus succeeded to his father's dominions, but was driven from the capital cities of Sparta, Mycenae, and Argos by the sons of Heracles, and took refuge with his army in Achaea. His son Cometes emigrated to Asia.

6

HERACLES

The Birth of Heracles

ELECTRYON, SON OF PERSEUS, High King of Mycenae and husband of Anaxo, marched vengefully against the Taphians and Teleboans. They had joined in a successful raid on his cattle, which had resulted in the death of Electryon's eight sons. While he was away, his nephew King Amphitryon of Troezen acted as regent. 'Rule well, and when I return victorious, you shall marry my daughter Alcmene,' Electryon cried in farewell. Amphitryon, informed by the King of Elis that the stolen cattle were now in his possession, paid the large ransom demanded, and recalled Electryon to identify them. Electryon, by no means pleased to learn that Amphitryon expected him to repay this ransom, asked harshly what right had the Eleans to sell stolen property, and why did Amphitryon condone in a fraud? Disdaining to reply, Amphitryon vented his annoyance by throwing a club at one of the cows which had strayed from the herd; it struck her horns, rebounded, and killed Electryon. Thereupon Amphitryon was banished from Argolis by his uncle Sthenelus.

Amphitryon, accompanied by Alcmene, fled to Thebes, where King Creon purified him and gave his sister Perimede in marriage to Electryon's only surviving son, Licymnius, a bastard borne by a Phrygian woman named Midea. But the pious Alcmene would not lie with Amphitryon until he had avenged the death of her eight brothers. Creon therefore gave him permission to raise a Boeotian army for this purpose. Then, aided by Athenian, Phocian, Argive, and Locrian contingents, Amphitryon overcame the Teleboans and Taphians, and bestowed their islands on his allies.

Meanwhile, Zeus, taking advantage of Amphitryon's absence, impersonated him and, assuring Alcmene that her brothers were now avenged – since Amphitryon had indeed gained the required victory that very morning – lay with her all one night, to which he gave the length of three. For Hermes, at Zeus's command, had ordered Helius to quench the solar fires, have the Hours unyoke his team, and spend the following day at home; because the procreation

opposite: *A cameo of Heracles (National Archaeological Museum, Athens)*

of so great a champion as Zeus had in mind could not be accomplished in haste. Hermes next ordered the Moon to go slowly, and Sleep to make mankind so drowsy that no one would notice what was happening. Alcmene, wholly deceived, listened delightedly to Zeus's account of the crushing defeat inflicted on Pterelaus at Oechalia, and sported innocently with her supposed husband for the whole thirty-six hours. On the next day, when Amphitryon returned, eloquent of victory and of his passion for her, Alcmene did not welcome him to the marriage couch so rapturously as he had hoped. 'We never slept a wink last night,' she complained. 'And surely you do not expect me to listen twice to the story of your exploits?' Amphitryon, unable to understand these remarks, consulted the seer Teiresias, who told him that he had been cuckolded by Zeus; and thereafter he never dared sleep with Alcmene again, for fear of incurring divine jealousy.

Nine months later, on Olympus, Zeus happened to boast that he had fathered a son, now at the point of birth, who would be called Heracles, which means 'Glory of Hera', and rule the noble House of Perseus. Hera thereupon made him promise that any prince born before nightfall to the House of Perseus should be High King. When Zeus swore an unbreakable oath to this effect, Hera went at once to Mycenae, where she hastened the pangs of Nicippe, wife of King Sthenelus. She then hurried to Thebes, and squatted cross-legged at Alcmene's door, with her clothing tied into knots, and her fingers locked together; by which means she delayed the birth of Heracles, until Eurystheus, son of Sthenelus, a seven-months' child, already lay in his cradle. When Heracles appeared, one hour too late, he was found to have a twin, Iphicles, Amphitryon's son, younger by a night. At first, Heracles was called Alcaeus, or Palaemon.

When Hera returned to Olympus, and calmly boasted of her success in keeping Eileithyia, goddess of childbirth, from Alcmene's door, Zeus fell into a towering rage; seizing his eldest daughter Ate, who had blinded him to Hera's deceit, he took a mighty oath that she should never visit Olympus again. Whirled around his head by her golden hair, Ate was sent hurtling down to earth. Though Zeus could not go back on his word and allow Heracles to rule the House of Perseus, he persuaded Hera to agree that, after performing whatever twelve labours Eurystheus set him, his son should become a god.

Now, unlike Zeus's former human loves, from Niobe onwards, Alcmene had been selected not so much for his pleasure as with a view to begetting a son powerful enough to protect both gods and men against destruction. Alcmene was the last mortal woman with whom Zeus lay, and he honoured her so highly that, instead of roughly violating her, he disguised himself as Amphitryon and wooed her with affectionate words and caresses. He knew Alcmene to be incorruptible and when he presented her with a Carchesian goblet, she accepted it without question as spoil won in the victory.

The Youth of Heracles

Alcmene, fearing Hera's jealousy, exposed her newly-born child in a field outside the walls of Thebes; and here, at Zeus's instigation, Athene took Hera for a casual stroll. 'Look, my dear! What a wonderfully robust child!' said Athene, pretending surprise as she stopped to pick him up. 'His mother must have been out of her mind to abandon him in a stony field! Come, you have milk. Give the poor little creature suck!' Thoughtlessly Hera took him and bared her breast, at which Heracles drew with such force that she flung him down in pain, and a spurt of milk flew across the sky and became the Milky Way. 'The young monster!' Hera cried. But Heracles was now immortal, and Athene returned him to Alcmene with a smile, telling her to guard and rear him well. Hera was thus Heracles's foster-mother, if only for a short while; and the Thebans therefore style him her son, and say that he had been Alcaeus before she gave him suck, but was renamed in her honour.

One evening, when Heracles had reached the age of eight or ten months and was still unweaned, Alcmene having washed and suckled her twins, laid them to rest under a lamb-fleece coverlet, on the broad brazen shield which Amphitryon had won from Pterelaus. At midnight, Hera sent two prodigious azure-scaled serpents to Amphitryon's house, with strict orders to destroy Heracles. The gates opened as they approached; they glided through, and over the marble floors to the nursery – their eyes shooting flames, and poison dripping from their fangs.

The twins awoke, to see the serpents writhed above them, with darting, forked tongues; for Zeus again divinely illumined the chamber. Iphicles screamed, kicked off the coverlet and, in an attempt to escape, rolled from the shield to the floor. His frightened cries, and the strange light shining under the nursery door, roused Alcmene. 'Up with you, Amphitryon!' she cried. Without waiting to put on his sandals, Amphitryon leaped from the cedar-wood bed, and seized his sword. At that moment the light in the nursery went out. Shouting to his drowsy slaves for lamps and torches, Amphitryon rushed in; and Heracles, who had not uttered so much as a whimper, proudly displayed the serpents, which he was in the act of strangling, one in either hand.

While Alcmene comforted the terror-stricken Iphicles, Amphitryon spread the coverlet over Heracles again, and returned to bed. At dawn, when the cock had crowed three times, Alcmene summoned the aged Teiresias and told him of the prodigy. Teiresias, after foretelling Heracles's future glories, advised her to strew a broad hearth with dry faggots of gorse, thorn and brambles, and burn the serpents upon them at midnight. In the morning, a maid-servant must collect their ashes, take them to the rock where the Sphinx had perched, scatter them to the winds, and run away without looking back. On her return, the palace must be purged with fumes of

Heracles and Hera. Amphora (British Museum)

Heracles (National Museum, Naples)

sulphur and salted spring water; and its roof crowned with wild olive. Finally, a boar must be sacrificed at Zeus's high altar. All this Alcmene did.

When Heracles ceased to be a child, Amphitryon taught him how to drive a chariot, and how to turn corners without grazing the goal. Castor gave him fencing lessons, instructed him in weapon drill, in cavalry and infantry tactics, and in the rudiments of strategy. One of Hermes's sons became his boxing teacher, and Eurytus taught him archery. But Heracles surpassed all archers ever born, even his companion Alcon, father of Phalerus the Argonaut, who could shoot through a succession of rings set on the helmets of soldiers standing in file, and could cleave arrows held up on the points of swords or lances.

Eumolpus taught Heracles how to sing and play the lyre; while Linus, son of the River-god Ismenius, introduced him to the study of literature. Once, when Eumolpus was absent, Linus gave the lyre lessons as well; but Heracles, refusing to change the principles in which he had been grounded by Eumolpus, and being beaten for his stubbornness, killed Linus with a blow of the lyre. At his trial for murder, Heracles quoted a law of Rhadamanthys, which justified forcible resistance to an aggressor, and thus secured his own acquittal. Nevertheless Amphitryon, fearing that the boy might commit further crimes of violence, sent him away to a cattle ranch, where he remained until his eighteenth year, outstripping his contemporaries in height, strength, and courage. It is not known who taught Heracles astronomy and philosophy, yet he was learned in both.

Heracles's eyes flashed fire, and he had an unerring aim, both with javelin and arrow. He ate sparingly at noon; for supper his favourite food was roast meat and Doric barley-cakes. His tunic was short-skirted and neat; and he preferred a night under the stars to one spent indoors. A profound knowledge of augury led him especially to welcome the appearance of vultures, whenever he was about to undertake a new labour. 'Vultures', he would say, 'are the most righteous of birds; they do not attack even the smallest living creature.'

Heracles claimed never to have picked a quarrel, but always to have given aggressors the same treatment as they intended for him. One Termerus used to kill travellers by challenging them to a butting match; Heracles's skull proved the stronger, and he crushed Termerus's head as though it had been an egg. Heracles was, however, naturally courteous, and the first mortal who freely yielded the enemy their dead for burial.

The Daughters of Thespius
In his eighteenth year, Heracles left the cattle ranch and set out to destroy the lion of Cithaeron, which was havocking the herds of Amphitryon and his neighbour, King Thespius, the Athenian

Erechtheid. The lion had another lair on Mount Helicon, at the foot of which stands the city of Thespiae.

King Thespius had fifty daughters by his wife Megamede, daughter of Arneus. Fearing that they might make unsuitable matches, he determined that every one of them should have a child by Heracles, for Heracles lodged at Thespiae for fifty nights running. 'You may have my eldest daughter Procris as your bed-fellow,' Thespius told him hospitably. But each night another of his daughters visited Heracles, until he had lain with every one. Some say, however, that he enjoyed them all in a single night, except one, who declined his embraces and remained a virgin until her death, serving as his priestess in the shrine at Thespiae. But he had begotten fifty-one sons on her sisters: Procris, the eldest, bearing him the twins Antileon and Hippeus; and the youngest sister, another pair.

Having at last tracked down the lion, and despatched it with an untrimmed club cut from a wild-olive tree which he uprooted on Helicon, Heracles dressed himself in its pelt and wore the gaping jaws for a helmet.

Erginus

Some years before these events, during Poseidon's festival at Onchestus, a trifling incident vexed the Thebans, whereupon Menoeceus's charioteer flung a stone which mortally wounded the Minyan King Clymenus. Clymenus was carried back, dying, to Orchomenus where, with his last breath, he charged his sons to avenge him. The eldest of these, Erginus, whose mother was the Boeotian princess Budeia, mustered an army, marched against the Thebans, and utterly defeated them. By the terms of a treaty the Thebans would pay Erginus an annual tribute of one hundred cattle for twenty years in requital for Clymenus's death.

Heracles, on his return from Helicon, fell in with the Minyan heralds as they went to collect the Theban tribute. When he enquired their business, they replied scornfully that they had come once more to remind the Thebans of Erginus's clemency in not lopping off the ears, nose and hands of every man in the city. 'Does Erginus indeed hanker for such tribute?' Heracles asked angrily. Then he maimed the heralds in the very manner that they had described, and sent them back to Orchomenus.

When Erginus instructed King Creon at Thebes to surrender the author of this outrage, he was willing enough to obey, because the Minyans had disarmed Thebes; nor could he hope for the friendly intervention of any neighbour, in so bad a cause. Yet Heracles persuaded his youthful comrades to strike a blow for freedom. Making a round of city temples, he tore down all the shields, helmets, breastplates, greaves, swords, and spears, which had been dedicated there as spoils. Thus Heracles armed every Theban of fighting age, taught them the use of their weapons, and himself assumed command. An

above: *The First Labour: Heracles battling with the Nemean Lion (University of Pennsylvania Museum)*

right: *The Second Labour: Heracles and the Lernaean Hydra. Red-figured vase (British Museum)*

*The Third Labour: Heracles pursuing the Ceryneian
Hind. Detail of Attic vase (British Museum)*

oracle promised him victory if the noblest-born person in Thebes would take his own life. All eyes turned expectantly towards Antipoenus, a descendant of the Sown Men; but, when he grudged dying for the common good, his daughters Androcleia and Alcis gladly did so in his stead.

Presently, the Minyans marched against Thebes, but Heracles ambushed them in a narrow pass, killing Erginus and the greater number of his captains. This victory, won almost single-handed, he exploited by making a sudden descent on Orchomenus, where he battered down the gates, sacked the palace, and compelled the Minyans to pay a double tribute to Thebes. Unfortunately, Amphitryon, his foster-father, was killed in the fighting.

The Madness of Heracles

Heracles's defeat of the Minyans made him the most famous of heroes; and his reward was to marry King Creon's eldest daughter Megara, and be appointed protector of the city; while Iphicles married the youngest daughter. Some say that Heracles had two sons by Megara; others that he had three, four, or even eight. They are known as the Alcaids.

Heracles next vanquished Pyraechmus, King of the Euboeans, an ally of the Minyans, when he marched against Thebes; and created terror throughout Greece by ordering his body to be torn in two by colts and exposed unburied beside the river Heracleius.

Hera, vexed by Heracles's excesses, drove him mad. He first attacked his beloved nephew Iolaus, Iphicles's eldest son, who managed to escape his wild lunges; and then, mistaking six of his own children for enemies, shot them down, and flung their bodies into a fire, together with two other sons of Iphicles, by whose side they were performing martial exercises.

When Heracles recovered his sanity, he shut himself up in a dark chamber for some days, avoiding all human intercourse and then, after purification by King Thespius, went to Delphi, to enquire what he should do. The Pythoness, addressing him for the first time as Heracles, rather than Palaemon, advised him to reside at Tiryns; to serve Eurystheus for twelve years; and to perform whatever Labours might be set him, in payment for which he would be rewarded with immortality. At this, Heracles fell into deep despair, loathing to serve a man whom he knew to be far inferior-to himself, yet afraid to oppose his father Zeus. Many friends came to solace him in his distress; and finally, when the passage of time had somewhat alleviated his pain, he placed himself at Eurystheus's disposal.

It has been said that when Heracles set forth on his Labours, Hermes gave him a sword, Apollo a bow and smooth-shafted arrows, feathered with eagle feathers; Hephaestus a golden breastplate; and Athene a robe. Athene and Hephaestus, it is added, vied with one another throughout in benefiting Heracles: she gave him enjoyment of peaceful pleasures; he, protection from the dangers of war. The gift of Poseidon was a team of horses; that of Zeus, a magnificent and unbreakable shield. Many were the stories worked on this shield in enamel, ivory, electrum, gold, and lapis lazuli; moreover, twelve serpents' heads carved about the boss clashed their jaws whenever Heracles went into battle, and terrified his opponents. The truth, however, is that Heracles scorned armour and, after his first Labour, seldom carried even a spear, relying rather on his club, bow and arrows. He had little use for the bronze-tipped club which Hephaestus gave him, preferring to cut his own from wild-olive: first on Helicon, next at Nemea. This second club he later replaced with a third, also cut from wild-olive, by the shores of the Saronic Sea: the club which, on his visit to Troezen, he leaned against the image of Hermes. It struck root, sprouted, and became a stately tree.

His nephew Iolaus shared in the Labours as his charioteer, or shield-bearer.

The First Labour: The Nemean Lion

The First Labour which Eurystheus imposed on Heracles, when he came to reside at Tiryns, was to kill and flay the Nemean, or Cleonaen lion, an enormous beast with a pelt proof against iron, bronze, and stone.

Arriving at Cleonae, between Corinth and Argos, Heracles lodged in the house of a day-labourer, or shepherd, named Molorchus, whose son the lion had killed. When Molorchus was about to offer a ram in propitiation of Hera, Heracles restrained him. 'Wait thirty days,' he said. 'If I return safely, sacrifice to Saviour Zeus; if I do not, sacrifice to me as a hero!'

Heracles reached Nemea at midday, but since the lion had depopulated the neighbourhood, he found no one to direct him; nor were any tracks to be seen. Having first searched Mount Apesas – so called after Apesantus, a shepherd whom the lion had killed – Heracles visited Mount Tretus, and presently descried the lion coming back to its lair, bespattered with blood from the day's slaughter. He shot a flight of arrows at it, but they rebounded harmlessly from the thick pelt, and the lion licked its chops, yawning. Next, he used his sword, which bent as though made of lead; finally he heaved up his club and dealt the lion such a blow on the muzzle that it entered its double-mouthed cave, shaking its head – not for pain, however, but because of the singing in its ears. Heracles, with a rueful glance at his shattered club, then netted one entrance of the cave, and went in by the other. Aware now that the monster was proof against all weapons, he began to wrestle with it. The lion bit off one of his fingers; but, holding its head in chancery, Heracles squeezed hard until it choked to death.

Carrying the carcass on his shoulders, Heracles returned to

From the Fourth Labour: a miniature showing Eurystheus hiding in the bronze jar (Archaeological Museum, Delphi)

Cleonae, where he arrived on the thirtieth day, and found Molorchus on the point of offering him a heroic sacrifice; instead, they sacrificed together to Saviour Zeus. When this had been done, Heracles cut himself a new club and, after making several alterations in the Nemean Games hitherto celebrated in honour of Opheltes, and rededicating them to Zeus, took the lion's carcass to Mycenae. Eurystheus, amazed and terrified, forbade him ever again to enter the city; in future he was to display the fruits of his Labours outside the gates.

For a while, Heracles was at a loss how to flay the lion, until by divine inspiration, he thought of employing its own razor-sharp claws, and soon could wear the invulnerable pelt as armour, and the head as a helmet. Meanwhile, Eurystheus ordered his smiths to forge him a bronze jar, which he buried beneath the earth. Henceforth, whenever the approach of Heracles was signalled, he took refuge in it and sent his orders by a herald – a son of Pelops, named Copreus, whom he had purified for murder.

The Second Labour: The Lernaean Hydra

The Second Labour ordered by Eurystheus was the destruction of the Lernaean Hydra, a monster born to Typhon and Echidne, and reared by Hera as a menace to Heracles.

Lerna stands beside the sea, some five miles from the city of Argos. To the west rises Mount Pontinus, with its sacred grove of plane-trees. Every year, secret nocturnal rites were held at Lerna in honour of Dionysus, who descended to Tartarus at this point when he went to fetch Semele; and, not far off, the Mysteries of Lernaean Demeter were celebrated in an enclosure which marks the place where Hades and Persephone also descended to Tartarus.

This fertile and holy district was once terrorized by the Hydra, which had its lair beneath a plane-tree at the sevenfold source of the river Amymone and haunted the unfathomable Lernaean swamp near by, the grave of many an incautious traveller. The Hydra had a prodigious dog-like body, and eight or nine snaky heads, one of them immortal; but some credit it with fifty, or one hundred, or even ten thousand heads. At all events, it was so venomous that its very breath, or the smell of its tracks, could destroy life.

Athene had pondered how Heracles might best kill this monster and, when he reached Lerna, driven there in his chariot by Iolaus, she pointed out the Hydra's lair to him. On her advice, he forced the Hydra to emerge by pelting it with burning arrows, and then held his breath while he caught hold of it. But the monster twined around his feet, in an endeavour to trip him up. In vain did he batter at its heads with his club: no sooner was one crushed, than two or three more grew in its place.

An enormous crab scuttered from the swamp to aid the Hydra, and nipped Heracles's foot; furiously crushing its shell, he shouted to Iolaus for assistance. Iolaus set one corner of the grove alight and then, to prevent the Hydra from sprouting new heads, seared their roots with blazing branches; thus the flow of blood was checked.

Now using a sword, or a golden falchion, Heracles severed the immortal head, part of which was of gold, and buried it, still hissing, under a heavy rock beside the road to Elaeus. The carcass he disembowelled, and dipped his arrows in the gall. Henceforth, the least wound from one of them was invariably fatal.

In reward for the crab's services, Hera set its image among the twelve signs of the Zodiac; and Eurystheus would not count this Labour as duly accomplished, because Iolaus had supplied the firebrands.

The Third Labour: The Ceryneian Hind

Heracles's Third Labour was to capture the Ceryneian Hind, and bring her alive from Oenoe to Mycenae. This swift, dappled creature had brazen hooves and golden horns like a stag, so that some call her a stag. She was sacred to Artemis who, when only a child, saw five hinds, larger than bulls, grazing on the banks of the dark-pebbled Thessalian river Anaurus at the foot of the Parrhasian Mountains; the sun twinkled on their horns. Running in pursuit, she caught four of them, one after the other, with her own hands, and harnessed them to her chariot; the fifth fled across the river Celadon to the Ceryneian Hill – as Hera intended, already having Heracles's Labours in mind.

Loth either to kill or wound the hind, Heracles performed this Labour without exerting the least force. He hunted her tirelessly for one whole year, his chase taking him as far as Istria and the Land of the Hyperboreans. When, exhausted at last, she took refuge on Mount Artemisium, and thence descended to the river Ladon, Heracles let fly and pinned her forelegs together with an arrow, which passed between bone and sinew, drawing no blood. He then caught her, laid her across his shoulders, and hastened through Arcadia to Mycenae. Artemis came to meet Heracles, rebuking him for having ill-used her holy beast, but he pleaded necessity, and put the blame on Eurystheus. Her anger was thus appeased, and she let him carry the hind alive to Mycenae.

The Fourth Labour: The Erymanthian Boar

The Fourth Labour imposed on Heracles was to capture alive the Erymanthian Boar: a fierce, enormous beast which haunted the cypress-covered slopes of Mount Erymanthus, and the thickets of Arcadian Mount Lampeia; and ravaged the country around Psophis.

Heracles, passing through Pholoë on his way to Erymanthus – where he killed one Saurus, a cruel bandit – was entertained by the Centaur Pholus, whom one of the ash-nymphs bore to Silenus. Pholus set roast meat before Heracles, but himself preferred the raw, and dared not open the Centaurs' communal wine jar until Heracles reminded him that it was the very jar which, four generations earlier,

The Fourth Labour:
Heracles and the
Erymanthian Boar. Detail
of vase (British Museum)

The Fourth Labour: Heracles and the Erymanthian Boar. Detail of vase (British Museum)

Dionysus had left in the cave against this very occasion. The Centaurs grew angry when they smelt the strong wine. Armed with great rocks, uprooted fir-trees, firebrands, and butchers' axes, they made a rush at Pholus's cave. While Pholus hid in terror, Heracles boldly repelled Ancius and Agrius, his first two assailants, with a volley of firebrands. Nephele, the Centaurs' cloudy grandmother, then poured down a smart shower of rain, which loosened Heracles's bow-string and made the ground slippery. However, he showed himself worthy of his former achievements, and killed several Centaurs, among them Oreus and Hylaeus. The rest fled as far as Malea, where they took refuge with Cheiron, their king, who had been driven from Mount Pelion by the Lapiths.

A parting arrow from Heracles's bow passed through Elatus's arm, and stuck quivering in Cheiron's knee. Distressed at the accident to his old friend, Heracles drew out the arrow and, though Cheiron himself supplied the vulneraries for dressing the wound, they were of no avail and he retired howling in agony to his cave; yet could not die, because he was immortal. Prometheus later offered to accept immortality in his stead, and Zeus approved this arrangement.

Pholus, in the meantime, while burying his dead kinsmen, drew out one of Heracles's arrows and examined it. 'How can so robust a creature have succumbed to a mere scratch?' he wondered. But the arrow slipped from his fingers and, piercing his foot, killed him there and then. Heracles broke off the pursuit and returned to Pholoë, where he buried Pholus with unusual honours at the foot of the mountain which has taken his name.

Heracles now set off to chase the boar by the river Erymanthus. To take so savage a beast alive was a task of unusual difficulty; but he dislodged it from a thicket with loud halloos, drove it into a deep snow drift, and sprang upon its back. He bound it in chains, and carried it alive on his shoulders to Mycenae; but when he heard that the Argonauts were gathering for their voyage to Colchis, dropped the boar outside the market place and, instead of waiting for further orders from Eurystheus, who was hiding in his bronze jar, went off with Hylas to join the expedition. It is not known who despatched the captured boar, but its tusks were preserved in the temple of Apollo at Cumae.

The Fifth Labour: The Stables of Augeias

Heracles's Fifth Labour was to cleanse King Augeias's filthy cattle yard in one day. Eurystheus gleefully pictured Heracles's disgust at having to load the dung into baskets and carry these away on his shoulders. Augeias, King of Elis, was the son of Helius, by Naupiadame, a daughter of Amphidamus. Others call him the son of Poseidon. In flocks and herds he was the wealthiest man on earth: for, by a divine dispensation, his were immune against disease and inimitably fertile, nor did they ever miscarry. Although in almost every case they produced female offspring, he nevertheless had three hundred white-legged black bulls and two hundred red stud-bulls; besides twelve outstanding silvery-white bulls, sacred to his father Helius. These twelve defended his herds against marauding wild beasts from the wooded hills.

Now, the dung in Augeias's cattle yard and sheepfolds had not been cleared away for many years, and though its noisome stench did not affect the beasts themselves, it spread a pestilence across the whole Peloponnese. Moreover, the valley pastures were so deep in dung that they could no longer be ploughed for grain.

Heracles hailed Augeias from afar, and undertook to cleanse the yard before nightfall in return for a tithe of the cattle. Augeias laughed incredulously, and called Phyleus, his eldest son, to witness Heracles's offer. 'Swear to accomplish the task before nightfall,' Phyleus demanded. The oath which Heracles now took by his father's name was the first and last one he ever swore. Augeias likewise took an oath to keep his side of the bargain.

On the advice of Menedemus the Elean, and aided by Iolaus, Heracles first breached the wall of the yard in two places, and next diverted the neighbouring rivers Alpheus and Peneius, so that their streams rushed through the yard, swept it clean and then went on to cleanse the sheepfolds and the valley pastures. Thus Heracles accomplished this Labour in one day, restoring the land to health, and not soiling so much as his little finger. But Augeias, on being informed by Copreus that Heracles had already been under orders from Eurystheus to cleanse the cattle yards, refused to pay the reward and even dared deny that he and Heracles had struck a bargain.

Heracles suggested that the case be submitted to arbitration; yet when the judges were seated, and Phyleus, subpoenaed by Heracles, testified to the truth, Augeias sprang up in a rage and banished them both from Elis, asserting that he had been tricked by Heracles, since the River-gods, not he, had done the work. To make matters even worse, Eurystheus refused to count this Labour as one of the ten, because Heracles had been in Augeias's hire.

The Sixth Labour: The Stymphalian Birds

Heracles's Sixth Labour was to remove the countless brazen-beaked, brazen-clawed, brazen-winged, man-eating birds, sacred to Ares, which, frightened by the wolves of Wolves' Ravine on the Orchomenan Road, had flocked to the Stymphalian Marsh. Here they bred and waded beside the river of the same name, occasionally taking to the air in great flocks, to kill men and beasts by discharging a shower of brazen feathers and at the same time muting a poisonous excrement, which blighted the crops.

On arrival at the marsh, which lay surrounded by dense woods, Heracles found himself unable to drive away the birds with his arrows; they were too numerous. Moreover, the marsh seemed

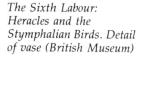

The Sixth Labour: Heracles and the Stymphalian Birds. Detail of vase (British Museum)

neither solid enough to support a man walking, nor liquid enough for the use of a boat. As Heracles paused irresolutely on the bank, Athene gave him a pair of brazen castanets, made by Hephaestus; or it may have been a rattle. Standing on a spur of Mount Cyllene, which overlooks the marsh, Heracles clacked the castanets, or shook the rattle, raising such a din that the birds soared up in one great flock, mad with terror. He shot down scores of them as they flew off to the Isle of Ares in the Black Sea, where they were afterwards found by the Argonauts.

The Seventh Labour: The Cretan Bull

Eurystheus ordered Heracles, as his Seventh Labour, to capture the Cretan Bull withheld by Minos from sacrifice to Poseidon, which sired the Minotaur on Pasiphaë. At this time it was ravaging Crete, especially the region watered by the river Tethris, rooting up crops and levelling orchard walls.

When Heracles sailed to Crete, Minos offered him every assistance in his power, but he preferred to capture the bull single-handed, though it belched scorching flames. After a long struggle, he brought the monster across to Mycenae, where Eurystheus, dedicating it to Hera, set it free. Hera however, loathing a gift which redounded to Heracles's glory, drove the bull first to Sparta, and then back through Arcadia and across the Isthmus to Attic Marathon, whence Theseus later dragged it to Athens as a sacrifice to Athene.

The Eighth Labour: The Mares of Diomedes

Eurystheus ordered Heracles, as his Eighth Labour, to capture the four savage mares of Thracian King Diomedes – it is disputed whether he was the son of Ares and Cyrene, or born of an incestuous relationship between Asterië and her father Atlas – who ruled the warlike Bistones, and whose stables, at the now vanished city of Tirida, were the terror of Thrace. Diomedes kept the mares tethered with iron chains to bronze mangers, and fed them on the flesh of his unsuspecting guests.

With a number of volunteers Heracles set sail for Thrace, visiting his friend King Admetus of Pherae on the way. Arrived at Tirida, he overpowered Diomedes's grooms and drove the mares down to the sea, where he left them on a knoll in charge of his minion Abderus, and then turned to repel the Bistones as they rushed in pursuit. His party being outnumbered, he overcame them by ingeniously cutting a channel which caused the sea to flood the low-lying plain; when they turned to run, he pursued them, stunned Diomedes with his club, dragged his body around the lake that had now formed, and set it before his own mares, which tore at the still living flesh. Their hunger being now fully assuaged – for, while Heracles was away, they had also devoured Abderus – he mastered them without much trouble.

left: *The Seventh Labour: Heracles capturing the Cretan Bull. Detail of vase (British Museum)*

right: *The Eighth Labour: Heracles harnessing the Mares of Diomedes*

The Ninth Labour: Hippolyte's Girdle

Heracles's Ninth Labour was to fetch for Eurystheus's daughter Admete the golden girdle of Ares worn by the Amazonian queen Hippolyte. Taking one ship and a company of volunteers, among whom were Iolaus, Telamon of Aegina, Peleus of Iolcus and, according to some accounts, Theseus of Athens, Heracles set sail for the river Thermodon.

The Amazons were children of Ares by the Naiad Harmonia, born in the glens of Phrygian Acmonia; but some call their mother Aphrodite, or Otrere, daughter of Ares. At first they lived beside the river Amazon, now named after Tanais, a son of the Amazon Lysippe, who offended Aphrodite by his scorn of marriage and his devotion to war. In revenge, Aphrodite caused Tanais to fall in love with his mother; but, rather than yield to an incestuous passion, he flung himself into the river and drowned. To escape the reproaches of his ghost, Lysippe then led her daughters around the Black Sea coast, to a plain by the river Thermodon, which rises in the lofty Amazonian mountains. There they formed three tribes, each of which founded a city.

The Amazons reckoned descent only through the mother, and Lysippe had laid it down that the men must perform all household tasks, while the women fought and governed. The arms and legs of infant boys were therefore broken to incapacitate them for war or travel. These unnatural women, whom the Scythians call Oeorpata, showed no regard for justice or decency, but were famous warriors, being the first to employ cavalry. They carried brazen bows and short shields shaped like a half moon; their helmets, clothes, and girdles were made from the skins of wild beasts. Lysippe, before she fell in battle, built the great city of Themiscyra, and defeated every tribe as far as the river Tanais. With the spoils of her campaigns she raised temples to Ares, and others to Artemis Tauropolus whose worship she established. Her descendants extended the Amazonian empire westward across the river Tanais, to Thrace; and again, on the southern coast, westward across the Thermodon to Phrygia. Three famous Amazonian queens, Marpesia, Lampado, and Hippo, seized a great part of Asia Minor and Syria, and founded the cities of Ephesus, Smyrna, Cyrene, and Myrine. It was on this expedition that the Amazons captured Troy, Priam being then still a child. But while detachments of the Amazonian army went home laden with vast quantities of spoil, the rest, staying to consolidate their power in Asia Minor, were driven out by an alliance of barbarian tribes, and lost their queen Marpesia.

By the time that Heracles came to visit the Amazons, they had all returned to the river Thermodon, and their three cities were ruled by Hippolyte, Antiope, and Melanippe. On his way, he put in at the island of Paros, famous for its marble, which King Rhadamanthys had bequeathed to one Alcaeus, a son of Androgeus; but four of Minos's sons, Eurymedon, Chryses, Nephalion, and Philolaus, had also settled there. When a couple of Heracles's crew, landing to fetch water, were murdered by Minos's sons, he indignantly killed all four of them, and pressed the Parians so hard that they sent envoys offering, in requital for the dead sailors, any two men whom he might choose to be his slaves. Satisfied by this proposal, Heracles raised the siege and chose King Alcaeus and his brother Sthenelus, whom he took aboard his ship. Next, he sailed through the Hellespont and Bosphorus to Mariandyne in Mysia, where he was entertained by King Lycus the Paphlagonian, son of Dascylus and grandson of Tantalus. In return, he supported Lycus in a war with the Bebrycans, killing many, including their king Mygdon, brother of Amycus, and recovered much Paphlagonian land from the Bebrycans; this he restored to Lycus, who renamed it Heracleia in his honour. Later, Heracleia was colonized by Megarians and Tanagrans on the advice of the Pythoness at Delphi, who told them to plant a colony beside the Black Sea, in a region dedicated to Heracles.

Arrived at the mouth of the river Thermodon, Heracles cast anchor in the harbour of Themiscyra, where Hippolyte paid him a visit and, attracted by his muscular body, offered him Ares's girdle as a love gift. But Hera had meanwhile gone about, disguised in Amazon dress, spreading a rumour that these strangers planned to abduct Hippolyte; whereupon the incensed warrior-women mounted

From the Ninth Labour: a bronze of an Amazon (British Museum)

their horses and charged down on the ship. Heracles, suspecting treachery, killed Hippolyte off hand, removed her girdle, seized her axe and other weapons, and prepared to defend himself. He killed each of the Amazon leaders in turn, putting their army to flight after great slaughter.

On his return from Themiscyra, Heracles came again to Mariandyne, and competed in the funeral games of King Lycus's brother Priolas, who had been killed by the Mysians. Heracles boxed against the Mariandynian champion Titias, knocked out all his teeth and killed him with a blow to the temple. In proof of his regret for this accident, he subdued the Mysians and the Phrygians on Dascylus's behalf; but he also subdued the Bithynians, as far as the mouth of the river Rhebas and the summit of Mount Colone, and claimed their kingdom for himself. Pelops's Paphlagonians voluntarily surrendered to him. However, no sooner had Heracles departed, than the Bebrycans, under Amycus, son of Poseidon, once more robbed Lycus of his land, extending their frontier to the river Hypius.

Sailing thence to Troy, Heracles rescued Hesione from a sea-monster; and continued his voyage to Thracian Aenus, where he was entertained by Poltys; and, just as he was putting to sea again, shot and killed on the Aenian beach Poltys's insolent brother Sarpedon, a son of Poseidon. Next, he subjugated the Thracians who had settled in Thasos, and bestowed the island on the sons of Androgeus, whom he had carried off from Paros; and at Torone was challenged to a wrestling match by Polygonus and Telegonus, sons of Proteus, both of whom he killed.

Returning to Mycenae at last, Heracles handed the girdle to Eurystheus, who gave it to Admete. As for the other spoil taken from the Amazons: he presented their rich robes to the Temple of Apollo at Delphi, and Hippolyte's axe to Queen Omphale, who included it among the sacred regalia of the Lydian kings. Eventually it was taken to a Carian temple of Labradian Zeus, and placed in the hand of his divine image.

The Tenth Labour: The Cattle of Geryon

Heracles's Tenth Labour was to fetch the famous cattle of Geryon from Erytheia, an island near the Ocean stream, without either demand or payment. Geryon, a son of Chrysaor and Callirrhoë, a daughter of the Titan Oceanus, was the King of Tartessus in Spain, and reputedly the strongest man alive. He had been born with three heads, six hands, and three bodies joined together at the waist. Geryon's shambling red cattle, beasts of marvellous beauty, were guarded by the herdsman Eurytion, son of Ares, and by the two-headed watchdog Orthrus – formerly Atlas's property – born of Typhon and Echidne.

During his passage through Europe, Heracles destroyed many wild beasts and, when at last he reached Tartessus, erected a pair of pillars facing each other across the straits, one in Europe, one in Africa. (These Pillars of Heracles are usually identified with Mount Calpe in Europe, and Abyle, or Abilyx in Africa.) Some hold that the two continents were formerly joined together, and that he cut a channel between them, or thrust the cliffs apart; others say that, on the contrary, he narrowed the existing straits to discourage the entry of whales and other sea-monsters.

Helius beamed down upon Heracles who, finding it impossible to work in such heat, strung his bow and let fly an arrow at the god. 'Enough of that!' cried Helius angrily. Heracles apologized for his ill-temper, and unstrung his bow at once. Not to be outdone in courtesy, Helius lent Heracles his golden goblet, shaped like a water-lily, in which he sailed to Erytheia; but the Titan Oceanus, to try him, made the goblet pitch violently upon the waves. Heracles again drew his bow, which frightened Oceanus into calming the sea.

On his arrival, he ascended Mount Abas. The dog Orthrus rushed at him, barking, but Heracles's club struck him lifeless; and Eurytion, Geryon's herdsman, hurrying to Orthrus's aid, died in the same manner. Heracles then proceeded to drive away the cattle. Menoetes, who was pasturing the cattle of Hades near by, took the news to Geryon. Challenged to battle, Heracles ran to Geryon's flank and shot him sideways through all three bodies with a single arrow. As

Hera hastened to Geryon's assistance, Heracles wounded her with an arrow in the right breast, and she fled. Thus he won the cattle, without either demand or payment, and embarked in the golden goblet, which he then sailed across to Tartessus and gratefully returned to Helius. From Geryon's blood sprang a tree which, at the time of the Pleiades' rising, bears stoneless cherry-like fruit.

How he then drove the cattle to Mycenae is much disputed, but according to a probable account he passed through the territory of Abdera, a Phoenician settlement, and then through Spain, leaving behind some of his followers as colonists. In the Pyrenees, he courted and buried the Bebrycan princess Pyrene, from whom this mountain range takes its name. He then visited Gaul, where he abolished a barbarous native custom of killing strangers, and won so many hearts by his generous deeds that he was able to found a large city, to which he gave the name Alesia, or 'Wandering', in commemoration of his travels. The Gauls honoured Alesia as the hearth and mother-city of their whole land and claimed descent from Heracles's union with a tall princess named Galata, who chose him as her lover and bred that warlike people.

When Heracles was driving Geryon's cattle through Liguria, two sons of Poseidon named Ialebion and Dercynus tried to steal them from him, and were both killed. At one stage of his battle with hostile Ligurian forces, Heracles ran out of arrows, and knelt down, in tears, wounded and exhausted. The ground being of soft mould, he could find no stones to throw at the enemy – Ligys, the brother of Ialebion, was their leader – until Zeus, pitying his tears, overshadowed the earth with a cloud, from which a shower of stones hailed down; and with these he put the Ligurians to flight. Zeus set among the stars an image of Heracles fighting the Ligurians, known as the constellation Engonasis. Another memorial of this battle survives on earth: namely the broad, circular plain lying between Marseilles and the mouths of the river Rhône, about fifteen miles from the sea, called 'The Stony Plain', because it is strewn with stones the size of a man's fist; brine springs are also found there.

In his passage over the Ligurian Alps, Heracles carved a road fit for his armies and baggage trains; he also broke up all robber bands that infested the pass, before Cis-alpine Gaul and Etruria. Only after wandering down the whole coast of Italy, and crossing into Sicily, did it occur to him: 'I have taken the wrong road!' The Romans say that, on reaching the Albula – afterwards called the Tiber – he was welcomed by King Evander, an exile from Arcadia. At evening, he swam across, driving the cattle before him, and lay down to rest on a grassy bed. In a deep cave near by, lived a vast hideous, three-headed shepherd named Cacus, a son of Hephaestus and Medusa, who was the dread and disgrace of the Aventine Forest, and puffed flames from each of his three mouths. Human skulls and arms hung nailed above the lintels of his cave, and the ground inside gleamed

opposite above: *The Tenth Labour: Heracles fetching the Cattle of Geryon. Attic cup (Antikensammlung, Munich)*

opposite below: *The Tenth Labour: Heracles and Geryon. Attic cup (Louvre)*

white with the bones of his victims. While Heracles slept, Cacus stole the two finest of his bulls; as well as four heifers, which he dragged backwards by their tails into his lair.

At the first streak of dawn, Heracles awoke, and at once noticed that the cattle were missing. After searching for them in vain, he was about to drive the remainder onward, when one of the stolen heifers lowed hungrily. Heracles traced the sound to the cave, but found the entrance barred by a rock which ten yoke of oxen could hardly have moved; nevertheless, he heaved it aside as though it had been a pebble and, undaunted by the smoky flames which Cacus was now belching, grappled with him and battered his face to pulp.

Aided by King Evander, Heracles then built an altar to Zeus, at which he sacrificed one of the recovered bulls, and afterwards made arrangements for his own worship. According to the Romans, Heracles freed King Evander from the tribute owed to the Etruscans; killed King Faunus, whose custom was to sacrifice strangers at the altar of his father Hermes; and begot Latinus, the ancestor of the Latins, on Faunus's widow, or daughter. Heracles is also believed to have founded Pompeii and Herculaneum; to have fought giants on the Phlegraean Plain of Cumae; and to have built a causeway one mile long across the Lucrine Gulf, called the Heracleian Road, down which he drove Geryon's cattle.

It is further said that, as he lay down to rest near the frontier of Rhegium and Epizephyrian Locris, a bull broke away from the herd and, plunging into the sea, swam over to Sicily. Heracles, going in pursuit, found it concealed among the herds of Eryx, King of the Elymans, a son of Aphrodite by Butes. Eryx, who was a wrestler and boxer, challenged him to a fivefold contest. Heracles accepted the challenge, on condition that Eryx would stake his kingdom against the runaway bull, and won the first four events; finally, in the wrestling match, he lifted Eryx high into the air, dashed him to the ground and killed him – which taught the Sicilians that not everyone born of a goddess is necessarily immortal. In this manner, Heracles won Eryx's kingdom, which he left the inhabitants to enjoy until one of his own descendants should come to claim it.

Continuing on his way through Sicily, Heracles came to the site where now stands the city of Syracuse; there he offered sacrifices, and instituted the annual festival beside the sacred chasm of Cyane, down which Hades snatched Core to the Underworld. To those who honoured Heracles in the Plain of Leontini, he left undying memorials of his visit. Close to the city of Agyrium, the hoof marks of his cattle were found imprinted on a stony road, as though in wax; and, regarding this as an intimation of his own immortality, Heracles accepted from the inhabitants those divine honours which he had hitherto consistently refused. Then, in acknowledgement of their favours, he dug a lake four furlongs in circumference outside the city walls, and established local sanctuaries of Iolaus and Geryon.

Returning to Italy in search of another route to Greece, Heracles drove his cattle up the eastern coast, proposing to drive them through Istria into Epirus, and thence to the Peloponnese by way of the Isthmus. But at the head of the Adriatic Gulf Hera sent a gadfly, which stampeded the cows, driving them across Thrace and into the Scythian desert. There Heracles pursued them and, having recovered most of the strayed cattle, drove them back across the river Strymon, which he dammed with stones for the purpose, and encountered no further adventures until the giant herdsman Alcyoneus, having taken possession of the Corinthian Isthmus, hurled a rock at the army which once more followed Heracles, crushing no less than twelve chariots and double that number of horsemen. This was the same Alcyoneus who twice stole Helius's sacred cattle: from Erytheia, and from the citadel of Corinth. He now ran forward, picked up the rock again, and this time hurled it at Heracles, who bandied it back with his club and so killed the giant.

The Eleventh Labour: The Apples of the Hesperides

Heracles had performed these Ten Labours in the space of eight years and one month; but Eurystheus, discounting the Second and the Fifth, set him two more. The Eleventh Labour was to fetch fruit from the golden apple-tree, Mother Earth's wedding gift to Hera, with which she had been so delighted that she planted it in her own divine garden. This garden lay on the slopes of Mount Atlas, where the panting chariot-horses of the Sun complete their journey, and where Atlas's sheep and cattle, one thousand herds of each, wander over their undisputed pastures. When Hera found, one day, that Atlas's daughters, the Hesperides, to whom she had entrusted the tree, were pilfering the apples, she set the ever-watchful dragon Ladon to coil around the tree as its guardian.

Though the apples were Hera's, Atlas took a gardener's pride in them and, when Themis warned him: 'One day long hence, Titan, your tree shall be stripped of its gold by a son of Zeus,' Atlas, who had not then been punished with his terrible task of supporting the celestial globe upon his shoulders, built solid walls around the orchard, and expelled all strangers from his land.

Heracles, not knowing in what direction the Garden of the Hesperides lay, marched through Illyria to the river Po, the home of the oracular sea-god Nereus. When Heracles came, the river-nymphs, daughters of Zeus and Themis, showed him Nereus asleep. He seized the hoary old sea-god and, clinging to him despite his many Protean changes, forced him to prophesy how the golden apples could be won.

Nereus had advised Heracles not to pluck the apples himself, but to employ Atlas as his agent, meanwhile relieving him of his fantastic burden; therefore on arriving at the Garden of the Hesperides, he asked Atlas to do him a favour. Atlas would have undertaken almost

The Eleventh Labour: Heracles holding up the world while Atlas brings him the Apples of the Hesperides. White-ground vase (National Archaeological Museum, Athens)

any task for the sake of an hour's respite, but he feared Ladon, whom Heracles thereupon killed with an arrow shot over the garden wall. Heracles now bent his back to receive the weight of the celestial globe, and Atlas walked away, returning presently with three apples plucked by his daughters. He found the sense of freedom delicious. 'I will take these apples to Eurystheus myself without fail,' he said, 'if you hold up the heavens for a few months longer.' Heracles pretended to agree but, having been warned by Nereus not to accept any such offer, begged Atlas to support the globe for one moment more, while he put a pad on his head. Atlas, easily deceived, laid the apples on the ground and resumed his burden; whereupon Heracles picked them up and went away with an ironical farewell.

After some months Heracles brought the apples to Eurystheus, who handed them back to him; he then gave them to Athene, and she returned them to the nymphs, since it was unlawful that Hera's property should pass from their hands. Feeling thirsty after this Labour, Heracles stamped his foot and made a stream of water gush out, which later saved the lives of the Argonauts when they were cast up high and dry on the Libyan desert. Meanwhile Hera, weeping for Ladon, set his image among the stars as the constellation of the Serpent.

Heracles did not return to Mycenae by a direct route. He first traversed Libya, whose King Antaeus, son of Poseidon and Mother Earth, was in the habit of forcing strangers to wrestle with him until they were exhausted, whereupon he killed them; for not only was he a strong and skilful athlete, but whenever he touched the earth, his strength revived. He saved the skulls of his victims to roof a temple of Poseidon. It is not known whether Heracles, who was determined to end this barbarous practice, challenged Antaeus, or was challenged by him. Antaeus, however, proved no easy victim, being a giant who lived in a cave beneath a towering cliff, where he feasted on the flesh of lions, and slept on the bare ground in order to conserve and increase his already colossal strength.

In preparation for the wrestling match, both combatants cast off their lion pelts, but while Heracles rubbed himself with oil in the Olympic fashion, Antaeus poured hot sand over his limbs lest contact with the earth through the soles of his feet alone should prove insufficient. Heracles planned to preserve his strength and wear Antaeus down, but after tossing him full length on the ground, he was amazed to see the giant's muscles swell and a healthy flush suffuse his limbs as Mother Earth revived him. The combatants grappled again, and presently Antaeus flung himself down of his own accord, not waiting to be thrown; upon which, Heracles, realizing what he was at, lifted him high into the air, then cracked his ribs and, despite the hollow groans of Mother Earth, held him aloft until he died.

Next, Heracles visited the Oracle at Ammon, and then struck

south, and founded a hundred-gated city, named Thebes in honour of his birthplace; but some say that Osiris had already founded it. All this time, the King of Egypt was Antaeus's brother Busiris, a son of Poseidon by Lysianassa, the daughter of Epaphus. Now, Busiris's kingdom had once been visited with drought and famine for eight or nine years, and he had sent for Greek augurs to give him advice. His nephew, a learned Cyprian seer, named Phrasius, son of Pygmalion, announced that the famine would cease if every year one stranger were sacrificed in honour of Zeus. Busiris began with Phrasius himself, and afterwards sacrificed other chance guests, until the arrival of Heracles, who let the priests hale him off the to the altar. They bound his hair with a fillet, and Busiris, calling upon the gods, was about to raise the sacrificial axe, when Heracles burst his bonds and slew Busiris, Busiris's son Amphidamas, and all the priestly attendants.

Next, Heracles traversed Asia and finally reached the Caucasus Mountains, where Prometheus had been fettered while every day a griffon-vulture, born of Typhon and Echidne, tore at his liver. Zeus had long repented of his punishment, because Prometheus had since sent him a kindly warning not to marry Thetis, lest he might beget one greater than himself; and now, when Heracles pleaded for Prometheus's pardon, granted this without demur. Having once, however, condemned him to everlasting punishment, Zeus stipulated that, in order still to appear a prisoner, he must wear a ring made from his chains and set with Caucasian stone – and this was the first ring ever to contain a setting. But Prometheus's sufferings were destined to last until some immortal should voluntarily go to Tartarus in his stead; so Heracles reminded Zeus of Cheiron, who was longing to resign the gift of immortality ever since he had suffered his incurable wound. Thus no further impediment remained, and Heracles, invoking Hunter Apollo, shot the griffon-vulture through the heart and set Prometheus free.

The Twelfth Labour: The Capture of Cerberus

Heracles's last, and most difficult, Labour was to bring the dog Cerberus up from Tartarus. As a preliminary, he went to Eleusis where he asked to partake of the Mysteries and wear the myrtle wreath. Since in Heracles's day Athenians alone were admitted, Theseus suggested that a certain Pylius should adopt him. This Pylius did, and when Heracles had been purified for his slaughter of the Centaurs, because no one with blood-stained hands could view the Mysteries, he was duly initiated by Orpheus's son Musaeus, Theseus acting as his sponsor.

Thus cleansed and prepared, Heracles descended to Tartarus from Laconian Taenarum. He was guided by Athene and Hermes – for whenever, exhausted by his Labours, he cried out in despair to Zeus, Athene always came hastening down to comfort him. Terrified by Heracles's scowl, Charon ferried him across the river Styx without

The Twelfth Labour:
Heracles capturing
Cerberus. Red-figured
vase (Louvre)

Heracles with Apollo's
tripod. Detail of
red-figured vase (Wagner
Museum, Würzburg)

Heracles and the Cercopes twins. White-ground vase (Cinquantennaire, Brussels)

demur. As Heracles stepped ashore from the crazy boat, all the ghosts fled, except Meleager and the Gorgon Medusa. At sight of Medusa he drew his sword, but Hermes reassured him that she was only a phantom; and when he aimed an arrow at Meleager, who was wearing bright armour, Meleager laughed. 'You have nothing to fear from the dead,' he said, and they chatted amicably for a while, Heracles offering in the end to marry Meleager's sister Deianeira.

Near the gates of Tartarus, Heracles found his friends Theseus and Perithous fastened to cruel chairs, and wrenched Theseus free, but was obliged to leave Peirithous behind; next, he rolled away the stone under which Demeter had imprisoned Ascalaphus; and then, wishing to gratify the ghosts with a gift of warm blood, slaughtered one of Hades's cattle. Their herdsman, Menoetes, or Menoetius, the son of Ceuthonymus, challenged him to a wrestling match, but was seized around the middle and had his ribs crushed. At this, Persephone, who came out from her palace and greeted Heracles like a brother, intervened and pleaded for Menoetes's life.

When Heracles demanded Cerberus, Hades, standing by his wife's side, replied grimly: 'He is yours, if you can master him without using your club or your arrows.' Heracles found the dog chained to the gates of Acheron, and resolutely gripped him by the throat – from which rose three heads, each maned with serpents. The barbed tail flew up to strike, but Heracles, protected by the lion pelt, did not relax his grip until Cerberus choked and yielded.

With Athene's assistance, Heracles recrossed the river Styx in safety, and then half-dragged, half-carried Cerberus up the chasm near Troezen, through which Dionysus had conducted his mother Semele. When Heracles brought him to Mycenae, Eurystheus, who was offering a sacrifice, handed him a slave's portion, reserving the best cuts for his own kinsmen; and Heracles showed his just resentment by killing three of Eurystheus's sons: Perimedes, Eurybius, and Erypilus.

The Murder of Iphitus
When Heracles returned to Thebes after his Labours, he gave Megara, his wife, now thirty-three years old, in marriage to his nephew and charioteer Iolaus, who was only sixteen, remarking that his own union with her had been inauspicious. He then looked about for a younger and more fortunate wife; and, hearing that his friend Eurytus, a son of Melanius, King of Oechalia, had offered to marry his daughter Iole to any archer who could outshoot him and his four sons, took the road there. Eurytus had been given a fine bow and taught its use by Apollo himself, whom he now claimed to surpass in marksmanship, yet Heracles found no difficulty in winning the contest. The result displeased Eurytus excessively and, when he learned that Heracles had discarded Megara after murdering her children, he refused to give him Iole. Having drunk a great deal of wine to gain

confidence, 'You could never compare with me and my sons as an archer,' he told Heracles, 'were it not that you unfairly use magic arrows, which cannot miss their mark. This contest is void, and I would not, in any case, entrust my beloved daughter to such a ruffian as yourself! Moreover, you are Eurystheus's slave, and like a slave, deserve only blows from a free man.' So saying, he drove Heracles out of the Palace. Heracles did not retaliate at once, as he might well have done; but swore to take vengeance.

Three of Eurytus's sons, namely Didaeon, Clytius, and Toxeus, had supported their father in his dishonest pretensions. The eldest, however, whose name was Iphitus, declared that Iole should in all fairness have been given to Heracles; and when, soon afterwards, twelve strong-hooved brood-mares and twelve sturdy mule-foals disappeared from Euboea, he refused to believe that Heracles was the thief. As a matter of fact, they had been stolen by the well-known thief Autolycus, who magically changed their appearance and sold them to the unsuspecting Heracles as if they were his own. Iphitus followed the tracks of the mares and foals and found that they led towards Tiryns, which made him suspect Heracles was, after all, avenging the insult offered him by Eurytus. Coming suddenly face to face with Heracles, who had just returned from his rescue of Alcestis, he concealed his suspicions and merely asked for advice in the matter. Heracles did not recognize the beasts from Iphitus's description as those sold to him by Autolycus, and with his usual heartiness promised to search for them if Iphitus would consent to become his guest. Yet he now divined that he was suspected of theft, which galled his sensitive heart. After a grand banquet, he led Iphitus to the top of the highest tower in Tiryns. 'Look about you,' he demanded, 'and tell me whether your mares are grazing anywhere in sight.' 'I cannot see them,' Iphitus admitted. 'Then you have falsely accused me in your heart of being a thief!' Heracles roared, distraught with anger, and hurled him to his death.

Heracles presently went to Neleus, King of Pylus, and asked to be purified; but Neleus refused, because Eurytus was his ally. Nor would any of his sons, except the youngest, Nestor, consent to receive Heracles, who eventually persuaded Deiphobus, the son of Hippolytus, to purify him at Amyclae. However, he still suffered from evil dreams, and went to ask the Delphic Oracle how he might be rid of them. The Pythoness Xenoclea refused to answer this question. 'You murdered your guest,' she said. 'I have no oracles for such as you!' 'Then I shall be obliged to institute an oracle of my own!' cried Heracles. With that, he plundered the shrine of its votive offerings and even pulled away the tripod on which Xenoclea sat. 'Heracles of Tiryns is a very different man from his Canopic namesake,' the Pythoness said severely as he carried the tripod from the shrine; she meant that the Egyptian Heracles had once come to Delphi and behaved with courtesy and reverence.

top: *Two coins of Heracles (Pennisi Collection, Acireale, Sicily)*

bottom: *Heracles saves Hesione from the sea-monster. Black-figured vase (Archaeological Museum, Taranto)*

opposite: *Head of Pan (National Archaeological Museum, Rome)*

A river god (British Museum)

kicked him across the grotto. Hearing a loud crash and a howl, Omphale sprang up and called for lights, and when these came she and Heracles laughed until they cried to see Pan sprawled in a corner, nursing his bruises. After that day, Pan abhorred clothes, and summoned his officials naked to his rites; it was he who revenged himself on Heracles by spreading the rumour that his whimsical exchange of garments with Omphale was habitual and perverse.

Hesione

After serving as a slave to Queen Omphale, Heracles returned to Tiryns, his sanity now fully restored, and at once planned an expedition against Troy. His reasons were as follows. He and Telamon, either on their way back from the country of the Amazons, or when they landed with the Argonauts at Sigeium, had been astonished to find Laomedon's daughter Hesione, stark naked except for her jewels, chained to a rock on the Trojan shore. It appeared that Poseidon had sent a sea-monster to punish Laomedon for having failed to pay him and Apollo their stipulated fee when they built the city walls and tended his flocks. Some say that he should have sacrificed to them all the cattle born in his kingdom that year; others,

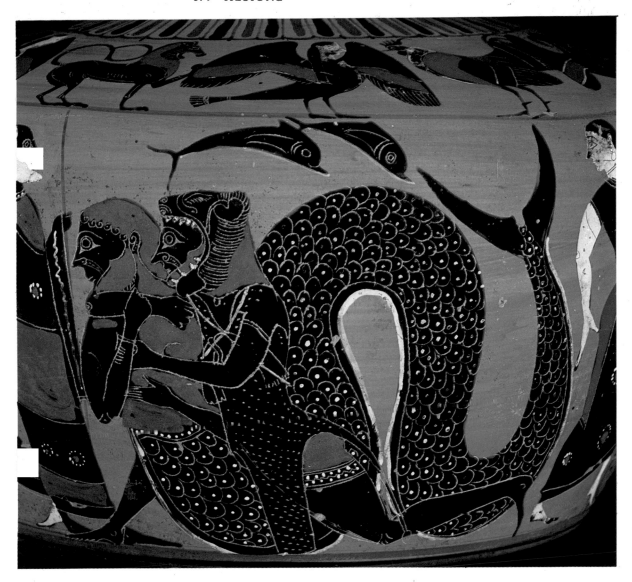

that he had promised them only a low wage as day-labourers, but even so cheated them of more than thirty Trojan drachmae. In revenge, Apollo sent a plague, and Poseidon ordered this monster to prey on the plainsfolk and ruin their fields by spewing sea water over them.

Laomedon visited the Oracle of Zeus Ammon, and was advised by him to expose Hesione on the seashore for the monster to devour. Yet he obstinately refused to do so unless the Trojan nobles would first let him sacrifice their own daughters. In despair, they consulted Apollo who, being no less angry than Poseidon, gave them little satisfaction. Most parents at once sent their children abroad for safety, but

Heracles wrestling with Achelous in his serpent shape. Detail of black-figured vase (British Museum)

left: *Heracles with his wife Deianeira. Detail of red-figured vase (Ashmolean Museum, Oxford)*

opposite: *The Apotheosis of Heracles. Black-figured vase (Paestum Museum, Italy)*

below: *Heracles in Olympus. Black-figured vase (British Museum)*

in the heart of Elis, the Corinthians intervened by proclaiming the Isthmian Truce. Among those wounded by the Moliones was Heracles's twin brother Iphicles; his friends carried him fainting to Pheneus in Arcadia, where he eventually died and became a hero.

When Heracles returned to Tiryns, Eurystheus accused him of designs on the high kingship in which he had himself been confirmed by Zeus, and banished him from Argolis. With his mother Alcmene, and his nephew Iolaus, Heracles then rejoined Iphicles at Pheneus, where he took Laonome, daughter of Guneus, as his mistress.

Afterwards, hearing that the Eleans were sending a procession to honour Poseidon at the Third Isthmian Festival, and that the Moliones would witness the games and take part in the sacrifices, Heracles ambushed them from a roadside thicket below Cleonae, and shot both dead; and killed their cousin, the other Eurytus, as well, a son of King Augeias.

Molione soon learned who had murdered her sons, and made the Eleans demand satisfaction from Eurystheus, on the ground that Heracles was a native of Tiryns. When Eurystheus disclaimed responsibility for the misdeeds of Heracles, whom he had banished, Moline asked the Corinthians to exclude all Argives from the Isthmian Games until satisfaction had been given for the murder. This they declined to do, whereupon Molione laid a curse on every Elean who might take part in the festival.

Heracles now borrowed the black-maned horse Arion from Oncus, mastered him, raised a new army in Argos, Thebes, and Arcadia, and sacked the city of Elis. Some say that he killed Augeias and his sons, restored Phyleus, the rightful king, and set him on the Elean throne; others, that he spared Augeias's life at least.

The Capture of Pylus
Heracles next sacked and burned the city of Pylus, because the Pylians had gone to the aid of Elis. He killed all Neleus's sons, except the youngest, Nestor, who was away at Gerania, but Neleus himself escaped with his life.

Athene, champion of justice, fought for Heracles; and Pylus was defended by Hera, Poseidon, Hades, and Ares. While Athene engaged Ares, Heracles made for Poseidon, club against trident, and forced him to give way. Next, he ran to assist Athene, spear in hand, and his third lunge pierced Ares's shield, dashing him headlong to the ground; then, with a powerful thrust at Ares's thigh, he drove deep into the divine flesh. Ares fled in anguish to Olympus, where Apollo spread soothing unguents on the wound and healed it within the hour; so he renewed the fight, until one of Heracles's arrows pierced his shoulder, and forced him off the field for good. Meanwhile, Heracles had also wounded Hera in the right breast with a three-barbed arrow.

Neleus's eldest son, Periclymenus the Argonaut, was gifted by

Poseidon with boundless strength and the power of assuming whatever shape he pleased, whether of bird, beast, or tree. On this
occasion he turned himself first into a lion, then into a serpent and
after a while, to escape scrutiny, perched on the yoke-boss of Heracles's horses in the form of an ant, or fly, or bee. Heracles, nudged by
Athene, recognized Periclymenus and reached for his club, whereupon Periclymenus became an eagle, and tried to peck out his eyes,
but a sudden arrow from Heracles's bow pierced him underneath his
wing. He tumbled to earth, and the arrow was driven through his
neck by the fall, killing him.

Heracles gave the city of Messene to Nestor, in trust for his own
descendants, remembering that Nestor had taken no part in robbing
him of Geryon's cattle; and soon came to love him more even than
Hylas and Iolaus. It was Nestor who first swore an oath by Heracles.

Deianeira

After spending four years in Pheneus, Heracles decided to leave the
Peloponnese. At the head of a large Arcadian force, he sailed across
to Calydon in Aetolia, where he took up his residence. Having now
no legitimate sons, and no wife, he courted Deianeira, the supposed
daughter of Oeneus, thus keeping his promise to the ghost of her
brother Meleager. But Deianeira was really the daughter of the god
Dionysus, by Oeneus's wife Althaea.

Many suitors came to Oeneus's palace in Pleuron, demanding the
hand of lovely Deianeira, who drove a chariot and practised the art of
war; but all abandoned their claims when they found themselves in
rivalry with Heracles and the River-god Achelous. It is common
knowledge that immortal Achelous appears in three forms: as a bull,
as a speckled serpent, and as a bull-headed man. Streams of water
flow continually from his shaggy beard, and Deianeira would rather
have died than marry him.

Heracles, when summoned by Oeneus to plead his suit, boasted that
if he married Deianeira, she would not only have Zeus for a father-in-
law, but enjoy the reflected glory of his own Twelve Labours.

Achelous (now in bull-headed form) scoffed at this, remarking that
he was a well-known personage, the father of all Greek waters, not a
footloose stranger like Heracles, and that the Oracle of Dodona had
instructed all visitants to offer him sacrifices. Then he taunted Heracles: 'Either you are not Zeus's son, or your mother is an adulteress!'

Heracles scowled. 'I am better at fighting than debating,' he said,
'and I will not hear my mother insulted!'

Achelous cast aside his green garment, and wrestled with Heracles
until he was thrown on his back, whereupon he deftly turned into a
speckled serpent and wriggled away.

'I strangled serpents in my cradle!' laughed Heracles, stooping to
grip his throat. Next, Achelous became a bull and charged; Heracles
nimbly stepped aside and, catching hold of both his horns, hurled

him to the ground with such force that the right horn snapped clean off. Achelous retired, miserably ashamed, and hid his injury under a chaplet of willow-branches.

After marrying Deianeira, Heracles marched with the Calydonians against the Thesprotian city of Ephyra – later Cichyrus – where he overcame and killed King Phyleus. Among the captives was Phyleus's daughter Astyoche, by whom Heracles became the father of Tlepolemus; though some say that Tlepolemus's mother was Astydameia, daughter of Amyntor, whom Heracles abducted from Elean Ephyra, a city famous for its poisons.

At a feast three years later, Heracles grew enraged with a young kinsman of Oeneus, named Eunomus, the son of Architeles, who was told to pour water on Heracles's hands, and clumsily splashed his legs. Heracles boxed the boy's ears harder than he intended, and killed him. Though forgiven by Architeles for this accident, Heracles decided to pay the due penalty of exile, and went away with Deianeira, and their son Hyllus, to Trachis, the home of Amphitryon's nephew Ceyx.

On his way, he came with Deianeira to the river Evenus, then in full flood, where the Centaur Nessus, claiming that he was the gods' authorized ferryman and chosen because of his righteousness, offered, for a small fee, to carry Deianeira dry-shod across the water while Heracles swam. He agreed, paid Nessus the fare, threw his club and bow over the river, and plunged in. Nessus, however, instead of keeping to his bargain, galloped off in the opposite direction with Deianeira in his arms; then threw her to the ground and tried to violate her. She screamed for help, and Heracles, quickly recovering his bow, took careful aim and pierced Nessus through the breast from half a mile away.

Wrenching out the arrow, Nessus told Deianeira: 'If you mix the seed which I have spilt on the ground with blood from my wound, add olive oil, and secretly anoint Heracles's shirt with the mixture, you will never again have cause to complain of his unfaithfulness.' Deianeira hurriedly collected the ingredients in a jar, which she sealed and kept by her without saying a word to Heracles on the subject.

By Deianeira, Heracles had already become the father of Hyllus, Ctesippus, Glenus, and Hodites; also of Macaria, his only daughter.

Heracles and Cycnus

Heracles now came to Itonus, a city of Phthiotis, where the ancient temple of Athene stands. Here he met Cycnus, a son of Ares and Pelopia, who was constantly offering valuable prizes to guests who dared fight a chariot duel with him. The ever-victorious Cycnus would cut off their heads and use the skulls to decorate the temple of his father Ares. This, by the way, was not the Cycnus whom Ares had begotten on Pyrene and transformed into a swan when he died.

Apollo, growing vexed with Cycnus, because he waylaid and carried off herds of cattle which were being sent for sacrifice to Delphi, incited Heracles to accept Cycnus's challenge. It was agreed that Heracles should be supported by his charioteer Iolaus, and Cycnus by his father Ares. Heracles, though this was not his usual style of fighting, put on the polished bronze greaves which Hephaestus had made for him, the curiously wrought golden breast-plate given him by Athene, and a pair of iron shoulder-guards. Armed with bow and arrows, spear, helmet, and a stout shield which Zeus had ordered Hephaestus to supply, he lightly mounted his chariot.

Heracles pursuing Nessus. Detail of vase (British Museum)

Athene, descending from Olympus, now warned Heracles that, although empowered by Zeus to kill and despoil Cycnus, he must do no more than defend himself against Ares and, even if victorious, not deprive him of either his horses or his splendid armour. She then mounted beside Heracles and Iolaus, shaking her aegis, and Mother Earth groaned as the chariot whirled forward. Cycnus drove to meet them at full speed, and both he and Heracles were thrown to the ground by the shock of their encounter, spear against shield. Yet they sprang to their feet and, after a short combat, Heracles thrust Cycnus through the neck. He then boldly faced Ares, who hurled a spear at him; and Athene, with an angry frown, turned it aside. Ares ran at Heracles sword in hand, only to be wounded in the thigh for his pains, and Heracles would have dealt him a further blow as he lay on the ground, had not Zeus parted the combatants with a thunderbolt. Heracles and Iolaus then despoiled Cycnus's corpse, while Athene led the fainting Ares back to Olympus. Cycnus was buried by Ceyx in the valley of the Anaurus but, at Apollo's command, the swollen river washed away his headstone.

Iole

At Trachis Heracles mustered an army of Arcadians, Melians, and Epicnemidian Locrians, and marched against Oechalia to revenge himself on King Eurytus, who refused to surrender the princess Iole, fairly won in an archery contest; but he told his allies no more than that Eurytus had been unjustly exacting tribute from the Euboeans. He stormed the city, riddled Eurytus and his son with arrows and, after burying certain of his comrades who had fallen in the battle, namely Ceyx's son Hippasus, and Argeius and Melas, sons of Licymnius, pillaged Oechalia and took Iole captive. Rather than yield to Heracles, Iole had allowed him to murder her entire family before her very eyes, and then leaped from the city wall; yet she survived, because her skirts were billowed out by the wind and broke the fall. Now Heracles sent her, with other Oechalian women, to Deianeira at Trachis, while he visited the Euboean headland of Cenaeum. It should be noted here that when taking leave of Deianeira, Heracles had divulged a prophecy: at the end of fifteen months, he was fated either to die, or to spend the remainder of his life in perfect tranquillity. The news had been conveyed to him by the twin doves of the ancient oak oracle at Dodona.

The Apotheosis of Heracles

Having consecrated marble altars and a sacred grove to his father Zeus on the Cenaean headland, Heracles prepared a thanksgiving sacrifice for the capture of Oechalia. He had already sent Lichas back to ask Deianeira for a fine shirt and a cloak of the sort which he regularly wore on such occasions.

Deianeira, comfortably installed at Trachis, was by now resigned to Heracles's habit of taking mistresses; and, when she recognized Iole as the latest of these, felt pity rather than resentment for the fatal beauty which had been Oechalia's ruin. Yet was it not intolerable that Heracles expected Iole and herself to live together under the same roof? Since she was no longer young, Deianeira decided to use Nessus's supposed love-charm as a means of holding her husband's affection. Having woven him a new sacrificial shirt against his safe return, she covertly unsealed the jar, soaked a piece of wool in the mixture, and rubbed the shirt with it. When Lichas arrived she locked the shirt in a chest which she gave to him, saying: 'On no account expose the shirt to light or heat until Heracles is about to wear it at the sacrifice.' Lichas had already driven off at full speed in his chariot when Deianeira, glancing at the piece of wool which she had thrown down into the sunlit courtyard, was horrified to see it burning away like saw-dust, while red foam bubbled up from the flag-stones. Realizing that Nessus had deceived her, she sent a courier post-haste to recall Lichas and, cursing her folly, swore that if Heracles died she would not survive him.

The courier arrived too late at the Cenaean headland. Heracles had by now put on the shirt and sacrificed twelve immaculate bulls as the first-fruits of his spoils: in all, he had brought to the altar a mixed herd of one hundred cattle. He was pouring wine from a bowl on the altars and throwing frankincense on the flames when he let out a sudden yell as if he had been bitten by a serpent. The heat had melted the Hydra's poison in Nessus's blood, which coursed all over Heracles's limbs, corroding his flesh. Soon the pain was beyond endurance and, bellowing in anguish, he overturned the altars. He tried to rip off the shirt, but it clung to him so fast that his flesh came away with it, laying bare the bones. His blood hissed and bubbled like spring water when red-hot metal is being tempered. He plunged headlong into the nearest stream, but the poison burned only the fiercer; these waters then became scalding hot and were called Thermopylae, or 'hot passage'.

Ranging over the mountain, tearing up trees as he went, Heracles came upon the terrified Lichas crouched in the hollow of a rock, his knees clasped with his hands. In vain did Lichas try to exculpate himself: Heracles seized him, whirled him thrice about his head and flung him into the Euboean Sea. There he was transformed: he became a rock of human appearance, projecting a short distance above the waves, which sailors called Lichas and on which they were afraid to tread, believing it to be sentient. The army, watching from afar, raised a great shout of lamentation, but none dared approach until, writhing in agony, Heracles summoned Hyllus, and asked to be carried away to die in solitude. Hyllus conveyed him to the foot of Mount Oeta in Trachis (a region famous for its white hellebore), the Delphic Oracle having already pointed this out to Licymnius and Iolaus as the destined scene of their friend's death.

Aghast at the news, Deianeira hanged herself or, some say, stabbed herself with a sword in their marriage bed. Heracles's one thought had been to punish her before he died, but when Hyllus assured him that she was innocent, as her suicide proved, he sighed forgivingly and expressed a wish that Alcmene and all his sons should assemble to hear his last words. Alcmene, however, was at Tiryns with some of his children, and most of the others had settled at Thebes. Thus he could reveal Zeus's prophecy, now fulfilled, only to Hyllus: 'No man alive may ever kill Heracles; a dead enemy shall be his downfall.' Hyllus then asked for instructions, and was told: 'Swear by the head of Zeus that you will convey me to the highest peak of this mountain, and there burn me, without lamentation, on a pyre of oak-branches and trunks of the male wild-olive. Likewise swear to marry Iole as soon as you come of age.' Though scandalized by these requests, Hyllus promised to observe them.

When all had been prepared, Iolaus and his companions retired a short distance, while Heracles mounted the pyre and gave orders for its kindling. But none dared obey, until a passing Aeolian shepherd named Poeas ordered Philoctetes, his son by Demonassa, to do as Heracles asked. In gratitude, Heracles bequeathed his quiver, bow, and arrows to Philoctetes and, when the flames began to lick at the pyre, spread his lion-pelt over the platform at the summit and lay down, with his club for pillow, looking as blissful as a garlanded guest surrounded by wine-cups. Thunderbolts then fell from the sky and at once reduced the pyre to ashes.

In Olympus, Zeus congratulated himself that his favourite son had behaved so nobly. 'Heracles's immortal part', he announced, 'is safe from death, and I shall soon welcome him to this blessed region. But if anyone here grieves at his deification, so richly merited, that god or goddess must nevertheless approve it willy-nilly!' All the Olympians assented, and Hera decided to swallow the insult, which was clearly aimed at her, because she had already arranged to punish Philoctetes, for his kindly act, by the bite of a Lemnian viper.

The thunderbolts had consumed Heracles's mortal part. He no longer bore any resemblance to Alcmene but, like a snake that has cast its slough, appeared in all the majesty of his divine father. A

Bronze head of Zeus (Archaeological Museum, Olympia)

cloud received him from his companions' sight as, amid peals of thunder, Zeus bore him up to heaven in his four-horse chariot; where Athene took him by the hand and solemnly introduced him to her fellow deities.

Now, Zeus had destined Heracles as one of the Twelve Olympians, yet was loth to expel any of the existing company of gods in order to make room for him. He therefore persuaded Hera to adopt Heracles by a ceremony of rebirth: namely, going to bed, pretending to be in labour, and then producing him from beneath her skirts – which was the adoption ritual in use among many barbarian tribes. Henceforth, Hera regarded Heracles as her son and loved him next only to Zeus. All the immortals welcomed his arrival; and Hera married him to her pretty daughter Hebe, who bore him Alexiares and Anicetus. And, indeed, Heracles had earned Hera's true gratitude in the revolt of the Giants by killing Pronomus, when he tried to violate her.

7

THE ARGONAUTS AND MEDEA

The Argonauts Assemble

AFTER THE DEATH OF KING CRETHEUS the Aeolian, Pelias, son of Poseidon, already an old man, seized the Iolcan throne from his half-brother Aeson, the rightful heir. An oracle presently warning him that he would be killed by a descendant of Aeolus, Pelias put to death every prominent Aeolian he dared lay hands upon, except Aeson, whom he spared for his mother Tyro's sake, but kept a prisoner in the palace; forcing him to renounce his inheritance.

Now, Aeson had married Polymele, who bore him one son, by name Diomedes. Pelias would have destroyed the child without mercy, had not Polymele summoned her kinswomen to weep over him, as though he were still-born, and then smuggled him out of the city to Mount Pelion; where Cheiron the Centaur reared him, as he did with Asclepius, Achilles, Aeneas, and other famous heroes.

A second oracle warned Pelias to beware a one-sandalled man and when, one day on the seashore, a group of his princely allies joined him in a solemn sacrifice to Poseidon, his eye fell upon a tall, long-haired Magnesian youth, dressed in a close-fitting leather tunic and a leopard-skin. He was armed with two broad-bladed spears, and wore only one sandal.

The other sandal he had lost in the muddy river Anaurus by the contrivance of a crone who, standing on the farther bank, begged passers-by to carry her across. None took pity on her, until this young stranger courteously offered her his broad back; but he found himself staggering under the weight, since she was none other than the goddess Hera in disguise. For Pelias had vexed Hera by with-holding her customary sacrifices, and she was determined to punish him for this neglect.

When, therefore, Pelias asked the stranger roughly: 'Who are you, and what is your father's name?', he replied that Cheiron, his foster-father, called him Jason, though he had formerly been known as Diomedes, son of Aeson.

Pelias glared at him balefully. 'What would you do,' he enquired

The Argonauts about to begin their voyage. Handle of a box (National Museum, Villa Giulia, Rome)

suddenly, 'if an oracle announced that one of your fellow-citizens were destined to kill you?'

'I should send him to fetch the golden ram's fleece from Colchis,' Jason replied, not knowing that Hera had placed those words in his mouth. 'And, pray, whom have I the honour of addressing?'

When Pelias revealed his identity, Jason was unabashed. He boldly claimed the throne usurped by Pelias, and, since he was strongly supported by his uncle Pheres, king of Pherae, and Amathaon, king of Pylus, who had come to take part in the sacrifice, Pelias feared to deny him his birthright. 'But first,' he insisted, 'I require you to free our beloved country from a curse!'

Jason then learned that Pelias was being haunted by the ghost of Phrixus, who had fled from Orchomenus a generation before, riding on the back of a divine ram, to avoid being sacrificed. He took refuge in Colchis where, on his death, he was denied proper burial; and, according to the Delphic Oracle, the land of Iolcus, where many of

Jason's Minyan relatives were settled, would never prosper unless his ghost were brought home in a ship, together with the golden ram's fleece. The fleece now hung from a tree in the grove of Colchian Ares, guarded night and day by an unsleeping dragon. Once this pious feat had been accomplished, Pelias declared, he would gladly resign the kingship, which was becoming burdensome for a man of his advanced years.

Jason could not deny Pelias this service, and therefore sent heralds to every court of Greece, calling for volunteers who would sail with him. He also prevailed upon Argus the Thespian to build him a fifty-oared ship; and this was done at Pagasae, with seasoned timber from Mount Pelion; after which Athene herself fitted an oracular beam into the *Argo*'s prow, cut from her father Zeus's oak at Dodona.

Many different muster-rolls of the Argonauts – as Jason's companions are called – have been compiled at various times; but the following names are those given by the most trustworthy authorities:

Acastus, son of King Pelias
Actor, son of Deion the Phocian
Admetus, prince of Pherae
Amphiaraus, the Argive seer
Great Ancaeus of Tegea, son of Poseidon
Little Ancaeus, the Lelegian of Samos
Argus the Thespian, builder of the *Argo*
Ascalaphus the Orchomenan, son of Ares
Asterius, son of Cometes, a Pelopian
Atalanta of Calydon, the virgin huntress
Augeias, son of King Phorbas of Elis
Butes of Athens, the bee-master
Caeneus the Lapith, who had once been a woman
Calais, the winged son of Boreas
Canthus the Euboean
Castor, the Spartan wrestler, one of the Dioscuri
Cepheus, son of Aleus the Arcadian
Coronus the Lapith, of Gyrton in Thessaly
Echion, son of Hermes, the herald
Erginus of Miletus
Euphemus of Taenarum, the swimmer
Eurylas, son of Mecisteus, one of the Epigoni
Eurydamas the Dolopian, from Lake Xynias
Heracles of Tiryns, the strongest man who ever lived, now a god
Hylas the Dryopian, squire to Heracles
Idas, son of Aphareus of Messene
Idmon the Argive, Apollo's son
Iphicles, son of Thestius the Aetolian
Iphitus, brother of King Eurystheus of Mycenae
Jason, the captain of the expedition

The Argonauts with Athene. Large two-handled bowl (Louvre)

Laertes, son of Acrisius the Argive
Lynceus, the look-out man, brother to Idas
Melampus of Pylus, son of Poseidon
Meleager of Calydon
Mopsus the Lapith
Nauplius the Argive, son of Poseidon, a noted navigator
Oïleus the Locrian, father of Ajax
Orpheus, the Thracian poet
Palaemon, son of Hephaestus, an Aetolian
Peleus the Myrmidon
Peneleos, son of Hippalcimus, the Boeotian
Periclymenus of Pylus, the shape-shifting son of Poseidon
Phalerus, the Athenian archer
Phanus, the Cretan son of Dionysus
Poeas, son of Thaumacus the Magnesian
Polydeuces, the Spartan boxer, one of the Dioscuri
Polyphemus, son of Elatus, the Arcadian
Staphylus, brother of Phanus
Tiphys, the helmsman, of Boeotian Siphae
Zetes, brother of Calais

– and never before or since was so gallant a ship's company gathered together.

The Argonauts are often known as Minyans, because they brought back the ghost of Phrixus, grandson of Minyas, and the fleece of his ram; and because many of them, including Jason himself, sprang from the blood of Minyas's daughters. This Minyas, a son of Chryses, had migrated from Thessaly to Orchomenus in Boeotia, where he founded a kingdom, and was the first king ever to build a treasury.

The Lemnian Women and King Cyzicus

Heracles, after capturing the Erymanthian Boar, appeared suddenly at Pagasae, and was invited by a unanimous vote to captain the *Argo*; but generously agreed to serve under Jason who, though a novice, had planned and proclaimed the expedition. Accordingly, when the ship had been launched, and lots drawn for the benches, two oarsmen to each bench, it was Jason who sacrificed a yoke of oxen to Apollo of Embarkations. As the smoke of his sacrifice rose propitiously to heaven in dark, swirling columns, the Argonauts sat down to their farewell banquet, at which Orpheus with his lyre appeased certain drunken brawls. Sailing thence by the first light of dawn, they shaped a course for Lemnos.

About a year before this, the Lemnian men had quarrelled with their wives, complaining that they stank, and made concubines of Thracian girls captured on raids. In revenge, the Lemnian women murdered them all without pity, old and young alike, except King Thoas, whose life his daughter Hypsipyle secretly spared, setting him adrift in an oarless boat. Now, when the *Argo* hove in sight and the Lemnian women mistook her for an enemy ship from Thrace, they donned their dead husbands' armour and ran boldly shoreward, to repel the threatened attack. The eloquent Echion, however, landing staff in hand as Jason's herald, soon set their minds at rest; and Hypsipyle called a council at which she proposed to send a gift of food and wine to the Argonauts, but not to admit them into her city of Myrine, for fear of being charged with the massacre. Polyxo, Hypsipyle's aged nurse, then rose to plead that, without men, the Lemnian race must presently become extinct. 'The wisest course', she said, 'would be to offer yourselves in love to those well-born adventurers, and thus not only place our island under strong protection, but breed a new and stalwart stock.'

This disinterested advice was loudly acclaimed, and the Argonauts were welcomed to Myrine. Hypsipyle did not, of course, tell Jason the whole truth but, stammering and blushing, explained that after much ill-treatment at the hands of their husbands, her companions had risen in arms and forced them to emigrate. The vacant throne of Lemnos, she said, was now his for the asking. Jason, although gratefully accepting her offer, declared that before settling in fertile Lemnos he must complete his quest of the Golden Fleece. Nevertheless, Hypsipyle soon persuaded the Argonauts to postpone their departure; for each adventurer was surrounded by numerous young women, all itching to bed with him. Hypsipyle claimed Jason for herself, and royally she entertained him; it was then that he begot Euneus, and his twin Nebrophonus, whom some call Deiphilus, or Thoas the Younger. Euneus eventually became king of Lemnos and supplied the Greeks with wine during the Trojan War.

Many children were begotten on this occasion by the other Argonauts too and, had it not been for Heracles, who was guarding the *Argo* and at last strode angrily into Myrine, beating upon the house doors with his club and summoning his comrades back to duty, it is unlikely that the golden fleece would ever have left Colchis. He soon forced them down to the shore; and that same night they sailed for Samothrace, where they were duly initiated into the mysteries of Persephone and her servants, the Cabeiri, who save sailors from shipwreck.

The Argonauts sailed on, leaving Imbros to starboard and, since it was well known that king Laomedon of Troy guarded the entrance to the Hellespont and let no Greek ship enter, they slipped through the Straits by night, hugging the Thracian coast, and reached the Sea of Marmara in safety. Approaching Dolionian territory, they landed at the neck of a rugged peninsula, named Arcton, which is crowned by Mount Dindymum. Here they were welcomed by King Cyzicus, the son of Aeneus, Heracles's former ally, who had just married Cleite of Phrygian Percote and warmly invited them to share his wedding banquet. While the revelry was still in progress, the *Argo*'s guards were attacked with rocks and clubs by certain six-handed Earth-born giants from the interior of the peninsula, but beat them off.

Afterwards, the Argonauts dedicated their anchor-stone to Athene and, taking aboard a heavier one, rowed away with cordial farewells, shaping a course for the Bosphorus. But a north-easterly wind suddenly whirled down upon them, and soon they were making so little way that Tiphys decided to about ship, and ran back to the lee of the peninsula. He was driven off his course; and the Argonauts, beaching their ship at random in the pitch-dark, were at once assailed by well-armed warriors. Only when they had overcome these in a fierce battle, killing some and putting the remainder to flight, did Jason discover that he had made the eastern shore of Arcton, and that noble King Cyzicus, who had mistaken the Argonauts for pirates, lay dead at his feet. Cleite, driven mad by the news, hanged herself; and the nymphs of the grove wept so piteously that their tears formed the fountain which now bears her name.

The Argonauts held funeral games in Cyzicus's honour, but remained weather-bound for many days more. At last a halcyon fluttered above Jason's head, and perched twittering on the prow of the *Argo*; whereupon Mopsus, who understood the language of birds, explained that all would be well if they placated the goddess Rhea. She had exacted Cyzicus's death in requital for that of her sacred lion's, killed by him on Mount Dindymum, and was now vexed with the Argonauts for having caused such carnage among her six-armed Earth-born brothers. They therefore raised an image to the goddess, carved by Argus from an ancient vine-stock, and danced in full armour on the mountain top. Rhea acknowledged their devotion: she made a spring gush from the neighbouring rocks. A fair breeze then arose, and they continued the voyage. The Dolionians, however, prolonged their mourning to a full month, lighting no fires, and subsisting on uncooked foods, a custom which was observed during the annual Cyzican Games.

Hylas, Amycus and Phineus

At Heracles's challenge the Argonauts now engaged in a contest to see who could row the longest. After many laborious hours, relieved only by Orpheus's lyre, Jason, the Dioscuri, and Heracles alone held out; their comrades having each in turn confessed themselves beaten. Castor's strength began to ebb, and Polydeuces, who could not otherwise induce him to desist, shipped his own oar. Jason and Heracles, however, continued to urge the *Argo* forward, seated on opposite sides of the ship, until presently, as they reached the mouth of the river Chius in Mysia, Jason fainted. Almost at once Heracles's oar snapped. He glared about him, in anger and disgust; and his weary companions, thrusting their oars through the oar-holes again, beached the *Argo* by the riverside.

While they prepared the evening meal, Heracles went in search of a tree which would serve to make him a new oar. He uprooted an enormous fir, but when he dragged it back for trimming beside the camp fire, found that his squire Hylas had set out, an hour or two previously, to fetch water from the near-by pool of Pegae, and not yet returned; Polyphemus was away, searching for him.

Crying 'Hylas! Hylas!', Heracles plunged frantically into the woods, and soon met Polyphemus, who reported: 'Alas, I heard Hylas shouting for help; and ran towards his voice. But when I reached Pegae I found no signs of a struggle either with wild beasts or with other enemies. There was only his water-pitcher lying abandoned by the pool side.' Heracles and Polyphemus continued their search all night, and forced every Mysian whom they met to join in it, but to no avail; the fact being that Dryope and her sister-nymphs of Pegae had fallen in love with Hylas, and enticed him to come and live with them in an underwater grotto.

At dawn, a favourable breeze sprang up and, since neither Heracles nor Polyphemus appeared, though everyone shouted their names until the hillsides echoed, Jason gave orders for the voyage to be resumed. This decision was loudly contested and, as the *Argo* drew farther away from the shore, several of the Argonauts accused him of having marooned Heracles to avenge his defeat at rowing. They even tried to make Tiphys turn the ship about; but Calais and Zetes interposed, which is why Heracles later killed them in the island of Tenos.

*Nymphs (Archaeological
Museum, Delphi)*

After threatening to lay Mysia waste unless the inhabitants continued their search for Hylas, dead or alive, and then leading a successful raid on Troy, Heracles resumed his Labours; but Polyphemus settled near Pegae and built the city of Crius, where he reigned until the Chalybians killed him in battle.

Next, the *Argo* touched at the island of Bebrycos, also in the Sea of Marmara, ruled by the arrogant King Amycus, a son of Poseidon. This Amycus fancied himself as a boxer, and used to challenge strangers to a match, which invariably proved their undoing; but if they declined, he flung them without ceremony over a cliff into the sea. He now approached the Argonauts, and refused them food or water unless one of their champions would meet him in the ring. Polydeuces, who had won the boxing contest at the Olympic Games, stepped forward willingly, and drew on the raw-hide gloves which Amycus offered him.

Amycus and Polydeuces went at it, hammer and tongs, in a flowery dell, not far from the beach. Amycus's gloves were studded with brazen spikes, and the muscles on his shaggy arms stood out like boulders covered with seaweed. He was by far the heavier man, and the younger by several years; but Polydeuces, fighting cautiously at first, and avoiding his bull-like rushes, soon discovered the weak points in his defence and, before long, had him spitting blood from a swollen mouth. After a prolonged bout, in which neither showed the least sign of flagging, Polydeuces broke through Amycus's guard, flattened his nose with a straight left-handed punch, and dealt further merciless punishment on either side of it, using hooks and jolts. In pain and desperation, Amycus grasped Polydeuces's left fist and tugged at it with his left hand, while he brought up a powerful right swing; but Polydeuces threw himself in the direction of the tug. The swing went wide, and he countered with a stunning right-handed hook to the ear, followed by so irresistible an upper cut that it broke the bones of Amycus's temple and killed him instantly.

When they saw their king lying dead, the Bebrycans sprang to arms, but Polydeuces's cheering companions routed them easily and sacked the royal palace. To placate Poseidon, Amycus's father, Jason then offered a holocaust of twenty red bulls, which were found among the spoils.

The Argonauts put to sea again on the next day, and came to Salmydessus in Eastern Thrace, where Phineus, the son of Agenor, reigned. He had been blinded by the gods for prophesying the future too accurately, and was also plagued by a pair of Harpies: loathsome, winged, female creatures who, at every meal, flew into the palace and snatched victuals from his table, befouling the rest, so that it stank and was inedible. When Jason asked Phineus for advice on how to win the golden fleece, he was told: 'First rid me of the Harpies!' Phineus's servants spread the Argonauts a banquet, upon which the Harpies immediately descended, playing their usual tricks. Calais and Zetes, however, the winged sons of Boreas, arose sword in hand, and chased them into the air and far across the sea. Some say that they caught up with the Harpies at the Strophades islands, but spared their lives when they turned back and implored mercy; for Iris, Hera's messenger, intervened, promising that they would return to their cave in Cretan Dicte and never again molest Phineus.

Phineus instructed Jason how to navigate the Bosphorus, and gave him a detailed account of what weather, hospitality, and fortune to expect on his way to Colchis. He added: 'And once you have reached Colchis, trust in Aphrodite!'

Now, Phineus had married first Cleopatra, sister to Calais and Zetes and then, on her death, Idaea, a Scythian princess. Idaea was jealous of Cleopatra's two sons, and suborned false witnesses to accuse them of all manner of wickedness. Calais and Zetes, however, detecting the conspiracy, freed their nephews from prison, and Phineus restored them to favour, sending Idaea back to her father.

From the Symplegades to Colchis

Phineus had warned the Argonauts of the terrifying rocks called Symplegades which, perpetually shrouded in sea mist, guarded the entrance to the Bosphorus. When a ship attempted to pass between them, they drove together and crushed her; but, at Phineus's advice, Euphemus let loose a dove to fly ahead of the *Argo*. As soon as the rocks had nipped off her tail feathers, and recoiled again, the Argonauts rowed through with all speed, aided by Athene and by Orpheus's lyre, and lost only their stern ornament. Thereafter, in accordance with a prophecy, the rocks remained rooted, one on either side of the straits, and though the force of the current made the ship all but unmanageable, the Argonauts pulled at their oars until they bent like bows, and gained the Black Sea without disaster.

Coasting along the southern shore, they presently touched at the islet of Thynias. Thence they sailed to the city of Mariandyne and were warmly welcomed by King Lycus. News that his enemy, King Amycus, was dead had already reached Lycus by runner, and he gratefully offered the Argonauts his son Dascylus to guide them on their journey along the coast. The following day, as they were about to embark, Idmon the seer was attacked by a ferocious boar lurking in the reed-beds of the river Lycus, which gashed his thigh deeply with its great tusks. Idas sprang to Idmon's assistance and, when the boar charged again, impaled it on his spear; however, Idmon bled to death despite their care, and the Argonauts mourned him for three days. Then Tiphys sickened and died, and his comrades were plunged in grief as they raised a barrow over his ashes, beside the one that they had raised for Idmon. Great Ancaeus first, and after him Erginus, Nauplius and Euphemus, all offered to take Tiphys's place as navigator; but Ancaeus was chosen, and served them well.

From Mariandyne they continued eastward under sail for many

days, until they reached Sinope in Paphlagonia, where Jason found recruits to fill three of the vacant seats on his benches: namely the brothers Deileon, Autolycus, and Phlogius, of Tricca, who had accompanied Heracles on his expedition to the Amazons but, being parted from him by accident, were now stranded in this outlandish region.

The *Argo* then sailed past the country of the Amazons; and that of the iron-working Chalybians, who neither till the soil, nor tend flocks, but live wholly on the gains of their forges; and the country of the Tibarenians, where it is the custom for husbands to groan, as if in child-bed, while their wives are in labour; and the country of the Mossynoechians, who live in wooden castles, couple promiscuously, and carry immensely long spears and white shields in the shape of ivy-leaves.

Near the islet of Ares, great flocks of birds flew over the *Argo*, dropping brazen plumes, one of which wounded Oileus in the shoulder. At this, the Argonauts, recalling Phineus's injunctions, donned their helmets and shouted at the top of their voices; half of them rowing, while the remainder protected them with shields, against which they clashed their swords. Phineus had also counselled them to land on the islet, and this they now did, driving away myriads of birds, until not one was left. That night they praised his wisdom, when a huge storm arose and four Aeolians clinging to a baulk of timber were cast ashore, close to their camp; these castaways proved to be Cytisorus, Argeus, Phrontis, and Melanion, sons of Phrixus by Chalciope, daughter to King Aeëtes of Colchis, and thus closely related to many of those present. They had been shipwrecked on a journey to Greece, where they were intending to claim the Orchomenan kingdom of their grandfather Athamas. Jason greeted them warmly, and all together offered sober sacrifices on a black stone in the temple of Ares. When Jason explained that his mission was to bring back the soul of Phrixus to Greece, and also recover the fleece of the golden ram on which he had ridden, Cytisorus and his brothers found themselves in a quandary: though owing devotion to their father's memory, they feared to offend their grandfather by demanding the fleece. However, what choice had they but to make common cause with these cousins who had saved their lives?

The *Argo* then coasted past the island of Philyra, and soon the Caucasus Range towered above the Argonauts, and they entered the mouth of the broad Phasis river, which waters Colchis. First pouring a libation of wine mixed with honey to the gods of the land, Jason concealed the *Argo* in a backwater, and called a council of war.

The Seizure of the Fleece

In Olympus, Hera and Athene were anxiously debating how their favourite, Jason, might win the golden fleece. At last they decided to approach Aphrodite, who undertook that her naughty little son Eros

Jason plucking the Golden Fleece from a tree. Red-figured vase (Metropolitan Museum of Art, New York)

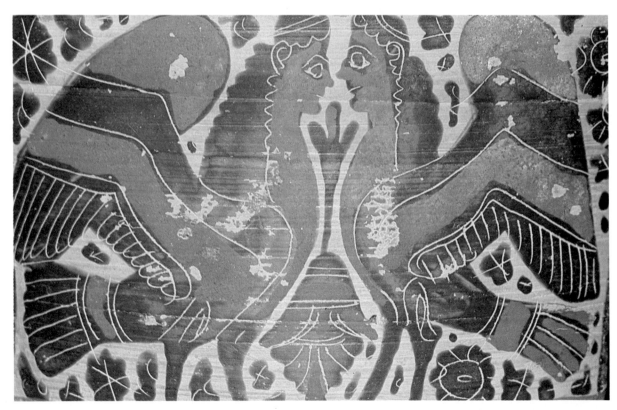

would make Medea, King Aeëtes daughter, conceive a sudden passion for him.

Meanwhile, at the council of war held in the backwater, Jason proposed going with Phrixus's sons to the near-by city of Colchian Aea, where Aeëtes ruled, and demanding the fleece as a favour; only if this were denied would they resort to guile or force. All welcomed his suggestion, and Augeias, Aeëtes's half-brother, joined the party.

As Jason and his companions approached, they were met first by Chalciope, who was surprised to see Cytisorus and her other three sons returning so soon and, when she heard their story, showered thanks on Jason for his rescue of them. Next came Aeëtes, accompanied by Eidyia and showing great displeasure – for Laomedon had undertaken to prevent all Greeks from entering the Black Sea – and asked Aegeus, his favourite grandson, to explain the intrusion. Aegeus replied that Jason, to whom he and his brothers owed their lives, had come to fetch away the golden fleece in accordance with an oracle. Seeing that Aeëtes's face wore a look of fury, he added at once: 'In return for which favour, these noble Greeks will gladly subject the Sauromatians to your Majesty's rule.' Aeëtes gave a contemptuous laugh, then ordered Jason to return whence they came, before he had their tongues cut out and their hands lopped off.

At this point, the princess Medea emerged from the palace, and when Jason answered gently and courteously, Aeëtes, somewhat ashamed of himself, undertook to yield the fleece, though on what seemed impossible terms. Jason must yoke two fire-breathing brazen-footed bulls, creations of Hephaestus; plough the Field of Ares to the extent of four ploughgates; and then sow it with the serpent's teeth given him by Athene, a few left over from Cadmus's sowing at Thebes. Jason stood stupefied, wondering how to perform these unheard-of feats, but Eros aimed one of his arrows at Medea, and drove it into her heart, up to the feathers.

Chalciope, visiting Medea's bedroom that evening, to enlist her help on behalf of Cytisorus and his brothers, found that she had fallen head over heels in love with Jason. When Chalciope offered herself as a go-between, Medea eagerly undertook to help him yoke the fire-breathing bulls and win the fleece; making it her sole condition that she should sail back in the *Argo* as his wife.

Jason was summoned, and swore by all the gods of Olympus to keep faith with Medea for ever. She offered him a flask of lotion, blood-red juice of the two-stalked, saffron-coloured Caucasian crocus, which would protect him against the bulls' fiery breath. Jason gratefully accepted the flask and, after a libation of honey, unstoppered it and bathed his body, spear and shield in the contents. He was thus able to subdue the bulls and harness them to a plough with an adamantine yoke. All day he ploughed, and at nightfall sowed the teeth, from which armed men immediately sprouted. He provoked these to fight one against another, as Cadmus had done on a similar occasion, by throwing a stone quoit into their midst; then despatched the wounded survivors.

King Aeëtes, however, had no intention of parting with the fleece, and shamelessly repudiated his bargain. He threatened to burn the *Argo* and massacre her crew; but Medea, in whom he had unwisely confided, led Jason and a party of Argonauts to the precinct of Ares, some six miles away. There the fleece hung, guarded by a loathsome and immortal dragon of a thousand coils, larger than the *Argo* herself, and born from the blood of the monster Typhon, destroyed by Zeus. She soothed the hissing dragon with incantations and then, using freshly-cut sprigs of juniper, sprinkled soporific drops on his eyelids. Jason stealthily unfastened the fleece from the oak-tree; and together they hurried down to the beach where the *Argo* lay.

An alarm had already been raised by the priests of Ares and, in a running fight, the Colchians wounded Iphitus, Meleager, Argus, Atalanta, and Jason. Yet all of them contrived to scramble aboard the waiting *Argo*, which was rowed off in great haste, pursued by Aeëtes's galleys. Iphitus alone succumbed to his wounds; Medea soon healed the others with vulneraries of her own invention.

The Murder of Apsyrtus

Many different accounts survive of the *Argo's* return to Thessaly, though it is generally agreed that, following Phineus's advice, the Argonauts sailed counter-sunwise around the Black Sea. Some say that when Aeëtes overtook them, near the mouth of the Danube, Medea killed her young half-brother Apsyrtus, whom she had brought aboard, and cut him into pieces, which she consigned one by one to the swift current. This cruel stratagem delayed the pursuit, because obliging Aeëtes to retrieve each piece in turn for subsequent burial at Tomi.

The most circumstantial and coherent account, however, is that Apsyrtus, sent by Aeëtes in pursuit of Jason, trapped the *Argo* at the mouth of the Danube, where the Argonauts agreed to set Medea ashore on a near-by island sacred to Artemis, leaving her in charge of a priestess for a few days; meanwhile a king of the Brygians would judge the case and decide whether she was to return home or follow Jason to Greece, and in whose possession the fleece should remain. But Medea sent a private message to Apsyrtus, pretending that she had been forcibly abducted, and begging him to rescue her. That night, when he visited the island and thereby broke the truce, Jason followed, lay in wait and struck him down from behind. He then cut off Apsyrtus's extremities, and thrice licked up some of the fallen blood, which he spat out again each time, to prevent the ghost from pursuing him. As soon as Medea was once more aboard the *Argo*, the Argonauts attacked the leaderless Colchians, scattered their flotilla, and escaped.

After Apsyrtus's murder, the *Argo* returned by the Bosphorus, the

A terracotta Siren (Archaeological Museum, Palermo, Sicily)

opposite: Medea pretending to rejuvenate Pelias (Museo Gregoriano Profano, Vatican)

way she had come, and passed through the Hellespont in safety, because the Trojans could no longer oppose her passage. For Heracles, on his return from Mysia, had collected six ships and surprised and destroyed the Trojan fleet. He then battered his way into Troy with his club, and demanded from King Laomedon the man-eating mares of King Diomedes, which he had left in his charge some years previously. When Laomedon denied any knowledge of these, Heracles killed him and all his sons, except the infant Podarces, or Priam, whom he appointed king in his stead.

Jason and Medea were no longer aboard the *Argo*. Her oracular beam had spoken once more, refusing to carry either of them until they had been purified of murder, and from the mouth of the Danube they had set out overland for Aeaea, the island home of Medea's aunt Circe. Medea led Jason there by the route down which the straw-wrapped gifts of the Hyperboreans are yearly brought to Delos. Circe, to whom they came as suppliants, grudgingly purified them with the blood of a young sow.

Now, their Colchian pursuers had been warned not to come back without Medea and the fleece and, guessing that she had gone to Circe for purification, followed the *Argo* across the Aegean Sea, around the Peloponnese, and up the Illyrian coast, rightly concluding that Medea and Jason had arranged to be fetched from Aeaea.

The 'Argo' Returns to Greece
Arrived at Corcyra, which was then named Drepane, the Colchians found the *Argo* beached opposite the islet of Macris; her crew were joyfully celebrating the successful outcome of their expedition. The Colchian leader now visited King Alcinous and Queen Arete, demanding on Aeëtes's behalf the surrender of Medea and the fleece. Arete, to whom Medea had appealed for protection, kept Alcinous awake that night by complaining of the ill-treatment to which fathers too often subject their errant daughters: finally prevailing upon Alcinous to tell her what judgement he would deliver next morning, namely: 'If Medea is still a virgin, she shall return to Colchis; if not, she is at liberty to stay with Jason.'

Leaving him sound asleep, Arete sent her herald to warn Jason what he must expect; and he married Medea without delay in the Cave of Macris, the daughter of Aristaeus and sometime Dionysus's nurse. The Argonauts celebrated the wedding with a sumptuous banquet and spread the golden fleece over the bridal couch. Judgement was duly delivered in the morning, Jason claimed Medea as his wife, and the Colchians could neither implement Aeëtes's orders nor, for fear of his wrath, return home. Some therefore settled in Corcyra, and others occupied those Illyrian islands, not far from Circe's Aeaea.

When, a year or two later, Aeëtes heard of these happenings, he nearly died of rage and sent a herald to Greece demanding the person of Medea and requital for the injuries done him; but was informed that no requital had yet been made for Io's abduction by men of Aeëtes's race (though the truth was that she fled because a gadfly pursued her) and none should therefore be given for the voluntary departure of Medea.

Jason now needed only to double Cape Malea, and return with the fleece to Iolcus. He cruised in safety past the Islands of the Sirens, where the ravishing strains of these bird-women were countered by the even lovelier strains of Orpheus's lyre. Butes alone sprang over-board in an attempt to swim ashore, but Aphrodite rescued him; she took him to Mount Eryx by way of Lilybaeum, and there made him her lover.

The Argonauts then sailed in fine weather along the coast of East-ern Sicily, where they watched the matchless white herds of Helius grazing on the shore, but refrained from stealing any of them. Sud-denly they were struck by a frightful North Wind which, in nine days' time, drove them to the uttermost parts of Libya; there, an enormous wave swept the *Argo* over the perilous rocks which line the coast and retreated, leaving her high and dry a mile or more inland. A lifeless desert stretched as far as the eye could see, and the Argonauts had already prepared themselves for death, when the Triple-goddess Libya, clad in goat skins, appeared to Jason in a dream and gave him reassurance. At this, they took heart and, setting the *Argo* on rollers, moved her by force of their shoulders to the salt Lake Tritonis, which lay several miles off, a task that occupied twelve days. All would have died of thirst, but for a spring which Heracles, on his way to fetch the golden apples of the Hesperides, had recently caused to gush from the ground.

Canthus was now killed by Caphaurus, a Garamantian shepherd whose flocks he was driving off, but his comrades avenged him. And hardly had the two corpses been buried than Mopsus trod upon a Libyan serpent which bit him in the heel; a thick mist spread over his eyes, his hair fell out, and he died in agony. The Argonauts, after giving him a hero's burial, once more began to despair, being unable to find any outlet to the Lake.

Jason, however, before he embarked on this voyage, had consulted the Pythoness at Delphi who gave him two massive brazen tripods, with one of which Orpheus now advised him to propitiate the deities of the land. When he did so, the god Triton appeared and took up the tripod without so much as a word of thanks, but Euphemus barred his way and asked him politely: 'Pray, my lord, will you kindly direct us to the Mediterranean Sea?' For answer, Triton merely pointed towards the Tacapae river but, as an afterthought, handed him a clod of earth. Euphemus acknowledged the gift with the sacrifice of a sheep, and Triton consented to draw the *Argo* along by her keel, until once more she entered the Mediterranean Sea.

Heading northward, the Argonauts reached Crete, where they

were prevented from landing by Talos the bronze sentinel, a creation of Hephaestus, who pelted the *Argo* with rocks, as was his custom. Medea called sweetly to this monster, promising to make him immortal if he drank a certain magic potion; but it was a sleeping draught and, while he slept, she removed the bronze nail which stoppered the single vein running from his neck to his ankles. Out rushed the divine ichor, a colourless liquid serving him for blood, and he died.

On the following night, the *Argo* was caught in a storm from the south, but Jason invoked Apollo, who sent a flash of light, revealing to starboard the island of Anaphe, one of the Sporades, where Ancaeus managed to beach the ship. In gratitude, Jason raised an altar to Apollo.

Sailing to Aegina, they held a contest: as to who could first draw a pitcher of water and carry it back to the ship. From Aegina it was a simple voyage to Iolcus, such as scores of ships make every year, and they made it in fair weather without danger.

The Death of Pelias

One autumn evening, the Argonauts regained the well-remembered beach of Pagasae, but found no one there to greet them. Indeed, it was rumoured in Thessaly that all were dead; Pelias had therefore been emboldened to kill Jason's parents, Aeson and Polymele, and an infant son, Promachus, born to them since the departure of the *Argo*. Aeson, however, asked permission to take his own life and, his plea being granted, drank bull's blood and thus expired; whereupon Polymele killed herself with a dagger after cursing Pelias, who mercilessly dashed out Promachus's brains on the palace floor.

Jason, hearing this doleful story from a solitary boatman, forbade him to spread the news of the *Argo*'s homecoming, and summoned a council of war. All his comrades were of the opinion that Pelias deserved death, but when Jason demanded an immediate assault on Iolcus, Acastus remarked that he could hardly be expected to oppose his father; and the others thought it wiser to disperse, each to his own home and there, if necessary, raise contingents for a war on Jason's behalf. Iolcus, indeed, seemed too strongly garrisoned to be stormed by a company so small as theirs.

Medea, however, spoke up and undertook to reduce the city singlehanded. She instructed the Argonauts to conceal their ship, and themselves, on some wooded and secluded beach within sight of Iolcus. When they saw a torch waved from the palace roof, this would mean that Pelias was dead, the gates open, and the city theirs for the taking.

During her visit to Anaphe, Medea had found a hollow image of Artemis and brought it aboard the *Argo*. She now dressed her twelve Phaeacian bond-maidens in strange disguises and led them, each in turn carrying the image, towards Iolcus. On reaching the city gates

opposite: Medea and Pelias with the cauldron. Amphora (British Museum)

Medea, who had given herself the appearance of a wrinkled crone, ordered the sentinels to let her pass. She cried in a shrill voice that the goddess Artemis had come from the foggy land of the Hyperboreans, in a chariot drawn by flying serpents, to bring good fortune to Iolcus. The startled sentinels dared not disobey, and Medea with her bond-maidens, raging through the streets like maenads, roused the inhabitants to a religious frenzy.

Awakened from sleep, Pelias enquired in terror what the goddess required of him. Medea answered that Artemis was about to acknowledge his piety by rejuvenating him, and thus allowing him to beget heirs in place of the unfilial Acastus, who had lately died in a shipwreck off the Libyan coast. Pelias doubted this promise, until Medea, by removing the illusion of old age that she had cast about herself, turned young again before his very eyes. 'Such is the power of Artemis!' she cried. He then watched while she cut a bleary-eyed old ram into thirteen pieces and boiled them in a cauldron. Using Colchian spells, which he mistook for Hyperborean ones, and solemnly conjuring Artemis to assist her, Medea then pretended to rejuvenate the dead ram – for a frisky lamb was hidden, with other magical gear, inside the goddess's hollow image. Pelias, now wholly deceived, consented to lie on a couch, where Medea soon charmed him to sleep. She then commanded his daughters, Alcestis, Evadne, and Amphinome, to cut him up, just as they had seen her do with the ram, and boil the pieces in the same cauldron.

Alcestis piously refused to shed her father's blood in however good a cause; but Medea, by giving further proof of her magic powers, persuaded Evadne and Amphinome to wield their knives with resolution. When the deed was done, she led them up to the roof, each carrying a torch, and explained that they must invoke the Moon while the cauldron was coming to a boil. From their ambush, the Argonauts saw the distant gleam of torches and, welcoming the signal, rushed into Iolcus, where they met with no opposition.

Jason, however, fearing Acastus's vengeance, resigned the kingdom to him, neither did he dispute the sentence of banishment passed on him by the Iolcan Council: for he hoped to sit upon a richer throne elsewhere.

As for Pelias's daughters: Alcestis married Admetus of Pherae, to whom she had long been affianced; Evadne and Amphinome were banished by Acastus to Mantinea in Arcadia where, after purification, they succeeded in making honourable marriages.

Medea at Ephyra

Jason first visited Boeotian Orchomenus, where he hung up the golden fleece in the temple of Laphystian Zeus; next, he beached the *Argo* on the Isthmus of Corinth, and there dedicated her to Poseidon.

Now, Medea was the only surviving child of Aeëtes, the rightful king of Corinth, who when he emigrated to Colchis had left behind as his regent a certain Bunus. The throne having fallen vacant, by the death without issue of the usurper Corinthus, son of Marathon (who styled himself 'Son of Zeus'), Medea claimed it, and the Corinthians accepted Jason as their king. But, after reigning for ten prosperous and happy years, he came to suspect that Medea had secured his succession by poisoning Corinthus; and proposed to divorce her in favour of Glauce the Theban, daughter of King Creon.

Medea, while not denying her crime, held Jason to the oath which he had sworn at Aea in the name of all the gods, and when he protested that a forced oath was invalid, pointed out that he also owed the throne of Corinth to her. He answered: 'True, but the Corinthians have learned to have more respect for me than for you.' Since he continued obdurate Medea, feigning submission, sent Glauce a wedding gift by the hands of the royal princes – for she had borne Jason seven sons and seven daughters – namely, a golden crown and a long white robe. No sooner had Glauce put them on, than unquenchable flames shot up, and consumed not only her – although she plunged headlong into the palace fountain – but King Creon, a crowd of other distinguished Theban guests, and everyone else assembled in the palace, except Jason; who escaped by leaping from an upper window.

At this point Zeus, greatly admiring Medea's spirit, fell in love with her, but she repulsed all his advances. Hera was grateful: 'I will make your children immortal,' said she, 'if you lay them on the sacrificial altar in my temple.' Medea did so; and then fled in a chariot drawn by winged serpents, a loan from her grandfather Helius, after bequeathing the kingdom to Sisyphus.

Medea in Exile
Medea fled first to Heracles at Thebes, where he had promised to shelter her should Jason ever prove unfaithful, and cured him of the madness that had made him kill his children; nevertheless, the Thebans would not permit her to take up residence among them because Creon, whom she had murdered, was their King. So she went to Athens, and King Aegeus was glad to marry her. Next, banished from Athens for her attempted poisoning of Theseus, she sailed to Italy and taught the Marrubians the art of snake-charming. After a brief visit to Thessaly, where she unsuccessfully competed with Thetis in a beauty contest judged by Idomeneus the Cretan, she married an Asian king.

Hearing, finally, that Aeëtes's Colchian throne had been usurped by her uncle Perses, Medea went to Colchis with Medeius, who killed Perses, set Aeëtes on his throne again, and enlarged the kingdom of Colchis to include Media. Some pretend that she was by that time reconciled to Jason, but the truth is that Jason, having forfeited the favour of the gods, whose names he had taken in vain when he broke faith with Medea, wandered homeless from city to city, hated of men.

In old age he came once more to Corinth, and sat down in the shadow of the *Argo* remembering his past glories, and grieving for the disasters that had overwhelmed him. He was about to hang himself from the prow, when it suddenly toppled forward and killed him. Poseidon then placed the image of the *Argo*'s stern, which was innocent of homicide, among the stars.

Medea never died, but became an immortal and reigned in the Elysian Fields where some say that she, rather than Helen, married Achilles.

As for Athamas, whose failure to sacrifice Phrixus had been the cause of the Argonauts' expedition, he was on the point of being himself sacrificed at Orchomenus, as the sin-offering demanded by the Oracle of Laphystian Zeus, when his grandson Cytisorus returned from Aeaea and rescued him.

opposite: *Medea and her children. Terracotta (Archaeological Museum, Avignon)*

INDEX

Les Secrets
de la Terre

Les Secrets
de la Terre

Sélection
du Reader's Digest

PARIS BRUXELLES MONTRÉAL ZURICH

Les Secrets de la Terre

publié par Sélection du Reader's Digest,
est l'adaptation française de *Geheimnisse der Erde*.

Équipe de Sélection du Reader's Digest

DIRECTION ÉDITORIALE : Gérard Chenuet
DIRECTION ARTISTIQUE : Dominique Charliat
SÉCRÉTARIAT GÉNÉRAL : Elizabeth Glachant
MAQUETTE : Françoise Boismal
LECTURE-CORRECTION : Béatrice Argentier, Catherine Decayeux,
Emmanuelle Dunoyer
FABRICATION : Marie-Pierre de Clinchamp

Nous remercions tous ceux qui ont contribué à cet ouvrage :

RÉALISATION DE LA VERSION FRANÇAISE : Initiales publishing
TRADUCTION : Liliane Charrier, Brigitte de Montgolfier,
Annick de Scribat, Pascale Hervieux
CONSULTANTS : Xavier Mauduit, Simon Parlier
RELECTURE : Marie-Thérèse Ménager

Code produit : GR 951/IC

PREMIÈRE ÉDITION
Premier tirage

© 2004 Sélection du Reader's Digest, SA,
5 à 7, avenue Louis-Pasteur, 92220 Bagneux
© 2004 NV Reader's Digest, SA,
20, boulevard Paepsem, 1070 Bruxelles
© 2004 Sélection du Reader's Digest, SA,
Räffelstrasse 11, « Gallushof », 8021 Zurich
© 2004, Sélection du Reader's Digest (Canada), Limitée,
1100, boulevard René-Lévesque Ouest, Montréal (Québec) H3B 5H5

Site Internet français: www.selectionclic.com
Site Internet canadien: www.selectionrd.ca

ISBN 2-7098-1582-6

Imprimé au Canada
Printed in Canada

AVANT-PROPOS

Des générations de savants ont étudié l'histoire de la Terre
et de sa formation. Les bibliothèques sont pleines de livres
qui accumulent les données scientifiques sur le sujet, toujours aussi difficile
d'accès pour les non-spécialistes.

Chaque paysage n'est que le résultat d'un processus d'évolution extrêmement
long et complexe. Les chercheurs ont aujourd'hui à leur disposition de multiples
méthodes qui leur permettent de sonder les profondeurs obscures de la Terre
et de reconstituer une histoire parfois très ancienne. L'ambition de cet ouvrage
est de retracer les stades successifs d'une évolution qui s'étend souvent sur
des millions d'années, en les illustrant de schémas très explicites.

Il donne une synthèse de processus géologiques fort complexes et met en évidence
les facteurs décisifs de ces évolutions. Le schéma ci-dessous montre par
exemple le Black Tusk, situé dans les massifs côtiers du Canada.
De ce volcan éteint depuis longtemps il ne reste plus que le bouchon
de basalte logé jadis à l'intérieur de sa cheminée.
Le lecteur trouvera dans cet ouvrage un choix
éclectique de paysages géologiques. Sans rien
perdre de leur singularité, ils sont
représentatifs d'innombrables autres
paysages de la Terre.

**Volcan en activité
il y a 170 000 ans**

**Aujourd'hui : bouchon
de basalte à l'emplacement
de l'ancienne cheminée**

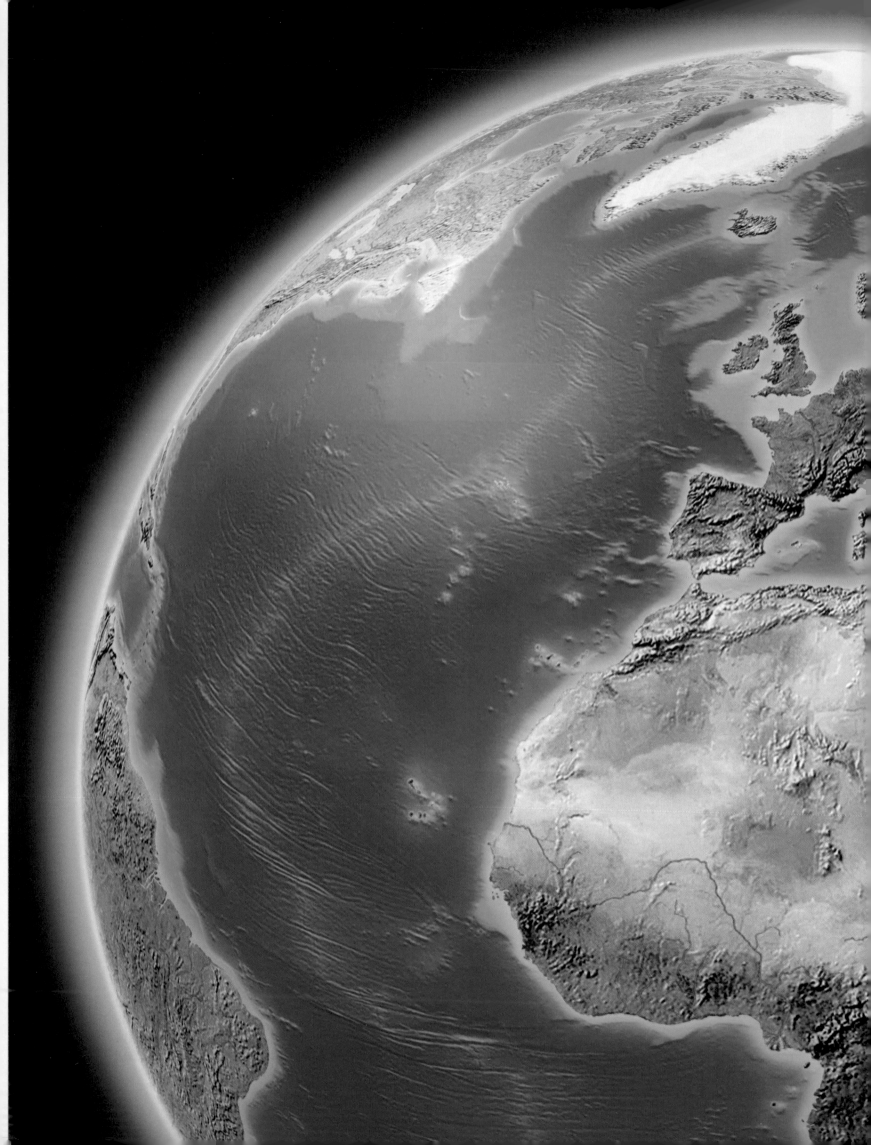

Europe
Une grande diversité sur peu d'espace

L'Islande
Cette terre de feu
et de glace est sillonnée
d'énormes fissures éruptives
(p. 128).

Le Great Glen
Le nord-ouest de l'Écosse
est traversé de bout en
bout par une faille
rectiligne (p. 106).

Les Alpes suisses
La formation des Alpes
a commencé par une
série de mouvements
de la croûte terrestre
(p. 174).

La Corse
L'île de Beauté, en
Méditerranée, surprend
par ses rochers de granit
étrangement érodés
(p. 221).

Les fjords norvégiens
Le pays européen des records offre les plus profonds fjords, les plus larges hauts plateaux et les plus grands glaciers (p. 78).

La mer Baltique
Depuis la dernière époque glaciaire, le soulèvement de la Scandinavie s'accompagne d'une baisse du niveau de la mer (p. 86).

La vallée du Rhin héroïque
Le fleuve romantique a été détourné à plusieurs reprises et a finalement été capturé par son propre lit (p. 50).

Le Karst
Des eaux d'infiltration font les choses en grand dans cette montagne calcaire (p. 61).

La Campanie
Le sous-sol du Vésuve est en perpétuelle ébullition (p. 92).

Les Dolomites
Cette énorme montagne est née dans les eaux d'une mer tropicale (p. 164).

Afrique
La magie d'un vieux continent

Les îles Canaries
Ces sept îles volcaniques
offrent un champ
d'expériences variées
de l'évolution (p. 225).

**Le Namib
des dunes**
Dans une région
extrêmement sèche,
des dunes monumentales
s'enveloppent d'un
brouillard frais
(p. 115).

Le Cap-Ouest
La flore de ce bout du monde
est mystérieusement liée
à celle des autres continents
(p. 256).

L'Ennedi
Au beau milieu du plus grand désert du monde, d'anciennes eaux alimentent des lacs bleus (p. 193).

La Rift Valley
Le Vieux Continent se brise à l'endroit où se trouvait le berceau de l'humanité (p. 188).

Les Seychelles
Les fragments du Gondwana – l'Ancien Continent – sont rongés par une intense érosion (p. 297).

Madagascar
Depuis des millions d'années, isolé du reste du monde, le « huitième » continent abrite un trésor de l'évolution (p. 236).

Le Zambèze
Un fleuve tropical indolent se métamorphose soudain en chutes d'eau impétueuses (p. 136).

Amérique du Nord

Un mur de montagnes à l'ouest

La Coast Range
Sur la montagneuse
côte pacifique,
l'Amérique du Nord
poursuit sa croissance
(p. 97).

**Les montagnes
Rocheuses
canadiennes**
Une mer fossilisée
témoigne du temps où
explosait la vie terrestre
(p. 161).

**La vallée
du Yosemite**
Les périodes glaciaires
ont laissé de gigantesques
cascades et cathédrales
de granit
(p. 72).

Le Grand Canyon
En aucun autre endroit
la Terre ne dévoile
autant son histoire
(p. 168).

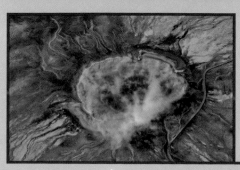

Yellowstone
Ces fantastiques paysages
d'eau et de vapeur cachent
une bombe à retardement
d'une force inimaginable
(p. 36).

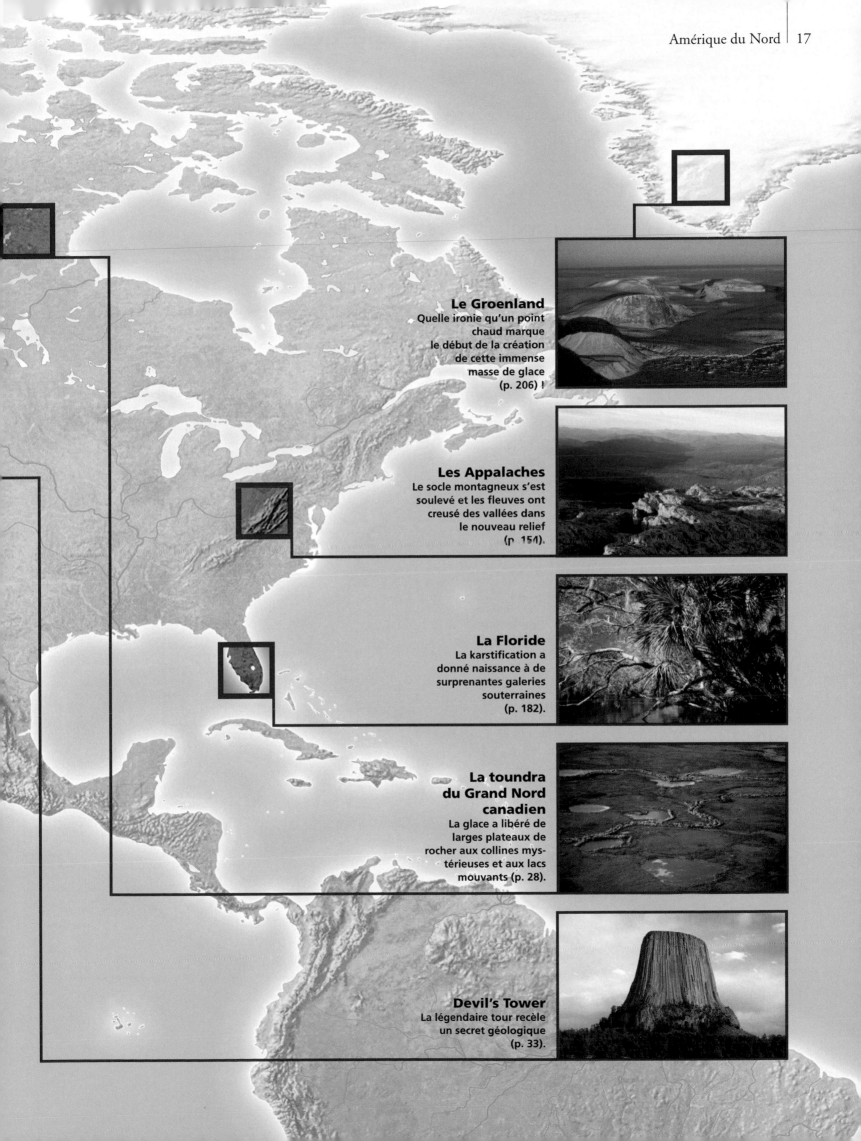

Le Groenland
Quelle ironie qu'un point
chaud marque
le début de la création
de cette immense
masse de glace
(p. 206) !

Les Appalaches
Le socle montagneux s'est
soulevé et les fleuves ont
creusé des vallées dans
le nouveau relief
(p. 154).

La Floride
La karstification a
donné naissance à de
surprenantes galeries
souterraines
(p. 182).

**La toundra
du Grand Nord
canadien**
La glace a libéré de
larges plateaux de
rocher aux collines mys-
térieuses et aux lacs
mouvants (p. 28).

Devil's Tower
La légendaire tour recèle
un secret géologique
(p. 33).

Amérique du Sud

De la forêt tropicale aux glaciers éternels

Le Yucatán
De mystérieuses
fontaines karstiques
dans l'empire disparu
des Mayas
(p. 202).

**La route
des volcans
et l'Altiplano**
Cette région de sommets
volcaniques enneigés est
l'une des plus explosives
de la Terre
(p. 140).

La Patagonie
Des fleuves glacials
détruisent tout ce
qui s'oppose à eux
(p. 52).

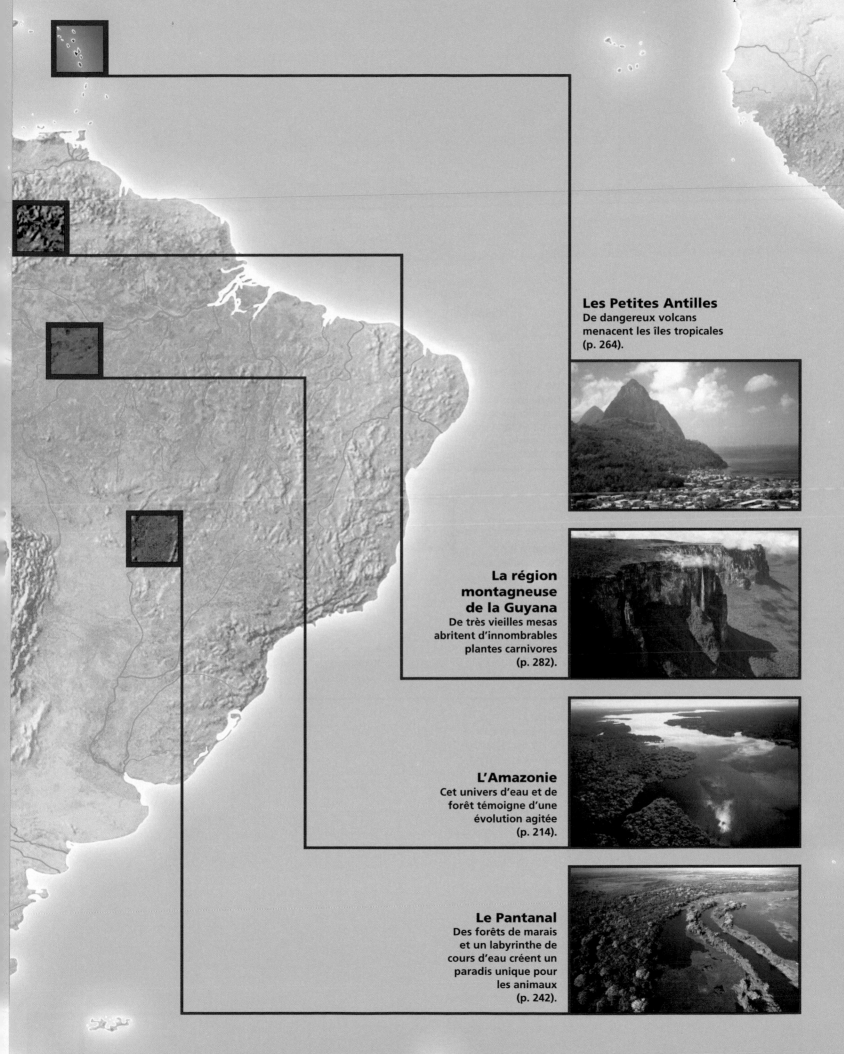

Les Petites Antilles
De dangereux volcans
menacent les îles tropicales
(p. 264).

**La région
montagneuse
de la Guyana**
De très vieilles mesas
abritent d'innombrables
plantes carnivores
(p. 282).

L'Amazonie
Cet univers d'eau et de
forêt témoigne d'une
évolution agitée
(p. 214).

Le Pantanal
Des forêts de marais
et un labyrinthe de
cours d'eau créent un
paradis unique pour
les animaux
(p. 242).

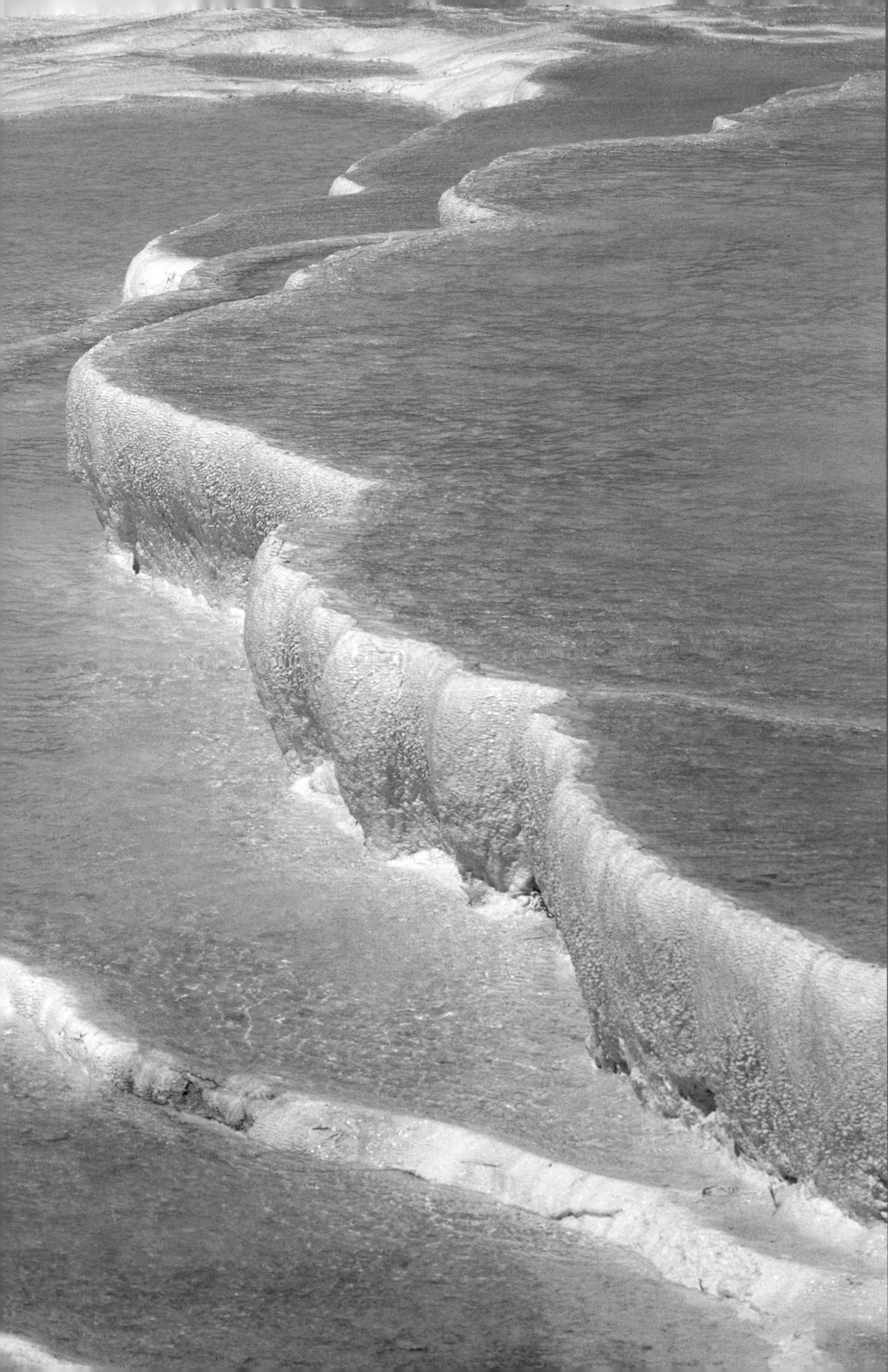

LES HUMEURS DE LA NATURE

LES CHEMINÉES DE

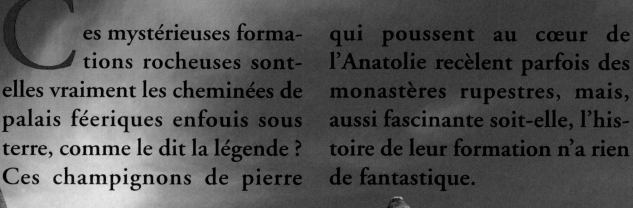

Ces mystérieuses formations rocheuses sont-
elles vraiment les cheminées de
palais féeriques enfouis sous
terre, comme le dit la légende ?
Ces champignons de pierre
qui poussent au cœur de
l'Anatolie recèlent parfois des
monastères rupestres, mais,
aussi fascinante soit-elle, l'histoire de leur formation n'a rien
de fantastique.

FÉES

Au pays des merveilles

La Cappadoce, ainsi baptisée par un peuple perse de l'Antiquité, est une région d'Anatolie centrale située sur le cours supérieur et moyen du Kizil Irmak, le fleuve Rouge. Elle est en majeure partie occupée par un plateau couvert d'une steppe aride et monotone, ponctuée de dépressions cernées de sommets arrondis. À l'ouest de Kayseri, l'ancienne Césarée, capitale de la Cappadoce, dans le triangle délimité par les villages de Göreme, Zelve et Ürgüp, le paysage offre néanmoins un spectacle inattendu. On dirait que les architectes de la préhistoire s'y sont livrés à un grand concours de créativité. D'innombrables pyramides et obélisques se dressent parfois à plus de 30 m de haut, étranges formations rocheuses qui évoquent autant de ruches et de champignons géants et que la tradition populaire a surnommées cheminées de fées ou demoiselles coiffées. La magie de ce paysage fabuleux s'accroît encore lorsque l'on découvre que nombre de ces cônes et pitons de pierre sont criblés de portes et de fenêtres. En jetant un regard à l'intérieur, on s'aperçoit que beaucoup sont entièrement évidés et qu'il n'en reste que de minces parois rocheuses.

Un dédale de monastères et d'ermitages

Le voile ne tarde pas à se lever sur le secret des cavités dès que le visiteur remarque les traces d'outils qui entaillent les plafonds et les parois. Hormis quelques rares grottes naturelles, les cavernes de Cappadoce sont l'œuvre de l'homme. Les plus anciennes remontent probablement à la période paléochrétienne – dès le IVᵉ siècle, en effet, les premiers ermites vinrent chercher refuge dans les replis rocheux de ces contrées reculées. Jusqu'au Moyen Âge, la Cappadoce se peupla ainsi d'une myriade de chapelles, ermitages et cellules, ainsi que de cités et de monastères souterrains, creusés à même la pierre sur plusieurs niveaux, parfois à plus de 50 m sous terre. Reliées entre elles par des galeries et des volées de marches, ces habitations troglodytiques forment un gigantesque labyrinthe.

Rares sont les roches qui se révèlent suffisamment solides et tendres pour se prêter à l'aménagement de logis rupestres. Six seulement réunissent ces deux conditions, dont le tuf volcanique, composé de cendres et de petits fragments de lave solidifiés – l'un des matériaux dans lequel ont été creusées les habitations troglodytiques.

Parmi les autres roches volcaniques qui forment la région, citons le basalte, composé de flots de lave figée, et l'ignimbrite, dont le nom pourrait se traduire par « pierre du nuage de feu ». Il est vrai que l'ignimbrite naît littéralement d'un nuage de feu, d'une émulsion en fusion de gaz et de particules de lave de taille variable. Voici 3 millions d'années, de violentes éruptions volcaniques ébranlèrent la région, puis les matériaux les plus lourds s'agrégèrent sur le sol, tandis que les gaz, plus légers, formaient des nuages incandescents.

Le journal de Vulcain : une lecture édifiante

La lave en fusion et les nuées ardentes peuvent recouvrir des centaines de kilomètres carrés en un rien de temps. Les températures atteignent alors de tels sommets que les particules de lave se soudent en un bloc extrêmement solide. Aussi

Vivre dans les entrailles de la Terre

Aujourd'hui, certaines cavités rupestres de Cappadoce sont encore habitées. Si elles ne protègent plus l'homme de l'ennemi, elles le préservent toujours du froid hivernal et de la chaleur estivale. À quelques mètres sous terre, les températures annuelles moyennes varient déjà de quelques degrés par rapport aux températures extérieures. Tandis que, à l'air libre, se succèdent des périodes de froid mordant et de chaleur écrasante, la roche maintient une atmosphère plus clémente. L'été, elle prodigue une fraîcheur agréable, tout en emmagasinant une partie de la chaleur atmosphérique pour la restituer l'hiver.

le tuf composé de cendres volcaniques cimentées se distingue-t-il à peine de la lave figée.

Ces épaisses strates de tuf, entre lesquelles s'intercalent des sédiments calcaires, vestiges du fond de mers depuis longtemps disparues, représentent en quelque sorte les pages d'un journal où Vulcain, le dieu du feu, aurait consigné les faits et gestes de ses disciples. Les premières pages du chapitre sur l'Anatolie centrale restent pratiquement indéchiffrables, puis viennent les écritures remontant à une dizaine de millions d'années avant notre ère, plus distinctes et détaillées. C'est à cette époque que s'accéléra le glissement de la plaque arabique vers le nord, sous la plaque iranienne. En s'enfonçant, elle commença à fondre dans les entrailles de la Terre et la pression de la roche en fusion engendra les deux grandes chaînes volcaniques de la région. De violentes éruptions ébranlèrent la région, tapissant de vastes étendues de couches successives de roches volcaniques,

qui se soudèrent en un plateau. Il semble que les dernières éruptions des monts Erciyas et Hasan datent du IVe siècle seulement. C'est donc l'activité volcanique qui, dans une certaine mesure, fournit le matériau des étonnants reliefs de Cappadoce, tandis que les phénomènes d'érosion s'en firent les architectes inspirés, révélant des strates aux nuances variées, du blanc crème au noir de jais en passant par le rose, l'ocre et le brun.

Au commencement était le versant

Tout aussi fascinantes que le déploiement de couleurs, les étranges silhouettes de pierre sculptées par l'eau, le soleil, le vent et le gel demeurent une source inépuisable d'étonnement. Les plus spectaculaires restent les cheminées de fées, dont la plupart sont couronnées d'un bloc d'ignimbrite, une roche très dure. Dès que l'érosion com-

mence à désolidariser ce chapeau de la roche plus tendre qu'il coiffe, le destin du cône de pierre est définitivement scellé. Desséchée par le soleil, la surface de la roche a beau durcir et se transformer en une véritable carapace offrant une grande résistance aux éléments, le cône de tuf est condamné à plus ou moins longue échéance.

Combien de temps s'écoule entre la formation et la disparition de ces étranges monuments ? Difficile à dire… Des siècles peut-être, ou des millénaires. Une certitude demeure, toutefois, c'est que tous naissent sur les versants de la dépression creusée par le Kizil Irmak dans les imposantes strates

Genèse volcanique

Voici quelque 3 millions d'années, l'actuelle Cappadoce fut dévastée par une violente éruption volcanique. Projetés haut dans le ciel, les nuées ardentes retombèrent en pluie de cendres, tandis que les coulées de lave en fusion se répandaient sur plus de 300 km² dans un bassin cerné de montagnes, la plupart ne cessant leur course que lorsqu'elles rencontraient un lac.

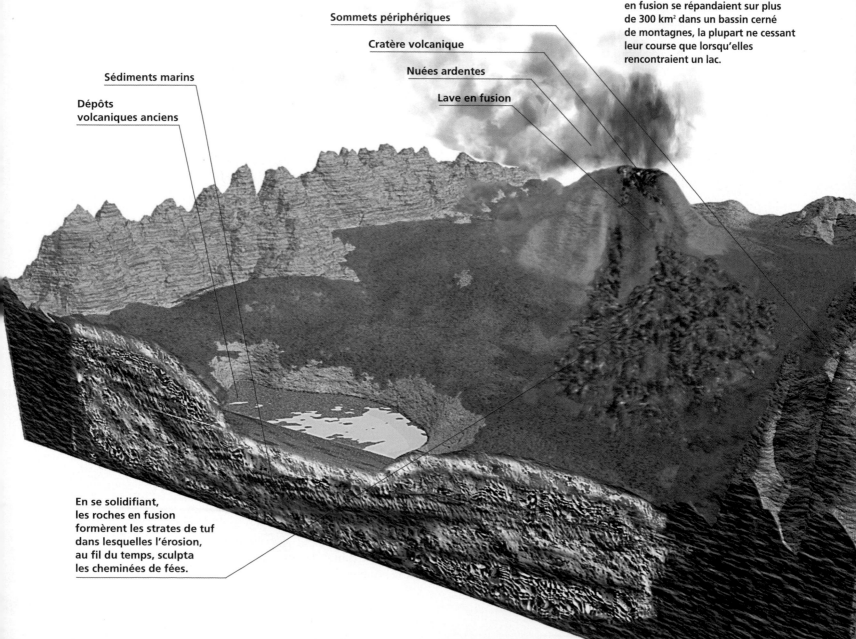

Sommets périphériques

Cratère volcanique

Nuées ardentes

Lave en fusion

Sédiments marins

Dépôts volcaniques anciens

En se solidifiant, les roches en fusion formèrent les strates de tuf dans lesquelles l'érosion, au fil du temps, sculpta les cheminées de fées.

C'est ici, au pied des versants, que l'on observe les plus anciennes cheminées de fées, certaines étant déjà « décapitées ». Les plus récentes et les plus petites, en revanche, dont quelques-unes sont encore reliées par les arêtes, se forment en haut des pentes.

Si l'érosion de l'eau contribue à la création des étranges silhouettes de pierre de Cappadoce, elle est également responsable de leur destruction. Elle sculpte d'abruptes parois rocheuses et taille les flancs à pic des pyramides et autres cheminées de fées pendant de longues années, mais, peu à peu, la roche en butte aux intempéries incessantes finit par s'user et disparaître.

Creusées dans la roche par les pluies violentes, de profondes ravines aux crêtes acérées lacèrent les versants qui délimitent le pays des cheminées de fées, au cœur du haut plateau de Cappadoce, où les effets de l'érosion sont moins spectaculaires.

rocheuses de Cappadoce. Rares mais violentes, les pluies burinent un dédale de ravines dans les versants. Dans la partie supérieure, où les précipitations sont le plus fortes, où l'écoulement est le plus rapide et, par conséquent, l'érosion le plus forte, les sillons sont plus profonds. En aval, où la vitesse d'écoulement ralentit, les rigoles se creusent moins vite. Or la quantité d'eau n'est pas moindre – au contraire, elle redouble souvent au confluent des ravines, qui tendent à s'élargir pour recevoir toute cette eau, empiétant sur la base des formations rocheuses.

Anatomie des cheminées de fées

Cette coupe d'un champignon de pierre illustre clairement le rapport entre la dureté de la pierre et l'intensité de l'érosion, et par conséquent la physionomie des formations rocheuses.

Le chapeau est en général composé de dépôts de lave en fusion, formant une roche relativement dure.

Le « cou », fait d'une roche plus tendre, tuf ou sédiments marins, offre une moindre résistance aux intempéries.

Le « pied » de tuf compact, relativement solide, se prête à l'aménagement d'habitations rupestres.

La toundra du Grand Nord canadien

L'EMPIRE DU GEL

Tout au long de l'an-
née, le gel main-
tient son emprise sur les im-
mensités du nord-ouest du Canada.
Jadis, une épaisse carapace de glace
modela ces plateaux rocheux, les buri-
nant d'impressionnantes stries (petite
photo). Aujourd'hui, à l'issue de milliards d'années d'une histoire
tourmentée, l'évolution géologique de cette région semble
définitivement figée. Pourtant, le paysage
ne cesse de se modifier : des lacs naissent
et se tarissent, tandis que d'autres se
déplacent à travers la plaine ou engen-
drent de mystérieuses buttes gelées.

L'Arctique : un univers de glaces en mouvement

Les vastes régions de l'Arctique ne sont pas aussi arides que le suggère leur nom anglais Barren Grounds (« terres nues »). Entre la mer de Beaufort, à l'ouest, et la terre de Baffin, à l'est, s'étend un immense territoire tapissé de résineux au sud et d'arbustes nains, de mousses et de lichens au nord. Parmi la végétation, la roche à nu affleure en saillies arrondies dont le vent balaie la protection neigeuse, les exposant à l'action du gel. Ici, le gel est quotidien, ou presque, même au plus fort de l'été arctique.

Durant la période glaciaire, le Canada se trouvait presque entièrement recouvert d'un bouclier de glace dont l'épaisseur atteignait 3 000 m par endroits. Dans le Grand Nord, ces énormes masses de glace, lestées de blocs de pierre arrachés au fond des glaciers, creusèrent et polirent la roche. Elles façonnèrent des bosses et des cuvettes où l'eau s'accumula lorsque les glaciers reculèrent, donnant naissance à une myriade de lacs.

C'est ainsi que la physionomie des paysages du Grand Nord est criblée de lacs, petits et grands. À environ un millier de kilomètres au sud-est du delta du Mackenzie, sur les rives du lac Acasta, affleurent les roches les plus anciennes du globe. Formées voici quelque 4 milliards d'années, ces roches issues des entrailles de la Terre furent jadis exposées à des températures atteignant 800 °C. Aujourd'hui, c'est le gel qui les tient sous sa coupe : le Grand Nord canadien est couvert de permafrost.

En Europe centrale, le sol connaît toujours des périodes de dégel l'été. Sous les latitudes arctiques du Canada, en revanche, le gel est permanent. Même pendant la saison « chaude », le sol reste gelé en profondeur et seule une mince couche se réchauffe à la surface. Or, lorsque le sol reste pris par le gel pendant au moins 2 ou 3 années de suite, il se forme ce que l'on appelle un permafrost ou pergélisol. Celui-ci peut être révélateur d'une période de climat froid, mais il existe aussi pendant les périodes plus tempérées, là où les températures annuelles moyennes restent inférieures à − 6 ou − 8 °C, comme dans le Grand Nord canadien. Plus le mercure tombe, plus la limite du permafrost est profonde – aux abords du lac Acasta, elle se situerait à environ 100 m sous terre, tandis qu'elle dépasserait par endroits 500 m sur les côtes de la mer de Beaufort et sur les îles de l'Arctique canadien.

Des buttes de terre au cœur de glace

Le permafrost recèle des zones de taille variable où le sol n'est pas constamment gelé. Celles-ci se trouvent en général sous les lacs, où l'eau, qui emmagasine la chaleur, préserve le sous-sol du gel. Dans le delta du Mackenzie, ce phénomène a engendré un curieux phénomène naturel : au fil du temps, des éminences coniques au sommet creusé d'un petit cratère ont émergé de la plaine, à un rythme de 1 à 2 m par an dans

Un vestige de la croûte terrestre originelle

Les roches qui, au fil de millions d'années, s'enfoncent sous la croûte terrestre, fondent en s'approchant des zones où les températures sont extrêmement élevées. Peu avant de se liquéfier, elles se déstructurent et les minéraux s'agrègent en paillettes et rubans, comme dans la roche métamorphique représentée ci-dessous, probablement issue du basalte. Le gneiss sombre d'Acasta, veiné de traces d'un blanc laiteux, est aussi une roche métamorphique, née voici 4 milliards d'années du granit, roche typique de la croûte terrestre continentale. Cela signifie qu'il existait déjà une croûte continentale solide, hypothèse confirmée par l'existence de minuscules cristaux de zircon dans les granits d'Australie, antérieurs de 200 millions d'années au gneiss canadien d'Acasta.

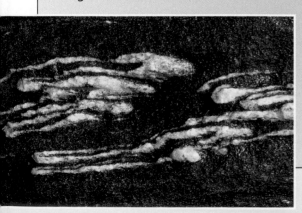

Dans le delta du Mackenzie se succèdent de petites collines de glace appelées pingos. Les schémas ci-contre illustrent les principales étapes de leur formation. Les indications de temps se rapportent à l'évolution d'un seul pingo.

Pingo au cœur de glace

L'eau est entièrement gelée (noyau de glace). Il n'est pas rare qu'une petite dépression se creuse au sommet par un phénomène de dilatation. C'est par ce cratère que le cœur de glace finira tôt ou tard par se réchauffer et fondre.

À l'origine s'étend un lac profond dont seule la surface est exposée au gel. Sous le lac, le permafrost présente une rupture, les eaux souterraines échappant à l'action du gel.

Strate retenant l'eau

À mesure que les sédiments s'accumulent au fond du lac, le gel s'infiltre par les côtés, emprisonnant la nappe phréatique comme dans une bulle. Sous la pression, l'eau remonte, voûtant la surface, et gèle par le haut.

« Bulle d'eau » souterraine

Il y a 8000 ans

Il y a environ 7200 ans

Aujourd'hui

Où naissent les pingos ?

Ces gigantesques buttes de glace se forment uniquement dans les régions de permafrost, et plus précisément dans les couches de sable et d'argile – elles demeurent rares dans les roches dures. Autre condition essentielle à leur formation : le permafrost doit inclure des talikis – des « bulles » d'eau qui ne gèlent pas.

Comme au premier jour

Au cœur de l'Anatolie, le temps semble s'être arrêté autour du Meketuzlasi, un volcan qui entra en éruption voici plus de 8000 ans. Depuis, au milieu du cratère parfaitement circulaire, le cône de cendres de 50 m de haut est resté intact. Comment est-ce possible ? La réponse est simple : les rares précipitations se sont infiltrées dans les cendres poreuses au lieu de s'écouler à la surface et de raviner le cône aux lignes parfaites.

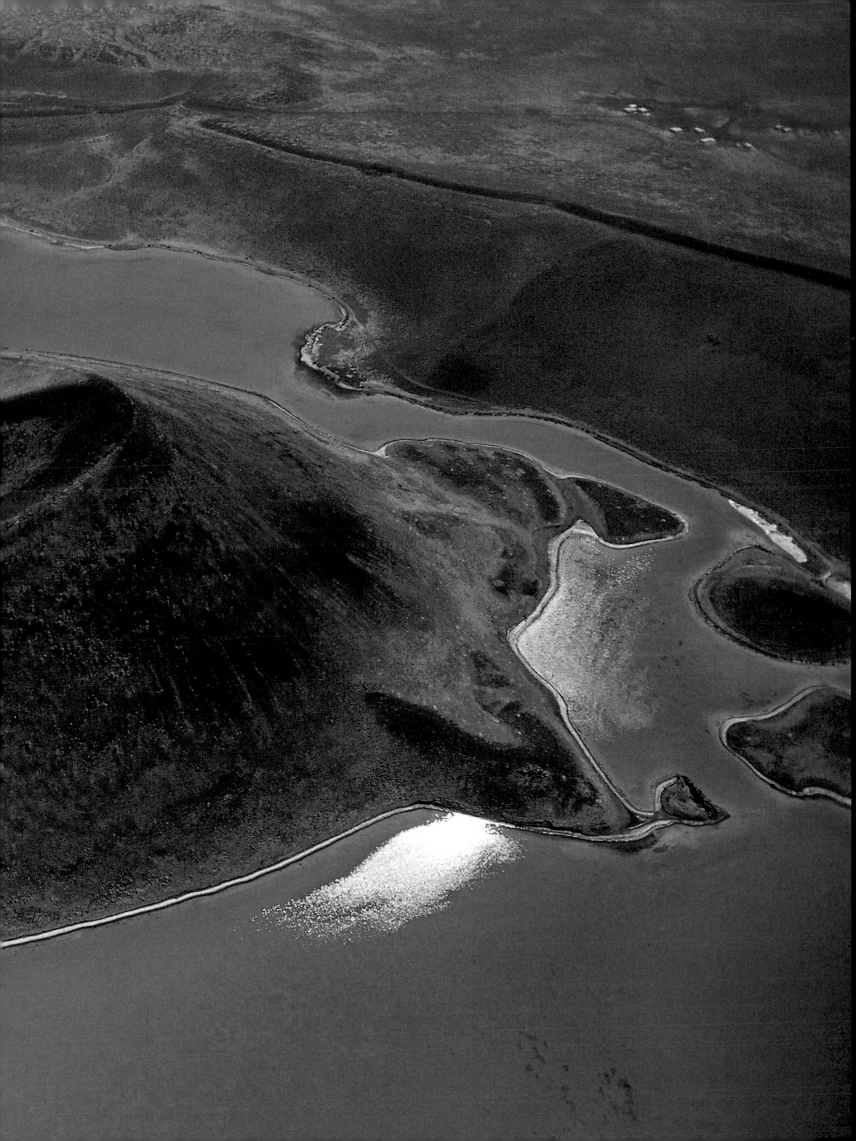

Le chaudron de la sorcière

Dans les eaux boueuses, le gaz forme des bulles grises qui enflent, puis éclatent. La caldeira de l'Uzon, un volcan éteint dans la péninsule du Kamtchatka, à l'extrémité orientale de la Russie, évoque la marmite d'une sorcière. Il est alimenté par une chambre magmatique qui, à 5 km sous terre, maintient en permanence les eaux souterraines en ébullition.

Devil's Tower

UNE LÉGENDE DE PIERRE

Selon une légende indienne dont les origines remontent à la nuit des temps, l'étrange rocher grisâtre qui se dresse au milieu des paysages vallonnés du Wyoming, en Amérique du Nord, aurait mystérieusement jailli du sol. Comme toutes les légendes, celle-ci recèle sa part de vérité. Au microscope, Devil's Tower (« la tour du Diable ») – ainsi fut-elle baptisée par les pionniers – livre enfin tous les secrets de sa formation, comme le montre la coupe ci-contre.

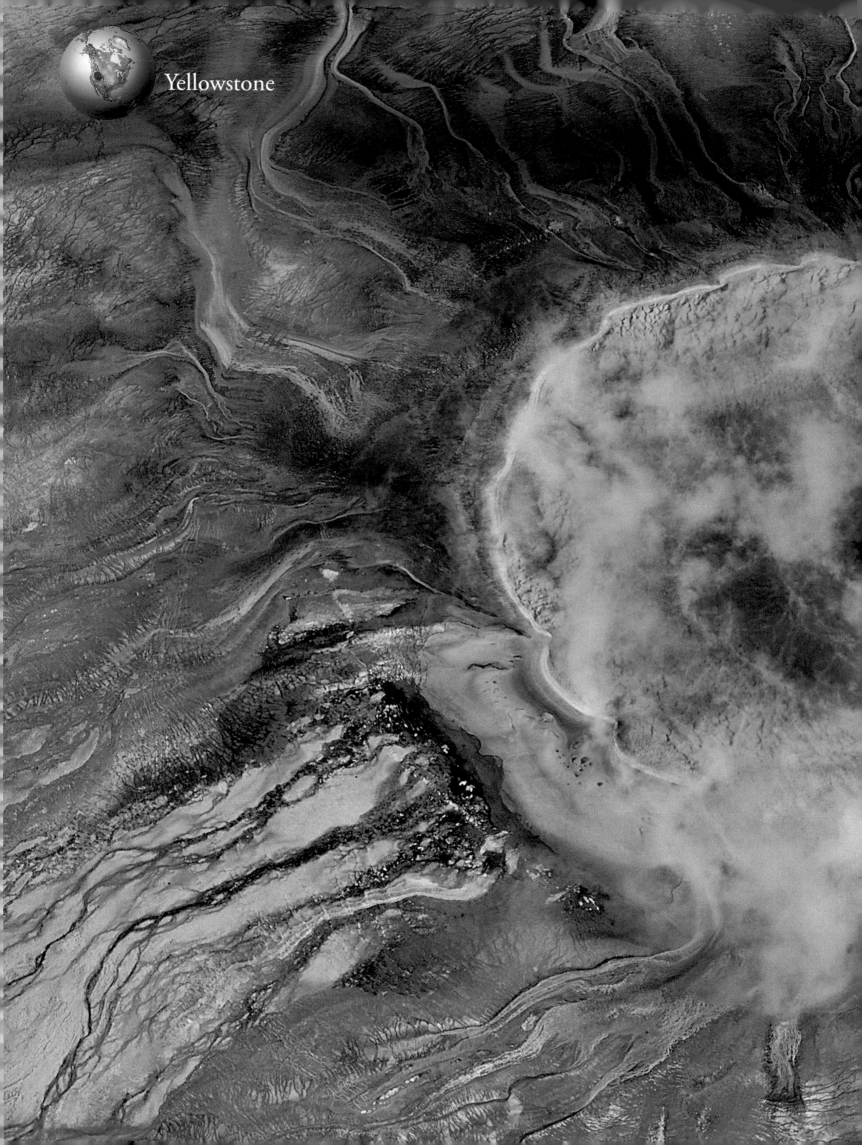

Yellowstone

LE GÉANT TRAVESTI

Le sol du parc de Yellowstone fume et bouillonne de toutes parts. Cet extraordinaire plateau des montagnes Rocheuses, en Amérique du Nord, a quelque chose de magique. Les geysers soufflent eau et vapeur à intervalles réguliers, tandis que les bassins alimentés par les sources chaudes, comme le Grand Prismatic Spring, scintillent de toutes les couleurs de l'arc-en-ciel. Mais, si bucoliques soient-ils, ces paysages d'eau et de vapeur trahissent une effervescence qui pourrait préluder à une gigantesque catastrophe.

La vie en couleur

Les sources chaudes de Yellowstone évoquent autant de pierres semi-précieuses aux nuances variées. Autour du cœur du bassin, en général d'un bleu d'azur, comme celui du Morning Glory, ci-dessous, se dessinent des cercles vert émeraude, jaune clair, orange et ocre. À chaque couleur correspond l'habitat de certains organismes vivants.

Au centre, au contact de l'eau bouillante, vivent de minuscules bactéries qui permettent à l'eau de refléter la couleur du ciel. Les quelques algues jaunâtres qui prolifèrent entre 70 et 80 °C donnent aux eaux peu profondes une couleur jaune, qui vire au vert à mesure que la profondeur augmente. D'autres organismes apparaissent entre 50 et 60 °C, notamment des algues ocre et des bactéries rouge orangé qui forment un épais tapis au fond du bassin.

Le fait qu'une plaque continentale dérive au-dessus du point chaud, lui-même statique, ne peut que décupler sa puissance. En effet, la plaque se compose en majeure partie de roches riches en silice, qui, au contact de la chaleur, donnent une matière en fusion très liquide susceptible de provoquer des éruptions dévastatrices.

Fidèle à la formule « point chaud + plaque continentale = caldeira », le plateau de Yellowstone a vu se former trois caldeiras en quelques millions d'années : l'une voici 2 millions d'années, l'autre environ 700 000 ans plus tard, suivi d'une dernière voici quelque 600 000 ans. Les éruptions les plus récentes ont creusé une cuvette d'environ 70 km de long sur 50 km de large et déposé à la surface plus de 1 000 km³ de roche volcanique, soit au moins dix fois plus que le Tambora indonésien en 1815.

En observant la chronologie des éruptions, il apparaît qu'elles sont survenues à des intervalles de 600 000 à 700 000 ans. Si la caldeira de Yellowstone respecte ce rythme, une nouvelle éruption serait imminente – à l'échelle géologique. Les nombreux séismes qui ébranlent la région ne font qu'étayer cette hypothèse : le compte à rebours d'une bombe à retardement serait bel et bien enclenché sous ce petit coin de paradis. Ils prouvent que les entrailles de la Terre sont soumises à de violents tiraillements. Les conséquences d'une éruption à Yellowstone seraient catastrophiques bien au-delà des frontières de la région et de l'Amérique du Nord, puisque les nuages de cendres qui se répandraient dans l'atmosphère provoqueraient des bouleversements climatiques dramatiques.

Le dernier souffle du volcan

Les volcans meurent extrêmement lentement. À l'éruption dévastatrice qui eut lieu voici 600 000 ans succédèrent d'innombrables petites éruptions jusqu'à 60 000 à 70 000 ans avant notre ère. Il fallut ensuite attendre plusieurs millénaires encore avant que la température du sol baisse. Durant cette phase de refroidissement, le volcan est à l'origine de divers phénomènes plus ou moins spectaculaires – sources chaudes, boues et geysers. Plus d'une dizaine de milliers de ces manifestations post-volcaniques peuvent être observées sur le plateau de Yellowstone, dont les plus impressionnantes restent les geysers, des jets d'eau chaude et de vapeur uniques au monde. Parmi les quelque 500 geysers de Yellowstone, deux se détachent du lot : l'Old Faithful, qui entre en action à intervalles réguliers – actuellement toutes les 90 minutes environ – et le Steamboat (« bateau à vapeur »), ainsi baptisé à cause du vacarme qu'il produit, qui se distingue par l'incroyable hauteur de son panache (plus de 115 m).

Indépendamment de la périodicité des jets, la plupart des geysers alternent phases de repos et d'activité plus ou moins longues. Durant les phases de repos, une eau relativement fraîche sourd des couches superficielles et s'infiltre dans les profondeurs, où elle s'accumule dans des cavités et forme une colonne fermée qui se réchauffe au contact de la roche. Comme la température

d'ébullition augmente avec la pression et que la pression est supérieure au pied des colonnes d'eau, l'eau bout non pas à 100 °C, mais à 20 ou à 30 °C de plus. Lorsque la température de l'eau atteint un seuil précis qui varie en fonction de la pression, l'eau surchauffée se transforme subitement en vapeur et pousse la colonne vers le haut. C'est pourquoi les geysers crachent toujours de l'eau dans un premier temps avant que jaillisse la vapeur, moteur du phénomène.

Un apport thermique permanent

Pour que jaillisse un geyser, il faut un réseau souterrain de cavités reliées entre elles par des crevasses. Le sous-sol du bassin supérieur, mais aussi des autres bassins de Yellowstone, recèle justement ce type de système. Décomposée par l'eau chaude en argile, la rhyolite permet à l'eau de s'accumuler au fond du bassin et les cavités se remplissent rapidement. Autre condition sine qua non à la formation d'un geyser : l'apport de chaleur. La quantité de chaleur fournie par les entrailles de la Terre à Yellowstone représente au moins la moitié des flux de chaleur dont bénéficierait une île volcanique dix fois plus vaste, par exemple. Ainsi les geysers de Yellowstone disposent-ils d'une source d'énergie inépuisable.

Aujourd'hui, c'est en général la foudre qui est responsable des feux de forêt sur le plateau de Yellowstone, jadis dévasté par les éruptions volcaniques, comme en témoignent plus d'une vingtaine de couches de cendres superposées, vestiges d'autant de forêts carbonisées.

Des chutes grandioses, comme les Lower Falls, dévalent des falaises de roche volcanique.

L'ŒUVRE DU DRAGON

Criblés d'innombrables grottes et envahis d'une végétation tropicale vierge, des milliers d'îlots rocheux s'élancent des eaux paisibles de la vaste baie, telles les tours d'une cité engloutie. L'univers fabuleux de cette étrange forêt enchantée n'en est pas moins exposé aux assauts des intempéries et des pholades (petite photo).

LABOURÉ PAR LES VENTS

Gobi – le pays sans eau –, c'est ainsi que les habitants de Mongolie appellent cet immense territoire d'Asie centrale couvert de steppes et de déserts. Les Chinois, pour leur part, l'ont baptisé Sha-mo (désert de sable) à cause des gigantesques dunes mouvantes que doivent affronter les caravanes de chameaux (petite photo). Par endroits, dans ce dédale de dunes, se dressent soudain de longues crêtes rocheuses…

Les sillons
d'une charrue géante

Ces crêtes rocheuses burinent le plateau d'Alashan (désert de Badain Jaran), en Chine. Les Ouigours d'Asie centrale les ont baptisées yardangs : « monts abrupts » ou îles. Si certaines ne dépassent pas quelques dizaines de centimètres de haut, d'autres atteignent la hauteur d'un immeuble. Elles sont en moyenne quatre fois plus longues que larges et la plupart se distinguent par une silhouette fuselée. Si certaines évoquent le dos d'une baleine ou un mur au sommet arrondi, d'autres présentent un profil en dents de scie. Le plus frappant, c'est que l'axe longitudinal des crêtes et des

sillons qui les séparent reste en général parallèle sur plusieurs kilomètres, comme s'ils avaient été tracés au cordeau.

Ce type de relief, qui reste rare, apparaît en présence de strates rocheuses quasi verticales, ne présentant pas toutes la même dureté. Peu à peu, les roches les plus résistantes émergent, formant des crêtes, à mesure que les plus tendres disparaissent, usées par l'érosion. Or les yardangs aux silhouettes étranges du plateau d'Alashan et d'autres paysages désertiques de Gobi sont, pour la plupart, constitués de couches sédimentaires horizontales, de l'argile aux éboulis, déposées par les lacs et les cours d'eau. Les eaux qui déposèrent les sédiments auraient-elles aussi pu les creuser ?

La formation d'un yardang commence souvent par une grosse crevasse dans les sédiments asséchés déposés par un fleuve ou un lac.

Grâce à ses lignes fuselées, le yardang reste en grande partie épargné par l'érosion.

L'érosion éolienne agit uniquement au-dessus de la surface de la nappe phréatique. S'ils sont aujourd'hui envahis par les eaux, les couloirs où s'engouffrait le vent se sont formés durant les périodes sèches.

d'herbes t
et 1960, se
sont aujou
migrer. Le
trouvaient
pour nou
meaux dar
aujourd'h
climat.
    Pour l'h
cation » o
inexorable
catégoriqu
    Pourtant,
disparaisse
alimentés
survivre à
surtout qu
et que les
comme ce
années. D
de la neig
blanche »,

La dis
sence
arbore
cours
Qu
les yar
le lon
enfin
la pre
se cor
l'un c
Proje
les gr
caden
crêtes
de mè
porté
dizair
de cet
tante
des ya

Vent j

Les « d
billons
les ani
dessus
de fines
en altitu
parfois
ces col
kosa er
Pacifiqu
sieurs m
du Nor
sur les p
sière vo
tives, s'
au fil de
au mon
Gobi so
poussiè

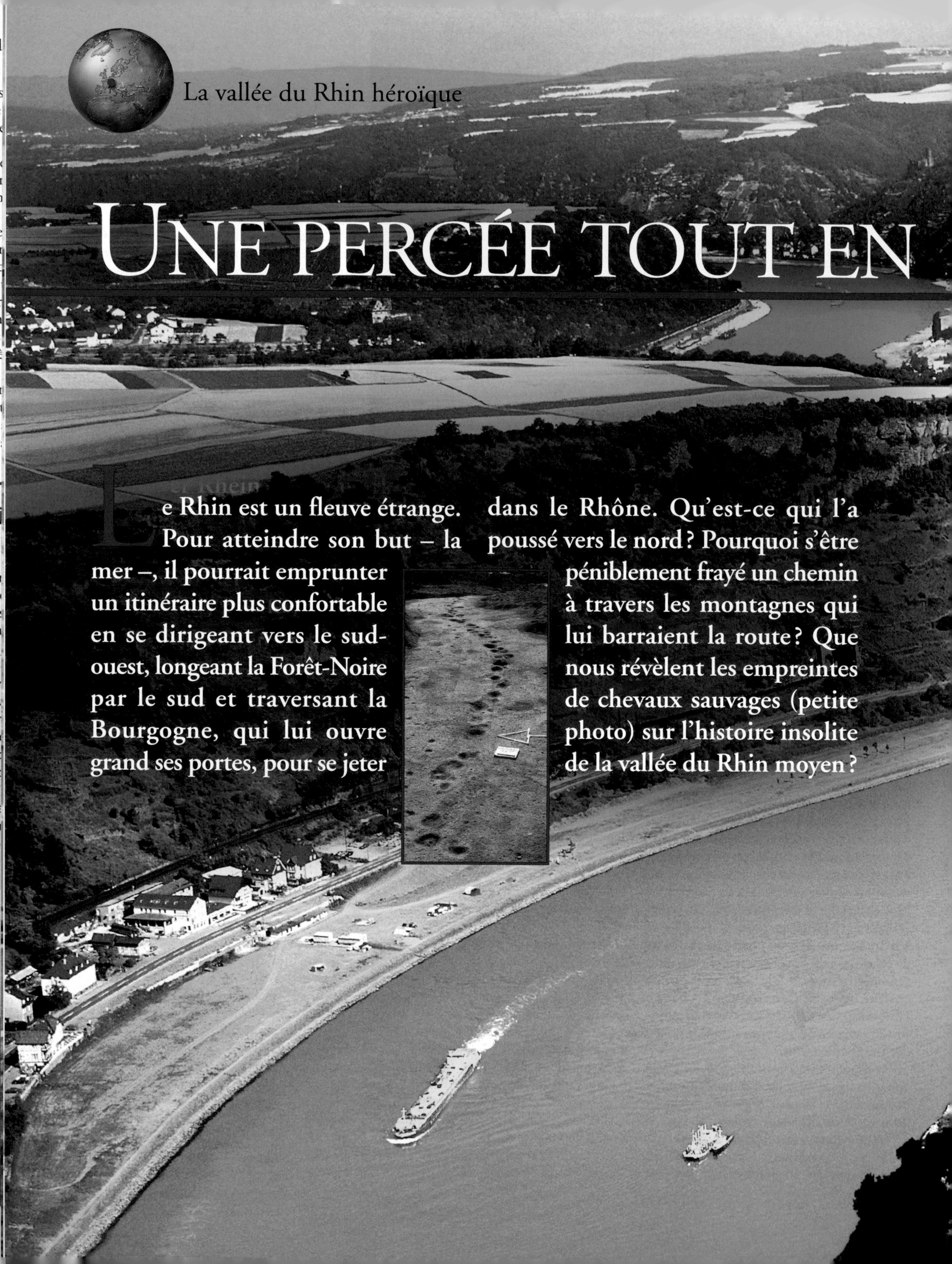

La vallée du Rhin héroïque

UNE PERCÉE TOUT EN

Le Rhin est un fleuve étrange. Pour atteindre son but – la mer –, il pourrait emprunter un itinéraire plus confortable en se dirigeant vers le sud-ouest, longeant la Forêt-Noire par le sud et traversant la Bourgogne, qui lui ouvre grand ses portes, pour se jeter dans le Rhône. Qu'est-ce qui l'a poussé vers le nord ? Pourquoi s'être péniblement frayé un chemin à travers les montagnes qui lui barraient la route ? Que nous révèlent les empreintes de chevaux sauvages (petite photo) sur l'histoire insolite de la vallée du Rhin moyen ?

MÉANDRES

Les processus de dissolution sont sensiblement plus lents dans le Karst « nu », dépourvu de toute végétation, ou presque – ici le parc national de Paklenica, en Croatie – que dans le Karst « couvert », revêtu d'un tapis de végétation.

Les montagnes karstiques abritent çà et là de vastes dépressions occupées par des plaines aux sols gras et argileux. Ces poljés (« plaines »), vastes dépressions fermées et fertiles, sont les seules régions du Karst se prêtant à l'agriculture.

souterraine ? La preuve en incombe à des spéléologues d'un genre particulier : des anguilles marquées qui, livrées aux eaux de la Reka à Skocjan, ressurgissent à Timavo au bout de quelques jours.

La réaction chimique qui provoque la dissolution du calcaire peut intervenir à rebours : lorsque la quantité de calcaire présente dans l'eau dépasse un plafond qui dépend de sa teneur en acide carbonique, le calcaire dissous se dépose à nouveau – à la grande joie des visiteurs des grottes, qui peuvent ainsi admirer de superbes stalactites, et

au grand dam des riverains, dont les cafetières et les machines à laver sont mises à rude épreuve par une eau dure et calcaire.

La nature bâtit ses barrages

Dans les grottes, les stalactites se développent en général très lentement – la plupart ne gagnent pas plus de 1 micromètre par an. Sur le sol, en revanche, le calcaire se dépose beaucoup plus rapidement sous forme de concrétions. Actuellement, les barrages de calcaire qui retiennent les eaux des lacs de Plitvice s'élèvent de 10 à 30 mm par an. Le plus ancien, et par conséquent le plus haut, atteint aujourd'hui une cinquantaine de mètres de haut. Si l'on compte une croissance de 20 mm par an en moyenne, ce barrage aurait 2 500 ans – un temps record à l'échelle géologique ! Sur le cours de la Korana, en Croatie, une vingtaine de lacs de toutes tailles s'étagent ainsi sur quelque 7 km, séparés par des barrières de concrétions calcaires. L'eau franchit ces barrages en cascades que l'on pourrait qualifier de « constructives », puisqu'au lieu de les user par érosion au fil du temps elles poursuivent leur édification d'année en année, en y déposant du calcaire.

Tout près des barrages que l'eau calcaire bâtit ainsi à une vitesse étonnante, d'étranges stries et cannelures burinent les versants rocheux de la vallée de la Korana. À certains endroits, ces sillons sont très rapprochés et presque parallèles. Souvent dotés

d'une arête acérée – on les appelle alors des lapiaz –, ils sont sculptés par les eaux de fonte et les pluies acides qui s'écoulent sur la roche à nu.

Les lapiaz sont caractéristiques des paysages karstiques. En dépit de leur aspect récent, ils ne se creusent que très lentement dans la roche et restent des phénomènes de corrosion négligeables. En 1 000 ans, l'eau entame la surface des versants calcaires de 1 à 2 cm seulement. Comparée à l'érosion souterraine, l'érosion superficielle des paysages karstiques arides reste négligeable. Le Karst se creuse bien plus de l'intérieur.

Les dolines trahissent les vides du sous-sol

On dénombre dans le seul Karst slovène plus de 3 500 grottes, dont certaines recèlent de véritables palais de stalactites, comme à Postojna. Les eaux qui s'engouffrent dans les grottes continent presque toujours nettement plus de calcaire dissous que celles qui, à l'air libre, strient les surfaces rocheuses d'étranges lapiaz. Si la teneur en calcaire est supérieure sous terre, c'est en partie parce que l'air du sous-sol contient sensiblement plus de gaz carbonique que l'air atmosphérique du fait des processus de décomposition. En outre, l'eau chargée d'acide s'infiltre très lentement dans le sol, restant ainsi plus longtemps en contact avec la roche soluble.

L'action de l'érosion interne reste en grande partie cachée. Ce n'est que lorsque le toit d'une cavité souterraine s'effondre, formant, en surface, une doline, un puits ou un entonnoir, que l'on se rend compte de l'ampleur des processus qui se jouent sous terre. En surface, rares sont les reliefs marquants sculptés par des processus de corrosion, car ils sont cantonnés aux strates dures et imperméables qui affleurent au fond des vallées des régions karstiques ou en périphérie. Incapable de s'infiltrer sous terre, l'eau acide se disperse et attaque les roches solubles sur les côtés ou au pied des versants. Au fil du temps, à mesure que les flancs reculent, apparaît un poljés, une dépression en général fermée où s'accumulent les matériaux fertiles trans-

UN ROCHER

DANS LE DÉSERT

Ayers Rock, Uluru pour les Aborigènes, se dresse en ermite au milieu d'une immense plaine. Contrairement à la plupart des sommets sur terre, qui s'intègrent à un massif ou s'inscrivent dans un relief montagneux, le colosse rouge fait cavalier seul. Uluru semble être planté là pour l'éternité. Et pourtant, lui aussi disparaîtra un jour, victime de l'érosion par le vent et la pluie qui, sans relâche, le taraudent à la base (petite photo).

L'EMPIRE DES GÉANTS

Au pays des fjords, tout semble plus grand. C'est en Norvège que s'étend le plus vaste plateau d'Europe, tapissé de lichens et d'arbustes nains (petite photo). C'est là que les plus grands glaciers du continent encapuchonnent les sommets, et que les fjords les plus longs et les plus profonds entaillent la côte – ici, Eidfjord. Tout un univers de superlatifs, façonné à la mesure des géants.

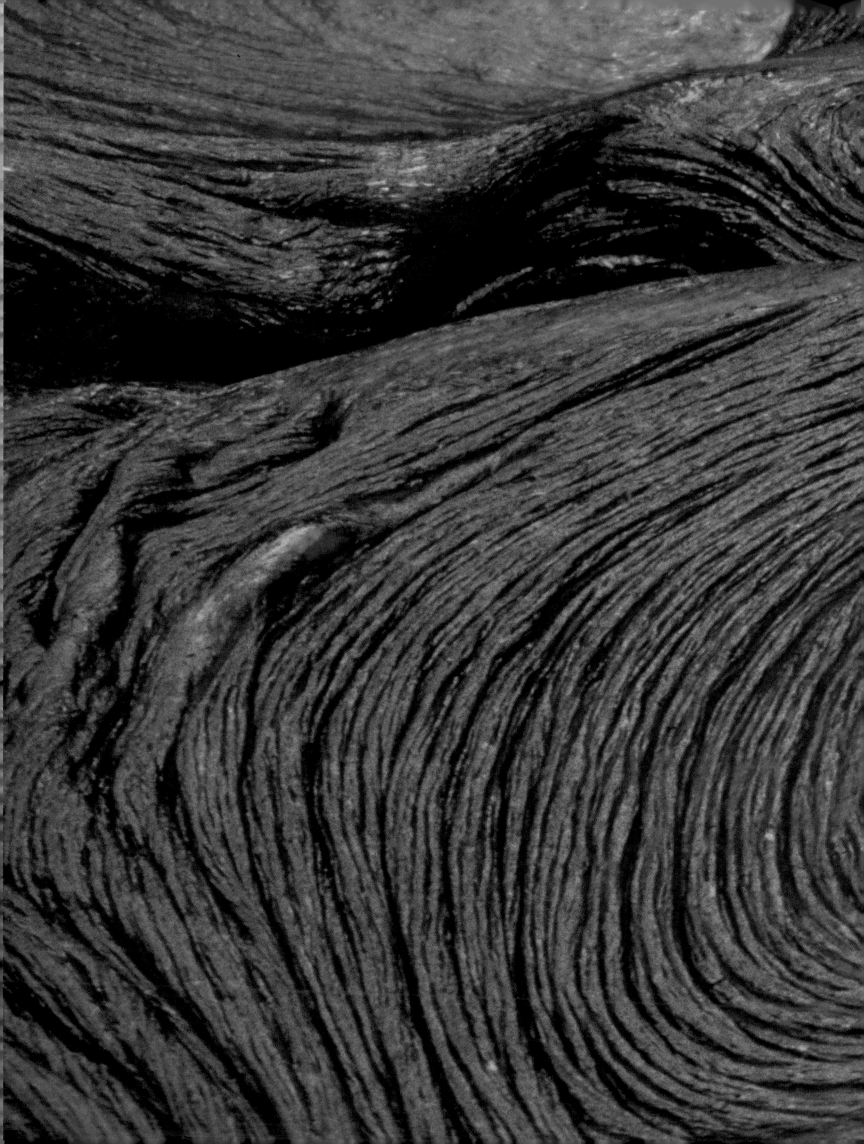

UNE TERRE SANS REPOS

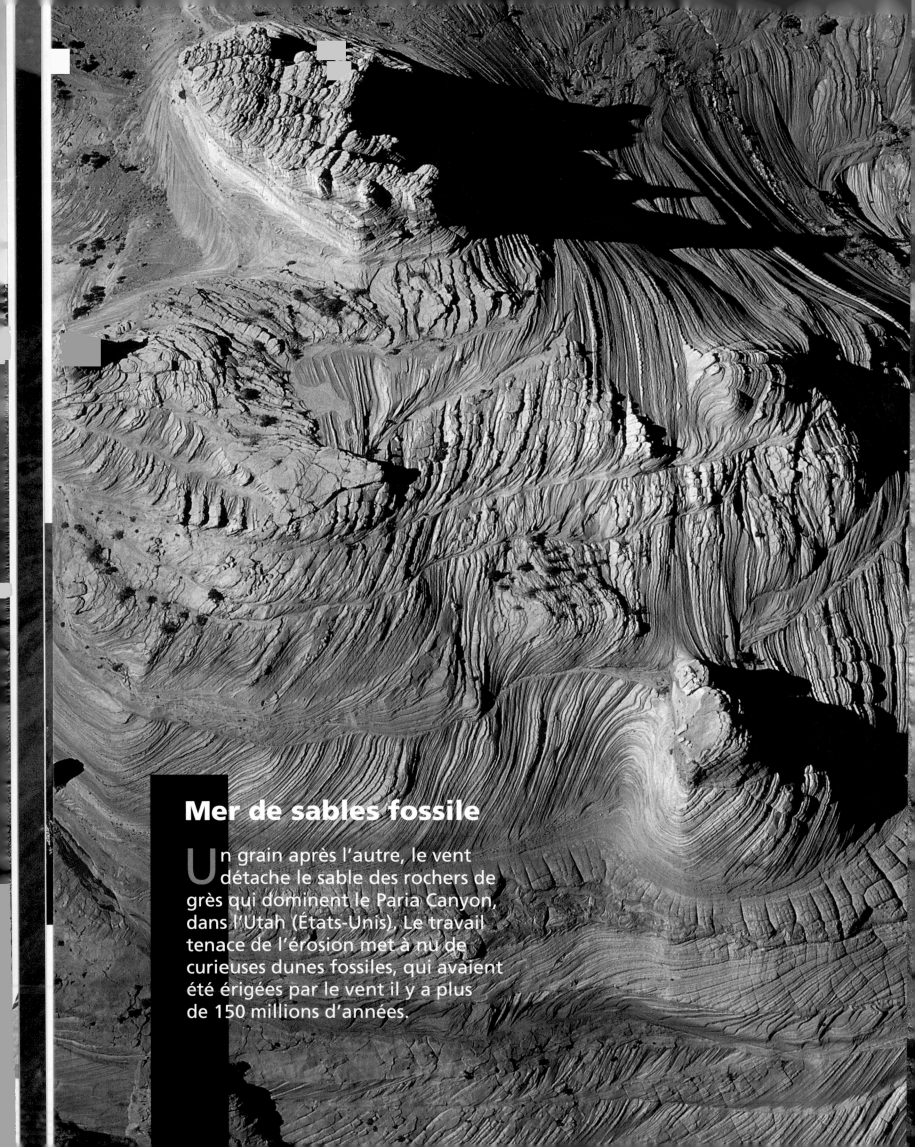

Mer de sables fossile

Un grain après l'autre, le vent détache le sable des rochers de grès qui dominent le Paria Canyon, dans l'Utah (États-Unis). Le travail tenace de l'érosion met à nu de curieuses dunes fossiles, qui avaient été érigées par le vent il y a plus de 150 millions d'années.

Une croûte terrestre
« sous tension »

D'un tracé rectiligne, la faille de San Andreas traverse une région semi-désertique de Californie. Cette profonde entaille ne cesse de se rouvrir sous l'effet des pressions énormes auxquelles elle est soumise. Depuis des millions d'années, le frottement à la limite des plaques pacifique et nord-américaine déplace des montagnes entières.

UN CONTINENT POURSUIT SA CROISSANCE

La plupart des volcans situés sur les régions côtières du Canada et de l'Alaska sont désormais éteints. Leurs curieuses silhouettes de lave – comme celle du Black Tusk (photo) – disparaissent le plus souvent sous une couche de neige et de glace. Mais le volcan Redoubt (petite photo) et ses cousins en activité continuent à offrir de temps à autre un spectacle impressionnant. Ils nous rappellent que l'Amérique du Nord n'a pas encore fini de grandir.

Volcans et microcontinents

Prairies et toundras, lacs et glaciers, hauts sommets enneigés des Rocheuses : telles sont les images qu'évoque généralement le Canada. Mais cet immense pays compte également deux douzaines de volcans et chaînes volcaniques – plus que tout autre État au monde, y compris par exemple l'Italie, le « classique » pays des volcans. Le volcan Mountain, dans le Grand Nord, et le mont Garibaldi, dans le Sud, appartiennent tous deux à la Coast Range, une chaîne de montagnes parallèle à la côte du Pacifique. Durant les deux à trois derniers millions d'années, elle comprenait au moins 100 volcans en activité. Les dernières éruptions du Lava Fork, sans doute le plus jeune volcan du Canada, ne datent que de 150 ans environ.

Les volcans du sud de la Colombie-Britannique sont considérés comme les plus dangereux. Ils ont tendance à avoir des éruptions explosives, comparables à celle – catastrophique – qui ravagea l'île de la Martinique en 1902. Situé dans la région volcanique du mont Garibaldi, le Black Tusk rappelle l'aiguille de lave d'une très grande viscosité qui fut expulsée cette

année-là par la cheminée de la montagne Pelée à la suite d'une explosion dévastatrice. Mais le Black Tusk – « croc noir » – ne présente plus aucun danger : il est éteint depuis quelque 170 000 ans. Énorme bouchon solidifié, l'aiguille de lave – ultime vestige d'un volcan jadis gigantesque – est restée logée à l'intérieur de la cheminée principale.

Des bombes à retardement enfouies sous la glace

Stratovolcans, volcans boucliers ou cônes de scories, la quasi-totalité des volcans est représentée dans l'ouest du Canada. Les *tuyas*, qui ont une histoire très mouvementée, n'ont pas du tout l'aspect d'un volcan. Dans l'extrême nord de la Colombie-Britannique, le Tuya Butte par exemple, bien que constitué de roches volcaniques, ressemble à un plateau de grès ou de calcaire. Formée de structures de lave en coussins, sa base est surmontée de couches de lave solidifiées et disloquées, puis de laves compactes sur le sommet. On pensait jadis que les *tuyas* étaient les vestiges d'un plateau de laves et de cendres ayant été soumis à l'érosion. Mais cette superposition de couches de lave indique qu'une éruption volcanique s'est produite sous la glace. Sous la masse glaciaire, un

Des maisons bâties sur de l'argile sensible

Un vrai cauchemar pour tout propriétaire : la roche sur laquelle reposent les fondations de sa maison devient soudain une sorte de bouillie et l'édifice s'enfonce dans le sol. L'argile sensible, un sédiment qui date de l'ère glaciaire, est l'une de ces roches sournoises. Lors du séisme qui secoua l'Alaska en 1964, plus de 70 maisons en furent victimes. Ces sédiments argileux ont une structure instable : les particules d'argile sont disposées à la manière d'un château de cartes, avec des interstices gorgés d'eau. Après l'effondrement de cette structure sous l'effet des secousses telluriques, l'expulsion de l'eau transforme l'argile en une masse pâteuse.

La croissance d'un continent

Les bords des plaques pacifique et américaine se superposent en partie. À diverses reprises durant l'histoire de la Terre, des fragments de croûte terrestre à la dérive, solidaires de la plaque pacifique, se sont soudés au continent nord-américain.

Le fragment d'un autre continent et un volcan surgi au-dessus d'un point chaud de la croûte océanique dérivent tous deux en direction de la plaque américaine.

Une partie du microcontinent (terrane) se rattache aux reliefs côtiers.

Les terranes, désormais soudés, donnent naissance aux massifs côtiers du Pacifique.

La croûte nord-américaine constitue le soubassement géologique du massif.

La plaque pacifique s'enfonce sous la plaque américaine.

lac d'eaux de fonte commence par se former à l'intérieur du cratère. Au fond de ce lac, la lave rejetée par le volcan se solidifie, engendrant ces structures en forme de coussins, typiques d'une éruption subaquatique. Plus le sommet du volcan émerge de la surface du lac et moins les masses d'eau pèsent sur les flots de lave, qui sont alors disloqués par les explosions successives. Dès que le sommet dépasse le niveau de l'eau, l'éruption reprend son cours « normal ». La lave s'écoule paisiblement sur la terre ferme, où elle se solidifie en couches épaisses.

La Coast Range, qui comprend des dizaines de volcans, se prolonge vers le nord-ouest sur les îles et les massifs côtiers de l'Alaska. Ses volcans les plus célèbres sont le Katmai, qui a connu une gigantesque éruption en juin 1912, le Great Sitkin – sur les îles Aléoutiennes –, un volcan encore très actif, et le Wrangell, dont la caldeira contient un volume de neige et de glace supérieur à celui de tout autre volcan. Cette association entre phénomènes volcaniques et glaciaires le rend particulièrement dangereux.

Un puzzle géologique énigmatique

Malgré la présence de ces nombreux volcans, les massifs côtiers de Colombie-Britannique et d'Alaska ne sont pas des reliefs volcaniques typiques. Les roches volcaniques dont l'origine peut être attribuée avec certitude à des centres éruptifs récents dans l'histoire de la Terre n'y sont que faiblement représentées. En revanche, on y trouve d'innombrables autres sortes de roches : granits, calcaires, schistes, etc. Ces massifs forment une mosaïque multicolore, dont l'alignement parallèle à la côte semble constituer la seule structure commune. Leurs roches datent de toutes les périodes. Des massifs âgés de plus de 500 millions d'années voisinent avec des strates géologiques datant de « seulement » 50 millions d'années.

Les théories habituelles sur la formation des reliefs ne donnent pas la clé de cette énigme. Elles considèrent le plus souvent qu'un massif s'est érigé en majeure partie à l'endroit même où il se trouve et qu'il n'a été déplacé que sur de courtes distances. Or ces massifs de la côte pacifique d'Amérique du Nord ont quelque chose de très insolite dans leur environnement géologique actuel. Ils évoquent plutôt des débris d'arcs insulaires, des sommets sous-marins ou encore des fragments de croûtes océanique ou continentale. Beaucoup d'entre eux semblent avoir parcouru un très long chemin.

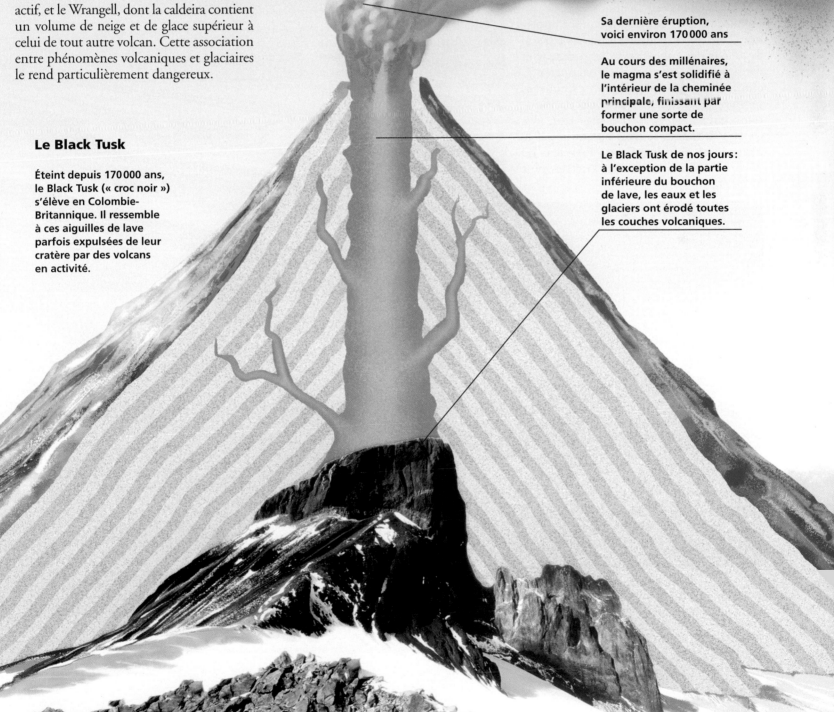

Le Black Tusk

Éteint depuis 170 000 ans, le Black Tusk (« croc noir ») s'élève en Colombie-Britannique. Il ressemble à ces aiguilles de lave parfois expulsées de leur cratère par des volcans en activité.

Sa dernière éruption, voici environ 170 000 ans

Au cours des millénaires, le magma s'est solidifié à l'intérieur de la cheminée principale, finissant par former une sorte de bouchon compact.

Le Black Tusk de nos jours : à l'exception de la partie inférieure du bouchon de lave, les eaux et les glaciers ont érodé toutes les couches volcaniques.

Au terme d'un long voyage

À l'heure actuelle, on suppose que les reliefs côtiers sont formés d'une mosaïque de microplaques soudées entre elles, les « terranes ». Il y a 200 millions d'années, d'importants fragments de la Colombie-Britannique et de l'Alaska se trouvaient encore à 1 500 ou 2 000 km plus au sud. Au cours des 100 derniers millions d'années, ces fragments de croûte ont dérivé à la rencontre du continent nord-américain. Certains plongèrent sous l'Amérique du Nord, tandis que d'autres, formés de roches plus légères, se soudèrent à la marge continentale. Une bande côtière de 600 à 700 km de large s'est ainsi formée peu à peu à l'emplacement actuel de la Colombie-Britannique. Chaque million d'années, elle gagnait quelques kilomètres vers le sud-ouest de l'océan Pacifique.

Aujourd'hui, ces microplaques continuent à dériver. Poussées à travers le Pacifique par des courants du manteau, elles finissent tôt ou tard par rencontrer le continent nord-américain. Les fréquents séismes qui secouent la côte du Pacifique témoignent de ce processus. L'un des centres sismiques se trouve dans la partie centrale et méridionale de l'Alaska. Le 27 mars 1964 s'y produisit l'un des plus

Le Denali (mont McKinley), le plus haut sommet d'Amérique du Nord, culmine à 6 194 m sur un socle instable. Sous ses pieds, la croûte terrestre se déplace de 1 à 2 cm par an.

Fougères, mousses
et autres végétaux
peuplent les épais sous-
bois de la forêt pluviale
dans les régions côtières
du Pacifique, qui
bénéficient d'un climat
extrêmement doux et
humide (ci-dessus).

Le geai de Steller
(à droite) possède une
queue et des plumes
d'un bleu lumineux, qui
répond au vert intense
des forêts pluviales du
littoral pacifique.

violents tremblements de terre de l'Histoire, qui fut accompagné d'importants déplacements de plaques.

Une ère glaciaire contemporaine

Un autre facteur continue tout autant à façonner la physionomie de la région : la circulation des masses d'air chaudes et humides de l'océan Pacifique qui rencontrent les hauts reliefs de l'arrière-pays côtier. En s'élevant le long des flancs montagneux, les masses d'air se refroidissent et la vapeur d'eau se transforme en nuages, lesquels déversent d'abondantes précipitations – une moyenne de 3 000 à 4 000 l/m² par an dans la Coast Range. En altitude, la majeure partie de ces précipitations tombe sous forme de neige. Cette portion de la côte pacifique d'Amérique du Nord est l'une des

Le glacier Malaspina s'étend
sur plus de 20 km, des massifs
montagneux à la plaine
côtière de l'Alaska. Il forme
des moraines élevées en
écrasant les débris rocheux.

régions du globe qui reçoit les plus importantes chutes de neige. Le record absolu est détenu par le mont Baker, où sont déjà tombés en l'espace d'une année près de 30 m de neige. Il se dresse dans l'État de Washington, légèrement au sud de la frontière qui sépare le Canada et les États-Unis d'Amérique.

À l'instar de nombreux sommets situés au nord-ouest du Pacifique, le mont Baker n'est surmonté que d'une petite calotte glaciaire. Mais plus l'on approche du cercle polaire et plus les glaciers sont étendus. Dans les seules chaînes montagneuses et très humides de la côte pacifique du Canada, ils couvrent une surface de plus de 37 000 km². L'ère glaciaire y est toujours d'actualité ! Dans les régions frontalières du Canada et de l'Alaska, les glaciers isolés se rejoignent à partir d'une altitude de plus de 5 000 m pour constituer de vastes réseaux glaciaires, comme dans les Alpes il y a environ 20 000 ans. Ils finissent par former deux glaciers gigantesques, uniques au monde, le Bering et le Malaspina. Alimentés par les neiges éternelles, ces deux glaciers débouchent des vallées pour s'écouler sur les contreforts des massifs.

LA MONTAGNE DES DIEUX

Depuis environ douze siècles, un temple est perché sur le sommet enneigé du Fuji-Yama, qui semble flotter au-dessus des nuages, en plein cœur du Japon. Les pèlerins font l'ascension pour vénérer leurs dieux.

Le volcan est loin d'être éteint, et beaucoup examinent avec inquiétude le fond du cratère. Le Fuji-Yama pourrait entrer en éruption à tout moment et couvrir de cendres la région alentour, extrêmement peuplée.

La vie sur une poudrière

Plus de 200 volcans furent en activité sur l'archipel japonais durant les temps historiques. Le premier rapport sur une éruption volcanique au Japon date de l'an 684. Plus de 800 éruptions postérieures attribuées à 60 volcans au moins sont attestées. Même si certains sont maintenant éteints, les pronostics des vulcanologues japonais demeurent très réservés. Un volcan qui n'a montré aucun signe d'activité pendant 1 000 ans peut avoir brusquement une éruption très destructrice.

Mais la nature de ces éruptions compte au moins autant que leur nombre. Et, à cet égard, les volcans du Japon sont parmi les plus dangereux du monde. Ils expulsent avant tout de la lave visqueuse, qui se solidifie souvent dans les conduits. Tel le bouchon d'une bouteille de champagne, elle empêche les gaz volcaniques de s'échapper. Lorsque la pression devient trop forte à l'intérieur du volcan, il se produit une énorme explosion qui ouvre un nouveau cratère dans le flanc de la montagne.

Une fleur de lotus « explosive »

Le Fuji-Yama, qui culmine à 3 776 m au-dessus du niveau de la mer, est le plus haut volcan du Japon. Depuis la fin du VIIIᵉ siècle, il a connu au moins 16 éruptions explosives de ce genre. Lors de la dernière – en décembre 1707 –, les gaz ouvrirent une énorme brèche dans le versant sud-est du géant. Près de 2 km³ de produits volcaniques furent propulsés dans les airs. Pluies de cendres et bombes volcaniques s'abattirent dans un large rayon autour du volcan. Même la ville d'Edo – l'actuelle Tokyo –, distante d'une centaine de kilomètres, fut plongée dans l'obscurité. Aujourd'hui, une semblable explosion aurait des conséquences très graves pour la mégapole japonaise et pour le pays tout entier.

Depuis quelques années, une augmentation de la fréquence des secousses sismiques a été enregistrée dans la région du Fuji-Yama. C'est le signe que les roches en fusion sont en train de remonter à l'intérieur du volcan et qu'une explosion pourrait être imminente. Après une longue période de repos, la prochaine éruption serait sans doute tout aussi dévastatrice que celle de 1707.

Le volcan le plus connu du Japon est déjà mentionné dans les chroniques les plus anciennes de l'empire. La plupart préfèrent évoquer la beauté parfaite de son cône plutôt que ses dangers potentiels. Certains de ses admirateurs affirment même reconnaître dans la dentelure du cratère principal les huit pétales d'une fleur de lotus. Et depuis toujours, l'explication préférée des poètes pour le mot *fu-ji* met en avant le caractère unique du volcan : « à nul autre pareil ».

La plupart des gens imaginent un volcan sous la forme d'un cône régulier, dont les flancs sont légèrement inclinés à la base, puis de plus en plus raides à l'approche des bords dentelés du cratère. Cette description correspond presque à celle du Fuji-Yama. Et pourtant, le Fuji-Yama n'a rien d'un volcan « classique ». Les volcans plus répandus sont les volcans boucliers, qui

Montagnes sacrées

De nombreux pays du monde célèbrent les montagnes, qu'ils considèrent comme le centre du monde. Mais le Japon est le pays des montagnes sacrées par excellence. Les divers cultes du Sangaku shinko (« hommage aux montagnes ») les vénèrent lors de cérémonies qui peuvent aller jusqu'au suicide rituel. Bien souvent, cette vénération repose sur des faits objectifs, comme chez les riziculteurs, pour qui l'eau venant des sommets a une importance vitale : elle est pour eux un don des dieux. De même, on considère au Japon que les hauts sommets abrupts sont un lien avec les cieux, ou encore une échelle réservée aux divinités célestes. Ainsi la légende affirme-t-elle que le petit-fils de la déesse du soleil est descendu sur terre par le sommet du volcan Takachiho, sur l'île de Kyushu.

D'innombrables montagnes sont censées héberger des divinités – bonnes ou mauvaises. Le Fuji-Yama abriterait par exemple la « princesse des Arbres en fleurs », à qui les Japonais apportent depuis des siècles leurs offrandes dans un temple perché au bord du cratère. Aux yeux des Occidentaux, le culte du Fuji-Yama prend parfois des formes insolites : pour permettre aux vieillards, aux infirmes et aux femmes – à qui l'ascension de la montagne sacrée était initialement interdite – de faire le pèlerinage, de nombreuses villes ont érigé des Fuji-Yama en miniature, hauts de quelques mètres.

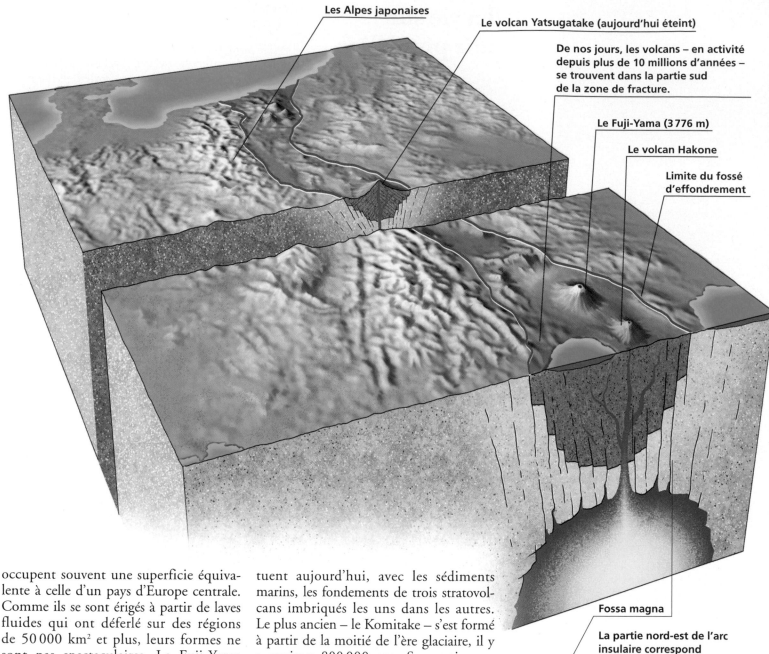

Les Alpes japonaises

Le volcan Yatsugatake (aujourd'hui éteint)

De nos jours, les volcans – en activité depuis plus de 10 millions d'années – se trouvent dans la partie sud de la zone de fracture.

Le Fuji-Yama (3 776 m)

Le volcan Hakone

Limite du fossé d'effondrement

Fossa magna

La partie nord-est de l'arc insulaire correspond à la zone de rencontre entre les plaques pacifique et eurasiatique.

Au sud-ouest de la Fossa magna, la plaque des Philippines plonge sous la plaque eurasiatique.

JAPON

Honshu

occupent souvent une superficie équivalente à celle d'un pays d'Europe centrale. Comme ils se sont érigés à partir de laves fluides qui ont déferlé sur des régions de 50 000 km² et plus, leurs formes ne sont pas spectaculaires. Le Fuji-Yama appartient quant à lui au groupe des stratovolcans, beaucoup plus rares. Par ailleurs, son cône, qui semble constituer une unité, comporte au moins trois édifices volcaniques différents.

Une croissance couche après couche

Comparée à celle d'un volcan bouclier, la surface au sol du Fuji-Yama – moins de 1 000 km² – semble minuscule. Ses produits volcaniques – cendres, scories, retombées ponceuses, coulées de laves – se sont accumulés, couche après couche, aux environs immédiats des conduits. Il y a plus de 5 millions d'années, des éruptions volcaniques – sous-marines – se produisirent déjà dans la région du Fuji-Yama. Ces premières couches de lave consti-

tuent aujourd'hui, avec les sédiments marins, les fondements de trois stratovolcans imbriqués les uns dans les autres. Le plus ancien – le Komitake – s'est formé à partir de la moitié de l'ère glaciaire, il y a environ 800 000 ans. Ses vestiges se trouvent encore sur le versant nord du cône de l'actuel volcan. Le Ko-Fuji – « vieux Fuji » – entra en activité il y a environ 80 000 ans et s'éteignit voici quelque 11 000 ans. Pendant la période de repos qui suivit, une terre noire et riche en humus recouvrit les anciennes roches volcaniques. Et enfin le « jeune Fuji » succéda au « vieux Fuji ». Depuis lors, l'activité du volcan se traduisit

La Fossa magna

L'alignement des volcans – du sud-ouest au nord-est – le long des quatre îles principales correspond à la limite entre les plaques pacifique/des Philippines au sud-est et eurasiatique au nord-ouest. De même, une ligne de volcans traverse l'île de Honshu à peu près en son milieu. Elle suit la Fossa magna, une zone de fracture située à l'aplomb de l'arc insulaire japonais.

tour à tour par des émissions de laves ou de cendres et des retombées de nuées ardentes. Les éruptions provenaient tantôt de la cheminée principale, tantôt des cheminées secondaires – une soixantaine – plus petites et réparties sur ses flancs.

Une alimentation abondante à la limite des plaques

Généralement, les stratovolcans ont une durée de vie comprise entre 100 000 ans et 10 millions d'années. Leur capacité intérieure est de 5 à 100 km³. Le volume du Fuji-Yama – en incluant ses fondations les plus anciennes – est évalué à plus de 1 000 km³. Et son existence de stratovolcan continental date d'un million d'années tout au plus. En comparaison avec les autres stratovolcans, le Fuji-Yama est donc relativement jeune et d'une dimension exceptionnelle.

Par conséquent, les cheminées du Fuji-Yama et de ses prédécesseurs ont dû expulser des entrailles de la Terre des quantités phénoménales de roches en fusion.

L'origine de cet inépuisable réservoir de magma demeura longtemps une énigme. Seule la théorie de la dérive des continents permit de fournir enfin une explication satisfaisante. Au nord-est de l'archipel japonais, la plaque pacifique plonge sous la plaque eurasiatique, à un rythme de plusieurs centimètres par an. Entrant en fusion dans les profondeurs, elle fournit des magmas volcaniques en abondance. Au sud-est, la plaque des Philippines disparaît sous la plaque eurasiatique, contribuant elle aussi à alimenter le Japon en flots de magma. La limite entre la plaque pacifique et celle des Philippines se trouve exactement à l'aplomb du Fuji-Yama, dans une profonde zone de fracture transversale appelée Fossa magna. Celle-ci facilite la migration des roches en fusion de ces deux réservoirs vers la surface de la Terre. Or, ce sont là des conditions idéales pour la croissance de ce stratovolcan.

Aux alentours du Fuji-Yama, des coulées de lave ont fermé de nombreux lacs. En divers endroits, les rivières franchissent des barrières de lave, comme celles des chutes de Shiraito, hautes de 26 m (ci-dessus).

Le volcan Hakone – voisin du Fuji-Yama – a fait éruption pour la dernière fois en 950 av. J.-C. Aujourd'hui, seules d'inoffensives émissions de vapeur et de soufre rappellent son activité passée (tout en haut).

LA GRANDE FAILLE ÉCOSSAISE

'Écosse est traversée par un étroit fossé rectiligne, dont le fond est occupé par les lochs légendaires. Glen More – la « Grande Vallée » – tel est le nom que les Écossais donnent à cette faille naturelle. Mais est-ce bien une vallée ? Et Nessie, le monstre mystérieux tapi dans les profondeurs du loch Ness, existe-t-il vraiment ? Il n'en demeure pas moins que le chardon des champs (petite photo), modeste fleur sauvage, est la plante nationale écossaise.

Une énigme géologique

Les Écossais l'appellent Glen More nan Albin et les Anglais Great Glen of Albin. Ces deux noms, qui signifient « grande vallée d'Albin », désignent une grande dépression qui traverse le nord de l'Écosse sur près de 100 km, de Moray Firth – près d'Inverness –, au nord-est, jusqu'au loch Linnhe – près de Fort William –, au sud-ouest. Mais cette dépression tectonique, au fond de laquelle s'étirent les trois lochs (lacs) Ness, Oich et Lochy, est-elle vraiment une vallée ?

Une vallée se caractérise, entre autres, par un fond plus ou moins raide, qui s'abaisse régulièrement dans la même direction. Or, dans le cas du Great Glen, le fond de la dépression commence par s'élever nettement au nord-est, puis il demeure à un même niveau sur une longue distance, avant de s'abaisser au sud-ouest.

Par ailleurs, Great Glen ne constitue en rien l'élément principal d'un réseau de vallées, même s'il est rejoint par quelques petites vallées adjacentes. En vérité, le Great Glen ressemble plutôt à un « corps étranger » qui traverse les Highlands écossais (Hautes Terres).

Une faille San Andreas au nord de l'Europe

Ce qui frappe le plus dans cette longue entaille qui parcourt les Highlands écossais, c'est son tracé parfaitement rectiligne orienté sud-ouest/nord-est. Le nord de la Grande-Bretagne comporte d'ailleurs d'autres structures analogues, comme l'important escarpement qui sépare les Hautes et les Basses Terres au cœur de l'Écosse. Une profonde fracture de la croûte terrestre, dont les fragments sont décalés quasiment à la verticale, y parcourt le pays en diagonale – de Firth of Clyde au sud-ouest à Stonehaven – près d'Aberdeen – au nord-est.

La fracture du Great Glen est très profonde elle aussi, mais sa faille relève d'un tout autre type. Le déplacement des blocs de croûte terrestre s'y fait surtout à l'horizontale, comme pour la faille californienne de San Andreas, exemple classique de faille transformante (à déplacement horizontal) et foyer sismique très actif. Les forces énormes qui agissent sur la croûte terrestre finissent par broyer les roches le long de la ligne de fracture. Or, le fond du Great Glen est considérablement disloqué sur près de 1 km de large. Et les forts tremblements de terre qui secouent régulièrement le centre des Highlands indiquent que les fragments de la croûte terrestre continuent à y coulisser, comme en Californie.

Des montagnes « jumelles »

Le fossé du Great Glen sépare deux massifs rocheux, très différents par leur âge et par leur nature. Ils sont constitués de gneiss très anciens et de dépôts stabilisés de sable ou d'éboulis – rouges pour la plupart – et plus jeunes de quelques millions d'années, ou de granit, de Foyers et de Strontian. Ces deux reliefs, aujourd'hui distants d'environ 100 km, se ressemblent tellement qu'ils ne formaient jadis, à l'évidence, qu'un seul et même massif granitique. Au nord de la ligne de fracture, les fragments de croûte terrestre ont sans doute coulissé de 120 km vers le sud-ouest. Ensuite, le mouvement changea d'orientation, et les massifs situés au sud migrèrent vers le nord-est. À cet endroit, la plus grande faille horizontale d'Europe se prolonge sous le fond de la mer du Nord jusqu'aux îles Shetland, et peut-être même sous la péninsule scandinave.

Mythe ou réalité ?

Les adeptes de la cryptozoologie – science des animaux légendaires et mystérieux – s'efforcent avec passion de démontrer l'existence du monstre du loch Ness. Les scientifiques tentent eux aussi de trouver une explication aux phénomènes étranges qui continuent à être observés dans le loch Ness. Certains jours, les eaux du lac sont en proie à une forte houle alors qu'il n'y a pas le moindre souffle d'air. Selon les scientifiques, il s'agirait de simples frémissements à la surface du lac, provoqués par des variations de pression et de température.

De même, la surface de l'eau présente parfois des rides ou un étrange bouillonnement, sans aucune raison apparente. Là aussi, il pourrait y avoir une explication objective : le lac surplombant une fracture de la croûte terrestre, des gaz volcaniques s'échapperaient des fissures sous l'effet de mini-secousses telluriques. Autre hypothèse : il s'agirait de méthane dégagé par les tourbes sédimentaires qui reposent au fond du lac.

La même faille de part et d'autre de l'Atlantique

Les lacs, qui occupent parfois le fossé tout entier, font le charme du Great Glen. Les sommets arrondis qui les surplombent sont principalement tapissés de bruyères. Or le même type de paysage, d'une austère beauté, se retrouve de l'autre côté de l'Atlantique, sur les deux rives du Grand Lac, dans le nord-ouest de Terre-Neuve. La seule différence, c'est que la partie inférieure des massifs y est couverte de conifères et les sommets de toundra. Le lac s'étire sur plus de 100 km dans l'arrière-pays du golfe du Saint-Laurent. Il occupe un fossé orienté lui aussi sud-ouest/nord-est, qui suit une profonde fracture de la croûte terrestre, la faille Cabot.

Le Grand Lac et le Great Glen correspondent tous deux à des fractures de la croûte terrestre dont les fragments ont coulissé à l'horizontale – ceux situés au nord de la faille vers le sud-ouest, et ceux situés au

La longue faille d'Écosse

Le Great Glen suit une fracture de la croûte terrestre, le long de laquelle des blocs de croûte ont coulissé quasiment à l'horizontale, en cassant un massif granitique. L'origine de cette faille horizontale est très ancienne. Elle appartenait à une ligne de fracture qui traversait le continent primitif de Laurasie jusqu'à l'actuelle Terre-Neuve.

Il y a environ 430 millions d'années : au cours de la formation des massifs – à l'ère calédonienne –, la croûte terrestre commence à se déplacer au milieu de la Laurasie. La majeure partie du massif granitique est encore intacte.

Aujourd'hui : les fragments du massif granitique situé sur la plus grande faille horizontale d'Europe se sont décalés d'une centaine de kilomètres.

Sur les hauteurs situées de part et d'autre du Great Glen, les étendues rocheuses sont tapissées principalement de bruyères et de mousses. Le Great Glen et ses vallées adjacentes sont peuplés des dernières forêts de conifères qui recouvraient jadis les terres les plus basses au nord de l'Écosse.

sud vers le nord-est. Les roches disloquées – granits, gneiss ou grès – présentent certaines similitudes.

Bien qu'éloignées de 3 000 km, ces deux failles appartenaient manifestement à la même entité. Longtemps avant la formation de l'océan Atlantique, une masse terrestre – la laurasie –, comprenant entre autres l'actuelle Écosse du Nord et Terre-Neuve, se divisa. Avec l'Avalonia, le Gondwana et d'autres, c'était l'un des continents originels du globe il y a environ 500 millions d'années.

D'abord dispersées au milieu d'un océan primitif, ces masses terrestres, poussées par les courants du manteau, dérivèrent les unes vers les autres. Elles finirent par entrer en collision – comme la Laurasie avec le Gondwana. Il y a environ 280 millions d'années, elles vinrent se souder pour former la Pangée, le continent originel le plus récent. L'étude de la dérive des plaques de la croûte terrestre a mis en évidence les conséquences de ces collisions interplaques : volcanisme, formation de massifs et fracture de la croûte terrestre en multiples fragments sous l'effet des tensions très fortes. Plus rigides, les plaques continentales ont davan-

tage tendance à se casser. Les fragments de plaque coulissent le plus souvent à l'horizontale, comme la faille commune au Great Lake et au Great Glen, très active il y a 340 à 380 millions d'années.

Mais le Great Glen écossais n'est pas aussi ancien que la faille dont il suit le tracé. Sa physionomie actuelle a été façonnée en majeure partie par les glaciers et les rivières d'eaux de fonte glaciaires durant les deux à trois derniers millions d'années.

Le Great Glen à l'ère glaciaire

Tel un entonnoir, la faille s'ouvre en direction du nord-est, où se trouvait jadis une avancée du glacier continental scandinave vers l'Écosse. Après avoir atteint le Great Glen, l'inlandsis parvint sans peine – avec l'aide des glaciers écossais – à raboter les roches disloquées par les déplacements de croûte de part et d'autre de la faille.

Il y a environ 20 000 ans, une calotte glaciaire atteignant jusqu'à 600 m d'épaisseur couvrait encore les Highlands écossais. Beaucoup moins épaisse que l'inlandsis scandinave, elle suffit pourtant à creuser de profondes cuvettes semblables à des fjords. Le loch Ness – le plus grand lac du Great Glen – mesure 240 m à son point le plus profond. Le fond du lac se trouve ainsi à 180 m en dessous du niveau de la mer. Et ses rives rocheuses sont très abruptes : à Foyers, la profondeur de l'eau atteint déjà 150 m à 20 m de la rive.

Le bord du lac est envahi de plantes aquatiques sur une étroite bande immergée. Ses eaux ne laissent pénétrer la lumière solaire que sur une profondeur de quelques mètres. Aussi les êtres réels ou imaginaires supposés peupler le loch Ness gardent-ils tout leur mystère.

Nessie et le loch Ness

La légende de Nessie date de près de 1 500 ans, depuis le jour où un monstre marin fut aperçu pour la première fois dans les eaux obscures et inquiétantes du loch. Une créature préhistorique avait-elle élu domicile dans le lac lorsque celui-ci était encore relié à la mer ? À l'époque postglaciaire, la croûte terrestre, libérée du poids des glaces, se releva. Ne pouvant rejoindre la mer, le « monstre » se serait retrouvé pris au piège.

Une voie d'eau naturelle : le canal calédonien

Trois grands lacs se succèdent dans le fossé du Great Glen, qui constitue une voie de navigation idéale pour relier la mer du Nord et l'océan Atlantique. Au XIXᵉ siècle, il ne fallut aménager qu'un tiers du canal calédonien – d'une longueur totale de 100 km. Le dénivelé de 32 m à peine put être surmonté grâce à une série de 29 écluses, dont les 8 écluses de l'escalier de Neptune, à la sortie sud-ouest du canal (ci-dessous). De nos jours, le canal n'est plus emprunté que par des bateaux de plaisance.

Hawaii

LES MAISONS DU FEU

UN
AU

Le sous-sol de l'île d'Hawaii, la plus vaste de l'archipel de même nom, connaît une intense activité volcanique. Au-dessus des sommets des volcans, l'air est néanmoins si pur que les astronomes, dans leurs observatoires (petite photo), parviennent à sonder les profondeurs de l'Univers. À plus de 2 000 km d'Hawaii, les îles Midway – un archipel corallien couvert de palmiers verdoyants – émergent à peine au-dessus du niveau de la mer. En dépit de leur très grande diversité, ces deux archipels ont pourtant une histoire commune.

L'Himalaya

LE SÉJOUR DES

La feuille
pacifique qu
millions d'a
vers l'ouest
à raison de
de la bougie
l'une de ces
dans le man
rapidement
terrestre. Q
flamme dar
aux volcan
feuille de p
reproduire l
par la déri
40 millions

La varia
du volca

Bien que d
tration ne
Pourquoi
commenc
de chang
de dérive
Commer
nisme ait
l'archipel
repos d'

Le silve
est orig
d'Amér
4 000 k
import
Ses feu
réserve
protég

NEIGES

L'Himalaya (« séjour des neiges » en sanskrit) est couronné de sommets dont les plus hauts – ici le mont Everest (à gauche), du côté tibétain – culminent à plus de 8 000 m. Aujourd'hui encore, cette gigantesque muraille continue à s'élever de quelques millimètres par an. Dans le même temps, le massif le plus imposant de la Terre est érodé par des torrents sauvages et couverts de débris rocheux (petite photo). Cette lutte entre les forces de la nature se poursuit depuis plus de 60 millions d'années.

TERRE DE FEU
ET DE GLACE

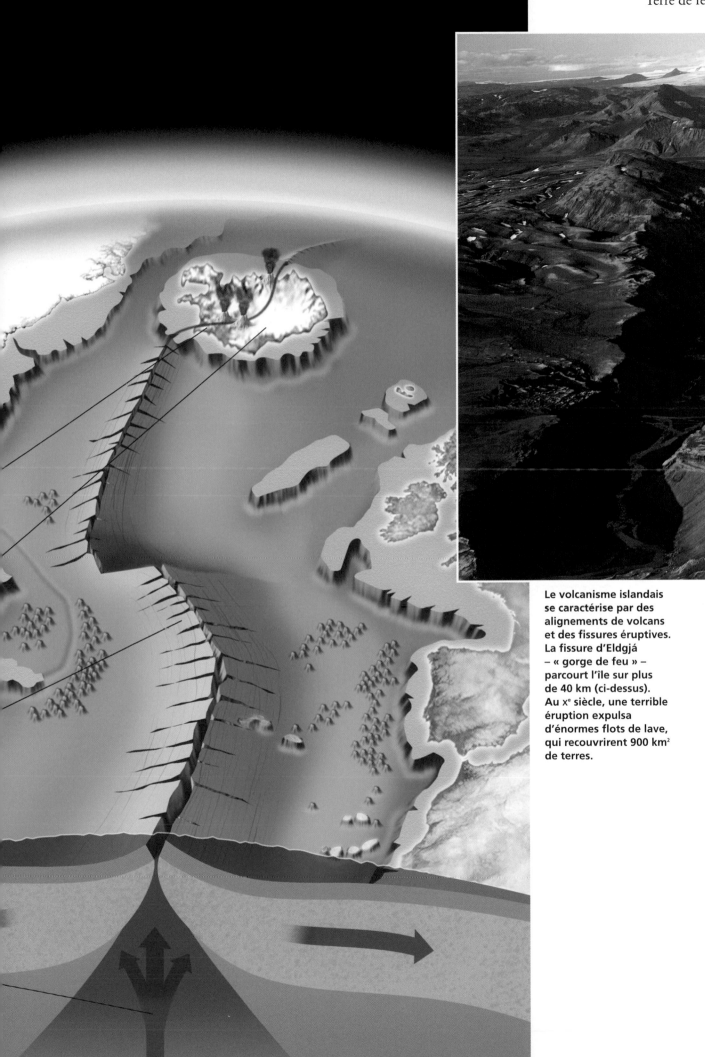

Le volcanisme islandais
se caractérise par des
alignements de volcans
et des fissures éruptives.
La fissure d'Eldgjá
– « gorge de feu » –
parcourt l'île sur plus
de 40 km (ci-dessus).
Au Xe siècle, une terrible
éruption expulsa
d'énormes flots de lave,
qui recouvrirent 900 km²
de terres.

une altitude étonnamment élevée : environ 600 m au nord-ouest, 1 000 m sur la côte septentrionale et au moins 1 200 m dans les régions élevées du Centre. Les sommets les plus hauts sont recouverts d'énormes calottes glaciaires, qui peuvent atteindre 1 000 m d'épaisseur. Les glaciers couvrent un bon dixième de la surface totale de l'île, faisant de l'Islande le plus grand pays de glaciers d'Europe.

Eaux noires des rivières : attention, danger

Les ruisseaux issus du Vatnajökull – le plus grand glacier d'Islande – s'écoulent vers l'aval, où ils forment d'innombrables rivières. Habituellement, les eaux de ces rivières sont d'un blanc jaunâtre, comme pour la plupart des rivières alimentées par les glaciers. Mais elles prennent une teinte noire lorsqu'elles charrient des cendres volcaniques. Les habitants de la côte méridionale d'Islande savent y reconnaître le signe d'un danger imminent. En l'espace de quelques jours, voire de quelques heures, le débit de la Skeidará – la rivière la plus importante, longue de près de 40 km – peut se multiplier par trois ou par quatre. Généralement, les masses d'eaux, qui emportent même des bâtiments, déferlent pendant quelques heures à peine. Elles se déversent dans la mer toute proche, abandonnant sur la plaine des blocs de glace et de gigantesques rochers.

Les Islandais appellent *jökulhlaup* (« cours d'eau de glaciers ») ces formidables crues glaciaires qui dévastent leurs terres à intervalles

Les éruptions des volcans cachés sous le glacier du Vatnajökull font fondre d'énormes quantités d'eau, dont le poids entraîne l'écroulement de la calotte glaciaire (grande photo).

Le Svartifoss (petite photo), l'une des innombrables cascades d'Islande, dégringole le long de parois de laves qui, en se solidifiant, ont formé des tuyaux d'orgue très caractéristiques.

LA FUMÉE QUI TONNE

Le Zambèze est un lent fleuve africain, aussi nonchalant que les crocodiles qui se dorent au soleil sur ses berges après un repas copieux. Mais, près de la ville de Livingstone (Maramba), le quatrième fleuve d'Afrique se métamorphose soudain en un cours d'eau impétueux après une chute de plus de 100 m dégageant de gros nuages de vapeur. Il dévale ensuite une gorge étroite et profonde. Les autochtones appellent « fumée qui tonne » cet impressionnant spectacle de la nature.

LES SOMMETS GLACÉS

DE LA CEINTURE DE FEU

Est-il monde plus inhospitalier que ces sommets couverts de glace, au pied desquels des lamas peu exigeants (petite photo) doivent chercher leur nourriture ? Mais la neige et la glace masquent des flots de lave en fusion qui bouillonnent à une grande profondeur avant de se frayer un chemin vers la surface. La ceinture de feu du Pacifique, dont font partie les jeunes cordillères d'Amérique du Sud et le volcan Cotopaxi (grande photo), s'étend sur toute une moitié du globe terrestre.

Le lac Titicaca (ci-dessus), qui s'étend entre deux cordillères, était une « mer sacrée » pour les Incas. Situé à 3 800 m d'altitude, c'est le plus haut lac navigable du monde.

Les feuilles capitonnées de l'azorelle (à droite) sont insensibles à la sécheresse et aux rayons solaires. Malgré leur aspect moelleux, elles sont très dures et constituent un bon combustible.

mais, plus à l'est, leur profondeur peut parfois atteindre 700 km. L'angle d'inclinaison de la plaque Nazca joue un rôle décisif dans le volcanisme des Andes. Si elle plongeait plus à l'horizontale, elle n'accéderait jamais aux profondeurs de l'écorce terrestre où la chaleur est suffisante pour faire fondre les roches. Plus verticale, elle parviendrait rapidement aux températures de fusion, mais la ceinture de volcans serait beaucoup plus étroite.

Vrais et faux records

Dans le cas des Andes, l'angle d'inclinaison de la plaque Nazca – 20 à 30° – semble donc idéal. Non seulement le nombre de volcans y est considérable, mais encore ils sont disséminés sur une bande large parfois de plus de 200 km.

Le Chimborazo – 6 310 m – est l'un des points culminants de la route des volcans. Ce volcan éteint fut longtemps considéré comme le plus haut sommet du monde, ce qui serait exact si l'on mesurait son altitude à partir des profondeurs de la Terre, et

non pas du niveau de la mer. Ici, à la hauteur de l'équateur, le globe terrestre présente en effet une sorte de bourrelet.

Mais le record véritable se situe dans le dénivelé de près de 15 000 m qui existe entre le fond de la fosse de l'Atacama, au large du port chilien d'Antofagasta, et le sommet du Llullaillaco, à environ 200 km à l'intérieur des terres. Le cas est unique au monde, surtout sur une aussi petite distance.

Cet énorme dénivelé résulte à la fois de l'immersion très rapide de la plaque Nazca et du soulèvement important des Andes. Ce double processus fit remonter à la surface des granits et autres roches de profondeur, qui constituent plus d'un sixième du massif. Situées à 15 à 20 km de profondeur, ces roches ne peuvent migrer vers la surface que si un massif est fortement soulevé et érodé en même temps.

Si l'on ne trouve pas de pareils dénivelés au cœur des Andes, les hauts sommets isolés sont nombreux. Ils dominent un vaste plateau – l'Altiplano – qui s'étend à des altitudes comprises entre 3 500 et 4 200 m entre les cordillères occidentale et orientale.

L'Altiplano

Pour les linguistes, l'Altiplano, au climat froid et sec, est un « haut plateau ». Mais pour les géologues, c'est un bassin subsident – qui s'enfonce lentement en profondeur – de plus de 1 000 km de longueur et 200 km de largeur s'étendant à l'intérieur du massif des Andes.

Les couches sédimentaires accumulées dans ce fossé depuis environ 80 millions d'années atteignent parfois une épaisseur de 14 000 m. L'Altiplano n'est parvenu à son altitude actuelle qu'au cours des cinq derniers millions d'années. À un soulèvement aussi rapide succède généralement une érosion tout aussi rapide. Mais une autre couche sédimentaire de 1 000 m d'épaisseur à peine, due à l'érosion des cordillères voisines, est venue s'ajouter par endroits. Parmi les rivières qui prennent leur source dans les flancs externes des deux chaînes, peu ont réussi à se frayer un chemin vers le haut plateau. Et les rares précipitations qui tombent chaque année sur l'Altiplano – parfois moins de 100 l/m² – ne permettent pas à ses propres cours d'eau de creuser une brèche dans les versants des cordillères pour rejoindre la mer. Ils se jettent un peu plus bas dans des lacs sans écoulement, vite asséchés en raison de l'évaporation, et y déposent le sable et la boue qu'ils charrient. Plus de 75 de ces lacs sont disséminés sur l'Altiplano, dont le Salar de Uyuni, qui mesure 10 000 km². Hormis durant la saison des pluies, où il se remplit d'une eau saumâtre, ce n'est plus qu'une vaste plaine de sel. Il y a environ 20 000 ans, le climat était plus frais et un immense lac d'eau douce se trouvait à cet endroit.

Des coulées meurtrières de braises et de boue

Près de La Paz, la capitale bolivienne, un fleuve venu des basses terres amazoniennes s'est frayé un chemin jusqu'à l'Altiplano, creusant de profondes gorges dans les couches sédimentaires. Celles-ci mettent au jour l'histoire très mouvementée du haut plateau : fines couches sédimentaires

Chronique d'une catastrophe annoncée

Un tremblement de terre, des éruptions de vapeur et de petits nuages de cendres furent les signes précurseurs. Puis, dans l'après-midi du 11 septembre 1985, les premières coulées de boue commencèrent à se former. Mais les autorités ne tinrent aucun compte de ces avertissements. L'éruption du Nevado del Ruiz, un volcan bouclier couvert de glaces et situé dans le nord des Andes, se produisit le 13 novembre 1985, à 21 h 09. Les 25 000 habitants d'Armero, une petite ville située à une cinquantaine de kilomètres du cratère, auraient eu tout juste deux heures et demie pour évacuer la ville. À 23 h 35, un fleuve de boue froide (photo ci-dessous) – mélange de cendres et d'eaux de fonte –

s'abattit sur Armero, engloutissant la quasi-totalité de ses habitants. Et encore, l'éruption n'avait fait fondre que 5 à 10 % de la calotte glaciaire du volcan. Dans le cas contraire, le nombre de victimes aurait pu être beaucoup plus important encore.

UN MUSÉE PRÉHISTORIQUE

À CIEL OUVERT

Les dugongs qui peuplent les eaux turquoise de Shark Bay, en Australie-Occidentale, y vivaient déjà il y a 30 millions d'années. Pourtant, ces massifs mammifères marins ne sont que de jeunes habitants de la Terre comparés aux organismes de plus de 3 milliards d'années, dont les étranges édifices ornent la baie.

LA MONTAGNE

Semblables à une mer infinie aux vagues pétrifiées, les crêtes des Appalaches s'étirent sur 3 000 km

à travers la partie orientale de l'Amérique du Nord avant de disparaître à l'horizon, tout comme les origines géologiques de la chaîne montagneuse se perdent quelque part dans les débuts des temps géologiques. Les fossiles tels que cet « animal intermédiaire » (petite photo), mi-aquatique, mi-terrestre, font mesurer l'incroyable ancienneté de son existence.

RESSUSCITÉE

Les Appalaches du Nord connaissent leurs dernières modifications de relief à la période glaciaire. Leurs vastes étendues rocheuses sont émaillées d'entailles profondes laissées par le passage des glaciers, comme ici à Cadillac Mountain, dans le Maine, aux États-Unis.

Les chutes d'eau telles que Dark Hollow Falls, dans le parc national de Shenandoah (à gauche), révèlent qu'au cours de leur récent passé géologique ces montagnes ont été formées par des soulèvements et des éboulements violents.

jusqu'à ce que l'océan Atlantique originel se soit entièrement fermé et que les mouvements souterrains qui ne cessaient de projeter des fragments de la plaque africaine vers l'Amérique du Nord se soient apaisés.

Les vestiges d'une montagne qui faisait autrefois le tour de la Terre

La naissance des Appalaches n'est donc qu'un acte d'une pièce de théâtre plus longue, jouée depuis les temps les plus reculés sur la scène géologique mondiale. Elle se termine par la réunion des fragments de

Au nord, les Appalaches se terminent dans le golfe du Saint-Laurent par des formations rocheuses monumentales telles que le rocher Percé, dans la péninsule de Gaspésie, un massif calcaire vieux de plus de 300 millions d'années (ci-dessus).

croûte terrestre et la constitution du continent originel de la Pangée. La chaîne montagneuse s'est soulevée au cœur de ce continent originel. Seule une dépression plate la séparait du massif des Mauritanides, situé du côté oriental de l'Atlantique. À l'instar de ce massif ouest-africain érodé jusqu'aux fondations, elle faisait partie d'un ensemble montagneux mondial qui s'étendait sur 8 000 km, de l'Eurasie à l'Amérique du Sud.

Cette montagne s'est brisée en plusieurs morceaux, parfois distants aujourd'hui les uns des autres de plusieurs milliers de kilomètres ; à peine 50 millions d'années après la constitution de la Pangée, ce conti-

nent a lui aussi été détruit. De nouveaux océans sont nés, tandis qu'ailleurs les plaques de la croûte terrestre entraient de nouveau en collision.

Tel un phénix renaissant de ses cendres

Piedmont est le nom donné à la ceinture qui borde les Appalaches depuis le sud-est de la Pennsylvanie jusqu'à la Géorgie du Sud. Ce paysage, avec ses collines arrondies et ses crêtes basses, ne constitue pas une montagne, mais un relief prémontagneux situé au « pied du mont ». Pourtant, du point de vue géologique, un piémont est une montagne, tout comme la plaine côtière atlantique. Sa surface en pente douce dissimule, en effet, des sédiments marins fortement plissés, déformés par la chaleur et la pression, vestiges d'archipels et de plusieurs fragments primaires de croûte ter-

restre africaine. Cette partie des Appalaches montre la fin que connaîtront un jour ou l'autre toutes les montagnes de la Terre : elles s'aplanissent, souvent très rapidement, plus vite en tout cas qu'elles ne s'étaient constituées.

En 500 millions d'années, à la fin de l'ère primaire, les Appalaches étaient devenues une montagne de format himalayen, mais, 50 ou 100 millions d'années à peine après la fin de leur formation, elles s'étaient de nouveau érodées – notamment sous l'effet des cours d'eau. La preuve de ce phénomène se trouve dans les couches sédimentaires jurassiques de la zone prémontagneuse, vieilles de 144 à 206 millions d'années, qui reposent sur des structures aplanies, séparées du socle plus ancien par une surface presque horizontale. Ce type de structures aplanies entre les formations jurassiques et des couches plus récentes prouve que le processus d'érosion s'est poursuivi il y a 50 et 60 millions d'années. Ensuite, la chaîne des Appalaches s'est de nouveau soulevée, tel un phénix renaissant de ses cendres, pour atteindre son altitude actuelle.

Les plus hauts sommets appalachiens se situent dans la chaîne de Blue Ridge, où le mont Mitchell dépasse les 2 000 m. La Valley-and-Ridge (région « des crêtes et des vallées »), zone de montagne plissée par excellence, présente les paysages les plus spectaculaires. De longues crêtes montagneuses

Forêt de conifères pétrifiée

Des forêts dont les conifères atteignaient 60 m de haut et 3 m de diamètre recouvraient autrefois le sud-ouest aujourd'hui sec des États-Unis. La forêt pétrifiée (Petrified Forest) d'Arizona n'a pu subsister que parce qu'elle a été recouverte de cendres volcaniques il y a 200 millions d'années.

Dans les pas des géants

Sortie en famille au jurassique : cinq dinosaures se sont promenés en toute harmonie là où l'actuel fleuve Purgatoire serpente au fond de la vallée dans l'État du Colorado. 150 millions d'années se sont écoulées depuis. Le sable s'est désormais transformé en grès, mais les empreintes sont restées.

MERS PÉTRIFIÉES

Les Rocheuses canadiennes abritent des lacs cristallins comme le lac Emerald (ci-contre), des forêts denses et des parois rocheuses escarpées, mais point de mer. En réalité, celle-ci a laissé sa trace dans le sous-sol, emprisonnée dans d'épaisses couches rocheuses constituées des restes d'animaux marins très anciens. Les montagnes abritent même des animaux préhistoriques fossilisés comme cet arthropode primitif (petite photo).

Un empilement de couches d'époques géologiques différentes

Les montagnes Rocheuses font partie de la série de cordillères qui longent la côte pacifique de l'Amérique du Nord et du Sud sur 15 000 km, de l'Alaska à la Terre de Feu. Si sa partie sud, constituée par les Andes, reste cohérente d'un point de vue géologique, ses formations deviennent de plus en plus complexes en remontant vers le nord. Dans la zone canadienne de la cordillère, les strates apparemment si étroitement imbriquées se décomposent, dans la moitié occidentale, en une mosaïque inextricable de massifs différents, tandis que dans la moitié orientale les couches rocheuses s'empilent les unes sur les autres comme un jeu de cartes.

La mosaïque géologique de l'ouest des Rocheuses est constituée de dizaines de microplaques. Il s'agit, pour la plupart, de fragments allongés de croûte terrestre, d'origine et de constitution diverses, qui ont dérivé vers l'est avec la plaque pacifique jusqu'au bord de l'Amérique, où ils se sont soudés au socle continental. Depuis la zone de collision, les ondes de choc se sont étendues, il y a 50 millions d'années, au continent, dont les bords étaient recouverts de mers peu profondes. Pareilles

L'« empilement » des montagnes Rocheuses

Depuis plus de 200 millions d'années, des fragments de croûte terrestre dérivant avec la plaque pacifique viennent se souder à l'Amérique du Nord. À chaque nouvelle collision, le précédent empilement sédimentaire subit une forte pression et un nouveau glissement.

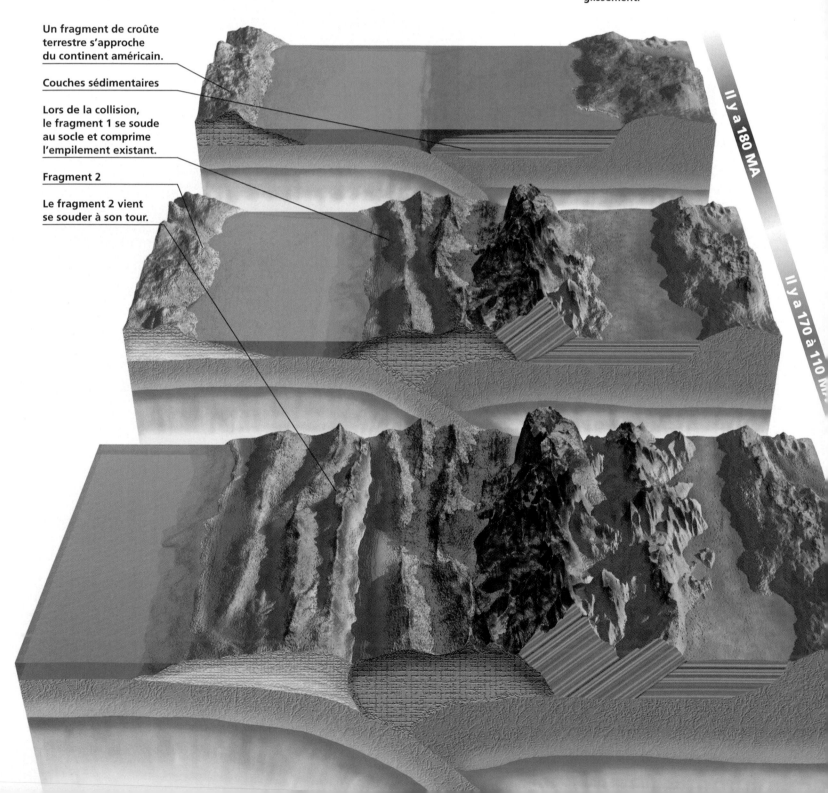

Un fragment de croûte terrestre s'approche du continent américain.

Couches sédimentaires

Lors de la collision, le fragment 1 se soude au socle et comprime l'empilement existant.

Fragment 2

Le fragment 2 vient se souder à son tour.

Il y a 180 MA

Il y a 170 à 110 MA

Les couches que l'on discerne sur les parois rocheuses du parc national de Banff (ci-dessus) se sont empilées pendant des millions d'années.

Les gisements de Burgess Pass (à gauche) représentent la plus grande vitrine du monde sur le cambrien.

à des bulldozers, elles ont repoussé les couches sédimentaires les unes sur les autres. Dans la partie sud des Rocheuses canadiennes, l'empilement des couches s'est ainsi réduit à la moitié de sa largeur originelle. La rigidité du calcaire empêchant la formation de plissements étroits, les fragments rocheux ont été repoussés les uns sur les autres sur plusieurs kilomètres. Au cours dc ce processus, les couches les plus anciennes se sont retrouvées au-dessus des plus récentes.

L'âge des couches sédimentaires va du précambrien à l'époque moderne en passant par le cambrien, l'époque qui a vu exploser la vie sur la Terre, il y a 540 à 490 millions d'années. L'extraordinaire diversité de la faune des mers du cambrien est mise en évidence par le site fossilifère des shales de Burgess, dans le parc national Yoho. Au moins 170 espèces enfouies dans un schiste fin d'environ 506 millions d'années y ont été mises au jour, ce qui constitue une véritable vitrine de la période cambrienne. Outre la diversité de la faune – les vers, les éponges et les crabes côtoient de nombreuses espèces mystérieuses qui n'ont pas d'équivalent à l'époque moderne –, les chercheurs sont aussi fascinés par l'état exceptionnel de conservation des fossiles, dont les détails des parties molles sont parfois encore reconnaissables.

Pourquoi les animaux ont-ils été aussi parfaitement conservés à cet endroit précis ? Sans doute parce qu'ils se trouvaient dans les profondeurs des eaux. Leur habitat était une mer chaude peu profonde, plus exactement la plate-forme d'un récif sur laquelle le limon se déposait en couches épaisses. Il arrivait de temps à autre que le limon se détache, entraînant les animaux avec lui vers les profondeurs, où il les recouvrait. Le fond du gouffre était rempli d'une eau pauvre en oxygène où ne pouvaient vivre ni charognard ni bactérie.

DE GIGANTESQUES ROCHERS CORALLIENS

D'impressionnants massifs montagneux aux pics imposants et aux parois déchiquetées dominent l'extraordinaire paysage des Dolomites. Lorsque l'on observe la roche nue de près – ici, le massif du Monte Pez –, on y découvre un peu partout des coraux (petite photo) et d'autres organismes marins fossilisés. Pourtant, les mers du Sud, avec leurs atolls et leurs récifs, sont loin, et ces montagnes pelées n'évoquent en rien la féerie multicolore des récifs coralliens tropicaux.

De majestueux édifices naturels

De loin, le Monte Pez, le groupe de Sella, le légendaire groupe de Catinaccio ou le sommet dominant Selva di Val Gardena qui marque l'entrée de la vallée romantique de Vallunga, où trônait autrefois le palais d'une célèbre famille aristocratique du sud du Tyrol, paraissent abrupts et inhospitaliers. Ils se dressent tels d'inexpugnables bastions rocheux au-dessus de vallées boisées et de grasses prairies. Peu après la fonte des neiges, crocus, anémones et soldanelles déploient leurs pétales multicolores et recouvrent les herbages. En été, le rhododendron ferrugineux recouvre les pentes laissées à l'état sauvage.

Plus haut, dans la zone rocheuse, tout est différent. Pendant l'ascension, on découvre çà et là de belles fleurs alpestres comme l'androsace blanche d'Hausmann ou la campanule *morettiana* bleu-violet, qui s'accrochent de toutes leurs racines aux fentes rocheuses. Cependant, comparées à la flore luxuriante des herbages au pied des massifs montagneux, elles ne forment que quelques taches de couleur isolées. La zone rocheuse permet pourtant de faire d'autres découvertes étonnantes.

La roche que les géologues désignent sous le nom de dolomie a donné son nom au massif montagneux alpin. Proche parente du calcaire, elle ressemble souvent à du sucre pétrifié. Dans les Dolomites, elle est particulièrement compacte et massive. Les amateurs de fossiles l'évitent, car il est presque impossible d'en exhumer les restes abondants d'animaux et de plantes préhistoriques sans les abîmer. Par endroits, les silhouettes d'organismes vivants pétrifiés affleurent sur les parois rocheuses : algues calcaires, coquillages, escargots, coraux. Il s'agit exclusivement d'espèces marines. Il y a 230 à 240 millions d'années, la région des Dolomites actuelles était recouverte par une mer tropicale chaude présentant de nombreux hauts-fonds. Durant des millions d'années, les algues calcaires et d'autres organismes sécrétant du calcaire dissous dans l'eau de mer ont édifié de gigantesques récifs, une couche après l'autre, dans les zones les moins profondes. De la base au sommet, ces récifs peuvent mesurer jusqu'à 1 000 m.

Ceux qui se lancent à l'assaut des Dolomites escaladent en fait la paroi abrupte d'un récif corallien préhistorique. Les récifs de ce type ne se forment que dans les mers sous lesquelles la croûte terrestre s'abaisse progressivement. Ainsi, les organismes responsables de l'édification du

Avec le soulèvement des Alpes, le récif dolomitique fossile s'est libéré de sa gangue de dépôts rocheux. Il a ensuite été colonisé par de gigantesques glaciers lors des périodes glaciaires. Il y a encore 25 000 ans, il émergeait, telle une île rocheuse, de cette colossale carapace de glace.

Glacier de plateau

Récif fossile

Carapace de glace

Moraines

Porphyre à quartz

De somptueux jardins de coraux aux récifs et aux volcans ceints de colonies de crinoïdes ont vu le jour il y a plus de 200 millions d'années dans une mer tropicale. Les poissons préhistoriques chassaient entre les jardins de coraux.

Il y a 235 MA

récif restent toujours à fleur d'eau, où ils reçoivent une lumière suffisante, tandis que les coraux plus profonds, privés de lumière, meurent peu à peu.

L'action des volcans

Les mouvements et les déplacements dans la croûte terrestre font apparaître des failles par lesquelles le magma remonte et jaillit des volcans sous forme de lave. L'activité volcanique était intense entre les récifs anciens des Dolomites. Essentiellement sous-marine, elle a néanmoins entraîné la formation de quelques îles telles que la montagne porphyrique de Bolzano. Les roches volcaniques, souvent relativement tendres et riches en minéraux, apparaissent aujourd'hui entre les anciens récifs sous la forme de hauts plateaux aux ondulations aplaties ; elles constituent la base d'une flore très diversifiée.

Majestueuses, presque hautaines, les parois rocheuses du groupe de Sella se dressent au-dessus de la charmante vallée du val Gardena (ci-dessus).

Seules quelques plantes hautement adaptées telles que la physoplexis chevelue poussent sur le calcaire nu, où elles s'accrochent dans les moindres anfractuosités.

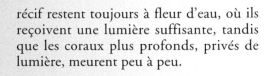

Il y a 25 000 ans　　　　　　　　　　　　　　　　　**Aujourd'hui**

Le Grand Canyon

L'HISTOIRE DE LA

TERRE À LIVRE OUVERT

En descendant vers le fond du Grand Canyon du Colorado, qui peut atteindre 1 600 m de profondeur, le randonneur remonte le temps à raison de 1 million d'années par mètre. Ce voyage à travers des mers, des marécages et des déserts préhistoriques est peuplé d'êtres vivants pétrifiés tels que ce trilobite (petite photo) depuis longtemps disparu.

Le journal intime du plateau du Colorado

La région du Colorado, dans le sud-ouest des États-Unis, porte le nom attribué par les conquistadors dans les années 1540 au fleuve, qui charriait alors une boue rougeâtre. En effet, *colorado* signifie rouge en espagnol. Les envahisseurs, chercheurs d'or avant tout, ne s'intéressaient sans doute pas à la géologie et n'auraient guère partagé l'enthousiasme du major John Wesley Powell, qui écrivait dans son journal, le 18 août 1869 : « Tout autour de moi se trouvent les témoins géologiques les plus

intéressants. Je peux y lire comme à livre ouvert tout en marchant ! »

Le premier explorateur du Grand Canyon comprenait le langage des strates rocheuses visibles sur les flancs de la gorge, témoins à travers ses couches successives sur une période de 2 milliards d'années de près de la moitié de l'histoire de la Terre. Ainsi, le grès de Coconino blanc, dans la partie supérieure, évoque un désert de hautes dunes, vieux de 260 millions d'années. Le schiste rouge est le limon solidifié d'un delta âgé de 270 millions d'années, le calcaire pourpre se compose des restes d'animaux marins de plus de 370 millions d'années et le grès de Tapeats évoque un littoral sableux où les trilobites (aujourd'hui disparus) barbotaient dans l'eau peu profonde au paléozoïque (de – 540 à – 250 millions d'années).

Le fleuve Colorado doit son origine à un lent fleuve de plaine qui, au fil des millénaires, a creusé ses méandres jusqu'à 1 600 m de profondeur dans le plateau.

Dans la partie supérieure du canyon, les strates sont presque horizontales. Les plus dures alternent avec les plus friables et façonnent les parois en grandes marches ou en balcons aplatis, selon leur résistance à l'érosion. Les stratifications intermédiaires inclinées remontent à plus de 540 millions d'années. Dans le fond de la gorge, les strates de schistes presque verticales, parcourues d'intrusions granitiques, sont vieilles de 1,7 milliard d'années. La position

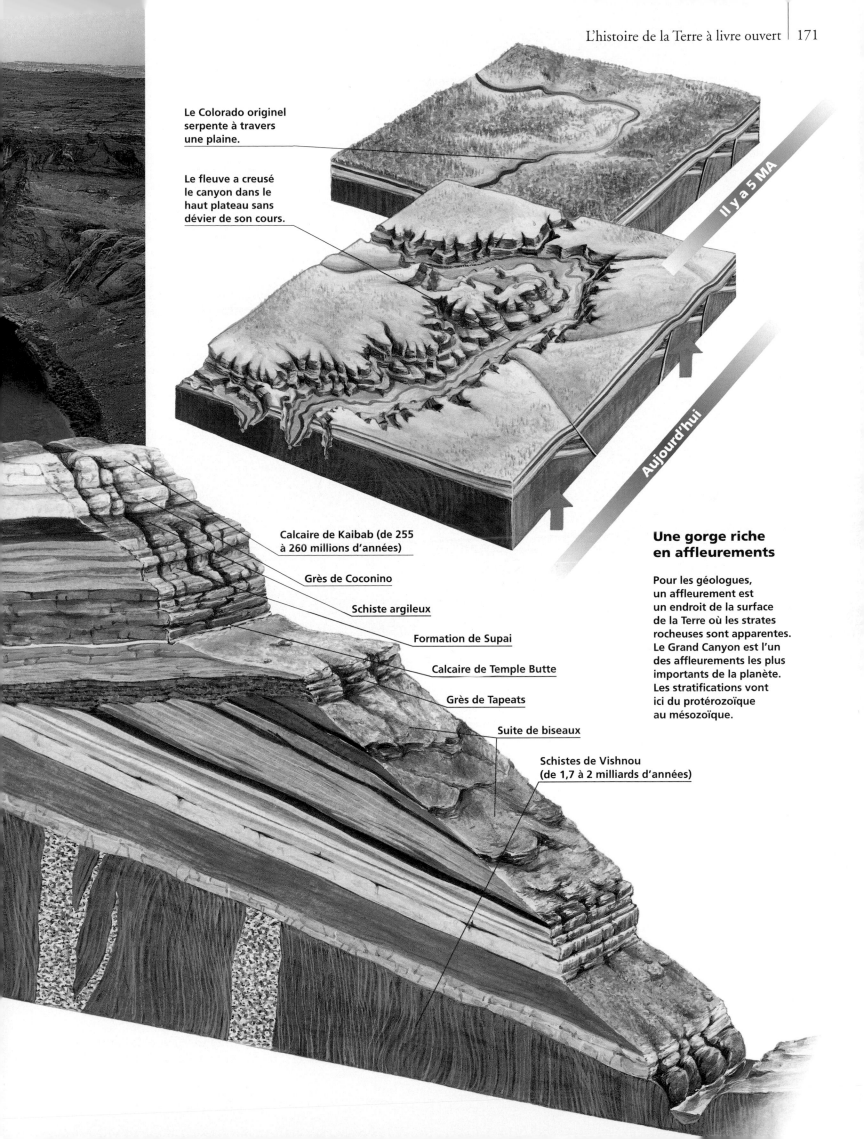

Le Colorado originel serpente à travers une plaine.

Le fleuve a creusé le canyon dans le haut plateau sans dévier de son cours.

Il y a 5 MA

Aujourd'hui

Calcaire de Kaibab (de 255 à 260 millions d'années)

Grès de Coconino

Schiste argileux

Formation de Supai

Calcaire de Temple Butte

Grès de Tapeats

Suite de biseaux

Schistes de Vishnou (de 1,7 à 2 milliards d'années)

Une gorge riche en affleurements

Pour les géologues, un affleurement est un endroit de la surface de la Terre où les strates rocheuses sont apparentes. Le Grand Canyon est l'un des affleurements les plus importants de la planète. Les stratifications vont ici du protérozoïque au mésozoïque.

Quelque 20 vallées sillonnent le plateau du Colorado. Il est difficile de dire laquelle est la plus imposante. Le Zion Canyon, le Bryce Canyon ou les Canyonlands ne sont pas moins impressionnants que le Grand Canyon. Chaque vallée du Colorado surprend par un paysage unique, résultat de forces d'érosion considérables. Ces formes multiples, étonnantes, semblent se modifier en fonction de la lumière, comme si la nature nous offrait un gigantesque diaporama.

inclinée ou verticale des deux strates inférieures révèle des mouvements puissants de la croûte terrestre, la formation de montagnes et leur nivellement. Ces strates sont surmontées de couches presque horizontales, comme si les 540 derniers millions d'années n'avaient plus connu de mouvements importants de la croûte terrestre.

Autour du plateau, les strates sont morcelées comme dans le Grand Bassin désertique (Great Basin) qui le borde à l'ouest, ou plissées comme dans les montagnes Rocheuses limitrophes au nord-est. Depuis la préhistoire, le plateau du Colorado lui-même est resté mystérieusement épargné par les mouvements de la croûte terrestre. Un bloc fixe mesurant jusqu'à 45 km de large a sans doute joué le rôle de socle sous le plateau, empêchant tout déplacement.

Des masses d'eau à travers le chas d'une aiguille

Sur la carte, le Colorado semble étirer paresseusement ses méandres à travers la plaine, mais en réalité, ses eaux sont puissantes et sauvages. En 1869, pour effectuer son voyage en bateau, qui se révéla plus dangereux que prévu, John Wesley Powell avait choisi la plus mauvaise période qui soit. En effet, avant d'être domestiqué par une succession de barrages, le Colorado connaissait chaque année des crues importantes. Il atteignait alors ponctuellement le débit quotidien moyen du Rhône à son delta (2 300 m³/s). Le Rhône est pourtant large de plusieurs centaines de mètres pour une déclivité réduite. Le Colorado, lui, ne fait que 90 m de large à hauteur de Grand Canyon Village, pour une déclivité de 1,70 m/km. Les masses d'eau qui se pressaient par ce chas d'aiguille charriaient une quantité phénoménale d'alluvions : près de 150 millions de tonnes annuelles. Lors d'une crue en 1927, ce volume a même atteint le niveau incroyable de 27 millions de tonnes en une journée au point de mesure de Bright Angel.

Aujourd'hui encore, la déclivité et les importants volumes charriés donnent

au Colorado une force d'érosion peu commune. En évaluant le volume d'alluvions pour calculer l'érosion moyenne par mètre carré, on obtient le résultat de 15 cm tous les 1 000 ans, soit 1 500 m en 10 millions d'années. Le canyon pourrait avoir atteint sa profondeur actuelle en un temps relativement court. Certains éléments laissent penser que la plus grande gorge de la planète serait même plus jeune encore. En effet, l'usure a été calculée pour l'ensemble du bassin versant, mais l'érosion concentrée dans le lit du fleuve était sans doute plus importante. Par ailleurs, pendant la période glaciaire, lorsque le climat était plus froid et plus humide, le Colorado charriait sans doute plus d'eau qu'à l'heure actuelle. Enfin, le fleuve se fraie aujourd'hui un chemin à travers les schistes et les granits plus durs du fond de la gorge, mais l'érosion des schistes argileux et des grès plus tendres des strates supérieures a dû être beaucoup plus facile.

Le Grand Canyon n'est que l'une des plus grandes vallées fluviales sillonnant le plateau du Colorado. Elles présentent presque toutes un tracé sinueux, ce qui est étonnant, car un fleuve impétueux creuse rapidement son lit sans faire de méandres, choisissant généralement le chemin le plus court. On peut alors supposer que le tracé tortueux des vallées remonte à des époques plus reculées.

Des méandres vestiges d'époques anciennes

Il y a encore 5 à 20 millions d'années, la Terre s'élevait ici à peine au-dessus du niveau de la mer. D'indolents fleuves de plaine s'écoulaient de l'ouest vers le centre du futur plateau. Lorsque la croûte terrestre fut soulevée sur une vaste zone, ces fleuves changèrent de direction pour s'écouler désormais vers les bords du plateau. Ils conservèrent leurs méandres, car ils avaient déjà creusé leur lit sur quelques mètres de profondeur. Il ne leur restait plus qu'à suivre leur ancien tracé avec leurs forces nouvelles.

Le Bryce Canyon (première photo, page de gauche) est un spectaculaire amphithéâtre rocheux creusé dans des strates de calcaire tendre.

Le parc national des Arches, au nord-est de Canyonlands National Park (deuxième photo à gauche), présente la plus grande collection mondiale d'arches rocheuses. Le vent et la pluie ont façonné cette arche délicate de grès rouge.

Dans le Zion Canyon se trouvent des « rochers pleureurs » (ci-dessus à gauche), des parois rocheuses desquelles l'eau ne cesse de suinter.

La mesa de l'Échiquier (ci-dessus à droite), qui surplombe le Zion Canyon, est formée de dunes pétrifiées, autrefois déposées ici par les vents du désert.

LE MONDE À L'ENVERS

Dans les Alpes, à 2 000 m d'altitude, on trouve encore des ammonites et d'autres animaux marins fossilisés. On rencontre même des morceaux de croûte terrestre africaine au cœur de ce haut massif si proche de nous. Les Alpes sont un gigantesque labyrinthe géologique dont les derniers bouleversements ont eu lieu pendant les périodes glaciaires. Le glacier du Gorner est un des exemples de ces mutations.

Des strates rocheuses contrevenant aux lois de la nature

La Suisse possède beaucoup de montagnes dont la notoriété n'est pas toujours liée à l'altitude. Le mont Cervin, par exemple, fascine par sa forme unique. Le Rigi, lui, célèbre pour la vue merveilleuse qu'offre son sommet, est un massif de 1 800 m moins impressionnant car il se compose de couches de molasse. Celle-ci, comme l'indique le latin *mollis*, est une roche relativement tendre ; les couches s'empilent à plat, les plus anciennes en bas, les plus récentes en haut, conformément au « principe de stratification » tel qu'il fut formulé par les pères de la géologie.

Toutefois, non loin de ce sommet le plus célèbre du centre de la Suisse, dans les Mythen, qui surplombent le lac des Quatre-Cantons, ce monde géologique se trouve inversé : les deux sommets constitués de strates vieilles de plus de 150 millions d'années se dressent sur un sous-sol rocheux plus jeune de quelque 100 millions d'années. La découverte d'animaux et de plantes fossilisés le prouve avec force.

Les Alpes suisses comptent de nombreux endroits où les couches plus anciennes surmontent les plus récentes. En outre, certaines strates elles-mêmes se présentent à l'envers. Il existe, dans les couches rocheuses, différents indices du processus de stratification, comme les tubes dans lesquels les vers et autres animaux marins vivaient au fond de la mer. Les terminaisons de ces tubes sont toujours orientées vers le haut. Si elles pointent aujourd'hui vers le bas, cela signifie que la stratification originale s'est inversée.

Des couches rocheuses nomades

Au sud-est du Rigi, dans les Alpes de Glaris, les couches rocheuses anciennes couvrent, là aussi, les plus récentes. La différence d'âge (200 millions d'années) est encore plus grande que dans les Mythen.

Il semble donc que le principe de stratification ne s'applique guère à de larges parties des Alpes suisses. Parfois, les roches anciennes forment des îlots sur les roches plus jeunes, parfois elles constituent une véritable couverture où seules quelques failles permettent de constater que le monde géologique s'est inversé.

Les géologues appellent nappes de charriage ces masses rocheuses qui reposent sur des roches plus jeunes et de types différents. Concrètement, les formations géologiques complexes des Alpes évoquent une pile de nappes fraîchement repassées qui seraient tombées par terre, se rabattant les unes sur les autres, se froissant et s'emmêlant. En d'autres termes, les masses rocheuses se sont

Les Mythen, qui surplombent le lac des Quatre-Cantons, se composent de calcaire dur et dessinent des sommets très découpés. Les strates rocheuses plus jeunes situées en contrebas s'érodent plus rapidement et forment des pentes douces (ci-dessus).

De tous côtés, les cirques glaciaires cernent le mont Cervin. Ce sommet est un vestige de l'ancienne plaque sud-alpine, voire de la plaque continentale africaine venue du sud-est et repoussée au-dessus de la croûte océanique et de la croûte européenne encore plus ancienne (à gauche).

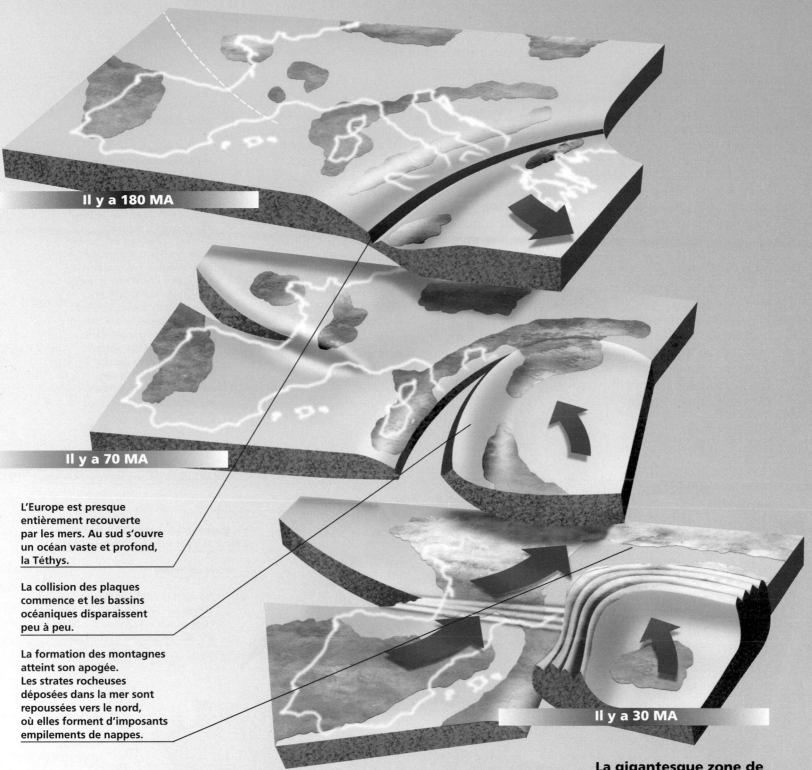

Il y a 180 MA

Il y a 70 MA

L'Europe est presque entièrement recouverte par les mers. Au sud s'ouvre un océan vaste et profond, la Téthys.

La collision des plaques commence et les bassins océaniques disparaissent peu à peu.

La formation des montagnes atteint son apogée. Les strates rocheuses déposées dans la mer sont repoussées vers le nord, où elles forment d'imposants empilements de nappes.

Il y a 30 MA

La gigantesque zone de déformation européenne

La formation des Alpes dure depuis maintenant 200 millions d'années. Les plaques de la croûte terrestre ont commencé à dériver, créant des bassins océaniques où se sont déposées d'importantes couches sédimentaires. La dérive des plaques s'est alors inversée et des fragments de la plaque africaine sont entrés en collision avec le continent européen, formant une zone de déformation au sein de laquelle les strates ont été compressées.

probablement empilées sous l'effet de forces souterraines avant de se renverser et de quitter leur lieu d'origine. Le fort rétrécissement de la croûte terrestre dans les Alpes suisses en témoigne également.

La danse des continents

Les Alpes et le sud de l'Europe sont présentés comme appartenant à la jeune Europe sur les cartes géologiques mondiales, ce qui ne signifie pas que cette partie du continent ne se compose que de roches jeunes. Seules les formations

géologiques de cette zone sont récentes, en particulier celles des Alpes, même s'il faut préciser que des montagnes bien plus anciennes existaient auparavant. Leurs socles se sont soudés aux montagnes plus jeunes.

L'ancêtre direct de la haute montagne actuelle est probablement une montagne depuis longtemps nivelée de la Pangée, le continent préhistorique. Il y a quelque 250 millions d'années, cette dernière était déjà en grande partie recouverte par une mer peu profonde. La formation des Alpes allait commencer très exactement 50 millions d'années plus tard, par une série de mouvements – encore en cours à l'heure actuelle – de la croûte terrestre, dont les fragments tournent, s'éloignent, se rapprochent et se pressent en une danse aussi lente qu'interminable.

Tout d'abord, la Pangée se disloque en deux parties, le Gondwana et la Laurasie. À l'est se forme l'océan Téthys, ancêtre de la Méditerranée, tandis qu'à l'ouest s'ouvre l'Atlantique. Il y a environ 110 millions d'années, l'océan, articulé en trois bassins dans la zone des Alpes, atteint sa plus grande largeur. La Laurasie commence alors une lente rotation dans le sens des aiguilles d'une montre et la Téthys disparaît peu à peu. Il y a 70 millions d'années, l'Afrique et l'Europe s'étaient de nouveau rapprochées, repoussant la croûte océanique à la fois sous et sur le continent européen. Au cours du tertiaire, la poussée de l'Afrique, ou plus exactement de fragments de la plaque africaine, allait augmenter, entraînant le plissement toujours plus serré et plus élevé des nappes alpines.

Ce que les poissons prisonniers des montagnes dévoilent aux géologues

Depuis des décennies, des poissons, des poissons préhistoriques et beaucoup d'autres animaux marins parfaitement conservés sont extraits du Monte San Giorgio, au-dessus de Lugano, à 1 000 m d'altitude. Même à 2 000 m au-dessus du niveau de la mer, les Alpes suisses recèlent de nombreuses roches marines, preuve de la puissance du soulèvement qui présida à la formation montagneuse encore en cours de nos jours. Les techniques de mesure modernes permettent désormais de connaître avec exactitude le niveau annuel de croissance. En Suisse, les sommets alpins grandissent chaque année de 1,5 mm en moyenne, ce qui donne une croissance de 1 500 m en un million d'années. Conclusion logique : si les Alpes ont grandi à une vitesse équivalente au cours du passé

La transformation des Alpes

Au début du tertiaire, les Alpes étaient encore une chaîne moyenne aux sommets peu marqués. La haute montagne actuelle, avec ses cirques, ses arêtes et ses crêtes rocheuses, a été sculptée par les glaciers au cours des différentes glaciations. Les « glaciers reliques » des Alpes suisses sont toujours imposants. Depuis la fin de la dernière période glaciaire, des torrents creusent des gorges dans les bouches des vallées secondaires, au-dessus de la vallée principale, où ils forment des cônes de déjection.

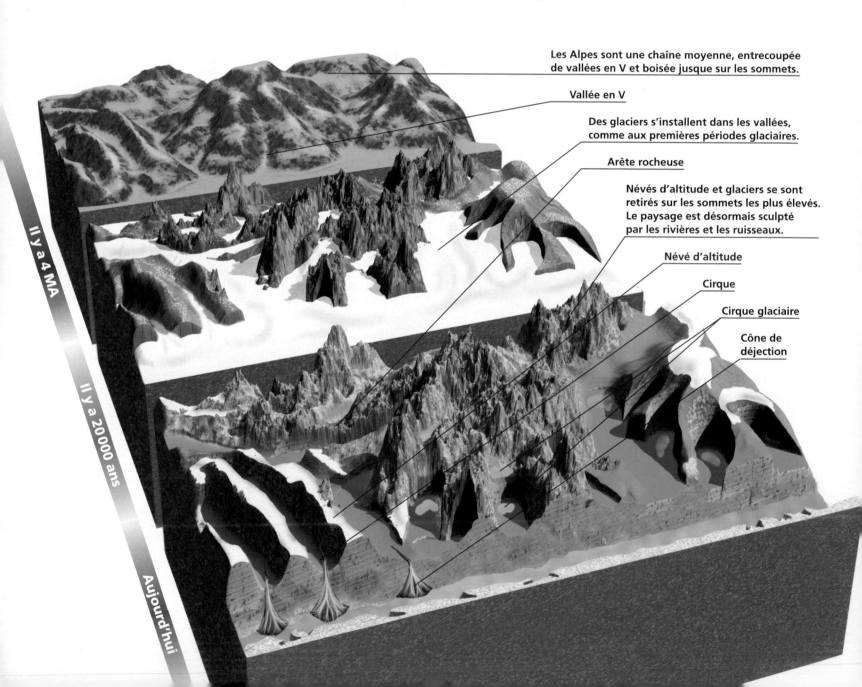

Les Alpes sont une chaîne moyenne, entrecoupée de vallées en V et boisée jusque sur les sommets.

Vallée en V

Des glaciers s'installent dans les vallées, comme aux premières périodes glaciaires.

Arête rocheuse

Névés d'altitude et glaciers se sont retirés sur les sommets les plus élevés. Le paysage est désormais sculpté par les rivières et les ruisseaux.

Névé d'altitude

Cirque

Cirque glaciaire

Cône de déjection

Il y a 4 MA

Il y a 20 000 ans

Aujourd'hui

terrestre récent, elles devaient être beaucoup plus basses il n'y a pas si longtemps. Au mieux atteignaient-elles l'altitude d'une montagne moyenne.

Les Alpes ne se sont hissées au rang des géants de ce monde qu'au cours des derniers millions d'années, comme le prouvent les sites au relief moins escarpé – pentes douces au bord supérieur de vallées abruptes – subsistant dans le paysage acéré de haute montagne. Ainsi, dans la vallée des Alpes du Valais aujourd'hui arrosée par la rivière issue du glacier du Gorner, les parois se dressent à la verti-

cale jusqu'à 300 à 400 m au-dessus du cours d'eau avant de s'évaser. Ce terrain aplati est probablement le fond d'une ancienne vallée en forme de cuvette qui accueillait autrefois un large fleuve.

Neiges d'antan

Devancé par le grand glacier d'Aletsch, le glacier du Gorner est le deuxième des quelque 2 000 glaciers de Suisse, avec ses 14 km de long et sa superficie de 64 km². Ce géant n'est pourtant qu'un nain

Une grotte permet aux visiteurs d'admirer de l'intérieur le glacier supérieur de Grindelwald. Les cours d'eau issus de glaciers jouent un rôle fondamental : l'actuel réchauffement climatique est donc observé avec inquiétude.

Les moraines des périodes glaciaires forment aujourd'hui de spectaculaires demoiselles coiffées, protégées de l'érosion par les gros blocs de pierre qui les surmontent.

Horn le plus connu, emblème de la Confédération helvétique, est le Matterhorn autrement dit le Cervin, qui culmine à 4 478 m dans les Alpes du Valais. Pour les géologues qui se préoccupent de formation montagneuse « de l'intérieur », ce sommet majestueux représente la klippe (élément isolé venu d'ailleurs) parfaite : c'est un lambeau de recouvrement presque entièrement érodé, composé de deux couches de croûte continentale (africaine en haut, européenne en bas) enserrant un fragment de croûte océanique. Le Cervin n'a

comparé à ses ancêtres qui remplissaient la vallée entière pendant les périodes glaciaires, s'unissaient à leurs voisins et formaient un gigantesque réseau couvrant l'ensemble des Alpes suisses, à l'exception de quelques sommets rocheux. Des langues glaciaires s'avançaient alors jusqu'à 10 km dans les terres, comme c'est le cas aujourd'hui dans les montagnes côtières du Pacifique, au Canada et en Alaska.

Au cours des deux à trois derniers millions d'années, les Alpes ont été couvertes au moins sept fois de glace. Les traces laissées par cette dernière sont encore fraîches et particulièrement impressionnantes en Suisse : cirques sauvages comme la vallée de Lauterbrunnen, dans les Alpes bernoises, lacs semblables à des fjords tel le lac des Quatre-Cantons, vallons glaciaires, niches

rocheuses creusées au flanc des montagnes par des glaciers plus petits, sans oublier les sommets extraordinaires appelés, selon l'endroit, aiguille, *Horn*, *piz* ou *becca*. Le

pris sa forme caractéristique que longtemps après la collision des continents, pendant la période glaciaire, lorsque les cirques le rongeaient de tous côtés.

Il y a 15 000 ans, les glaces ont reculé, les plantes ont recouvert le sol nu, les animaux ont repris possession des anciens déserts de glace, la nature a repris son souffle. Cette apparence de paix était trompeuse car elle annonçait des catastrophes naturelles majeures. Des versants de montagne entiers allaient s'effondrer dans les vallées, enterrant toute vie sous des tonnes de roches détritiques.

Des montagnes entières s'effondrent

Presque chaque vallée des Alpes suisses connaît depuis longtemps des glissements de terrain plus ou moins importants, mais les plus

Dans la plus grande marmite glaciaire du jardin des glaciers de Lucerne, les tourbillons des eaux de fonte et les graviers qu'elles charriaient ont creusé ces formes rocheuses caractéristiques appelées moulins glaciaires.

Derrière les agglomérats
des arènes alpines
de Flims s'est formé un lac
de plusieurs kilomètres de
long. L'eau finit par trouver
un chemin et creusa une gorge
de 600 m de profondeur
dans les strates : le Ruinaulta,
le « Grand Canyon suisse ».

ravageurs se sont produits dans la vallée du haut Rhin, sur le site de l'actuel village de Flims. La série d'éboulements commença il y a 14 000 ans et se poursuivit probablement jusqu'à il y a 9 000 ans. Sans cesse, de nouveaux massifs calcaires se mettaient en mouvement, glissaient et s'écroulaient sur les couches d'argile et de marne en contrebas, ne s'arrêtant parfois qu'à 15 km de leur point de départ et remplissant la vallée du haut Rhin jusqu'à 800 m de hauteur. En tout, plus de 10 milliards de mètres cubes se sont ainsi accumulés dans la vallée. C'est de loin le plus important glissement de terrain que les Alpes aient connu vers la fin de la récente période glaciaire.

Lorsque les glaciers soutenaient les montagnes

Les alpinistes le savent bien : lorsque le temps se réchauffe, au printemps, par exemple, ou le matin après une nuit froide, la glace fond dans les fentes et les crevasses, et les cailloux qu'elle retenait se mettent à rouler. Le sol sur les versants des sommets alpins est resté congelé pendant des millénaires. Avec l'augmentation de la température lors du dernier réchauffement, ce sol, appelé permafrost, a commencé à fondre. La glace qui maintenait les massifs rocheux de l'intérieur, comme un squelette, disparut et l'eau de fonte transforma les couches argileuses en véritables toboggans. Dans le même temps, les Alpes perdirent leur squelette extérieur, ces glaciers qui avaient rempli les vallées pendant la période glaciaire, empêchant les parois verticales de s'effondrer.

Le réchauffement atmosphérique actuel pourrait entraîner une recrudescence des glissements de terrain. La Suisse a perdu exactement 100 glaciers depuis le milieu du XIXe siècle. Pour les décennies à venir, on s'attend à une réduction d'au moins 50 %, qui aurait pour conséquence de rapprocher la limite inférieure du permafrost alpin de 700 m de la surface. Le squelette de glace rétrécit à vue d'œil.

VOYAGE DANS LE TERTIAIRE

Les plantes et les animaux pré-historiques tels que l'alligator (petite photo) ont pu survivre jusqu'à nos jours dans les vastes forêts marécageuses de Floride, longtemps restées inaccessibles à l'homme. Pourtant, aucun marécage ne devrait se trouver là, car la célèbre presqu'île nord-américaine repose sur du calcaire poreux qui, en temps normal, absorbe l'eau sans laisser de traces. Cette contradiction a une explication.

poreuse de
aujourd'hui
phréatique
régulièreme

Après la
réservoir
lorsque le
jourd'hui
sion à la s
artésiens.
expulsent

Lorsqu

Le sous-
une doll
vation d
de diam

Maré

Les forê
sembler
versants
au terti
L'espèc
cyprès
fère c
de hau
En t
marais
en par
de s'a
vent
cyprè
racin
assur
bois
pour
taux
d'ab
la p
Il
où
me
du
tar
Co
gr
su
fo
a
e
r
t

La Rift Valley

UN CONTINENT SE BRISE

Une grande faille semblable à une longue cicatrice s'étire à travers le haut plateau du Kenya ; la vue aérienne montre bien comment les fleuves et les éboulements montagneux l'ont comblée. Les forces colossales à l'œuvre des deux côtés du continent ont fait naître les lacs les plus profonds et les montagnes les plus hautes d'Afrique. Ce n'est peut-être pas un hasard si des découvertes sensationnelles de restes d'hommes préhistoriques (petite photo) ne cessent d'être faites à ce point de fracture.

Le berceau de l'humanité

Sur la photo satellite, il se reconnaît aisément. Le plus grand fossé d'effondrement du monde, qui s'étire sur plus de 6 400 km, naît dans la vallée du Jourdain et traverse la mer Rouge avant de se diviser en rift oriental et rift occidental, de se réunir au lac Malawi et de se terminer au Mozambique, dans le sud-est du continent. En maints endroits, la Rift Valley (ou Rifts est-africains) descend en dessous du niveau de la mer, tandis que ses flancs culminent parfois, de part et d'autre, à plus de 5 000 m. Vue de l'espace, cette suite de fossés d'effondrement évoque une plaie mal cicatrisée marquant profondément l'Est africain.

C'est le contraire qui est vrai en fait. La plaie est en train de s'ouvrir. La Rift Valley sous sa forme actuelle n'est qu'une étape intermédiaire d'un long processus de déchirement continental. Les gouffres profonds de cette « vallée africaine » se forment parce que la croûte terrestre se bombe sous l'effet de forces titanesques, un peu comme la croûte du pain éclate là où la chaleur de la cuisson agit le plus fortement sur la pâte. Les géophysiciens ont mis en évidence un bombement de la croûte terrestre de près de 10 km sur les quelque 1 000 km séparant les hauts plateaux éthiopiens de la côte somalienne.

Sous la faille, la croûte terrestre montre des faiblesses

Le géophysicien allemand Alfred Wegener (1880-1930) fut le premier, en 1912, à soupçonner que les continents se rapprochent et s'éloignent, au fil du temps, faisant disparaître d'anciens océans et en créant de nouveaux. Sa théorie de la dérive des continents est aujourd'hui universellement reconnue sous une forme modifiée.

Les grands fossés d'effondrement africains semblent être le début d'un processus de séparation dans lequel l'est de l'Afrique se sépare de la péninsule Arabique et du reste du continent. On ignore toutefois si les plaques concernées s'écartent activement ou si elles sont repoussées par du magma remontant de la partie supérieure du manteau. Les mesures confirment en tout cas que la croûte terrestre sous la Rift Valley est particulièrement fine et tendue. Elle est même crevassée en certains endroits de la zone centrale : dans la mer Rouge, le golfe d'Aden et la dépression d'Afar, en bordure sud de la mer Rouge. En ces endroits, le magma remonte directement à la surface de la Terre, élargissant le fossé.

Le Kilimandjaro est le plus grand massif volcanique d'Afrique. Il culmine à 5 895 m au-dessus de la savane, et son cratère, au sommet, mesure 2,5 km de diamètre.

Les premiers fossés de la zone se sont ouverts il y a 15 à 40 millions d'années. Une deuxième poussée a commencé il y a 5 millions d'années et se poursuit encore aujourd'hui. De nos jours, les bords de la mer Rouge s'écartent de 16 mm par an, ceux du golfe d'Aden, de 20 mm.

La source d'énergie responsable de ces événements se trouverait sous la dépression d'Afar, au point de rencontre des fossés de la mer Rouge, du golfe d'Aden et de l'Afrique de l'Est. L'intense activité volcanique de l'endroit y a totalement disloqué la croûte terrestre continentale, laissant remonter la lave. Le point chaud soupçonné sous la dépression d'Afar – une zone de fusion immobile à la base du manteau ter-

Les Massaïs nomment
ce volcan de 2 878 m
Ol Doinyo Lengai,
« la montagne des dieux ».
Dans son cratère, des
cheminées ou *hornitos*
crachent une lave riche
en sodium qui devient
blanche comme neige
en séchant.

restre – pourrait avoir de lourdes conséquences, car le continent africain ne s'est pratiquement pas déplacé depuis de nombreux millions d'années. Le point chaud a donc eu tout le temps nécessaire pour travailler la croûte terrestre.

Le lointain océan Atlantique permet d'anticiper l'avenir de la Rift Valley. Sa naissance, il y a environ 200 millions d'années, a été marquée par des effondrements qui ont brisé le continent originel – le Gondwana –, séparant l'Amérique du Sud et l'Afrique. Au niveau de la dorsale médio-atlantique, le magma continue de remonter à la surface, formant une nouvelle croûte océanique et élargissant l'Atlantique. La mer Rouge pourrait donc, elle aussi, être le modeste ancêtre d'un futur océan.

Les lacs salés abritent la vie

Les montagnes qui bordent le rift se composent de roches anciennes et de roches volcaniques, car le magma se fraie facilement un chemin à travers une croûte

terrestre tendue à l'extrême. Le mont Kenya (5 199 m) et le Kilimandjaro (5 895 m), les plus hautes montagnes volcaniques d'Afrique, se sont formés après le fossé d'effondrement.

Tandis que le Kilimandjaro est couronné de neiges éternelles, le sommet de l'Ol Doinyo Lengai (2 878 m), la montagne sacrée des Massaïs en Tanzanie, est recouvert d'une couche blanche de carbonate de sodium. Le volcan émet en effet une lave extrêmement riche en carbonate de sodium, un sel qui devient tout blanc au bout de quelques jours à l'air libre.

À 15 km au nord, le sel de sodium s'accumule également sur les rives du lac Natron, le plus spectaculaire d'une série de lacs salés de la Rift Valley. Son eau est chaude, salée et alcaline comme de l'eau de lessive. À certains endroits, des bactéries pourpres le teintent de rouge. Cet environnement d'apparence hostile abrite pourtant quelques espèces de cichlidés et accueille des centaines de milliers de flamants roses, environ la moitié de la population mondiale. Mais leur habitat est sérieusement menacé, car les lacs fermés ont de moins en moins d'eau et sont de plus en plus pollués. On a longtemps cru que le sel du lac Natron venait des volcans voisins, mais, en 1978, des geysers qui projetaient de l'eau salée chaude à la surface ont été découverts sous le lac.

Le lac Natron est salé et peu profond, mais le rift abrite également des étendues d'eau douce dont la grande profondeur empêche la salinisation en dépit d'une évaporation importante, comme le lac Tanganyika, le plus profond d'Afrique, avec

1 435 m. Tout comme son voisin, le lac Malawi, il abrite de nombreuses espèces de poissons qui n'existent nulle part ailleurs sur la planète.

Du fossé d'effondrement à l'évolution

La fracture d'un continent a des conséquences spectaculaires pour les régions concernées : à l'échelle géologique, de nouvelles montagnes et de nouvelles failles se

Un nouvel océan se forme

Le lac Tanganyika, au milieu de la Rift Valley, atteint une profondeur de 1 435 m. À cet endroit, les plaques de la croûte terrestre continuent de s'écarter lentement, le continent africain se brise. Selon les prévisions, la mer Rouge devrait s'enfoncer toujours plus avant dans la Rift Valley par la dépression d'Afar et former un nouvel océan en rejoignant les grands lacs.

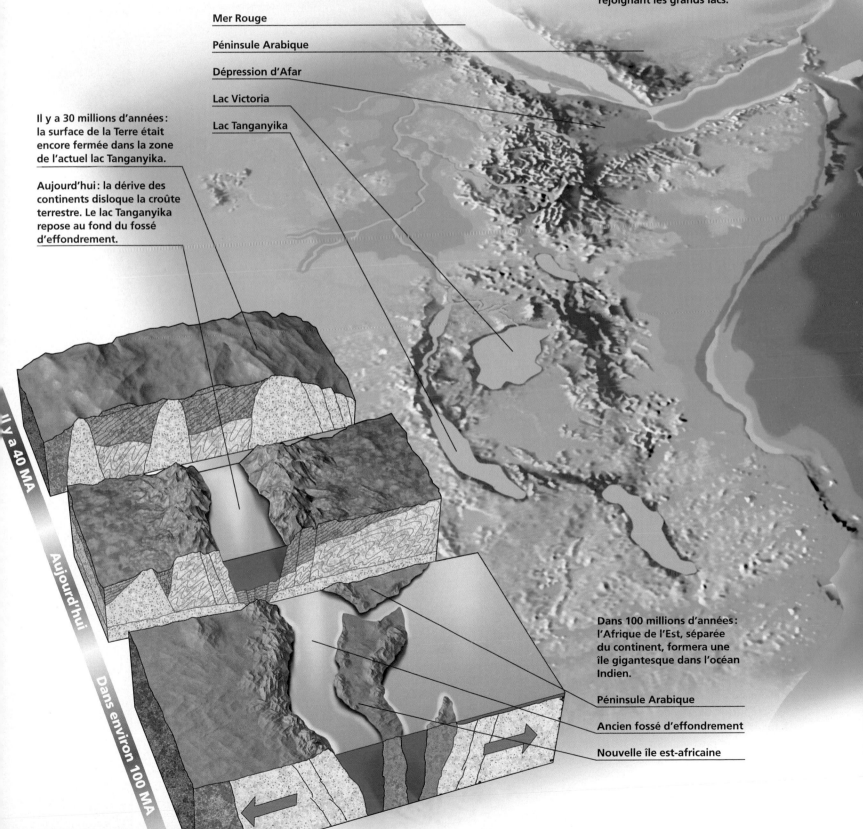

Mer Rouge

Péninsule Arabique

Dépression d'Afar

Lac Victoria

Lac Tanganyika

Il y a 30 millions d'années : la surface de la Terre était encore fermée dans la zone de l'actuel lac Tanganyika.

Aujourd'hui : la dérive des continents disloque la croûte terrestre. Le lac Tanganyika repose au fond du fossé d'effondrement.

Il y a 40 MA

Aujourd'hui

Dans environ 100 MA

Dans 100 millions d'années : l'Afrique de l'Est, séparée du continent, formera une île gigantesque dans l'océan Indien.

Péninsule Arabique

Ancien fossé d'effondrement

Nouvelle île est-africaine

forment, les fleuves modifient leur cours, les lacs se ferment et le tout s'accompagne d'effets climatiques importants. Toute forme de vie doit également s'adapter au changement environnemental. Ce n'est donc peut-être pas un hasard si l'évolution a pris un chemin particulièrement riche de conséquences dans cette vallée à la géologie et au climat si inhabituels.

Tout a-t-il commencé avec Lucy ?

En 1974, des chercheurs ont trouvé dans l'Afar éthiopien le squelette pétrifié d'un être de sexe féminin, apparenté à l'homme et vieux d'environ 4 millions d'années. Bien qu'adulte, le personnage ne dépassait pas 1 m et était apparemment mort jeune. C'était une découverte sensationnelle car il s'agissait de toute évidence d'un bipède. Les anthropologues Johanson, Coppens et Taieb venaient de trouver le plus vieil ancêtre de l'homme. S'inspirant d'une chanson des Beatles, ils baptisèrent l'arrière-grand-mère de l'humanité Lucy. Son cerveau n'était pas particulièrement grand, mais sa mâchoire ressemblait déjà fortement à celle d'un être humain. Lucy était donc un hominidé du groupe des hominiens, qui a donné naissance à la lignée humaine. Son espèce a reçu le nom scientifique d'*Australopithecus afarensis*. En 1978, des traces de pas de cet hominidé, datant de 3,5 millions d'années, furent découvertes dans la plaine entourant Laetoli, en Tanzanie.

D'autres découvertes importantes de fossiles indiquent que le berceau de l'humanité se trouvait en Afrique, sans doute dans la région de la Rift Valley, car aucun autre endroit n'a jusqu'à présent révélé autant de traces d'hominidés. Bien entendu, les événements naturels qui ont suivi la formation du fossé d'effondrement pourraient être responsables de cette accumulation de découvertes. Les restes de nos ancêtres ont été entièrement et rapidement ensevelis, ce qui, ajouté à la sécheresse du climat, a permis de les préserver parfaitement.

Par ailleurs, la Rift Valley était sans doute soumise aux conditions environnementales permettant au singe de se transformer en homme. Les primates existent depuis environ 60 millions d'années, les singes depuis 35 millions d'années. Le climat était alors tellement humide que les forêts tropicales s'étendaient jusqu'en Europe.

À l'époque de Lucy, le monde avait totalement changé. Il était devenu globalement plus froid et plus sec. Sur les hauts plateaux et dans les montagnes d'Afrique de l'Est, les

forêts étaient encore denses, mais, dans le fond du fossé d'effondrement et dans les régions plus éloignées de l'équateur, les savanes commençaient à s'étendre. La marche debout de Lucy et de ses congénères était bien adaptée à ces nouvelles conditions, et leurs descendants n'eurent plus besoin des doigts recourbés du singe pour se déplacer d'arbre en arbre.

En raison du climat plus sec, la plupart des hominidés se rapprochèrent des lacs. C'est près du lac Turkana que fut découvert le plus vieil *Homo rudolfensis*, qui tentait là de survivre à une période d'extrême sécheresse, il y a 2,5 millions d'années. Poussé par le manque de nourriture, il fut le premier représentant de l'espèce *Homo* à fabriquer des outils en pierre à l'aide desquels il fracassait les os et les crânes des cadavres pour atteindre la moelle et le cerveau. Dès lors, les meilleures chances de survie n'appartenaient plus seulement aux plus forts, mais aussi aux plus ingénieux.

Traces de pas d'*Australopithecus afarensis* en Tanzanie:
il y a 3,5 millions d'années,
les hominidés marchèrent
sur des cendres volcaniques
souples et humides qui
se pétrifièrent
peu après.

DES POISSONS DANS LE DÉSERT

Le lac Bokou scintille, tel un joyau précieux, entre les dunes et les contreforts rocheux de l'Ennedi, dans le sud-est du Sahara. Le désert s'étend à perte de vue, mais des poissons s'ébattent pourtant entre les roseaux dans les lacs d'Ounianga Serir. Ces inexplicables étendues d'eau témoignent d'une ère climatique bien particulière.

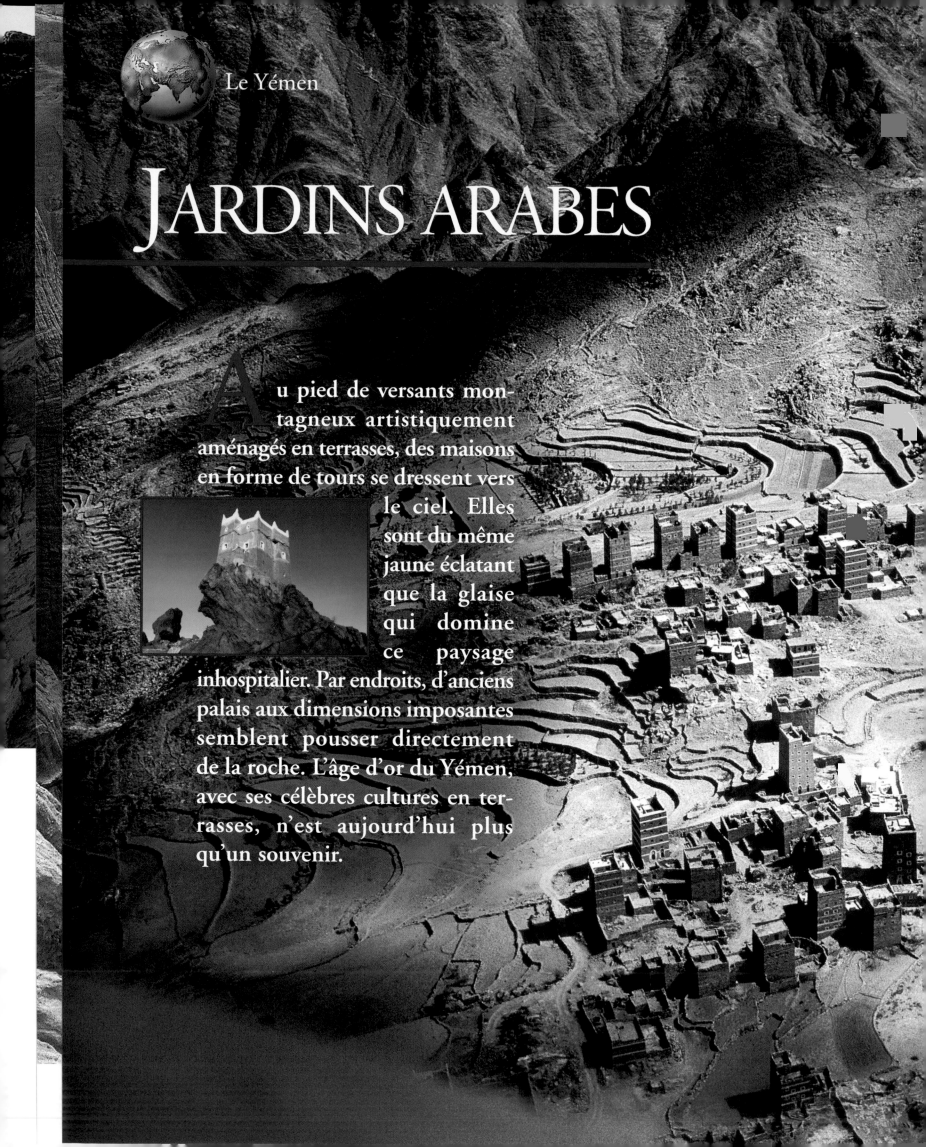

JARDINS ARABES

Au pied de versants montagneux artistiquement aménagés en terrasses, des maisons en forme de tours se dressent vers le ciel. Elles sont du même jaune éclatant que la glaise qui domine ce paysage inhospitalier. Par endroits, d'anciens palais aux dimensions imposantes semblent pousser directement de la roche. L'âge d'or du Yémen, avec ses célèbres cultures en terrasses, n'est aujourd'hui plus qu'un souvenir.

Les restes du jardin d'Éden

Chaque période de l'Histoire a connu son pays aux richesses légendaires : l'Égypte ancienne rêvait du Punt, perdu quelque part au cœur de l'Afrique, les conquérants ne pensaient qu'à l'Eldorado, le pays de l'or, caché dans les cordillères d'Amérique du Sud, l'Antiquité gréco-romaine ne jurait que par son *Arabia felix*. Si l'on en croit les textes antiques, cette Arabie heureuse, pays verdoyant aux denses forêts béni des dieux, dont « la terre contient de l'or fin et où l'argent est répandu dans les rues comme de la poussière », se trouvait dans le sud de la péninsule Arabique, à l'emplacement de l'actuel Yémen.

Les chroniqueurs qui, à l'époque déjà, doutaient de la réalité de cet Éden terrestre évoquaient la pseudo-Arabie heureuse. Si l'on considère le Yémen de nos jours, on aurait tendance à donner raison aux sceptiques. Al-Yaman, le « pays du Sud », est plutôt le frère pauvre de l'Arabie, et ses paysages ressemblent plus à ceux de l'*Arabia deserta*, ainsi que les textes anciens désignaient la péninsule Arabique.

Un pays de cocagne naît...

Le sud de l'Arabie est peuplé depuis au moins 700 000 ans. Les peintures rupestres réalisées à l'âge de la pierre montrent souvent des espèces animales dont les descendants actuels vivent dans les régions marécageuses plutôt que dans les déserts. Les régions montagneuses comprises entre la mer Rouge et la mer d'Oman ont donc temporairement connu un climat beaucoup plus humide que le climat désertique actuel. La géologie apporte elle aussi ses preuves : les sédiments marins retrouvés dans des zones totalement dépourvues d'eau, l'humus épais et brun qui ne peut se former que dans un climat humide et, surtout, les vastes wadis. Ces vallées sèches que l'eau ne traverse plus que rarement de part en part ont probablement été creusées par des cours d'eau. Au cours des derniers 50 000 ans, plusieurs périodes humides se sont succédé, principalement de 35 000 à 29 000 ans avant notre ère puis, après une interruption sèche de 18 000 ans, de 9 000 à 4 000 ans av. J.-C. Les masses d'air humide, poussées par les vents de mousson contre les flancs des montagnes yéménites, ont apporté la pluie et fait pousser des forêts denses et des prairies luxuriantes. Le nombre de gazelles, d'antilopes et d'autres animaux de la savane devait être important car on a retrouvé un peu partout des pièges caractéristiques composés de rangées de pierres en forme de Y. Les chasseurs y rabattaient les animaux par le côté ouvert pour les acculer et les tuer à la lance. Vu les conditions de vie difficiles dans les déserts actuels du sud de l'Arabie, les habitants de l'âge de la pierre vivaient presque dans un pays de cocagne, mais cela n'allait pas durer.

... et s'éteint

Il y a exactement 4 000 ans, le climat redevint plus aride. Ruisseaux et rivières s'asséchèrent, lacs et sources se tarirent, et le jardin d'Éden d'Arabie commença à se flétrir. Certaines peintures rupestres montrent clairement les effets catastrophiques du changement de climat sur la faune et la flore. Les gazelles et les buffles d'eau sont de moins en moins souvent représentés, tandis qu'apparaît l'oryx, une antilope du désert adaptée à une sécheresse extrême. Finalement, seuls les animaux domestiques tels que l'âne et la vache restent présents sur les peintures. C'est pourtant à cette époque, alors que les conditions de vie empiraient et que les hommes étaient contraints de se rapprocher pour survivre, qu'apparurent les premiers royaumes du sud de la péninsule Arabique. Le royaume

Un jardin d'Éden à l'âge de la pierre

Au milieu de la dernière période glaciaire, il y a tout juste 18 000 ans, les montagnes yéménites connaissaient un climat plutôt froid et humide. Leurs habitants menaient une vie de chasseurs et de cueilleurs nomades.

À partir du VIIIe millénaire av. J.-C., le climat se réchauffa et devint encore plus humide. Les vallées de l'actuel désert accueillaient des fleuves majestueux et les montagnes, aujourd'hui arides, étaient couvertes de végétation. Les hommes du néolithique se sédentarisèrent et édifièrent des villages semblables à ceux de l'actuelle Afrique de l'Est. Ils élevaient des vaches, des moutons et des chèvres, et chassaient dans la savane luxuriante, mais au bout de 5 000 ans, le climat commença à devenir plus sec.

de la légendaire reine de Saba est attesté il y a 3 000 ans. Il fut suivi d'une demi-douzaine d'autres, dont le dernier a disparu il y a environ 1 500 ans.

La solution : les terrasses

Au Yémen, les fenêtres sur l'Histoire sont grandes ouvertes. On peut remonter au miocène (de − 23,5 à − 5,3 millions d'années), lorsque l'Arabie s'est déplacée vers le nord-est et s'est séparée de l'Afrique par l'ouverture de la mer Rouge, ou pousser jusqu'au jurassique (de − 206 à − 144 millions d'années), lorsque les strates d'un merveilleux albâtre se sont déposées dans le fond d'une mer depuis longtemps disparue. Par comparaison, la période pendant laquelle les

Les trésors d'Arabie

Les textes de l'Antiquité célèbrent les fragrances d'Arabie : l'encens, la myrrhe, gomme-résine à l'odeur si agréable que les Égyptiens anciens utilisaient pour l'embaumement des momies, et bien d'autres parfums et épices accessibles à prix d'or. L'Éthiopie et le Yémen sont considérés comme les pays d'origine du café. Jusqu'au milieu du XVIIIe siècle, le Yémen était le seul à exporter ses graines de café (ci-dessous) et à bien en vivre. Aujourd'hui, seules quelques régions cultivent encore le café, qui a cédé la place au qat (*Catha edulis*), un arbuste dont les feuilles libèrent une substance hallucinogène très prisée et que l'on mâche comme stimulant. Il est déconseillé d'en faire autant avec les fleurs somptueuses du vénéneux brachychiton (ci-contre).

montagnes yéménites ont été transformées en un paysage unique au monde par la culture en terrasses est extrêmement courte. Elle n'a en effet duré que 3 000 ans, à peine un battement de cils à l'échelle géologique.

Il existe des cultures en terrasses dans de nombreux endroits au monde : des vignobles d'Europe centrale aux terrasses des Andes en passant par les rizières de l'Est et du Sud-Est asiatique. En tout, ce sont probablement plus de 2 millions de kilomètres carrés de la surface de la Terre qui ont ainsi été aménagés par l'homme, mais jamais l'aspect d'aucun autre pays n'a été aussi profondément modifié par les cultures en terrasses que le Yémen.

Leur création et leur entretien sont un travail difficile, surtout en l'absence de machines, mais cela en vaut la peine car les terrasses offrent des avantages certains. Elles constituent, sur les versants montagneux, la seule possibilité de cultiver la terre. Les animaux de trait ou de bât qui seraient incapables de gravir les parois en pente peuvent accomplir leur travail sur terrain plat. L'érosion du sol par l'eau est plus faible, d'une part parce que la pluie s'écoule plus lentement sur une surface horizontale, d'autre part parce que les terrasses sont divisées en de nombreuses petites unités incapables de retenir des masses d'eau importantes.

Lorsque la terre fertile d'une terrasse est entraînée par la pluie, elle s'accumule le plus souvent contre le muret de la suivante. Enfin, les terrasses favorisent la formation de nouvelles nappes phréatiques car la majeure partie de l'eau de pluie peut s'infiltrer dans leur sol.

De nouvelles recherches ont permis d'établir que les habitants des montagnes yéménites furent probablement les inventeurs des cultures en terrasses. Peut-être suivirent-ils pour cela l'exemple de la nature, car dans certaines régions du Yémen les versants sont étagés en strates basaltiques plus dures. C'est en tout cas il y a 4 000 à 5 000 ans que les premières terrasses furent construites dans le sud de l'Arabie, soit 1 000 ans plus tôt qu'en Chine. Elles ont toujours été exploitées depuis lors.

Les cultures en terrasses demandent beaucoup de travail. Il faut les entretenir sans arrêt car l'érosion peut les détruire en peu de temps. Pourtant, depuis quelques

décennies, c'est-à-dire depuis que les hommes vont travailler dans les riches États pétroliers du Proche-Orient, les exploitations manquent de bras et les terrasses s'abîment chaque jour un peu plus.

Des crues dispensatrices de vie

Au pied des terrasses, les vallées accueillent traditionnellement des cultures d'irriga-

tion dont l'exploitation semble primitive : des digues inclinées, aménagées dans le lit des rivières, permettent de détourner une partie de l'eau des crues et de la canaliser jusqu'aux champs. L'érosion du sol due à l'écoulement des eaux de crue s'avère particulièrement utile, car les particules dissoutes dans l'eau se déposent comme engrais naturel sur les terres cultivées. Pourtant cette méthode cache un risque mortel : les eaux d'irrigation peuvent ar-

racher les digues et anéantir des cultures entières, comme ce fut le cas au VIᵉ siècle lorsque céda la digue de Ma'rib. Cette catastrophe mit un terme à l'âge d'or des royaumes yéménites.

Les cultures en terrasses du Yémen ressemblent à des œuvres d'art. Elles constituent les dernières tentatives désespérées pour protéger les versants dénudés de l'érosion et pour maintenir quelques surfaces cultivables dans une région de plus en plus aride (ci-dessous).

Dans les vallées désertiques, les villages s'adossent aux flancs montagneux abrupts. Le fond de la vallée reste ainsi libre pour les cultures dans les oasis, de nos jours souvent irriguées par des puits (ci-contre).

La nécessité rend inventif et unit les hommes dans un même combat pour survivre. La création de terrasses sur les versants montagneux et l'irrigation des oasis étaient des tâches que nul clan n'était capable d'effectuer sans aide extérieure. Seule l'union pouvait permettre de les mener à bien (grande illustration).

LES PUITS DES DIEUX

La région karstique du Yucatán était étroitement liée à la culture des Mayas qui établirent leurs habitations à proximité de légendaires puits sacrificiels. Ces derniers constituent souvent l'entrée de labyrinthes caverneux peuplés de poissons aveugles (petite photo) et d'êtres qui ont probablement survécu à une gigantesque catastrophe naturelle.

Comme une île préhistorique

Le navigateur espagnol Antonio de Alaminos, l'un des premiers Européens à explorer les côtes d'Amérique centrale en 1517, était convaincu que le Yucatán était une île. Mais le plat pays bordé de récifs et de bancs de sable est solidement attaché au continent. Pourtant, Alaminos n'avait pas tout à fait tort. Bordé à l'ouest et au nord par le golfe du Mexique, à l'est par la mer des Caraïbes et au sud par une large ceinture forestière, le Yucatán est un monde en soi. Il possède une faune et une flore distinctes, ainsi qu'un climat sensiblement plus sec que celui du reste de l'Amérique centrale, dont la péninsule s'écarte comme un pouce tendu.

C'est par la géologie que le Yucatán diverge le plus du pont terrestre formé par l'Amérique centrale. Tandis que ce dernier présente des strates rocheuses plissées de toutes sortes, la péninsule se compose presque entièrement de couches de calcaire horizontales datant du tertiaire. La péninsule de Floride, qui lui fait face, se compose elle aussi de calcaire de cette même période, entre 65 et 2,5 millions d'années avant notre ère. On pourrait presque prendre les deux presqu'îles pour des jumelles, mais si leurs points communs sont bien réels, leurs différences sont encore plus nombreuses.

Beaucoup de pluie, mais peu d'eau

La Floride est imprégnée d'eau, qui alimente ses nombreux lacs, fleuves et marécages. En revanche, sa sœur centraméricaine est un pays presque dépourvu d'eau. Pas un seul fleuve n'arrose le nord du Yucatán. Cette absence ne peut pourtant pas être imputée au manque de pluie. Sur l'île de Cozumel, près de la pointe nord de la presqu'île, la pluviométrie annuelle moyenne est de 1 500 l/m², soit presque autant qu'à Miami. Les mois d'hiver sont un peu plus secs au Yucatán, mais l'été et l'automne connaissent souvent des pluies torrentielles. Même si on enlève 80 % du volume pour l'évaporation, il reste encore 300 litres d'eau par mètre carré pour l'écoulement. Et pourtant, nulle trace de cours d'eau.

Disparue de la surface de la Terre

Au Yucatán, les strates rocheuses du tertiaire sont essentiellement composées de calcaire, comme en Floride. Ces roches se

L'environnement karstique était intégré à la culture maya, comme le montre ce chemin reliant la pyramide de Kukulcán à Chichén Itzá au puits sacrificiel.

LE BLANC PAYS VERT

Les promontoires ro-cheux qui se dres-sent au-dessus de l'inland-sis au nord-ouest de la plus grande île de la Terre (grande photo) laissent deviner que l'uniforme cara-pace blanche dissimule des choses extraordinaires : certaines des roches les plus anciennes du monde, de scintillantes grottes de glace, des archives climatiques des dernières centaines de mil-liers d'années. Peut-être peut-on même y apprendre pourquoi cette île, où l'on ne trou-ve que de rares coins de verdure, comme dans le fjord Kangia, près d'Ilulissat, ancienne Jakobshavn (pe-tite photo), s'appelle le « Pays vert » (Groenland).

Une île de contradictions

L'origine du nom déroutant de l'île arctique remonte à Erik le Rouge, qui la découvrit en 982. Il la baptisa Groenland (Pays vert), se disant « que les gens préféreraient y aller si le pays avait un beau nom ». Belle imposture ! À la décharge du navigateur norvégien, il faut préciser que dans le sud-ouest du Groenland, à l'endroit où il fonda quelques colonies, une large bande côtière était effectivement libre de glace. Le Moyen Âge étant une période de réchauffement, elles étaient sans aucun doute beaucoup plus vertes qu'aujourd'hui.

D'autres questions subsistent pourtant. Comment de denses forêts peuvent-elles pousser en Europe bien au-delà du cercle polaire alors que, dans la zone équivalente outre-atlantique, cette île est verrouillée aux 4/5 par une épaisse carapace de glace ? Il y a encore deux millions d'années, des épicéas, des bouleaux et des mélèzes poussaient dans la partie la plus septentrionale du Groenland, comme aujourd'hui dans la taïga. Pourquoi les forêts se sont-elles transformées en déserts de glace et de roche ? Qu'est-ce qui a conduit, il y a plus de 30 millions d'années, à la constitution de la calotte glaciaire du Groenland ?

Les glaciers du Groenland chichement alimentés

Aucune masse de glace de l'hémisphère Nord n'est plus grande que celle du Pays vert : elle représente près de 1,7 million de kilomètres carrés et plus de 2,7 millions de kilomètres cubes. Ce volume pourrait recouvrir presque totalement les États membres de l'Union européenne d'une couche de glace de 1 km d'épaisseur. En moyenne, la calotte glaciaire descend à une profondeur d'environ 1 700 m, mais elle peut atteindre le double en certains endroits. Si les glaciers du Groenland devaient un jour fondre entièrement, le niveau de la mer augmenterait d'au moins 7 m.

On pourrait penser, au vu de ces dimensions colossales, que la calotte est nourrie par d'amples chutes de neige, mais ce n'est pas le cas. Au centre du Groenland il ne tombe en moyenne que 1 m de neige par an, ce qui correspond à un apport de glace de 30 à 40 cm. C'est sur les flancs est de la calotte, située sous les vents de pluie de l'ouest et du sud-ouest, là où le froid courant est Groenland freine l'arrivée de masses d'air humide, et donc la formation de nuages, qu'il neige le moins.

Le Gulf Stream apporte la neige

Les neiges sont beaucoup plus fréquentes dans l'Ouest et le sud-ouest de l'île, principalement à cause du Gulf Stream, ce « chauffe-eau » qui par ailleurs empêche le climat du Groenland de se répandre dans le nord de l'Europe. L'air au-dessus de la mer comparativement chaude contient tant d'humidité que la pointe sud de l'île connaît des précipitations annuelles de plus de 2 500 litres d'eau par mètre carré, sous forme de neige et de pluie. À l'extrémité opposée de l'île, dans le Peary Land (Terre de Peary), les précipitations atteignent à peine 1/10 de ce volume. C'est pourquoi la zone la plus septentrionale et la plus froide du Groenland est libre de glace.

Chaque année, les glaces du Groenland augmentent d'environ 500 km². Une masse équivalente se détache des glaciers qui aboutissent dans la mer en iceberg, ou se transforme en eau de fonte qui s'infiltre dans des crevasses et baigne d'imposantes grottes de glace. Au total, 2/5 des pertes de glace sont à attribuer aux icebergs. On estime que 30 000 à 50 000 icebergs se détachent chaque année des langues glaciaires du Groenland. Ils dérivent de 20 à 40 km

Retour vers le Pays vert ?

Imaginer que la deuxième masse de glace de la Terre pourrait disparaître a de quoi inquiéter. Le réchauffement de l'atmosphère terrestre ferait du Groenland un véritable pays vert, tandis que dans le reste du monde des contrées entières, densément peuplées, sombreraient dans la mer.

Certains indicateurs montrent que la calotte glaciaire du Groenland est en train de rétrécir. Dans le nord-ouest de l'île, l'inlandsis diminue de 10 à 15 cm par an depuis les années 1950, et le front du puissant cours d'eau glaciaire qui débouche dans le fjord Kangia, près d'Ilulissat (Kakobshavn), a reculé d'environ 25 km depuis 1850. Toutefois, le volume de glace a augmenté au cours des dernières décennies, notamment sur le flanc sud-ouest de la calotte, sans doute parce que l'atmosphère plus chaude contient plus d'humidité et alimente mieux les glaciers en neige.

L'océan Arctique, séparé des autres mers, ne reçoit ni eau chaude ni eau froide.

Vaste point chaud

Pont de terre de Thulé

Les plaques nord-américaine et eurasiatique s'écartent et les ponts de terre qui isolaient l'océan Arctique se brisent.

Point chaud

Dorsale médio-atlantique

Il y a 50 MA

Il y a 35 MA

Aujourd'hui

par jour sur la mer avant de disparaître. Les plus grands peuvent ainsi parcourir plus de 5 000 km.

L'île Uunartoq, près de la pointe sud du Groenland, offre une particularité surprenante : habitants et vacanciers peuvent s'y ébattre dans des sources d'eau chaude à 37 °C, tandis qu'à l'extérieur, les icebergs sillonnent le fjord. On ignore quel feu na-turel réchauffe l'eau, mais il s'agit sans doute d'un frag-ment de magma en train de refroidir dans le sous-sol.

Après le point chaud vint la glace

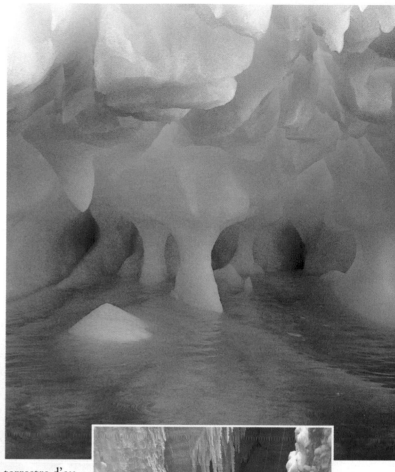

Cette partie de l'île connais-sait déjà des éruptions vol-caniques il y a 3,8 millions d'années. Les foyers des vol-cans sont éteints depuis longtemps et les roches vol-caniques sont devenues presque méconnaissables sous l'effet de la pression et de la chaleur. Toutefois, non loin de là s'étirent des zones volcaniques plus jeunes, notamment autour de la baie de Disko et le long de la côte est. Le premier foyer volcanique fixe, appelé point chaud, fut remarqué au cœur du Groenland il y a 60 millions d'années. Ses éruptions, accompagnées par une élévation de la croûte terrestre d'au moins 1 000 m, éclatèrent dans le centre de l'île. Lorsque la plaque nord-américaine – et le Groenland avec – dériva vers le nord-ouest au-dessus de ce point chaud, les éruptions volcaniques se déplacèrent vers le sud-est, dans l'Atlantique en for-mation. Une dorsale volcanique se créa, sur et sous la mer, reliant le Groenland, l'Is-lande, les îles Féroé et les îles Britanniques. Elle donna naissance au légendaire pont de terre de Thulé, qui a sans doute permis le passage de nombreuses espèces animales et végétales de l'Europe à l'Arctique et inversement.

Le Groenland devient une île de glace

Le développement de l'inlandsis du Groenland et l'histoire climatique de l'hémisphère Nord au cours des 30 à 40 derniers millions d'années sont intimement liés à l'ouverture de différentes routes maritimes entre l'Atlantique et l'océan Arctique à la suite de la dérive des continents. Des courants marins de l'Arctique ont conduit à un refroidissement du climat.

L'île, cernée par des courants marins froids et chauds, est recouverte d'une couche de glace dont l'épaisseur atteint par endroits 3 700 m.

Le Groenland en coupe transversale : sous le poids de la glace, la croûte terrestre s'est affaissée en forme de cuvette.

Les icebergs de l'Arctique proviennent essentiellem... de la côte ouest du Groenland. Le Sermeq Kujalleq, le glacier le plu... rapide du Grand Nord, a... une avancée de 20 m pa... jour, y assure la relève.

Au-dessus des barres rocheuses souterraines, les cours d'eau glaciaire entaillent des gorges particulièrement profondes (ci-dessus). Les crues de fonte s'y déversent en été et baignent de fascinantes grottes de glace.

Les masses de glace du Groenland contiennent souvent peu de bulles d'air et brillent d'intenses nuances bleutées (en haut). La glace plus aérée est blanche.

Pour les animau
terre était un che
courants marin
infranchissable. I
d'autres ponts,
Spitzberg et à l'Ar
laient presque ent
empêchant l'écha
Ces ponts ne se l
lions d'années. L
dans la zone du d
le Groenland et l
magma repoussé
se refroidirent et
des fragments re
entre les plaques
asiatique, brisant

LES PARADIS TERRESTRES

LE FLEUVE-MER

Lorsque Francisco de Orellana et ses troupes, en 1541, s'avancent bien au-delà des Andes sans connaître les lieux et sans provisions suffisantes, ils n'ont pour seul recours qu'un fleuve inconnu. Tandis qu'ils le descendent, ils rencontrent des Indiens chevelus qu'ils prennent pour les légendaires Amazones : le plus imposant fleuve du monde y a trouvé son nom. Des forêts pluviales baignant dans une brume humide bordent l'Amazone, dans laquelle on trouve même des dauphins (petite photo) et des poissons marins.

Un univers d'eau et de forêt

Le marché aux poissons d'Iquitos, sur le cours supérieur de l'Amazone, a longtemps étonné les scientifiques : on y trouve des requins, des soles, des raies et des sardines, tous des poissons d'eau de mer et tous pêchés dans l'Amazone ! Comment sont-ils arrivés à Iquitos, à 3 700 km de l'Atlantique, à contre-courant, en franchissant rapides et chutes d'eau ?

On a fini par découvrir que ces énigmatiques poissons étaient les descendants de poissons marins qui s'étaient adaptés à l'eau douce. De plus, ils ne venaient en aucun cas de l'Atlantique mais du Pacifique, au-delà des Andes !

Un poisson étant dans l'impossibilité de franchir les hautes montagnes plissées des Andes, cela induisait qu'ils étaient arrivés dans l'Amazone avant la formation de la cordillère : biologistes et géologues purent alors réunir leurs connaissances pour résoudre l'énigme du fleuve.

La formation de l'Amazone

L'histoire de l'Amazone remonte à 150 millions d'années. L'Afrique et l'Amérique du Sud faisaient alors partie d'un supercontinent, le Gondwana, parcouru par de profonds fossés d'effondrement. L'un d'eux deviendra plus tard l'Atlantique et l'autre donnera naissance au bassin de l'Amazone, en Amérique du Sud, et au bassin Bénoué/Niger, en Afrique, qui se termine dans le Sahara. Autrefois coulait dans cet immense fossé d'effondrement un fleuve qui se jetait dans une baie du Pacifique.

Tandis que l'Afrique et l'Amérique s'écartaient l'une de l'autre et que l'Atlantique devenait un océan, à l'ouest de l'Amérique du Sud la croûte océanique glissait sous le continent et les Andes se soulevaient à un rythme considérable, à l'échelle géologique tout du moins. C'est ainsi que l'Amazone originelle fut séparée du Pacifique et, avec elle, tous les poissons qui vivaient jusque-là dans son ancienne embouchure.

La loutre géante, qui peut atteindre 1,80 m de long, pêche dans les eaux blanches de l'Amazone, riches en argile et en vases.

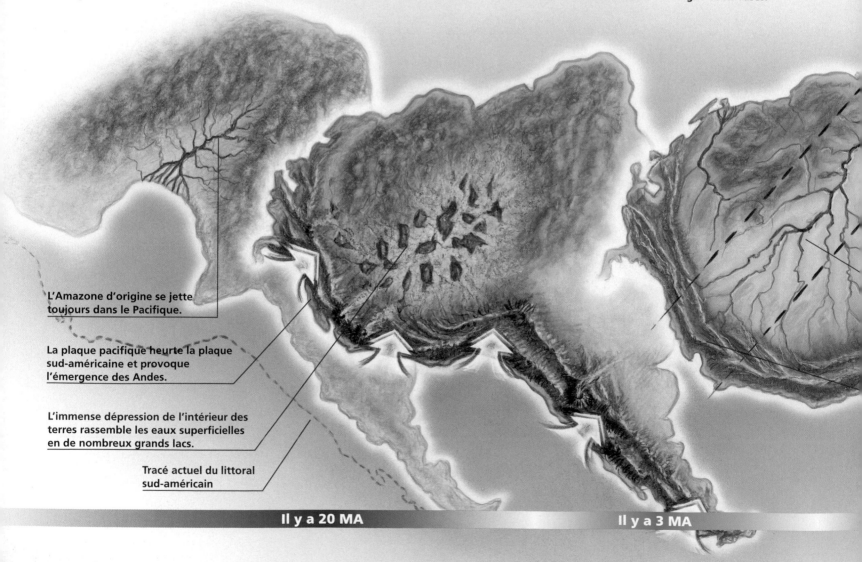

L'Amazone d'origine se jette toujours dans le Pacifique.

La plaque pacifique heurte la plaque sud-américaine et provoque l'émergence des Andes.

L'immense dépression de l'intérieur des terres rassemble les eaux superficielles en de nombreux grands lacs.

Tracé actuel du littoral sud-américain

Il y a 20 MA

Il y a 3 MA

Lorsque les fleuves se gonflent à la saison des pluies, les pêcheurs peuvent pénétrer profondément dans les forêts inondées, les *várzeas*, à bord de bateaux plats.

L'histoire de l'Amazone

Avant le soulèvement des Andes, l'actuel bassin supérieur de l'Amazone était encore une baie du Pacifique dans laquelle se jetait l'Amazone originel. Séparé de l'océan par cette nouvelle montagne, le fleuve et ses affluents formèrent sur place de nombreux lacs dans la dépression intérieure du pays. Un affaissement ultérieur du bassin inférieur permit aux lacs de s'écouler vers l'Atlantique et de former le système fluvial de l'Amazone.

Montagnes brésiliennes

Zone d'effondrement

Bassin de l'Amazone

Andes

Aujourd'hui

Des îles dans la savane

Tandis que les ères glaciaires modifiaient radicalement la végétation des zones tempérées, la forêt dense d'Amazonie subsistait sans pour autant s'étendre : à l'époque, le climat y était bien plus sec.

La carte ci-dessous montre l'Amazonie telle qu'elle était il y a environ 18 000 ans. La savane arborée (en jaune) recouvrait de vastes zones du bassin de l'Amazone. Les zones marginales encore plus sèches se caractérisaient par une savane épineuse (en orange). La forêt dense était limitée aux zones montagneuses et aux zones les plus humides proches de l'équateur (en vert).

Pendant les épisodes glaciaires, les forêts denses étaient isolées les unes des autres comme des îles. Or cela n'a pas empêché la progression de la biodiversité puisque chacun de ces îlots a développé ses propres espèces animales et végétales. À la fin des périodes glaciaires, une bonne partie d'entre elles s'est répandue dans la totalité de l'Amazonie à mesure que les forêts s'étendaient et se rejoignaient.

Petit à petit, la salinité des eaux a diminué et les mammifères marins et poissons d'eau de mer « piégés » se sont adaptés aux nouvelles conditions ou se sont éteints.

Un cinquième de l'eau douce de la Terre

À l'origine, le nom Amazone ne désignait que le fleuve se formant à Manaus par la confluence du Rio Negro et du Solimões. Aujourd'hui, il désigne la totalité du cours du fleuve, soit 7 025 km, de ses sources dans les Andes jusqu'à son embouchure, à Belém. Son bassin hydrographique, comprenant des forêts tropicales denses, des forêts d'inondation et des forêts de montagne, porte le nom d'Amazonie. Il couvre de vastes parties du Brésil et du Pérou et s'étend jusqu'en Bolivie, en Équateur, en Colombie et au Venezuela.

Ressemblant à un éventail, le bassin de l'Amazone compte plus de 1 000 grands et 100 000 petits affluents secondaires, ce qui, par sa superficie, le rapproche d'une mer. À la fin de la saison des pluies, il transporte un cinquième des eaux douces fluviales du globe se déversant dans les mers.

Mais un volume d'eau encore plus important circule dans le système hydrologique fermé de l'Amazonie. On estime que 75 % de l'eau qui s'évapore au-dessus des forêts et cours d'eau du

L'opossum-rat ou marmosa (ci-dessus), qui existe depuis fort longtemps, illustre la continuité de l'écosystème amazonien.

Dans la canopée, le paresseux bidactyle (à droite) n'est menacé que par les gros oiseaux de proie.

Originaire d'Afrique, le douroucouli (ci-dessous) prouve la dislocation du Gondwana.

bassin retombent sur place sous forme de pluie : de ce fait, la déforestation massive produit un effet désastreux sur le climat régional.

Un delta né aux périodes glaciaires

En contrebas des Andes, sur 4 000 km, la déclivité du lit de l'Amazone n'est que de quelques centimètres par kilomètre, et Manaus, au centre du continent, n'est situé qu'à 26 m au-dessus du niveau de la mer. Néanmoins, le lit du fleuve est profond car les glaciations du quaternaire ont été d'une telle ampleur qu'elles ont abaissé le niveau de la mer de plus de 100 m. Par conséquent, l'Amazone s'est creusé un lit profond dans lequel elle charriait d'énormes quantités de sédiments qui, déposés à son embouchure, ont formé un imposant delta. Du fait de la faible déclivité, les marées de l'océan Atlantique se font sentir jusqu'à 800 km en amont. Et aux changements de lune se produit une dangereuse vague déferlante, la *pororoca*, qui peut atteindre 5 m de hauteur et remonte loin vers l'amont. Il en résulte que les marées d'équinoxe de l'Atlantique bloquent périodiquement l'embouchure de l'Amazone.

Eaux noires pauvres et eaux blanches riches

À partir du point de confluence du Rio Negro et du Solimões (cours supérieur de l'Amazone au Brésil), les eaux sombres du premier et jaunâtres du second roulent encore ensemble sur un lit commun de 80 km avant de fusionner complètement.

Le Solimões et ses eaux blanches sont essentiels pour l'Amazonie. Les sédiments en provenance des Andes qui troublent ses eaux fournissent de précieux minéraux aux plantes aquatiques et aux forêts qui bordent ses rives.

Les eaux du Rio Negro (« fleuve Noir »), en revanche, sont extrêmement pauvres en nutriments. Depuis sa source, dans la partie nord du bassin amazonien, sa faible déclivité ne lui donne pas la puissance nécessaire pour éroder les roches dures et cela fait des millions d'années qu'il a lessivé les matières les plus tendres, absorbées depuis longtemps par les forêts. Sa couleur, en réalité brunâtre, est due à d'infimes quantités d'humus inutilisables pour les plantes. Même les algues et les plantes aquatiques y sont rares et les poissons doivent se nourrir de feuilles et de fruits tombant des arbres ou de pollen.

Le bassin hydrographique de l'Amazone s'étend en latitude du 5ᵉ degré nord au 18ᵉ degré sud. La presque totalité de son cours reçoit des précipitations toute l'année et, dans les zones marginales, se gonfle l'été des eaux de la saison des pluies. Son niveau monte alors de plus de 10 m et les crues peuvent pénétrer jusqu'à 100 km à l'intérieur des forêts : s'il s'agit d'eaux blanches, c'est une manne d'éléments nutritifs pour les sols.

Des nutriments venus d'Afrique

Les alizés sont une source importante de précieux nutriments. Toute l'année, ils transportent au-dessus de l'Atlantique et jusque dans la forêt dense d'Amazonie des millions de tonnes de fines poussières provenant de l'une des régions les plus désolées du monde : le sud du Sahara. Ces nuées de poussière sont nettement visibles sur les photos satellite et, sans elles, de nombreuses espèces botaniques d'Amazonie n'existeraient plus.

Les premiers Blancs à pénétrer dans la forêt très humide de l'Amazonie furent surpris par l'opulence de la végétation et l'abondance d'eau et de soleil. Constatant la quantité de plantes qui y poussaient apparemment sans difficulté, ils conclurent à une terre naturellement fertile. Mais l'impression est trompeuse : le sol de la forêt dense est extrêmement pauvre en nutriments et l'agriculture, limitée, n'est possible qu'au prix de gros efforts, à l'image de la lutte permanente de la faune et de la flore pour leur survie.

Parallèlement, on a dénombré jusqu'à présent 2 500 espèces d'arbres différentes en Amazonie, soit 10 fois plus que dans l'ensemble de l'Europe. Comment cela est-il possible ?

La concurrence stimule l'évolution

La biodiversité de la forêt tropicale d'Amazonie s'explique de plusieurs façons. Tout d'abord, l'évolution lui a laissé beaucoup de temps – 60 millions d'années – pour s'établir. Une autre raison tient aux conditions hostiles elles-mêmes : la lutte pour la survie oblige animaux et végétaux à développer des stratégies biologiques toujours plus sophistiquées pour s'imposer à leurs ennemis et à leurs concurrents.

Dans les zones tempérées, les forêts naturelles sont généralement très « ordonnées » : une hêtraie est dominée par les hêtres, une chênaie par les chênes, etc. Dans la forêt dense, en revanche, chaque nouvelle graine ne peut germer que le plus loin possible de la plante mère ; elle peut être transportée très loin par le vent ou les animaux. Car si elles sont trop nombreuses à s'implanter au même endroit, les graines doivent lutter pour survivre, même contre leurs proches parentes.

La compétition commence par la lutte pour la lumière. Dans la forêt dense, le rayonnement solaire ne touche dans sa totalité que la couronne des arbres, la canopée : seul 1 % parvient jusqu'au sol. Du fait de l'obscurité, le sous-bois est peu développé, les herbes et arbrisseaux sont clairsemés. Seules les forêts-galeries bordant les rives ensoleillées des cours d'eau autorisent un étroit rideau de verdure.

Un fleuve qui se remblaie lui-même

Du fait de leur faible pente, les cours d'eau du bassin de l'Amazone coulent lentement dans la grande plaine (1). Les sédiments qu'ils acheminent tombent au fond de l'eau et s'y accumulent, principalement près des rives, où le débit est le plus lent mais le plus fort en période de crue (2) : les eaux charrient alors davantage d'alluvions et sont freinées par la végétation. Lorsqu'elles se retirent, elles laissent derrière elles une seconde couche de remblais (3) sur les berges qui, du fait de l'alternance continue de hautes et de basses eaux, ne cessent de grossir.

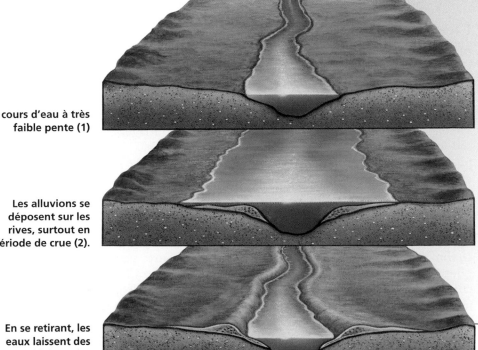

cours d'eau à très faible pente (1)

Les alluvions se déposent sur les rives, surtout en période de crue (2).

En se retirant, les eaux laissent des remblais sur les deux rives (3).

Toujours vers la lumière

Même les grands arbres commencent petits. À proximité du sol, ils surmontent les mauvaises conditions d'éclairement en développant de grosses feuilles qui captent le plus de lumière possible pour la photosynthèse. Le jeune arbre reste longtemps à ce stade et pousse très lentement. Ce n'est qu'au moment où la canopée s'ouvre un peu, par exemple lorsqu'un vieil arbre meurt, qu'il peut s'étirer vers le haut. Le tronc d'un arbre de 30 m de hauteur dépasse rarement un diamètre de 20 cm et sa couronne demeure peu étendue : il faut attendre que celle-ci soit formée pour que le tronc grossisse. Et, au sommet, il lui faut de petites feuilles pour contrer l'action desséchante du soleil et du vent. Dans la forêt dense, l'âpre concurrence pour la lumière génère de nombreuses espèces de lianes, spécifiquement adaptées à une croissance rapide vers le haut. De nombreux épiphytes (plantes non parasites se développant sur d'autres plantes), dont les principales espèces d'orchidées des tropiques, commencent leur vie dans les étages supérieurs de la forêt. Mais les nutriments et l'eau y étant rares, ces espèces aériennes, coupées du sol, stockent l'humidité dans leurs propres organes, à l'instar des plantes des déserts.

Chacun pour soi – mais avec les autres

Les nutriments font autant défaut que la lumière dans la forêt dense tropicale. Dans les zones tempérées, ils sont stockés dans le sol mais, dans la grande forêt amazonienne, ce sont les fleuves aux eaux blanches et les poussières du Sahara qui assurent l'approvisionnement en sels minéraux. L'engrais organique provenant des excréments animaux et des débris végétaux ne reste pas longtemps dans le sol : il retourne directement à la végétation dans le cadre d'une chaîne nutritionnelle très courte. C'est pourquoi les plantes développent des racines longues et plates qui leur permettent d'absorber rapidement les rares éléments nutritifs, avant qu'une autre plante ne s'en

empare. Certaines développent même des racines aériennes qui, comme leur nom l'indique, ne touchent jamais le sol.

Les champignons, du fait de leurs facultés de décomposition, jouent un rôle prépondérant dans la chaîne nutritionnelle. Nombre de plantes se trouvent avec eux dans des situations complexes d'interdépendance. Ce phénomène de communauté symbiotique se rencontre partout où les animaux et les végétaux cohabitent dans un écosystème restreint. Ils se protègent mutuellement contre leurs ennemis et partagent habitat ou

Ces Indiens Kayapos cherchent de l'or dans le Rio Blanco (« fleuve Blanc »). Les orpailleurs utilisent du mercure, très toxique, qui pollue les cours d'eau.

nourriture, ce qui leur donne un avantage notable par rapport à leurs concurrents.

L'opulence de la forêt pluviale va donc de pair avec des carences : en lumière pour les germes, en nutriments pour les plantes et en eau pour les épiphytes. La profusion est dans le nombre des prédateurs : c'est pourquoi ne survivent que les maîtres du camouflage, de l'adaptation et de la coopération.

L'écosystème complexe de l'Amazonie a pu se développer presque sans perturbation pendant 60 millions d'années, sous l'influence d'un climat tropical chaud et humide. Un grand nombre d'animaux et de végétaux ont disparu, tandis que d'autres passaient maîtres dans l'art de la survie. Chaque membre de la communauté, qu'il appartienne à la faune ou à la flore, joue un rôle prépondérant dans le maintien de l'ensemble.

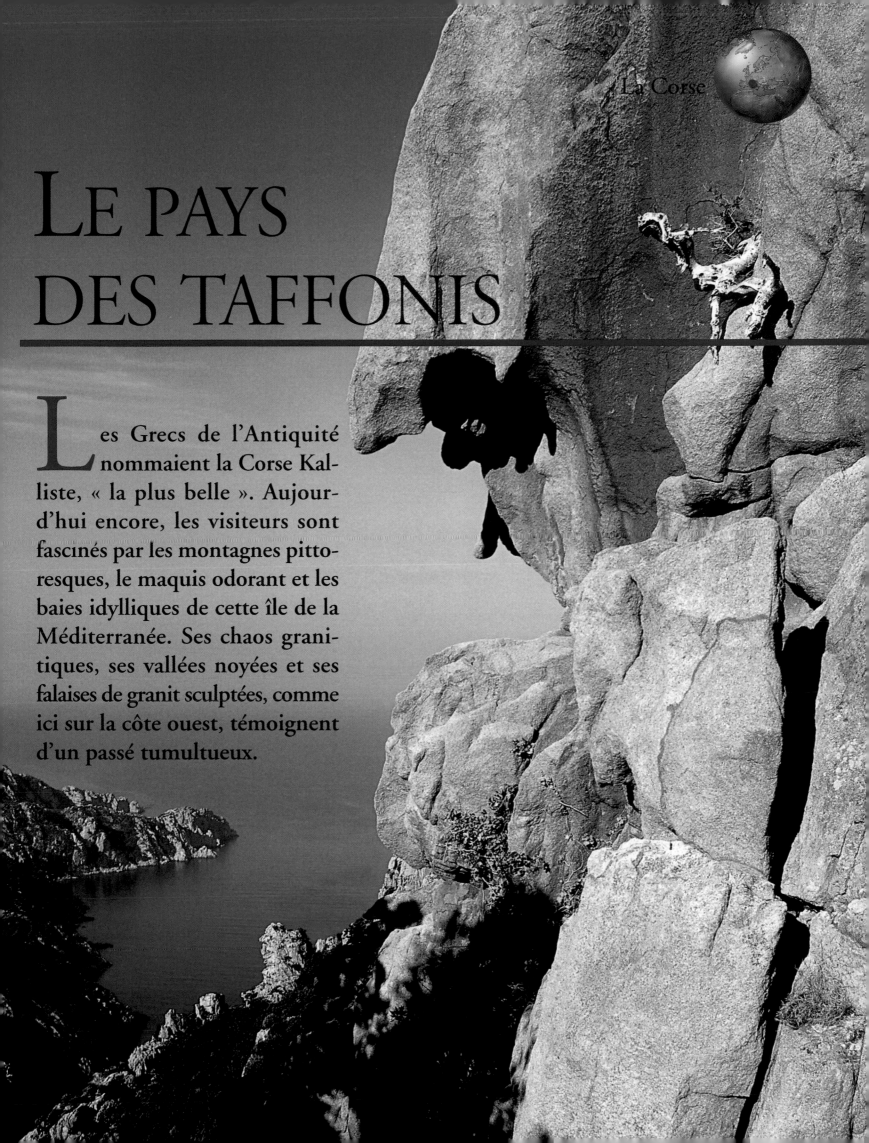

LE PAYS DES TAFFONIS

Les Grecs de l'Antiquité nommaient la Corse Kalliste, « la plus belle ». Aujourd'hui encore, les visiteurs sont fascinés par les montagnes pittoresques, le maquis odorant et les baies idylliques de cette île de la Méditerranée. Ses chaos granitiques, ses vallées noyées et ses falaises de granit sculptées, comme ici sur la côte ouest, témoignent d'un passé tumultueux.

Coincée entre deux continents

Le plus haut sommet de Corse, le monte Cinto, culmine à 2 710 m dans le nord-ouest de l'île, à 25 km de la mer Méditerranée. À partir de ce point, la montagne s'étire sur toute la longueur de l'île, jusqu'au sud-est. Les sommets escarpés et les profondes vallées témoignent d'une histoire mouvementée, sens dessus dessous au sens propre du terme ! C'est ainsi que l'on a trouvé dans les hautes montagnes corses des roches bien plus anciennes que nos continents et océans actuels, des gneiss et des schistes de la chaîne hercynienne d'origine, apparue il y a entre 400 et 500 millions d'années. D'où viennent ces vestiges ?

Entre 250 et 350 millions d'années avant l'époque actuelle, du magma est remonté des profondeurs de la Terre dans cette montagne hercynienne, pour y former un gros bloc granitique long de plus de 400 km. Pendant les quelques millions d'années qui ont suivi, à l'exception d'un socle résiduel, son enveloppe a été érodée et emportée dans la Thétys, un océan des temps anciens situé entre les précurseurs de nos continents : la Méditerranée contemporaine est un vestige de cette mer gigantesque.

Il y a environ 140 millions d'années, la Thétys a commencé à rétrécir lorsque la plaque continentale africaine, glissant vers le nord, est entrée en collision avec la plaque eurasiatique ; 100 millions d'années plus tard, la Corse et la Sardaigne d'origine se sont retrouvées prises dans cet étau, qui a exercé sur la Corse une rotation dans le sens contraire des aiguilles d'une montre et l'a fortement comprimée. C'est ainsi que ses strates de roches se sont plissées et ont glissé les unes sur les autres, juxtaposant du schiste et du gneiss hercynien aux couches granitiques déjà présentes. Cette

nouvelle montagne plissée a ensuite continué à se soulever et a légèrement basculé vers l'ouest : la Corse, haute montagne dans la Méditerranée, était née.

Eau, soleil et sel : l'énigme des roches creuses

Lorsqu'il ne reste d'un gros bloc de pierre qu'un toit en forme de bol renversé, on le désigne, dans le monde entier, sous le terme de taffoni, issu du corse *taffonare* (perforer) car on ne trouve nulle part ailleurs qu'en Corse une forme aussi achevée de ce phénomène. Les taffonis les plus spectaculaires se situent dans le nord-ouest de l'île, là où la montagne descend jusqu'au littoral.

Les scientifiques se sont longtemps demandé comment l'intérieur d'un bloc de granit pouvait s'émietter tandis que l'extérieur demeurait intact. Aujourd'hui, tous s'accordent à dire que c'est le résultat d'une alternance fréquente de fortes précipita-

Formation des taffonis

Le granit est une roche à grains grossiers composée de différents minéraux. Lorsque l'humidité s'infiltre dans les fissures (flèches bleues), les ions d'hydrogène dissocient les minéraux et les séparent en partie de l'ensemble. Petit à petit, à partir de la base, la roche devient friable.

Le soleil et le vent dessèchent la surface de la roche et « aspirent » l'humidité vers l'extérieur en emportant les substances dissociées (flèches jaunes). Celles-ci se déposent en surface et forment une fine patine dure, la croûte, tandis que la roche humide située au centre et à la base se désagrège progressivement.

Au stade final du processus, la roche émiettée est expulsée par les trous de la paroi ou emportée par le vent. Il ne reste plus que la croûte externe et une sous-couche rocheuse.

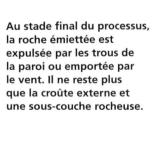

tions et de rayonnements solaires intenses. Néanmoins, ils ignorent toujours si la roche s'est simplement effritée ou si elle a également été soumise à des actions chimiques.

La croûte externe de nombreux taffonis, une patine brun-noir de quelques millimètres d'épaisseur, donne de précieux renseignements à ce sujet. Elle résulte de processus chimiques: l'eau acide percole dans le granit à travers de minuscules fissures, où elle dissocie certaines substances des minéraux le composant. Lorsque la surface de la roche se réchauffe sous l'action du soleil, l'eau qui remonte entraîne ces substances avec elle. Tandis qu'elle s'évapore, les oxydes de fer et de manganèse cimentent l'extérieur de la roche alors que, à l'intérieur, celle-ci continue à s'émietter.

Il existe certes des taffonis dépourvus de croûte. Dans ce cas, il s'agit d'une érosion typique de la roche, principalement due aux dépôts de sel: l'eau d'infiltration contient des sels provenant des embruns ou de l'air marin humide. Lorsque le sel

sèche, puis s'hydrate à nouveau, il subit une expansion de 30 à 100 % et exerce une énorme pression sur la roche. Cette expansion ameublit alors la texture de celle-ci, ce qui permet à l'humidité de s'infiltrer à nouveau, jusqu'à ce que, avec le temps, se forme une véritable cavité.

L'île parfumée

La Corse – 183 km de longueur et 83 km dans sa plus grande largeur – n'est pas une grande île. Toutefois, son histoire géologique tumultueuse a imprimé sur cette petite superficie une étonnante multiplicité de paysages et un climat extrêmement différencié: lorsque, l'été, la sécheresse et la chaleur règnent sur la côte, il peut faire très frais dans les montagnes encore souvent enneigées. Et des pentes d'éboulis arides

Les Calanches (calanques) de Piana, sur la côte ouest de l'île. Le feldspath potassique et l'oxyde de fer donnent à la roche une teinte orangée.

Le ciste, *mucchiu* en corse, a donné son nom au maquis, (*macchia*), cette formation arbustive impénétrable qui couvre la majeure partie de la Corse.

Lorsque la glace se brise

Des volcans sommeillent sous le Vatnajökull et d'autres glaciers d'Islande. En cas d'éruption, la glace fond et forme des cavités remplies d'eau. Lorsque l'eau s'échappe, la voûte de ces cavités s'effondre et met au jour la structure des glaces.

Une baie s'ensable

Les tracés des baies et des mers forment des paysages relativement éphémères à l'échelle géologique dont l'espérance de vie ne dépasse souvent pas quelques millénaires. Dans la province du Kwa-Zulu Natal, en Afrique du Sud, la baie de Kosi est progressivement envahie par le sable qu'apportent les marées.

L'ŒUVRE DE LA NATURE

D ans l'Atlantique, à 300 km au large des côtes africaines, un volcan puissant règne sur une douzaine d'îles : le Teide (grande photographie). Chacune des îles très visitées des Canaries a sa beauté propre et abrite une faune et une flore qui lui sont spécifiques. Le dragonnier (petite photo) ou dragon végétal, une plante de la famille des liliacées qui peut vivre, dit-on, jusqu'à mille ans, en est un exemple.

Une origine,
plusieurs visages

Culminant à 3 718 m, le pic de Teide, à Tenerife, dans l'archipel des Canaries intégré à l'Espagne dès le XVᵉ siècle, est le plus haut sommet du pays. Situées entre 100 et 300 km des côtes africaines, les sept îles principales (six autres sont inhabitées) ont émergé de l'Atlantique qui, dans cette zone,

forêts, Fuerteventura se caractérise par son aridité, Lanzarote, véritable paysage lunaire, possède les plus longs tunnels de lave de l'archipel, Tenerife a le plus haut volcan et La Gomera les plus vastes forêts de lauriers. De plus, les quatre parcs nationaux hébergent de nombreuses espèces végétales et animales introuvables ailleurs.

L'extraordinaire beauté des Canaries fascinait déjà les écrivains de l'Antiquité, qui les avaient baptisées *Insulae fortunatae* (les îles bienheureuses). Pour les scientifiques contemporains, les Canaries sont le terrain de recherche idéal pour étudier la forma-

tion des îles volcaniques et l'adaptation des animaux et des plantes aux conditions de vie extrêmes des régions isolées.

Point chaud et bulles de magma

L'activité volcanique des Canaries semble déroger à de nombreuses règles chères aux vulcanologues. À commencer par la forme des produits éruptifs : un volcan crachera de la lave fluide, un autre de la lave solide, tandis qu'un troisième rejettera des cendres et des bombes. Sur une île, la lave s'écoule

La Cueva de los Verdes, sur Lanzarote, fait partie de l'Atlántida, un tunnel de lave qui traverse la moitié de l'île, jusqu'à la mer.

atteint par endroits une profondeur de 3 000 m. Un cratère secondaire du Teide, le Chinyero, est entré en éruption en 1909. Sur La Palma, le Nambroque et le Teneguía étaient encore actifs, respectivement, en 1949 et 1971. À Lanzarote, sous le sol du parc national de las Montañas del Fuego (les montagnes du feu) ou de Timanfaya couve encore la chaleur des puissantes éruptions qui, au XVIIIᵉ siècle et pendant six ans d'affilée, ont changé de fond en comble la physionomie de l'île.

Toutes les îles de l'archipel sont d'origine volcanique et, sur la plupart d'entre elles, l'activité volcanique est loin d'avoir cessé. Toutefois, chacune a développé son propre paysage : La Palma est couverte d'épaisses

Tunnel de lave de Lanzarote

L'Atlántida s'est formé il y a entre 3 000 et 5 000 ans, lors de deux éruptions de la Corona. La seconde phase éruptive a créé une « galerie d'art » dans le tunnel.

La lave a creusé une profonde gouttière dans la roche. Elle s'est figée sur les parois et la surface du tunnel mais a continué à couler à l'intérieur.

lentement et, sur une autre, elle se solidifie au niveau de la cheminée ou fait exploser le sommet du volcan.

L'alignement et l'âge des volcans ne suivent les règles qu'à première vue. D'est en ouest, les îles sont de plus en plus jeunes. Lanzarote et Fuerteventura, âgées respectivement de 20,6 et de 15,5 millions d'années, sont les plus anciennes, contre 2 et 1,2 millions d'années pour les plus jeunes, La Palma et Hierro. Et l'on a découvert non loin de La Palma des volcans sous-marins qui formeront plus tard de nouvelles îles.

On a d'abord pensé à la présence d'un point chaud, une chambre magmatique fixe située dans le manteau terrestre, qui émet un panache chaud et ferait surgir l'un après l'autre les volcans des Canaries de la croûte océanique dérivant au-dessus de lui. Or, contrairement à Hawaii, où les volcans émergent de la mer et s'éteignent l'un après l'autre selon un certain alignement, aux Canaries les volcans forment un groupe non organisé et ne respectent pas le principe de succession dans le temps connu des spécialistes. C'est ainsi qu'à Lanzarote, l'une des îles les plus anciennes, des érup-

Rosa de piedra – rose de pierre : c'est le nom donné par les insulaires à cette magnifique rose de basalte dans les Cañadas de Tenerife. Le refroidissement, de l'extérieur vers l'intérieur, d'une coulée de lave a creusé ces crevasses et créé un motif floral.

tions ont encore eu lieu au XVIIIe siècle. Même les longues phases de repos entre les manifestations volcaniques irritent au plus haut point les chercheurs.

Des géophysiciens allemands semblent sur la bonne voie pour éclaircir ce mystère. Le problème viendrait de gigantesques bulles (en anglais : *blobs*) de lave visqueuse

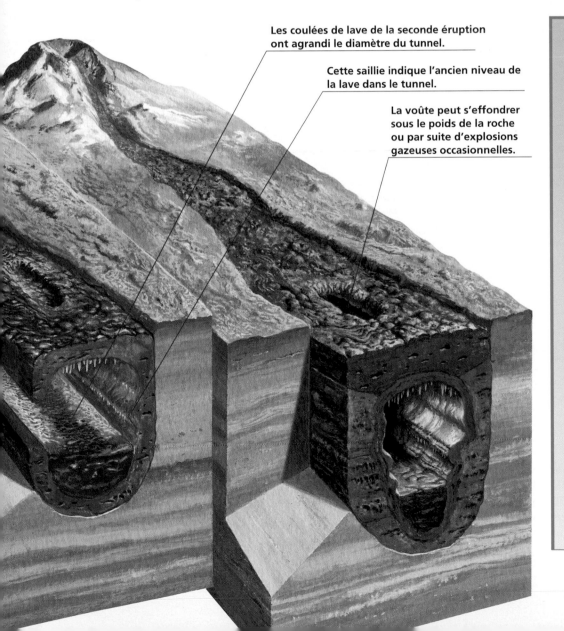

Les coulées de lave de la seconde éruption ont agrandi le diamètre du tunnel.

Cette saillie indique l'ancien niveau de la lave dans le tunnel.

La voûte peut s'effondrer sous le poids de la roche ou par suite d'explosions gazeuses occasionnelles.

Cultures en entonnoir

Lorsque les paysans de Lanzarote sont retournés chez eux après les éruptions volcaniques ininterrompues de 1730 à 1736, ils ont trouvé dans leurs champs des lapilli, débris de roches volcaniques, empilés sur plusieurs mètres de hauteur. Avec courage, ils ont creusé des entonnoirs pour atteindre le sol cultivable et ont découvert avec bonheur que, dans les entonnoirs, leurs cultures poussaient mieux qu'avant. En effet, les lapilli protègent le sol contre la sécheresse le jour et, la nuit, absorbent la rosée et la restituent aux plantes. Aujourd'hui, les agriculteurs utilisent les lapilli dans toutes les Canaries et la zone d'origine de cette méthode, la Gería (l'entonnoir), sur Lanzarote, s'est consacrée avec succès à la viticulture.

Les euphorbiacées

Euphorbia canariensis, l'euphorbe des Canaries, pousse dans les régions arides. Elle ressemble à un cactus, stocke l'eau comme un cactus, mais n'en est pas un. Elle appartient en fait à la grande famille des euphorbiacées, très représentée aux Canaries, dont les membres sont souvent toxiques. Elle contient un liquide laiteux. La *tabaiba dulce*, euphorbe sucrée, était autrefois employée pour fabriquer de la gomme à mâcher.

Les euphorbiacées et les cactées sont un superbe exemple d'évolution convergente: vivant dans les mêmes conditions, ces deux familles ont développé des stratégies identiques contre la sécheresse.

situées dans le manteau terrestre, sous les Canaries. Attisé par un point chaud, le magma remonte à la surface sur 400 km en traversant les bulles, dont chacune peut atteindre 100 km de longueur et correspond à la phase éruptive d'un volcan canarien. Le cœur très chaud d'une bulle, plus fluide que sa marge plus froide, expliquerait la diversité des roches que l'on trouve aux Canaries. Et là où la croûte terrestre a déjà été ouverte par des éruptions, les bulles ont la voie libre. Voilà pourquoi de nouvelles éruptions ne cessent de se produire sur les îles les plus anciennes.

Enfin, les mêmes scientifiques allemands expliquent l'alignement irrégulier des îles par la lenteur de la dérive de la plaque continentale africaine qui leur a donné naissance.

La diversité de la flore canarienne

Qu'un volcan s'ouvre dans une effrayante explosion en faisant sombrer la moitié de l'île dans la mer, comme sur Hierro, qu'un dôme volcanique s'effondre en laissant derrière lui une immense caldeira, comme sur La Palma, ou qu'une éruption ensevelisse une plaine fertile sous une épaisse couche de cendres et de débris rocheux poreux (lapilli), dans tous les cas, les effets sur l'environnement sont manifestes et, comme aux Canaries, très divers.

Dans de telles conditions, seules des espèces spécialisées peuvent s'imposer. Isolées du reste du monde, les îles Canaries ont développé une grande biodiversité sur une superficie restreinte. Un certain nombre d'animaux, citons le lézard géant de Hierro, et de végétaux, le dragonnier notamment, sont des fossiles vivants. Environ 2 000 espèces de plantes ont été répertoriées, dont plus d'un quart sont endémiques. On comprend donc pourquoi les Canaries sont qualifiées de « Galápagos des botanistes ». Ici, l'évolution n'est pas un vain mot.

Les éruptions volcaniques elles-mêmes, pourtant destructrices, ont contribué à cette biodiversité en donnant à des plantes pionnières l'occasion de s'établir sans risque de concurrence de la part de végétaux plus évolués. Après une éruption, les champs de lave et de cendres sont dépourvus de tout germe et la vie doit repartir de rien. Ce sont d'abord les bactéries qui colonisent les lieux, puis les lichens et, après une longue période, les premières plantes à fleurs. Mais de nombreuses générations de plantes doivent se décomposer avant que le sol ne convienne à l'établisssement de végétaux supérieurs. Les fleurs attirent les insectes, qui à leur tour font venir oiseaux et lézards. Quant aux gros mammifères, ce sont les hommes qui doivent les réintroduire dans les îles Canaries.

La vie revient avec les alizés

Le volcanisme a donc préparé le sol à une grande biodiversité sur l'archipel, mais ce sont les alizés et le courant des Canaries qui y ont introduit la vie. Car lorsque les vents de nord-est chauds rencontrent le courant des Canaries, frais, ils absorbent de l'humidité. En passant au-dessus des vieilles îles aplanies par l'érosion de Fuerteventura et Lanzarote, ils ne laissent pas tomber une seule goutte de pluie. En revanche, les masses d'air humide s'accumulent au-dessus des îles montagneuses, de sorte que, le matin, les sommets disparaissent régulièrement dans la brume ou les nuages de pluie. Les vents descendants

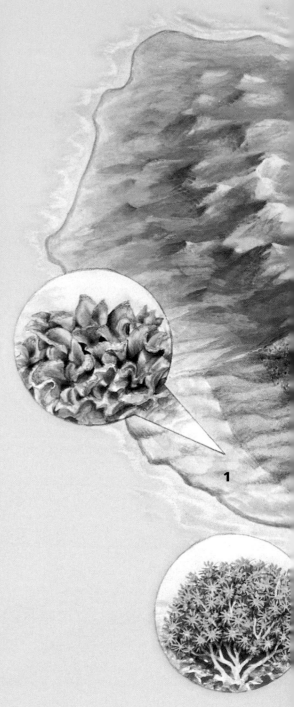

1

Les zones de végétation de Tenerife

Sur Tenerife, dominée par le Teide, la végétation se répartit entre six zones bien marquées et d'une typicité presque idéale, caractérisées par l'altitude et l'influence des alizés. Cette illustration montre le panorama de l'île selon un axe nord-est. Les cercles contiennent un dessin grossi des plantes typiques de chaque zone.

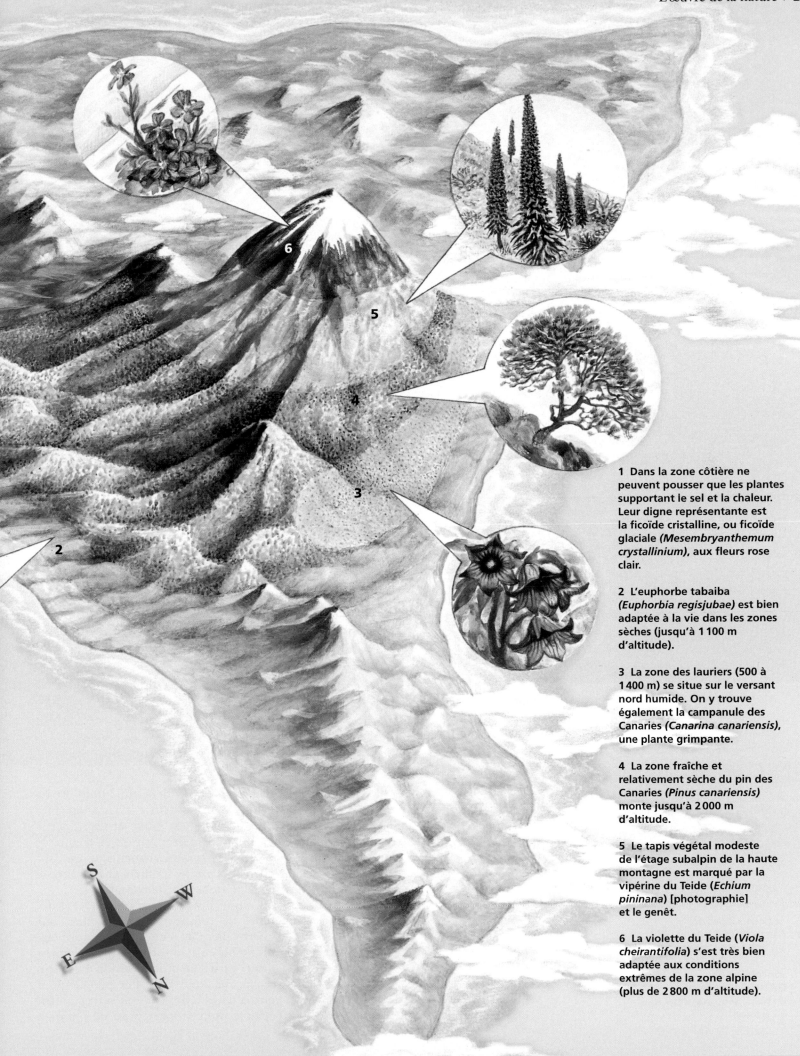

1 Dans la zone côtière ne peuvent pousser que les plantes supportant le sel et la chaleur. Leur digne représentante est la ficoïde cristalline, ou ficoïde glaciale *(Mesembryanthemum crystallinium)*, aux fleurs rose clair.

2 L'euphorbe tabaiba *(Euphorbia regisjubae)* est bien adaptée à la vie dans les zones sèches (jusqu'à 1 100 m d'altitude).

3 La zone des lauriers (500 à 1 400 m) se situe sur le versant nord humide. On y trouve également la campanule des Canaries *(Canarina canariensis)*, une plante grimpante.

4 La zone fraîche et relativement sèche du pin des Canaries *(Pinus canariensis)* monte jusqu'à 2 000 m d'altitude.

5 Le tapis végétal modeste de l'étage subalpin de la haute montagne est marqué par la vipérine du Teide *(Echium pininana)* [photographie] et le genêt.

6 La violette du Teide *(Viola cheirantifolia)* s'est très bien adaptée aux conditions extrêmes de la zone alpine (plus de 2 800 m d'altitude).

Le petit Sahara des
Canaries : Maspalomas,
sur la Grande Canarie.

Les collines de
Fuerteventura (tout
en haut) sont exposées
à l'érosion.

soufflant au-delà des crêtes, eux, sont secs car l'air en se réchauffant à cet endroit absorbe toute l'humidité restante. Dans la zone semi-désertique du sud-ouest des îles ne poussent presque que des plantes succulentes et la forte activité touristique s'est développée au détriment de la faune naturelle. Or, si les alizés arrosent toutes les îles de façon égale, la végétation s'est développée de façon très diverse de l'une à l'autre. Ce phénomène est par-ticulièrement évident sur Hierro et La Palma : dans les deux cas, les montagnes font obstacle aux vents africains, mais La Palma peut être considérée comme le jardin d'Éden des Canaries, alors que, sur Hierro, les plantes souffrent de la sécheresse en dépit de la forte pluviosité.

Ce phénomène s'explique par la diffé-rence de composition des roches. Sur Hierro, île plus jeune, la matière volca-nique poreuse absorbe immédiatement l'eau. Et il faut que l'érosion fasse son œuvre sur une très longue période pour que la couche de terre soit suffisamment épaisse pour stocker l'eau de pluie en

sont par ailleurs recouvertes d'une couche cireuse isolante. La famille des euphorbiacées, très représentée aux Canaries, ressemble par bien des aspects aux cactées succulentes du continent sud-américain.

Les forêts canariennes ne bénéficient pas d'une abondante pluviosité et les arbres doivent intercepter l'humidité directement dans l'air : c'est ce que l'on appelle les « précipitations horizontales ». De ce point de vue, le pin est bien pourvu : ses aiguilles, qui peuvent atteindre 30 cm de longueur, absorbent l'humidité des nuages et de la brume.

Les forêts de lauriers ont survécu aux ères glaciaires

Les forêts de lauriers, ou *laurisilvas*, de La Gomera s'alimentent elles aussi de l'humidité ambiante. Ces lauriers géants sont couverts de mousses et de longues barbes de lichens qui rejoignent les fougères du sous-bois. La bruyère arborescente, de la famille des éricacées, développe des troncs qu'un homme ne peut entourer de ses bras, et le pissenlit pousse à hauteur de taille. Plus grande forêt de lauriers du monde, le parc national de Garajonay et ses quatre espèces de lauriers indigènes a été inscrit au patrimoine naturel mondial. Il y a 60 millions d'années, de vastes régions du globe étaient couvertes de forêts de lauriers, qui ont dû reculer lors des glaciations au profit de plantes mieux adaptées au froid. Aux Canaries, les températures sont restées suffisamment élevées pour que le laurier survive à ses concurrents.

Une mosaïque de couleurs

Le dragonnier, emblème des Canaries, est un arbre fossile vivant. De par sa hauteur et sa couronne, il ressemble à un arbre, mais il s'agit en réalité d'une plante herbacée appartenant à la famille des agavacées. Son tronc contient une sève, le « sang de dragon », qui devient rouge en séchant et que l'on gratifie de vertus médicinales. Pour les habitants d'origine des Canaries, les Guanches, le dragonnier était sacré. Le tronc ne présentant pas de cernes de croissance, il est difficile de déterminer son âge : on a toujours attribué un âge canonique aux plus gros spécimens. Aujourd'hui encore, on parle de dragonniers millénaires. Toutefois, les scientifiques concèdent au plus vieux sujet connu, *Drago de Icod* (dragon d'Icod), sur Tenerife, un âge maximal de 365 ans.

Aux Canaries, les niches écologiques offrant un biotope particulier à certains êtres vivants sont très petites. Ainsi, le lac souterrain de la grotte de lave de Jameos del Agua, sur Lanzarote, est habité par de minuscules crabes aveugles et albinos, spécifiques à ce lieu. Ailleurs, ces crabes n'auraient pas eu la moindre chance de survie, mais ils n'ont aucun concurrent dans cette niche.

Aux Canaries, les biotopes sont isolés les uns des autres et du reste du monde par un désert de lave, une montagne ou même l'Atlantique. Cela explique qu'un grand nombre d'espèces ait pu s'y maintenir. Lorsque ces barrières entre les biotopes n'existent plus ou qu'un écosystème se trouve en concurrence avec des plantes et animaux extérieurs à l'archipel, les espèces natives les plus faibles sont rapidement éliminées. C'est pourquoi la faune et la flore des îles sont aujourd'hui menacées par les espèces introduites dans l'archipel, sans parler des infrastructures touristiques qui ne cessent de prendre de l'expansion.

Un fossile vivant

Des lézards géants régnaient sur l'ouest des Canaries avant l'arrivée des humains. Au début du xxᵉ siècle, on y trouvait encore des individus de 1,50 m de longueur. Le lézard géant de Hierro (ci-dessous) peut atteindre 60 cm. On le croyait éteint jusqu'à ce qu'un chercheur en retrouve la trace en 1974. En 2000, on a réintroduit cette espèce sur l'île inhabitée de Hierro, à l'abri des rats, des touristes curieux et des chats sauvages. En 1999, on a découvert sur La Gomera, dans la Valle Gran Rey, une espèce apparentée pouvant atteindre une longueur de 50 cm : le lézard géant de La Gomera.

surface. Par nécessité, les plantes des régions sèches ont donc déployé des stratégies fascinantes pour se procurer l'eau indispensable à leur survie.

Les plantes s'adaptent

Comme dans toutes les régions sèches de la Terre, les plantes des Canaries ont développé la capacité de stocker l'eau dans leurs tissus. Au cours de l'évolution, leurs feuilles se sont transformées en épines de façon à réduire l'évaporation, renforcée par le vent incessant. Un grand nombre d'entre elles

LE PLUS GRAND CHANTIER DU MONDE

Au large de la côte est de l'Australie, de minuscules animaux constructeurs de coraux comme le corail cerveau (petite photo) travaillent sur le plus grand chantier du monde, un monde merveilleux et labyrinthique de récifs, de passes, d'îles, de lagons et de bancs de sable. Mais la croissance de la Grande Barrière de corail ne s'est pas faite, et ne se fait pas, sans difficulté.

Des corpuscules bâtisseurs

Le capitaine anglais James Cook (1728-1779) est déjà depuis des semaines à une distance sûre de la côte est de l'Australie, encore inexplorée, lorsque, le 11 juin 1770 son vaisseau, l'*Endeavour*, se heurte à un récif. Le navigateur le plus célèbre de son époque comprend rapidement qu'il ne se trouve pas en haute mer, mais dans une passe ménagée dans un gigantesque récif. Cook vient de découvrir le plus grand complexe corallien de la planète, qui s'étire sur 2 000 km et une largeur de 300 km le long du littoral du cinquième continent.

Ce que Cook et les naturalistes de son temps ne savent pas encore, c'est que la Grande Barrière de corail, un labyrinthe monumental de 2 900 récifs, est l'œuvre des plus petits bâtisseurs qui soient au monde : les polypes coralliens, des animaux mesurant entre quelques millimètres et quelques centimètres.

Vorace et productive : la coopérative des coraux

Les polypes coralliens se composent principalement d'une cavité servant avant tout à leur digestion. Dans la Grande Barrière de corail cohabitent 400 espèces différentes de coraux durs et mous. Grâce à leur squelette calcaire, véritable matériau de construction, seuls les coraux durs contribuent à l'édification des récifs coralliens. Chacun ressemble à un petit calice, dans lequel le polype se retire le jour et dont il se projette la nuit pour capturer le plancton à l'aide de ses tentacules. Lorsqu'il meurt, son squelette calcaire est colonisé.

Pour construire un récif, il faut des myriades de coraux, qui se reproduisent de deux façons. Le bourgeonnement, asexué, consiste à fabriquer de nouveaux sujets par excroissance. Chaque espèce a son propre plan de construction, qui dépend des conditions de son environnement. Ainsi, certaines vont se déployer en forme d'éventail filigrané, tandis que d'autres, pour résister à un ressac plus puissant, développeront des sortes de branches épaisses ou, dans les grandes profondeurs, prendront une forme de champignon. Mais une nouvelle colonie ne peut s'implanter

uniquement par bourgeonnement et le corail doit également se reproduire de façon sexuée : après la pleine lune de novembre, tous les polypes émettent en même temps leurs œufs et leurs graines, ce qui a pour effet de troubler les eaux. La rencontre entre un œuf et un spermatozoïde donne naissance à une larve nageuse qui, si elle ne disparaît pas dans l'estomac d'un poisson, ira fonder ailleurs une nouvelle colonie.

Seuls les coraux durs acclimatés aux tropiques peuvent bâtir des récifs, mais ils ne peuvent le faire sans l'étroite collaboration d'une algue verte d'une espèce très spécifique, la zooxanthelle. Cet organisme unicellulaire niche dans la paroi cellulaire du polype corallien et fait bénéficier son hôte des produits métaboliques de la photosynthèse : il s'agit donc d'un échange de bons procédés entre l'algue et le corail. La zooxanthelle fournit notamment aux polypes l'énergie nécessaire, sous forme d'hydrates de carbone, pour prélever dans l'eau de mer le calcium qui leur permet de développer leur squelette calcaire. Et plus l'eau est claire, plus la zooxanthelle est généreuse en hydrates de carbone. C'est pourquoi les coraux vivent généralement juste en dessous de la surface, là où le rayonnement solaire leur parvient. À plus de 80 m de profondeur, ils ne peuvent survivre.

L'ennemi du récif

L'acanthaster ou étoile de mer épineuse (*Acanthaster planci*), le plus dangereux ennemi des coraux, peut mesurer jusqu'à 80 cm. Depuis 1962, trois invasions d'acanthasters ont fortement perturbé la vie du récif. Au cours de son existence, cette étoile de mer pond environ 1 milliard d'œufs et il suffit que les chances de survie des larves augmentent d'un rien pour que naissent des millions de nouveaux individus.

Depuis quelques années, une quantité croissante de nutriments provenant des déchets de la civilisation pénètre dans le récif par le biais des rivières et favorise la prolifération de ces étoiles de mer qui infligent de graves dégâts aux récifs.

Madagascar

UNE ÎLE QUI A TOUT

À Madagascar, les arbres ne ressemblent pas toujours à des arbres et certains animaux indigènes ont quelque chose d'improbable. Le baobab, comme ici près de Morondava, et le catta, un lémurien, sont deux des espèces très particulières de la quatrième île du monde par la taille.

D'UN CONTINENT

De la pluie
en suffisance

environnement. L'île proposant de nombreux biotopes différents, une grande biodiversité a pu s'y installer avec le temps.

Le socle montagneux âgé de 2 à 3 milliards d'années n'est plus visible que dans l'est de l'île. Suivant l'imposant escarpement qui suit une série de failles rectilignes, la ligne côtière orientale semble avoir été tracée à la règle. L'érosion a altéré les roches des zones de fracture provoquées par la séparation de Madagascar et de l'Inde. Les alizés de sud-est, saturés d'humidité, assurent toute l'année une forte pluviosité sur les versants de la montagne. Par conséquent, la dépression située entre le littoral et le haut plateau abrite de nombreuses plantes marécageuses spécialisées.

Les précipitations sont encore plus abondantes en bordure du haut plateau abrupt, région de forêt dense tropicale. Dans les zones éloignées, celle-ci ressemble à une véritable jungle et offre une profusion de plantes luxuriantes ordonnées en plusieurs étages, dont des orchidées, et de lémuriens, d'oiseaux bariolés et de papillons géants. À 800 m d'altitude, la forêt dense cède la place à la forêt de montagne tropicale, elle-même relayée, à 1 300 m, par la forêt de brouillard.

Le haut plateau central, appelé Hautes Terres, est le domaine du granit. Il présente de vastes étendues plates étagées sur plusieurs niveaux, de sorte que le relief évoque un escalier géant. La montagne qui s'élevait à cet endroit il y a fort longtemps s'est ensuite aplatie, puis à nouveau soulevée. Vers l'ouest, à l'abri des montagnes, le climat se fait de plus en plus sec. Les précipitations sont encore abondantes, mais nettement plus rares. Dans la plaine s'élèvent des chaos granitiques, un ensemble de blocs de granit désordonnés comme ceux que l'on peut observer en Corse.

Les forêts qui couvraient autrefois les Hautes Terres ont cédé la place à une véri-

table savane herbacée, où l'on rencontre en permanence des *lavaka*, des profonds ravinements de terrain au sol teinté de rouge par la latérite. Après la saison sèche, en effet, le sol argileux est dur comme de la pierre et fissuré, et les fortes pluies s'infiltrent dans les interstices jusqu'à l'interface entre la terre et la roche. L'argile devenue glissante dévale les pentes et laisse derrière elle des trous de plusieurs centaines de mètres de diamètre : les *lavaka*. Une forêt empêcherait ces effondrements, mais 90 % de la surface boisée d'origine ont été sacrifiés à la culture sur brûlis.

Les plantes élaborent
des stratégies savantes
contre la sécheresse

Au-dessus du haut plateau se dressent des chaînes montagneuses dont le point culminant, le Maromokotra, s'élève au nord à 2 876 m d'altitude. Le Maromokotra est l'un des nombreux volcans éteints de Madagascar. Les traces qu'il a laissées – coulées de lave, cônes de cendres et sommets érodés – multiplient dans le paysage les

Le déboisement et les fortes précipitations ont marqué le haut plateau de profondes blessures : ces ravinements portent le nom de *lavaka*.

petites niches écologiques habitées par des créatures spécialisées. Ainsi les plus grands prédateurs de l'île, les crocodiles, ont-ils élu domicile dans d'idylliques lacs volcaniques .

Sur les versants occidentaux, les alizés du sud-est sont des vents descendants secs, mais d'autres vents apportent la pluie. En été, dans l'hémisphère Sud, l'ouest se trouve dans la zone d'influence des vents de nord-est humides : la flore locale doit donc être apte à stocker l'eau pour les périodes sèches. Le tronc en forme de bouteille du baobab est éloquent quant à cette faculté. Plus grand arbre de la région, il n'est en aucun cas le végétal le plus étrange de la flore locale. Les euphorbiacées et les curieux pachypodes, notamment, ont déployé des stratégies remarquables contre la sécheresse.

Après une longue période sèche, une espèce de pachypode peut se retirer en totalité dans le sol. Elle perd ses quelques

Des fougères arborescentes poussent dans la forêt dense tropicale de la côte est. La population végétale primitive de l'île comptait des fougères semblables qui, dans la plupart des régions du monde, ont été remplacées par d'autres plantes.

feuilles, transfère dans ses racines l'humidité de son tronc en train de mourir et disparaît complètement dans la terre.

La région la plus sèche de Madagascar est toutefois le sud-ouest, où de rares vents d'ouest créent une dépression atmosphérique souvent liée à un cyclone. C'est le domaine des didiéracées, de petits arbres au tronc serpentiforme qui ressemblent à des cactées. Le tronc et les branches sont hérissés d'épines et l'arbre perd ses feuilles à la saison sèche.

Un havre de paix perturbé par l'homme

Il y a 60 millions d'années, les animaux émigrés d'Afrique ne trouvèrent certes pas un paradis à Madagascar, mais l'un des plus vastes habitats naturels coupés du reste du monde. Dans de telles conditions, la spécialisation des différentes espèces est allée très loin. Ainsi l'île abrite-t-elle 3 000 espèces de papillons. Presque toutes sont endémiques, mais beaucoup dépendent de plantes très particulières, elles aussi endémiques.

Mais la spécialisation n'est pas toujours un avantage : lorsqu'une certaine espèce bota-

Les didiéracées ressemblent à des cactées. Celles-ci, dans le parc Berenty, dans le sud de l'île, stockent l'eau dans leur tronc pour survivre aux longues périodes de sécheresse de la savane épineuse.

nique meurt, les organismes qui en dépendent perdent leur moyen de subsistance.

Les premiers êtres humains sont arrivés à Madagascar au début de notre ère, en provenance du Pacifique Sud. On ignore toujours s'ils ont parcouru tout ce chemin directement par la mer ou en passant par l'Afrique. Au regard de la longue période qu'il a fallu à l'évolution pour établir sur la grande île une faune et une flore incomparables, l'homme n'a pas mis beaucoup de temps pour changer la physionomie de l'île. Les brûlis massifs et l'utilisation des arbres comme bois de chauffage ont détruit près de 90 % du peuplement forestier. Cela explique qu'un grand nombre d'espèces se soient éteintes avant que l'on ait eu le temps de les découvrir et de les classifier.

En tout état de cause, Madagascar demeure un havre de paix biologique qui, dans un avenir peut-être proche, pourrait prendre une valeur économique considérable : on a utilisé avec succès contre la leucémie, chez des enfants, des substances actives provenant de la forêt sempervirente, un argument fort pour protéger ce trésor naturel. La recherche génétique commence à peine à comprendre les secrets de la vie.

AU GRÉ DES COURS D'EAU

Une fois par an, de violentes inondations submergent un tiers du gigantesque bassin à fond plat situé entre la région de hauts plateaux de l'est du Brésil et les Andes. On comprend alors que les spécialistes aient longtemps pris le Pantanal pour une ancienne mer. Cette région d'Amérique du Sud, la plus riche sur le plan faunique, est une véritable arche de Noé. Les extrêmes – crues et sécheresses – influent sur la vie de l'ensemble de ses habitants, dont le jabiru (petite photo).

Une mosaïque d'eau et de terre

Les conquérants portugais baptisèrent *pântano* (marécage) le bassin situé entre les Andes et les montagnes de l'est du Brésil, d'où le nom de Pantanal attribué à cette région. Selon la saison et la zone dans laquelle on se trouve, le paysage se fait savane ou marécage. On y trouve aussi bien de vastes prairies, des palmeraies et des forêts-galeries que des centaines d'étangs et de mares ponctuant la plaine, où les cours d'eau s'insinuant entre des digues naturelles alternent avec des lacs aux contours arrondis.

À la période de crue annuelle, 60 à 80 % du Pantanal se retrouvent submergés, ce qui donne tout son sens à son nom.

L'eau protège le Pantanal contre la présence humaine car ce labyrinthe de cours d'eau et de levées naturelles n'est alors plus accessible à pied ni par les gros bateaux. À ce jour, une seule route mène au Pantanal et de vastes portions de cette région d'eaux douces unique, d'une superficie de 187 818 ha, appartiennent alors entièrement aux poissons, oiseaux, jaguars et loutres géantes.

Un ancien bassin maritime ?

Sur la bordure nord et est du Pantanal s'élève le plateau en terrasses du centre du Brésil, dont la limite géologique est marquée par la cascade du Veú da Noiva (« voile de la mariée »). À cet endroit, le Cuiabá se déverse à la verticale, sur 85 m, le long d'une paroi de grès datant de 350 à 400 millions d'années, jusque dans la cuvette marécageuse plus jeune du Pantanal. Quelque 500 km plus loin vers l'ouest, le terrain entame son élévation vers les Andes.

On a longtemps pensé que cette gigantesque cuvette avait été occupée autrefois par une mer. Mais, dans les années 1960, l'étude de prélèvements minéralogiques n'a révélé aucune trace d'eau salée. Le Pantanal n'a jamais été une mer, bien au contraire : sa physionomie actuelle résulte de périodes de grande sécheresse.

De l'effet des glaciations

Aux périodes glaciaires, le Pantanal était une zone semi-désertique dotée d'une végétation clairsemée. La pluie était rare, mais diluvienne : les vallées sèches se transformaient alors en lits de fleuves tumultueux. Ces cours d'eau charriaient d'énormes quantités de sable arraché aux montagnes brésiliennes, qu'ils déversaient ensuite dans la cuvette, surtout vers la fin de la dernière phase glaciaire, il y a 11 000 ans. Ces alluvions, dites cônes de déjection, se sont accumulées par endroits sur une épaisseur

Aux chutes du Veú da Noiva, le Cuiabá se déverse sur 85 m dans le bassin du Pantanal.

d'une centaine de mètres et ont formé de vastes deltas intérieurs, dans lesquels les cours d'eau se ramifiaient sans jamais atteindre la mer : ils s'évaporaient ou se tarissaient dans la plaine.

Les cours d'eau bâtissent des digues

Aujourd'hui, les cours d'eau transportent principalement des particules très fines et les cônes de déjection des périodes de glaciation se sont ramifiés sur de telles étendues que le Pantanal est irrigué sur un large front. Certaines rivières s'enfoncent dans le sol pour ne resurgir que 200 km plus loin.

Parfois, les rivières sont bordées de hautes berges semblables à des digues. Pour certains chercheurs, ces levées naturelles sont des vestiges de dunes des ères glaciaires, un point de vue étayé par le parallélisme des cours d'eau avec les vents dominants de l'époque.

Cependant, les cours d'eau peuvent construire ces digues eux-mêmes : la dénivellation du Pantanal se limite à 1 ou 2 cm/km sur l'axe nord-sud, et 6 à 8 cm sur l'axe est-ouest. Les eaux s'écoulant donc lentement dans la plaine, leurs sédiments tombent et s'accumulent au fond, principalement près des berges, où le débit est particulièrement lent. C'est ainsi que s'édifient progressivement ces remblais naturels parallèles à la rive.

Ces cours d'eau bordés de levées coulent souvent très au-dessus du niveau du fond de la vallée. Par endroits, ils transportent de grandes îles flottantes formées de jacinthes d'eau, qui évoquent la superstructure d'un bateau voguant sur un canal artificiel.

Un ancien domaine de géants

Aux périodes glaciaires, d'énormes mammifères habitaient la savane sèche du Pantanal. On a retrouvé des fossiles de paresseux géant, ancêtre du paresseux actuel, qui avait la taille d'un éléphant. Il y avait également des tigres à dents de sabre, aux longs crocs acérés, et des tatous de la taille d'une petite voiture. Enfin, on a également trouvé des os pétrifiés de chevaux, une véritable curiosité puisque le cheval avait disparu d'Amérique du Sud avant l'arrivée des hommes et y a été réintroduit par les Européens.

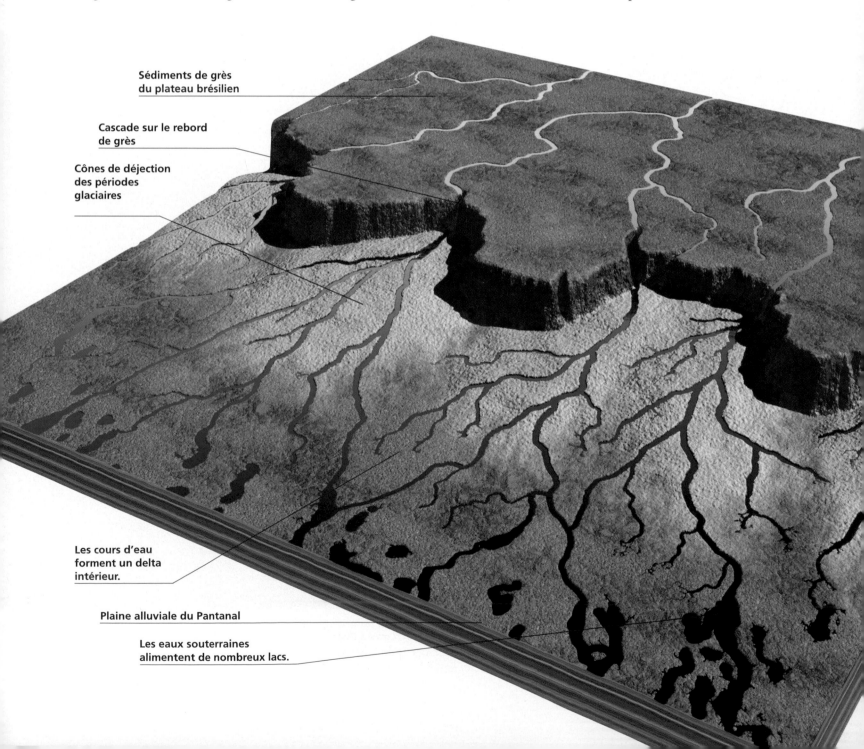

Sédiments de grès du plateau brésilien

Cascade sur le rebord de grès

Cônes de déjection des périodes glaciaires

Les cours d'eau forment un delta intérieur.

Plaine alluviale du Pantanal

Les eaux souterraines alimentent de nombreux lacs.

Pourquoi ces mammifères géants se sont-ils éteints il y a 11 000 ans ? L'explication vient peut-être du changement climatique majeur intervenu à la fin du dernier épisode glaciaire : les animaux adaptés à la sécheresse n'ont pu s'accommoder de ces crues annuelles.

Des inondations à retardement

De par sa situation en bordure des tropiques, le Pantanal connaît de longues périodes de sécheresse. La saison des pluies dure de novembre à février, mais les eaux n'atteignent qu'entre mai et juin une hauteur de 4 m au-dessus du niveau à sec. En effet, elles sont d'abord en grande partie absorbées par les cônes de déjection, puis vont alimenter les nappes souterraines, et il faut attendre plusieurs mois avant qu'elles ne remplissent les mares taries pour les transformer en lacs.

Dans les parties les plus hautes du Pantanal, environ 20 % des terres sont submergées pendant deux à trois mois sous 30 à 40 cm d'eau ; dans ses zones moyennes,

Le ara hyacinthe se nourrit principalement des noix du palmier aricuri (ci-contre), qu'il casse avec son bec puissant. Sa survie dépend du maintien de ces palmeraies.

Le Pantanal : un bassin gigantesque

Lorsque les cours d'eau du plateau brésilien atteignent le Pantanal, ils se heurtent à des cônes de déjection et à des deltas intérieurs datant des glaciations. Ils doivent donc dévier leur trajectoire et se divisent en bras secondaires.

la crue persiste trois à quatre mois ; et les portions basses et plates du bassin demeurent inondées la moitié de l'année sous 4 m d'eau.

Une réserve sauvage unique

Dans le Pantanal, la faune et la flore se sont adaptées aux caprices des eaux. À la saison des pluies, les animaux terrestres trouvent refuge sur les îles tandis que, à la saison

sèche, ils se précipitent vers les points d'eau subsistants. Ainsi, au début de la saison des pluies, les oiseaux aquatiques élisent leur terrain de pêche dans les eaux basses du sud du Pantanal, avant de s'aventurer plus haut lorsque les eaux montent. À la saison sèche, ils se nourrissent des poissons piégés dans les étangs.

Dans le Pantanal, les plantes aquatiques côtoient les grands palmiers, les feuillus, les herbes et les algues, et fournissent le gîte et le couvert à de nombreux animaux. 80 espèces de mammifères ont été recensées dans la région, auxquelles s'ajoutent 650 espèces d'oiseaux, 50 de reptiles et au moins 240 de poissons.

Parmi les palmiers paissent des cerfs des marais, des caïmans à lunettes chassent des capybaras, les aras hyacinthes se régalent des noix du palmier aricuri et le jabiru, emblème du Pantanal, cherche des serpents dans l'herbe. Jaguars, tatous, tapirs et anacondas sont également les hôtes de la région.

Le Sarawak

DES GROTTES DANS LA FORÊT DENSE

Telle une bouche béante dans la verdure de la forêt dense, une cavité gigantesque s'ouvre vers le monde extérieur. Qui s'aventure dans l'une des nombreuses grottes du nord de l'île de Bornéo s'aperçoit que les salles, gale-ries et cheminées de ce monde souterrain ne sont pas désertes: une vie étonnante se cache à l'abri de l'obscurité, que même le porte-lanterne (petite photo) ne pourrait éclairer: ses capacités luminescentes ne sont qu'une légende.

Un linceul de verdure

Dans les forêts du Sarawak malais, sur l'île de Bornéo, la nature fait naître des fleurs extraordinaires. La rafflésie, de 1 m de diamètre, est plus grande que l'agile muntjac, un cerf qui mesure 50 cm au garrot. Le petit univers souterrain de l'île est à nul autre pareil : les grottes de Gunung Mulu, fortes de plus de 100 km de galeries, sont les plus étendues du monde et la salle du Sarawak passe pour le plus grand dôme calcaire naturel de la planète.

Tout aussi spectaculaire est le nombre d'animaux et de végétaux répertoriés dans la région : 950 espèces de poissons, 530 d'oiseaux, 185 de mammifères, 166 de serpents, 104 de lézards et plus de 10 000 espèces d'insectes, auxquelles viennent s'ajouter plus de 8 000 espèces de plantes à fleurs, 4 500 de champignons et 615 de fougères. On y trouve notamment des tigres, des léopards, des rhinocéros et des orangs-outans.

Bornéo n'a pas toujours été une île

Cette exceptionnelle diversité naturelle est due avant tout à la situation géographique du Sarawak. La région se trouve près de l'équateur, dans le nord de Bornéo, sur la mer de Chine méridionale. Toute l'année, le climat y est humide et relativement chaud à très chaud : les conditions idéales pour une végétation luxuriante.

Mais l'insularité est à la fois un avantage et un inconvénient pour le développement floristique et faunique. D'un côté, animaux et plantes ont pu se développer sans crainte de concurrents et de prédateurs mais, de l'autre, l'isolement peut entraîner un appauvrissement des espèces puisqu'il empêche les migrations.

C'est pourquoi Bornéo est longtemps restée une énigme pour les biologistes. De fait, nombre de ses animaux et plantes sont endémiques, mais bien d'autres sont présents également dans les îles voisines de Java et Sumatra, en Inde, en Australie ou, plus loin, dans le Sud-Est asiatique. Cela est valable pour des animaux vivants, mais aussi pour des espèces depuis longtemps disparues dont on a retrouvé des fossiles. Il en a donc été conclu que Bornéo n'a pas toujours été une île.

La mer entourant Bornéo est peu profonde car l'île est située sur la plate-forme continentale de la Sonde. Lors des épisodes glaciaires, les glaciers ont englacé une telle quantité d'eau que le niveau de la mer était par endroits 100 m plus bas que le niveau actuel. La mer peu profonde de la plate-forme s'est donc asséchée, faisant de Bornéo une presqu'île entre le continent asiatique et la fosse de Java, au large de l'Australie. Les paléontologues appellent

De ces immenses grottes sortent chaque nuit des millions de chauves-souris et de salanganes, un martinet nocturne, à la recherche de nourriture dans les forêts denses du Sarawak.

pays de la Sonde cette langue de terre ferme aujourd'hui submergée, dont la Nouvelle-Guinée ne faisait pas partie à l'époque puisqu'elle était encore reliée à l'Australie.

Des périodes glaciaires sans conséquences

Au cours des 2 à 3 millions d'années passées, l'alternance de phases glaciaires et chaudes a été beaucoup plus fréquente que ne l'ont longtemps cru les climatologues. Selon eux, il n'y avait eu que quatre grands épisodes glaciaires en Europe, alors que l'on estime aujourd'hui ce chiffre à plusieurs dizaines. Cette alternance a provoqué l'apparition et la disparition de nombreuses liaisons terrestres entre les îles et les continents et, respectivement, l'arrivée et le départ d'espèces biologiques. Cela explique la complexité des liens de parenté entre espèces.

Dans la plupart des régions du monde, les ères glaciaires ont décimé la faune et la flore mais, dans le Sud-Est asiatique, un nombre relativement élevé d'animaux et de végétaux a résisté aux changements climatiques. En effet, tandis que d'autres régions étaient complètement englacées ou souffraient d'une pluviosité nettement insuffisante, le Sud-Est asiatique conservait un climat relativement humide et chaud, loin des grandes calottes glaciaires.

On y trouve donc des espèces qui n'existent plus ailleurs, dont le varan sourd, un crocodile qui ne vit plus qu'au Sarawak, et l'hippopotame de Sumatra.

Une karstification lourde de conséquences

La présence de ces gigantesques grottes calcaires du Sarawak s'explique aussi par le climat humide relativement régulier de la région. L'érosion du calcaire est due à la dissolution de son carbonate de calcium par le dioxyde de carbone des eaux, un processus de dégradation appelé karstification. Dans les zones tropicales humides, ce phénomène est particulièrement rapide car il est accéléré par les températures élevées et l'infiltration dans le sol des acides provenant de la décomposition des végétaux

morts. À proximité des grottes du Gunung Mulu, un labyrinthe surréaliste de rochers en forme d'aiguilles pouvant culminer à 60 m illustre cette intense karstification aérienne.

Dans le sous-sol, l'érosion chimique creuse d'abord au niveau de la nappe phréatique des tunnels elliptiques complètement submergés. Si le niveau de l'eau baisse, par suite d'un changement climatique, par exemple, l'eau peut ensuite s'écouler librement, comme un cours d'eau, et creuser de profonds sillons dans le plancher de ces tunnels. L'infiltration des eaux de pluie provoque ensuite la formation de concrétions calcaires. Enfin, si les voûtes s'effondrent, les grottes s'élargissent et s'ouvrent sur l'extérieur : une voie d'accès pour les animaux et les plantes.

Un paradis pour les chauves-souris et les salanganes

Les grottes du Sarawak ont une forte densité de population et sont notamment habitées par d'immenses colonies de chauves-souris. À l'entrée de la Deer Cave, on peut assister le soir, lorsque le temps le

Les colonies de grands rhinolophes comptent des milliers d'individus qui s'accrochent aux voûtes des grottes.

La grande grotte de Niah (tout en haut) était habitée par des êtres humains il y a 40 000 ans. Outre des os et des poteries, ils y ont laissé des peintures rupestres remarquables. La grotte est aujourd'hui une curiosité touristique.

permet, à un spectacle extraordinaire : plus d'un million de chauves-souris boule-dogues partent en plusieurs vagues à la recherche de nourriture. Cette envolée, qui dure plus d'une heure, est fort attendue par des rapaces comme la buse des chauves-souris, postés à l'entrée de la grotte.

Autres habitantes des grottes, les salanganes sont des martinets nocturnes dont certains, comme les chauves-souris, s'orientent dans la totale obscurité grâce à un sonar. Cela leur permet à la fois de chasser la nuit et de retrouver leur nid, parmi des centaines d'autres, dans le noir.

Cette extraordinaire quantité de chauves-souris et d'oiseaux fournit un biotope idéal à des millions de blattes et autres invertébrés, mais également un engrais très recherché.

Des espèces forestières spécialisées

Les deux tiers du Sarawak sont recouverts de forêts très dissemblables, qui n'abritent pas les mêmes animaux. Véritable

Pendant les périodes glaciaires, il y a entre 3 millions d'années et 11 000 ans, le niveau de la mer était bien plus bas qu'aujourd'hui. Les îles actuelles étaient donc reliées pour certaines au Sud-Est asiatique et, pour d'autres, à l'Australie.

Hainan
Thaïlande
Philippines
OCÉAN PACIFIQUE
Malaisie
Sumatra
Bornéo
Moluques
Sulawesi
Nouvelle-Guinée
I n d o n é s i e
Java
OCÉAN INDIEN
Australie

Le sanglier à barbe fait partie des rescapés des derniers épisodes glaciaires dans cette partie du monde.

Le népenthès (tout en haut) tire ses nutriments des insectes qu'il attire dans ses urnes. Le couvercle que l'on aperçoit empêche la pluie de diluer les sucs digestifs contenus dans les urnes.

Le nid de la salangane à nid noir est comestible. Avant de le préparer, il faut d'abord ôter avec soin les plumes qui le tapissent.

caricature de l'homme, le nasique, endémique à Bornéo, se plaît dans les mangroves de la côte et les tourbières acides de l'intérieur des terres.

L'orang-outan (« homme des bois » en malais) vit exclusivement à Sumatra et dans les forêts denses toujours humides du Sarawak, où plusieurs étages de végétation bénéficient des rayons du soleil. Contrairement au gorille et au chimpanzé, cet imposant singe anthropoïde vit principalement dans les cimes des arbres.

Arbres géants de l'est de l'Asie, filaos d'Australie

Les principales plantes de la forêt dense du Sarawak sont les diptérocarpacées, une famille d'arbres géants du Sud-Est asiatique comprenant de nombreuses espèces. Dépourvus de branches, les troncs peuvent mesurer 40 à 60 m de hauteur pour un diamètre de 1,50 m. Lorsqu'ils atteignent la canopée, ces arbres développent une couronne extrêmement étendue. Malgré l'absence de véritables saisons au Sarawak, toutes les diptérocarpacées fleurissent pratiquement en même temps dans un rayon de quelques kilomètres. L'air se remplit alors d'un parfum qui attire les insectes et les chauves-souris, qui assureront la pollinisation de l'espèce. Les fruits mûrissent eux aussi à peu près en même temps et sont consommés par les singes et les calaos.

Le bois des diptérocarpacées est très recherché par l'industrie du bois. C'est pourquoi de nombreuses zones du Sud-Est asiatique ont subi une déforestation massive, les secteurs proches du littoral ayant été particulièrement touchés. Dans les zones plus élevées et moins accessibles, la forêt demeure intacte pour l'essentiel : sa faune et sa flore ont été protégées par la création de 10 parcs nationaux.

Dans l'est du Sarawak se dresse la montagne la plus élevée de la région, le Gunung Murud, qui culmine à 2 438 m. Les forêts de montagne, plus claires et moins diversifiées, poussent sur un sol sableux très pauvre et tirent leur humidité d'une couverture nuageuse permanente. Parmi la flore typique de cette forêt, on compte le filao, une plante arrivée d'Australie par l'intermédiaire du vent et des oiseaux.

La plus grosse fleur du monde commence par un petit bouton

Ces sols sableux pauvres en nutriments donnent toutefois naissance à des plantes merveilleuses. Le botaniste Carl von Linné (1707-1778) a baptisé népenthès une plante carnivore d'Indonésie, du nom d'un breuvage magique figurant dans l'*Odyssée* d'Homère et qui, selon le poète, dissipe le chagrin, la rancœur et les souvenirs douloureux.

Comme toutes les plantes vertes, cette plante à urnes recourt à la photosynthèse, c'est-à-dire utilise l'eau et l'énergie solaire pour produire des hydrates de carbone. Mais le népenthès a besoin d'autres nutriments : grâce au nectar sucré contenu dans ses urnes, il attire des insectes qui, embrumés par l'alcool, tombent à l'intérieur de l'urne, dans les sucs digestifs de la plante. Le népenthès tire de ces insectes du nitrate, de l'azote et du phosphore, des nutriments essentiels que le sol pauvre ne peut lui procurer.

Toutes les forêts du Sarawak regorgent de plantes grimpantes et d'épiphytes, des plantes qui poussent sur d'autres végétaux sans leur causer de dommages. L'une d'elles, le rotang, est un palmier grimpant doté d'une longue tige mince très employée en vannerie.

La rafflésie, elle, est un parasite. L'espèce *Rafflesia tuanmudae*, qui porte la plus grosse fleur du règne végétal, ne pousse que dans le Sarawak. Son unique plante hôte est un cépage sauvage du genre *Tetrastigma*. Au départ, la rafflésie n'est qu'un petit bouton sur une tige de la plante hôte courant sur le sol. De nombreuses semaines plus tard, ce bouton grossit en une sorte de chou-fleur luisant et rosé avant de s'ouvrir en une fleur pouvant atteindre 1 m de diamètre et dont l'odeur de viande pourrie attire les insectes. La rafflésie ne vit que quelques jours.

Le nid d'hirondelle, un mets de choix pour les Chinois

Lorsqu'un clic métallique retentit dans une grotte du Sarawak, c'est que des salanganes ne sont pas loin : ces martinets nocturnes s'orientent dans l'obscurité à l'aide d'un sonar biologique. Les mâles ont sous leur langue des glandes sécrétant une épaisse salive qui sèche vite et leur sert à construire leur nid, couche après couche. Dans la cuisine chinoise, cette sécrétion est considérée depuis plus de 1000 ans comme un mets fin. Longtemps condamnée par le communisme comme diabolique, la soupe au nid d'hirondelle est redevenue un mets de luxe. Les nids « blancs » de l'espèce *Collocalia fuciphaga*, qui niche dans la grotte Baram, au Sarawak, sont les plus appréciés : ils rapportent jusqu'à 1 600 euros le kilo. Cela explique pourquoi la salangane s'est éteinte dans de nombreuses régions.

NI TERRE NI OCÉAN

Jour après jour, le Gange, le Brahmapoutre et le Meghna transportent d'imposantes masses de boue et d'eau jusqu'au golfe du Bengale. Dans la région côtière plate s'est formée une mosaïque multicolore de cours d'eau, de bancs de sable et d'îles arborées, refuges d'une faune et d'une flore exceptionnelles. Le plus grand delta du monde a par ailleurs constitué des mangroves uniques adaptées aux conditions régnant dans cette zone. Les vastes forêts sont le domaine des derniers tigres du Bengale.

Du toit du monde jusqu'à la mer

Les Sundarbans, paysage côtier spectaculaire du delta du Gange, du Brahmapoutre et du Meghna, ne doivent pas leur nom au hasard : celui-ci vient du mot *sundari*, désignation locale d'une espèce de palétuvier, *Heritiera fomes*. Le sundari supporte les eaux salées, comme tous les palétuviers, mais il est aussi le spécialiste des eaux douces. Et les puissants flots d'eau douce qui irriguent les Sundarbans sont vitaux pour les mangroves locales.

À la saison des pluies, le Gange et le Brahmapoutre enregistrent un débit de 82 000 m³ par seconde en direction de l'océan et charrient jusqu'au delta 13 millions de tonnes de boue par jour. Pour atteindre une telle capacité, un certain nombre de facteurs sont nécessaires : un grand bassin hydrographique, une forte pluviosité, d'énormes quantités de sédiments fins et suffisamment d'énergie pour le transport.

Un puissant tapis roulant alimenté en permanence

Le vaste système hydrographique du Gange draine une grande partie de l'Himalaya et du nord de l'Inde. Le Brahmapoutre prend sa naissance au Tibet, s'écoule le long du versant nord de l'Himalaya, traverse l'Assam et se jette dans le golfe du Bengale. Grossi par les précipitations des monts Khasi et Parkai, le Meghna débouche également dans le delta.

Ce gigantesque bassin hydrographique est l'un des plus arrosés du monde. L'été, lorsque les vents de mousson saturés d'humidité atteignent le continent et sont forcés de s'élever en se heurtant à la montagne, les pluies sont diluviennes. La presque totalité du bassin reçoit plus de 1 000 mm de pluie par an, le versant méridional de la montagne Khasi en recevant même plus de 10 000 mm en moyenne.

Dans l'Himalaya, les cours d'eau acheminent principalement des charges de fond mais, plus loin en aval, ils traversent des terrains très érodés, puis des terrasses fluviales de l'ère glaciaire comportant des matériaux fins, plus faciles à emporter. Quant à l'énergie nécessaire pour transporter ces charges, le Gange et le Brahma-

poutre n'en manquent pas. Certaines de leurs sources sont situées à plusieurs milliers de mètres d'altitude, sur le toit du monde : pour un fleuve, dénivellation est synonyme d'énergie.

Les cours d'eau charrient donc leur charge vers l'aval mais, quand celle-ci devient trop lourde ou que le régime ralentit, ils perdent en puissance. Ils déposent d'abord les alluvions les plus lourdes, puis les sables et les argiles. Il arrive fréquemment qu'ils obturent leur propre lit et se fraient alors un autre chemin et se ramifient en de nombreux bras secondaires. C'est ainsi, petit à petit, que se forme une importante accumulation d'alluvions, le delta. Les cours d'eau perdent leur puissance dès qu'ils atteignent la mer.

Le delta couvre aujourd'hui une superficie de 105 000 km². Mais il ne s'agit là que de sa partie visible : il se prolonge sous la mer au-delà du plateau continental, dans le golfe du Bengale et l'océan Indien, jusqu'à près de 3 000 km. On estime que ses alluvions sous-marines s'étendent sur plus de 1 000 km de largeur et 15 km d'épaisseur.

Le Gange, une artère vitale

Entre ses sources et le golfe du Bengale, le Gange s'écoule sur près de 2 500 km. Dans sa course, il entraîne tout sur son passage : eaux de fonte de l'Himalaya, terres agricoles du Népal, eaux usées de Dehli. Les Sundarbans se trouvent tout à fait à l'extrémité de cette chaîne, qui constitue un énorme danger. Si les glaciers de l'Himalaya se mettaient à fondre en raison du réchauffement climatique, les Sundarbans seraient totalement inondés. Le déboisement et l'érosion dans le nord de l'Inde remplissent les bras du fleuve de boues. De plus, à la saison sèche, 30 % des eaux du Gange sont détournées au profit de l'agriculture. De ce fait, la salinité de l'eau des Sundarbans augmente de telle façon que certaines espèces de palétuviers et de poissons sont réellement menacées.

Comment le delta peut-il atteindre de telles dimensions ? Sa formation remonte aux glaciations. Il y a 18 000 ans, le niveau de la mer était 100 m plus bas qu'aujourd'hui et la ligne côtière longeait pratiquement le rebord du plateau continental. À la fin de chaque épisode glaciaire, surtout, la maigre végétation était détruite par les eaux de fonte et rien ne faisait obstacle au dépôt d'énormes quantités de sédiments le long de la plate-forme.

Ces dépôts boueux dévalaient la pente raide du front du delta et, telle une avalanche, emportaient tout sur leur passage. Les canyons creusés dans les sédiments sous-marins témoignent de l'existence passée de ces coulées de boue, encore appelées courants de turbidité, qui continuent à se déverser et remettent en mouvement les matériaux précédemment déposés. Ils peuvent être provoqués par des séismes, des cyclones ou, plus simplement, une suraccumulation de boues.

De nos jours, la partie occidentale indienne du delta n'est plus active. Au rythme des marées, les anciens bras des fleuves se remplissent d'eau salée provenant de l'océan. Les grands fleuves d'eau douce s'écoulent désormais dans la partie orientale du système deltaïque, côté Bangladesh.

Les habitats de la mangrove

Seules les plantes spécialisées peuvent s'installer dans les boues instables d'un delta et s'accommoder aussi bien de l'eau douce que de l'eau salée. Les palétuviers sont les arbres les mieux adaptés à la vie dans les embouchures de fleuves tropicaux et les zones soumises aux marées. Un amas enchevêtré de racines-échasses leur permet de s'ancrer dans la vase et ils respirent par l'intermédiaire de pores, les lenticelles, et d'un tissu spécifique permettant les échanges gazeux avec l'air. Le palétuvier

sundari porte ces pores le long d'excroissances racinaires verticales qui émergent de l'eau. Une autre espèce de palétuvier des Sundarbans développe des racines en arceaux et une troisième respire par les lenticelles de son écorce.

Les racines des palétuviers filtrent et remuent les eaux troubles, de sorte que le sable et l'argile tombent au fond et finissent par former d'innombrables îles et îlots, biotopes de nombreuses créatures car les cours d'eau transportent dans leurs boues une grande quantité de nutriments. Les mangroves comptent parmi les écosystèmes les

Le delta du Gange

Avant de se jeter dans le golfe du Bengale, le Gange, le Brahmapoutre et le Meghna décélèrent et déposent par couches le sable et la boue qu'ils transportent, remblayant ainsi le delta de telle façon qu'il s'étire jusque loin dans le golfe.

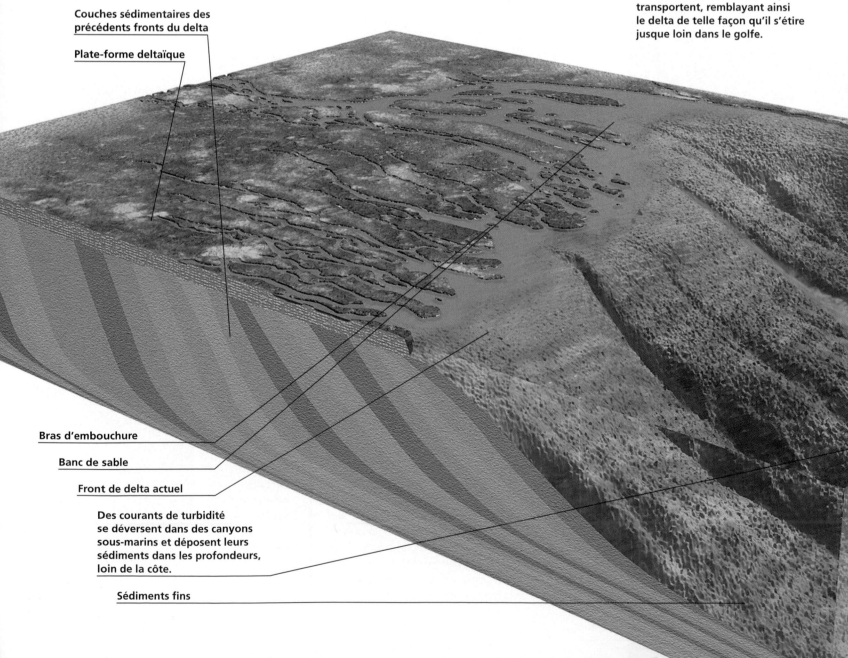

Couches sédimentaires des
précédents fronts du delta

Plate-forme deltaïque

Bras d'embouchure

Banc de sable

Front de delta actuel

Des courants de turbidité
se déversent dans des canyons
sous-marins et déposent leurs
sédiments dans les profondeurs,
loin de la côte.

Sédiments fins

Cette vue aérienne montre que les innombrables bras de l'embouchure transportent loin dans la mer leurs charges boueuses.

Le périophtalme, ou sauteur de boue, est un poisson doté de nageoires particulières qui lui permettent de sauter dans la vase à marée basse et de ramper sur les racines des palétuviers.

plus productifs de la Terre. Celles des Sundarbans, contrairement à celles qui ont une salinité plus élevée, se distinguent par une étonnante biodiversité.

Les eaux peu profondes et saumâtres pullulent de crustacés, proies de choix pour les poissons et les oiseaux. 315 espèces avicoles ont été recensées et plus de 400 de poissons. Les Sundarbans sont la nursery de nombreux poissons de haute mer. Les lézards, tortues, et mammifères y sont rares mais représentés.

Le maître incontesté des animaux du Sundarbans est le tigre royal. Il partage sa vie entre l'eau et la terre et se nourrit essentiellement de poissons, mais également de cochons sauvages, de cerfs mouchetés, de singes rhésus et de varans aquatiques. Il s'attaque aussi aux hommes, généralement ceux qui s'enfoncent dans les forêts pour récolter du miel.

Sur les milliers de tigres qui peuplaient autrefois les mangroves, il ne reste qu'environ 250 individus. La cause de leur disparition est la déforestation des Sundarbans, qui ne couvrent plus de nos jours qu'une superficie de 10 000 km² : convertie en rizières, la majeure partie du delta est aujourd'hui habitée. Enfin, les fréquents cyclones en provenance du golfe du Bengale amènent dans le delta des marées de tempête pouvant atteindre 7 à 9 m de haut et provoquant des inondations catastrophiques.

Les Sud-Africains sur-nomment le mur de fœhn qui recouvre la montagne de la Table, près de la ville du Cap, la Nappe. La Nappe n'apporte pas de précipitations sur la côte mais des vents chauds et secs. C'est pourquoi ici, à l'extrémité sud de l'Afrique, entre deux océans, est née une faune unique dont l'origine remonte loin dans le temps. La protée royale, fleur nationale du pays (petite photo), pour-rait raconter une histoire qui a com-mencé il y a plus de 160 millions d'années.

LES FLEURS ROYALES DU

GONDWANA

Un royaume botanique du bout du monde

La fleur de la protée royale peut mesurer jusqu'à 30 cm. Très appréciée dans de nombreux pays comme plante ornementale, elle est originaire de la province du Cap-Ouest (Western Cape), en Afrique du Sud. C'est là que les protéacées forment une famille homogène de 330 espèces. Leurs plus proches parents ne poussent pas en Afrique, mais en Australie et dans quelques endroits d'Amérique du Sud. Les botanistes se sont longtemps demandé comment les protéacées avaient bien pu traverser l'océan.

Lorsque l'on se trouve au cap de Bonne-Espérance, la question paraît sans réponse : 249 m séparent son sommet, Cape Point, de la mer. On se croirait au bout du monde si l'on ignorait que la Terre est ronde et que, par-delà l'horizon, se trouvent l'An-tarctique, l'Australie et l'Amérique du Sud jadis soudés à l'Afrique.

Le premier navigateur à doubler cette pointe sud de la presqu'île du Cap l'avait baptisée « cap des tempêtes », et les nombreuses épaves de navires justifient le bien-fondé de ce nom. C'est là que se rejoignent les océans Indien et Atlantique, une rencontre tumultueuse puisque le premier transporte les eaux chaudes du courant des Aiguilles, l'un des courants océaniques les plus puissants du monde, et le second les eaux froides du courant de Benguela. Mais les masses d'eau ne se mélangent qu'en partie et au niveau de la ligne de partage se massent souvent d'épais nuages qui enveloppent le phare et étaient autrefois très dangereux pour les navires.

Dans la ville du Cap, cette butte témoin s'appelle Lion's Head, « tête de lion ». Son socle granitique est surmonté par une couche de grès quartzeux.

L'escarpement de la côte prouve à quel point la mer est ici plus puissante que la terre. Le ressac sape la roche et emporte les éboulis dans la mer, surtout l'hiver, lorsque de violents vents d'ouest balaient le littoral.

Une montagne au cœur très ancien

Pour le plus grand bonheur des géologues, le ressac a dénudé dans le Cap-Ouest une formation géologique stratifiée de plusieurs centaines de mètres de hauteur, un affleurement qui est une véritable fenêtre sur la géochronologie de ce sol.

Ainsi, l'extérieur de la montagne de la Table, partie la plus haute de cette croupe montagneuse de 50 km de long et s'étirant sur la totalité de la presqu'île, se compose d'un grès quartzeux vieux de 350 à 410 millions d'années, tandis que le granit sous-jacent remonte au précambrien, il y a plus de 540 millions d'années.

La ville du Cap et la montagne de la Table

Enserrée entre les océans Atlantique et Indien et la montagne de la Table, la ville du Cap bénéficie d'un microclimat. Lorsque le vent souffle de l'est, la montagne se recouvre d'un nuage blanc : c'est un mur de fœhn, la Nappe. Mais les vents descendants sont toujours chauds et secs.

Mur de fœhn (la Nappe)

Vents descendants secs (fœhn)

Sédiments gréseux

Granit de la montagne de la Table (granit du Cap)

Lion's Head

Sur les traces de la protée royale

Le grès perméable se dégrade plus lentement que le granit. Au Cap, l'érosion a rongé le socle granitique, de sorte que le versant de la montagne n'a cessé de régresser vers l'intérieur des terres. L'étonnant Lion's Head, au beau milieu de la ville du Cap, est un relief résiduel, ou butte témoin. L'affleurement des roches et les fossiles retrouvés ont par ailleurs mis les géologues sur la piste des protéacées, qui les a emmenés jusqu'en Australie, en Amérique du Sud et en Antarctique, où se trouvent des successions de strates identiques dotées des mêmes fossiles. Or ces continents se trouvent à des milliers de milles marins de l'Afrique. Quel est le lien ?

La falaise de Cape Point, la pointe du Cap, offre une vaine résistance au ressac. Morceau après morceau, la mer grignote la roche.

Les immortelles (ci-contre) sont protégées du vent et du soleil par un duvet hirsute.

Les marguerites du Cap se plaisent dans les sols rocheux du littoral (ci-dessous).

Une histoire de séparation

À l'apogée du règne des dinosaures carnivores, il y a entre 149 et 160 millions d'années, l'Amérique du Sud, l'Afrique, l'Antarctique, l'Australie et l'Inde formaient un supercontinent, le Gondwana. Seule une petite mer intérieure entre l'Afrique du Sud et l'Antarctique, partie d'un fossé d'effondrement dans la croûte terrestre, indiquait la future dérive des continents. De violents séismes, associés à une forte activité volcanique, finirent par disloquer le Gondwana et provoquèrent le plissement des strates de roches. Un phénomène semblable peut être observé de nos jours dans la Rift Valley, en Afrique, où s'annonce la formation d'une nouvelle mer. On distingue nettement les strates plissées du Gondwana dans les montagnes de la presqu'île du Cap. La séparation de l'Amérique du Sud, l'Antarctique et l'Afrique du Sud s'est achevée il y a entre 100 et 140 millions d'années.

Des fossiles prouvent qu'il y avait déjà des protéacées à cette époque, ce qui explique le lien de la protée royale avec l'Australie et l'Amérique du Sud. D'autres plantes comme *Todea barbara*, une fougère arborescente, ne sont présentes qu'en Afrique du Sud, en Australie et en Nouvelle-Zélande.

Le lis orangé (ci-dessus) est l'une des nombreuses plantes à fleurs qui ont débuté au Cap leur carrière internationale.

Un pays de fleurs coupées

Au cours de l'histoire de la Terre sont apparues autour du globe sept zones de végétation, appelées empires floristiques par les botanistes. Ceux-ci ont donné à la petite extrémité sud-ouest de l'Afrique sa propre catégorie, qualifiée de flore du Cap. Couvrant une superficie égale à celle du Portugal, c'est la plus petite flore du monde. Par comparaison, l'Europe fait partie de la zone holarctique, qui comprend l'ensemble de l'hémisphère Nord, hormis les tropiques, car les végétations de l'Amérique, de l'Europe, de l'Asie et de l'Arctique ne sont pas si différentes les unes des autres.

Dans la minuscule zone du Cap prospère une plus grande variété de plantes que dans l'ensemble de la zone holarctique. Près de 9 000 espèces y ont été répertoriées, dont 6 000 sont endémiques. Seules quelques régions de forêt pluviale tropicale en comptent davantage.

En plus des protéacées poussent des carex, des éricacées et des plantes à bulbes ; l'alisier prospère sur les pentes humides. De nombreuses fleurs coupées répandues dans le monde entier sont originaires du Cap, dont les glaïeuls, les freesias, les amaryllis et les immortelles.

Le caractère unique de la flore du Cap s'explique par son isolement : elle est séparée d'autres régions par les océans et, de plus, les déserts et les zones sèches de ses limites nord et est ont empêché la propagation des plantes indigènes. Une question demeure : d'où tient-elle une telle diversité ?

Un climat de type méditerranéen

Lorsque les habitants du Cap voient la Nappe s'étendre au-dessus de la montagne de la Table, ils savent qu'ils n'auront pas besoin de leur parapluie, car à peine les nuages se gonflent-ils de façon menaçante qu'ils se transforment en air chaud. La station météorologique située sur la montagne enregistre trois fois plus de précipitations à 750 m au-dessus du niveau de la mer que dans la ville du Cap elle-même. L'été, la canicule s'abat sur la côte sud, alors que, sur le plateau, les plantes continuent de bénéficier de l'humidité des nuages.

Le climat du Cap connaît des étés secs et très chauds et des hivers doux et humides, traits caractéristiques d'un climat de type méditerranéen. L'hiver – de juin à septembre dans l'hémisphère Sud –, les vents d'ouest amènent sur la province des houles cycloniques porteuses de pluie. L'été, en revanche, le Cap se trouve dans la zone d'influence d'un anticyclone subtropical qui fait descendre les masses d'air au-dessus de l'Afrique du Sud. Du fait qu'elles se réchauffent en descendant, ces masses sont toujours sèches car l'air chaud absorbe davantage d'humidité que l'air froid. La zone côtière est toujours balayée par un léger vent du sud qui, passant au-dessus du courant froid de Benguela, n'apporte pas non plus de précipitations.

Dans le Cap-Ouest, ce climat est toutefois sujet à de grandes variations. Le microclimat de telle ou telle vallée, de tel ou tel promontoire dépend de l'altitude, de la latitude, de la situation par rapport à la mer et de l'exposition au vent.

Par ailleurs, l'intensité du gel et du rayonnement solaire, la composition du sous-sol et la qualité des sols diffèrent d'un lieu à l'autre et influent sur la végétation. Dès lors, comment s'étonner que la flore du Cap ait répondu à des conditions si diverses en développant un si grand nombre d'espèces ?

Le feu favorise certaines espèces

Le couvert végétal typique du Cap est le *fynbos*, « joli buisson » en afrikaans, une végétation arbustive proche de celle du maquis corse, qui ne dépasse pas 1,20 m de hauteur.

Les botanistes s'accordent à dire que les fréquents feux de brousse jouent un rôle prépondérant dans l'entretien du *fynbos*. Dès avant l'arrivée de l'homme, la foudre provoquait déjà des incendies à la saison sèche, auxquels la flore s'est adaptée : certaines espèces ne germent qu'après le passage du feu. Cette particularité offre de nombreux habitats aux animaux et aux plantes, leur permettant parfois de se développer.

Certains scientifiques, en revanche, estiment que la biodiversité du Cap tient davantage aux animaux pollinisateurs. Les plantes à fleurs, végétaux les plus évolués du monde, devraient essentiellement leur évolution à leurs rapports avec les animaux : elles leur fournissent nectar et fruits et, en retour, ils transportent leur pollen.

De nombreuses plantes du Cap dépendent donc fortement de la pollinisation par des insectes, oiseaux et mammifères spécifiques, une interaction favorable à la flore locale.

DES ÎLES SUR TERRE ET SUR MER

UN ARC INSULAIRE EXPLOSIF

S ociables, les îles se réunissent fréquemment en arcs élégants entre pays et continents. C'est le cas des nombreuses îles pittoresques des Antilles, dont Sainte-Lucie (grande photo), qui relient le nord et le sud du Nouveau Monde. Mais les archipels sont des formations fragiles. Les terribles éruptions volcaniques (la petite photo montre la Soufrière, sur Montserrat) qui s'y produisent laissent supposer sur quelles bases peu sûres ils reposent.

Là où le ciel et l'enfer se rencontrent

Les chroniqueurs de l'Antiquité parlaient d'une île imaginaire nommée Antilia, qui se trouvait quelque part au-delà du détroit de Gibraltar, son nom signifiant « l'île d'en face ». Lors de ses deux voyages de 1492 et 1493, Christophe Colomb découvre en fait les Antilles, le groupe d'îles des « Indes occidentales » dont seules les Bahamas ne font pas partie. Les Grandes Antilles sont Cuba, Haïti, la Jamaïque et Porto Rico,

prolongées au sud-est par les Petites Antilles. Le navigateur génois est émerveillé par la beauté de ce monde insulaire et impressionné par des phénomènes naturels comme les chutes du Carbet, en Guadeloupe, qui « tombent de si haut qu'on croirait qu'elles se jettent du ciel ». C'est à un spectacle infernal qu'il aurait assisté 170 ans plus tard : vers 1660 a lieu la première éruption de la Soufrière, en Guadeloupe. Ce stratovolcan a connu ses dernières grandes éruptions dans les années 1970 et son cratère ne rejette plus que de la vapeur d'eau et des fumerolles de soufre. À la fin des années 1990, la Soufrière de Montserrat est entrée en éruption. Et lorsque la mer bout devant l'île de Grenade, c'est que le Kick 'em Jenny, le seul volcan sous-marin des Petites Antilles,

reprend de l'activité. Ces dix mille dernières années, 17 volcans des Petites Antilles ont été en activité, qui font tous partie d'un type de volcan particulièrement dangereux. Les coulées de lave sont rares, mais les cheminées crachent des nuées ardentes de 800 °C qui dévalent leurs flancs à une vitesse vertigineuse et détruisent tout sur leur passage.

La montagne Pelée

Le 8 mai 1902, une éruption de la montagne Pelée, à la Martinique, fait plus de 29 000 morts dans la ville portuaire de Saint-Pierre. Le nom de Pelée lui a été attribué au XVIIᵉ siècle, en raison de la roche grise et nue surmontant son sommet.

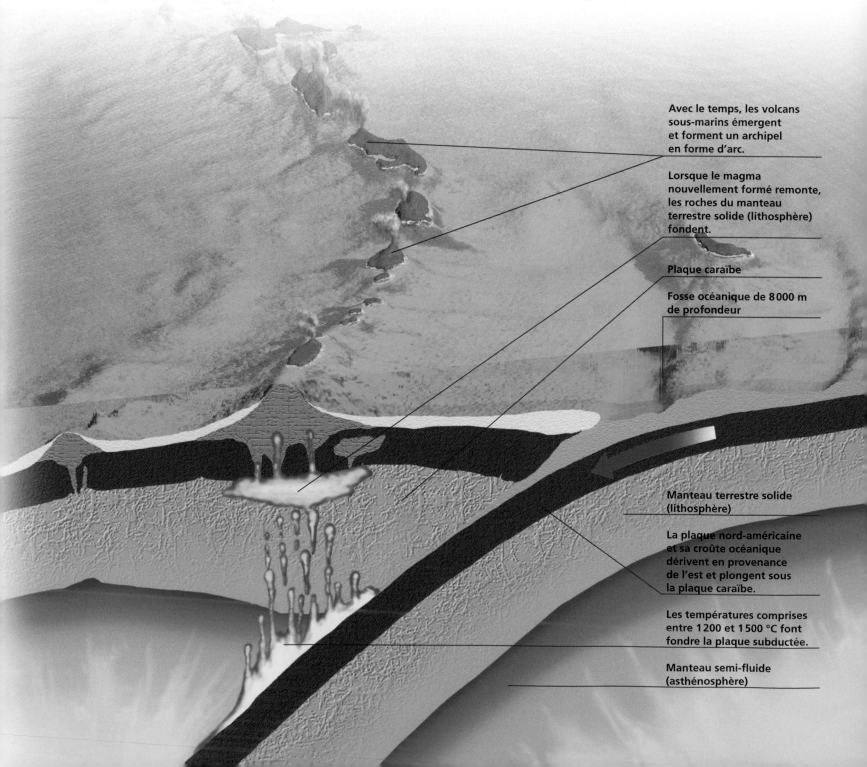

Avec le temps, les volcans sous-marins émergent et forment un archipel en forme d'arc.

Lorsque le magma nouvellement formé remonte, les roches du manteau terrestre solide (lithosphère) fondent.

Plaque caraïbe

Fosse océanique de 8 000 m de profondeur

Manteau terrestre solide (lithosphère)

La plaque nord-américaine et sa croûte océanique dérivent en provenance de l'est et plongent sous la plaque caraïbe.

Les températures comprises entre 1200 et 1500 °C font fondre la plaque subductée.

Manteau semi-fluide (asthénosphère)

Environ 6 mois après l'éruption de mai 1902, une nouvelle Pelée apparaît au sommet du volcan, un dôme de lave grise composée de magma comprimé qui grandit chaque jour de quelques mètres. En mai 1903, parmi les nuages de cendres et de vapeur, l'aiguille atteint une hauteur de 300 m au-dessus du fond du cratère. Des blocs de roche commencent à tomber et, quelques mois plus tard, elle s'effondre complètement.

Les nuées ardentes et les dômes de lave sont très typiques des volcans à magma acide, visqueux et riche en silice, alors que le magma pauvre en silice est plus fluide et s'écoule plus lentement. Cette teneur peut être élevée dès le départ mais, souvent, le magma s'enrichit en silice en remontant vers la surface car ses composants pauvres en silice se séparent à haute température et restent dans le sol. De plus, le magma peut incorporer des roches acides en montant, et plus la montée est longue, plus il est probable qu'il rencontre de telles roches.

Du combustible pour haut-fourneau

Les foyers des volcans des Antilles se trouvent à des profondeurs comprises entre 50 et 100 km, où la chaleur provoque la fusion de la plupart des roches. Les fragments de roche dotés des températures de fusion les plus basses, à savoir les minéraux relativement légers, fondent les premiers. Une fois fondue, la roche possède une densité plus faible qu'à l'origine et subit donc une forte poussée qui l'entraîne vers le haut. La température de fusion dépend de la composition chimique de la roche et de la pression exercée : elle baisse quand la pression diminue. Le magma situé dans les couches supérieures (lithosphère) de la croûte terrestre, où la pression est plus faible que plus bas, remonte, peut faire fondre les roches à des températures relativement basses et, ainsi, produire de nouveaux matériaux fondus.

La tectonique des plaques est responsable de la production permanente de magma : à raison de 1 à 2 cm par an, elle pousse vers l'ouest la croûte océanique nouvellement formée sur la dorsale médio-atlantique, vers la plaque caraïbe, et la fait plonger sous celle-ci, alimentant ainsi directement le « haut-fourneau » des entrailles de la Terre. La zone dans laquelle la plaque atlantique plonge (zone de subduction) sous celle de sa mer marginale est marquée par une fosse de plus de 8 000 m de profondeur devant les îles Vierges. L'arc de volcans sous-marins et d'îles volcaniques se trouve entre 100 et 200 km vers l'ouest,

Les Petites Antilles : un arc insulaire volcanique

Sur la dorsale médio-atlantique se forme en permanence une nouvelle croûte océanique. Sous l'arc insulaire des Petites Antilles, en revanche, elle fond totalement ou en partie. Tandis que le magma remonte vers la surface, sa composition change. Les laves émises par les volcans sont plus riches en silice et plus visqueuses que le magma basaltique d'origine.

Aucun des sept centres volcaniques de l'île de la Dominique n'a jamais été en activité. Très loin dans le sol, on trouve cependant des masses magmatiques encore chaudes qui portent l'eau à ébullition dans le fameux « lac bouillonnant ».

là où les températures de fusion sont extrêmement élevées dans les profondeurs, de sorte que la plaque qui plonge sous l'autre fond. Manifestement, la zone de subduction s'est déplacée vers l'ouest au fil du temps car il se trouve entre les Petites Antilles volcaniques et la fosse océanique un second arc de substratum volcanique plus ancien, aplani depuis longtemps et couronné de couches de calcaire. Anguilla et Antigua font partie de ces « Antilles calcaires » plates et karstiques, de même que Grande-Terre, la partie orientale de la Guadeloupe.

Où il est question de vent

Il est bien plus courant de diviser les Petites Antilles en fonction de leur climat que de leur géologie. Les îles constituant l'arc allant des îles Vierges, au nord, à Trinidad, au sud, sont appelées les îles du Vent. Celles situées au large de l'Amérique du Sud, en revanche, sont les îles Sous-le-Vent. Cela indique, tout simplement, leur

exposition aux alizés. Les îles du Vent sont donc face au vent dominant : leur climat est humide car les nuages s'accumulent et provoquent de fortes pluies au-dessus des versants des montagnes. « Humide » signifie en l'occurrence jusqu'à 10 000 litres de pluie par an et par mètre carré. Les îles Sous-le-Vent, quant à

elles, sont situées du côté à l'abri du vent, où règne un climat sec. La plupart ne reçoivent que 400 litres de précipitations par an et par mètre carré.

On pourrait également entendre par « sous le vent » le fait que ces îles soient particulièrement venteuses. De fait, l'île de Curaçao, qui fait partie des Antilles

Dans les zones calcaires des Petites Antilles, on rencontre de vastes étendues de karst écumoire. Ce karst résulte de la dissolution du calcaire, particulièrement intense sous les tropiques.

Les cactées de l'île Bonaire sont typiques des îles sèches. Entre les cactus cierges pouvant atteindre 6 m de hauteur, on aperçoit un dividivi qui, tel une girouette, modifie la direction de ses branches et de sa couronne en fonction du vent.

Formation du karst écumoire

Des dolines se forment d'abord dans les couches de calcaire.

Les dolines se transforment en gouffres karstiques. Par érosion chimique, une couche de limon fertile se forme sur le calcaire.

Une végétation arbustive s'implante sur les pitons arrondis arrivés à maturité.

néerlandaises, est en moyenne bien plus balayée par le vent que la côte de la mer du Nord, aux Pays-Bas. Considérant que les températures oscillent autour de 30 °C, le vent apporte aux insulaires une fraîcheur bienvenue, mais un stress permanent pour les plantes, du fait de la forte évaporation. De plus, une grande partie des rares pluies s'infiltre dans les couches de calcaire. Économiser et stocker l'eau est donc une question de survie pour la flore, une faculté dont disposent les cactées et les épineux qui dominent le couvert végétal. À l'extrémité occidentale des Petites Antilles, le nombre d'espèces est particulièrement limité. La flore de Curaçao, par exemple, ne compte que sept espèces endémiques et la faune se distingue davantage par sa forte densité d'un nombre restreint d'espèces, dont les flamants, qui peuplent par centaines les lacs d'eau salée.

Les îles Sous-le-Vent n'ont pas toujours été aussi sèches et arides. Un réseau de vallées creusées dans le calcaire, d'où l'eau est pratiquement absente, des vestiges de sols fortement érodés sur les plateaux karstiques et des grottes ornées de superbes concrétions indiquent un climat plus humide par le passé. Ce sont les cactées qui ont le mieux résisté à des siècles de surpâturage.

Une grande diversité dans un petit espace

Même sur les îles du Vent, plus humides, certains endroits sont extrêmement secs. Selon son exposition aux alizés et son altitude, chaque secteur possède son propre climat, qui se reflète de façon étonnante dans la diversité floristique. Sur la Dominique, par exemple, plus de 1 000 espèces de plantes à fleurs sont endémiques et un seul hectare peut compter 60 espèces d'arbres, autant que dans l'ensemble de l'Europe de l'Ouest. Près de 170 espèces d'arbres n'existent que sur les îles du Vent, où elles forment d'épaisses forêts tropicales. Malgré l'abondance des précipitations et des températures tournant toute l'année autour de 25 °C, les véritables forêts pluviales sont étonnamment rares. Cela est probablement dû aux cyclones qui ravagent de vastes zones forestières et empêchent leur développement. Car il faut des siècles, voire des millénaires, pour qu'une vraie forêt primaire parvienne à maturité.

Hormis les chauves-souris, les mammifères sont rares dans les Petites Antilles, sauf à Trinidad qui, jusqu'à la fin de la dernière période glaciaire, était reliée au continent sud-américain. La faune en est d'autant plus bigarrée et variée : presque chacune des grandes îles du Vent possède son espèce endémique, notamment l'amazone de Saint-Vincent et l'amazone de Sainte-Lucie sur les îles du même nom.

Petites îles, petits animaux

Le gecko nain (ci-dessous) ne mesure que 8 cm, mais c'est un géant comparé à son cousin des îles Vierges, qui tiendrait sur une pièce de 1 euro. Les créatures miniatures sont fréquentes aux Antilles. Citons la grenouille siffleuse, qui mesure 1 cm, un colibri qui pèse 2 g ou le serpent aveugle des Antilles, fin comme une mine de crayon. En général, les très petits animaux sont répandus sur les îles, sans doute parce qu'il y manque de nombreuses espèces ou des groupes d'espèces entiers. Ainsi, d'autres espèces peuvent occuper ces niches, mais elles doivent adapter leur taille et leur comportement. Le gecko nain des îles Vierges, le plus petit de tous les reptiles, joue en fait le rôle d'une araignée.

UNE OASIS EN SIBÉRIE

Un lac qui serait à la fois une mer et une île : cela paraît impossible. Cette triple contradiction existe pourtant. C'est le lac Baïkal, en Sibérie, qui contient autant d'eau qu'une mer.

On y rencontre des phoques qui se sont adaptés à l'eau douce. Et son écosystème, isolé depuis des millions d'années à la façon d'une île, a développé une biodiversité qu'aucun autre lac ne peut concurrencer.

Le lac de tous les superlatifs

Les Bouriates l'ont baptisé Baïkal, qui signifie « création la plus sublime de la nature » ou, plus simplement, le « lac riche ». Les guides touristiques parlent de « perle de la Sibérie » ou d'« œil bleu de la Sibérie ». La littérature scientifique reflète elle aussi la fascination qu'exerce ce lac, même sur ceux dont il n'est qu'un sujet d'études. Après plus de 250 ans de recherche, le Baïkal est sans doute le lac le mieux connu du monde, mais il demeure le plus énigmatique.

Comment un lac contenant plus d'eau que la mer Baltique peut-il se trouver au cœur de l'Asie ? Il faudrait que toutes les rivières du monde s'y déversent pendant un an pour le remplir. Pourquoi est-il aussi profond ? En son point le plus bas, il atteint près de 1 200 m sous le niveau de la mer et, si l'on tient compte de l'exhaussement constitué par les sédiments déposés au fil du temps, son bassin mesure 8 000 m de profondeur. C'est une véritable fosse océanique au beau milieu d'un continent. D'où tient-il ses eaux transparentes ? Quelle est la cause de son infime teneur en miné-raux alors que celle en oxygène est élevée ? Pourquoi est-il peuplé d'animaux à l'origine marins, comme le nerpa, un phoque d'eau douce ? L'océan le plus proche se trouve pourtant à 1 700 km !

Pas moins de 336 rivières alimentent le lac, mais une seule y prend sa source, l'Angara. Principalement durant la fonte des neiges, ces rivières charrient des masses de sable et d'alluvions pris aux montagnes proches, qui culminent à 2 000 m, et déposent ces sédiments au fond du lac. La couche de matériaux plus meubles recouvrant le sous-sol cristallin mesure 6 000 m d'épaisseur. Ce gigantesque bassin long de 650 km, d'une largeur maximale de 80 km et d'une profondeur moyenne de 730 m se remplira-t-il un jour à rabord de sédiments ? Et, comme des millions d'autres lacs, finira-t-il par s'assécher ?

Un bassin en expansion

Le lac Baïkal n'est pas près de s'assécher. Au contraire, son bassin s'agrandit chaque année de quelques millimètres, l'écart entre ses rives s'allonge et son fond s'affaisse. En moyenne, son volume croît de 20 millions de mètres cubes par an, soit la contenance d'un petit lac-réservoir.

Mais cette expansion ne se fait pas sans dégâts. Jusqu'à 2 000 secousses sismiques agitent chaque année ses berges et son fond. Certaines sont d'une grande magnitude, comme en 1959, lorsque le fond du lac s'est affaissé par endroits de 12 à 20 m. En 1862, un séisme a même précipité dans le lac 200 km² de rives et les villages qui y étaient bâtis. Ces séismes et les failles constatées dans le sous-sol de la montagne proche montrent que le Baïkal est un lac tectonique typique. Il s'est formé par déplacement de la croûte terrestre dans une zone de faille, toujours active, et continue à se déformer. Cette zone de faille s'étend sur plus de 1 000 km à travers la Sibérie. D'un côté, elle marque un déplacement latéral provoquant le rapprochement, sur un plan plus ou moins horizontal, de fragments de la croûte terrestre et, de l'autre, elle constitue un fossé d'effondrement, à savoir des lignes de failles entre lesquelles d'étroits fragments de croûte se sont affaissés sur une profondeur sans équivalent sur d'autres continents.

Des liens avec l'Inde

L'ensemble de l'Eurasie orientale est sillonné de zones de failles. En Sibérie, en Mongolie et en Chine prévalent des zones d'extension dans lesquelles, comme au lac Baïkal, des corps magmatiques en forme de coussin ont provoqué le bombement et la distension de la croûte, dont le sommet s'est ouvert en fossé d'effondrement. Les sources thermales jaillissant au fond du lac forment en rencontrant les eaux profondes d'une température de 3 à 4 °C une oasis de chaleur

Les puces de mer vivent généralement dans les océans. Elles sont pourtant très nombreuses dans le lac Baïkal, telle cette espèce endémique.

Gneiss

L'affaissement du bassin a débuté il y a entre 25 et 30 millions d'années le long de lignes de failles escarpées.

Formations du cambrien

Masses d'eau

Sédiments marins

La profondeur maximale du lac est de 1 637 m. Son fond recouvert de sédiments mesure 6 000 m d'épaisseur.

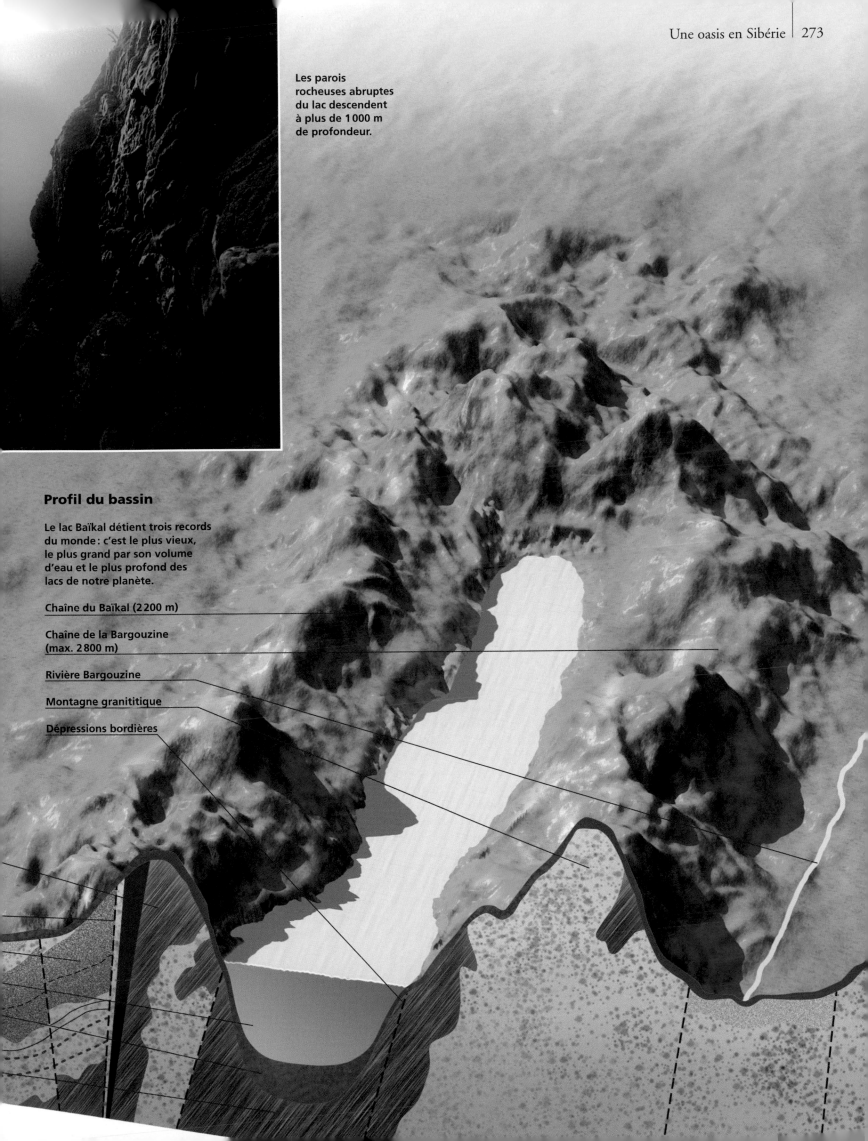

Les parois rocheuses abruptes du lac descendent à plus de 1 000 m de profondeur.

Profil du bassin

Le lac Baïkal détient trois records du monde : c'est le plus vieux, le plus grand par son volume d'eau et le plus profond des lacs de notre planète.

Chaîne du Baïkal (2 200 m)

Chaîne de la Bargouzine (max. 2 800 m)

Rivière Bargouzine

Montagne granititique

Dépressions bordières

Le lac Baïkal se situe dans la zone de transition entre la steppe mongole et la taïga sibérienne. Grâce à son effet adoucissant sur le climat, son pourtour compte des prairies d'une grande biodiversité.

Cette pêche fructueuse est trompeuse : la production de poissons exploitable sur le plan économique se monte en moyenne à 2,5 kg/ha, un chiffre extrêmement faible.

dotée d'une faune très particulière et indiquent des accumulations de magma sous le bassin du lac. Vers le sud, en direction du haut plateau tibétain et de l'Inde, les conditions géologiques s'inversent progressivement : les zones d'extension et d'affaissement de la croûte terrestre sont relayées par des zones de resserrement et de forte surrection des fragments de manteau. C'est dans l'Himalaya, où la plaque indienne – morceau du supercontinent originel, le Gondwana – entre en collision avec l'Eurasie et s'encastre dans le nord du continent, que resserrement et surrection atteignent leur paroxysme. La fragmentation de la croûte dans la moitié orientale de l'Eurasie pourrait avoir débuté dans cette puissante zone de collision entre les continents. Cette hypothèse est confirmée par les dates géologiques. Selon elles, l'effondrement du Baïkal remonte à 25-30 millions d'années, soit à l'époque où la collision entre l'Inde et l'Eurasie était la plus forte. L'effondrement du fossé est parti de la section centrale du bassin du lac, là où l'écho-sonde a mesuré la profondeur maximale de 1 637 m. Le nord et le sud du bassin sont plus plats et plus jeunes et se sont probablement effondrés il y a 3 à 10 millions d'années. La durée de vie de la plupart des lacs étant limitée à quelques millénaires, le lac Baïkal est de loin le plus vieux du globe.

Un véritable chauffe-eau

Si, en moyenne annuelle, le Baïkal est aussi ensoleillé que la Costa del Sol espagnole, ses eaux affichent une température maximale de 15 °C, ce qui n'incite pas à la baignade. En dessous de 200 m environ, la température oscille toute l'année entre 3 et 4 °C, véritable bénédiction pour la faune et la flore locales. Dans les lacs tropicaux, le climat uniformément chaud organise les masses d'eau en couches de température superposées qui varient peu au fil des ans. Peu brassées, les couches profondes se caractérisent souvent par un manque d'oxygène. Dans le cas du Baïkal, la forte amplitude thermique entre l'hiver et l'été sibériens empêche toute stabilité des différentes couches et provoque un brassage de l'eau jusqu'au fond du bassin. Ainsi, l'oxygène fait rarement défaut. De plus, la glace recouvrant le lac de décembre-janvier à mai-juin est exceptionnellement claire. La photosynthèse du plancton est donc possible sous la couche de glace et l'oxygène émis par les plantes sature parfois l'eau.

Le lac Baïkal démontre de façon impressionnante qu'un lac froid peut réchauffer le climat de façon sensible. Sur ses rives règne un climat presque océanique caractérisé par des étés plus frais et, par conséquent, des écarts de température saisonniers nettement moins marqués. En automne et en hiver, en revanche, le lac restitue lentement la chaleur emmagasinée l'été et la température moyenne de l'air sur les berges peut afficher jusqu'à 10 °C de plus que dans l'environnement immédiat. Dans toute la Sibérie, la seule station climatique enregistrant une température annuelle moyenne supérieure à 0 °C se situe au bord du lac Baïkal.

Un paradis naturel

Des eaux isolées depuis des millions d'années au cœur d'un continent, qui offraient une oasis libre de glace durant la période la plus froide de la dernière glaciation et donnent aujourd'hui à la faune et à la flore un habitat peu marqué par des écarts de température : l'évolution ne pouvait trouver de meilleures conditions. Un bon cinquième de la population faunique et floristique du lac est endémique. Elle comprend plus de 1 000 espèces de plantes aquatiques, 300 d'unicellulaires, à peu près autant de puces de mer, une bonne centaine de mollusques, plus de 50 de poissons, des vers, des éponges, des insectes et, grande particularité du lac, le nerpa, un phoque d'eau douce dont le seul

parent habite le lac des Loups-Marins, au Québec. Ce mammifère, marin à l'origine, aurait migré de l'océan Glacial Arctique vers le Baïkal lors des ères glaciaires en passant par les fleuves Ienisseï et Angara. Au fil des millénaires, c'est devenu un véritable mammifère d'eau douce.

Les puces de mer, dont les amphipodes, de la taille d'un grain de riz, occupent quelque 90 % du biotope et constituent la principale source alimentaire du lac. Par ailleurs, elles assurent la propreté de l'eau. En un an, elles filtrent au moins trois fois les 50 m supérieurs des masses d'eau et, nécrophages, elles nettoient les restes de poissons et autres animaux morts, au grand dépit des pêcheurs, qui ne trouvent que des squelettes dans leurs filets s'ils ne les remontent pas à temps.

Les risques écologiques d'un lac profond

Jusqu'au siècle dernier, le lac Baïkal a été à peu près épargné et par la nature et par l'homme. Il est alimenté par des ruisseaux

Ici et là, des protubérances cristallines émergent des eaux. Le fond du lac se compose principalement de gneiss et de granits que l'érosion laisse à peu près intacts.

de montagne issus de roches pauvres en nutriments qui, par conséquent, ne le surchargent pas en éléments nutritifs. Grâce à sa population d'amphipodes, il dispose d'un système d'autonettoyage unique, une sorte d'usine naturelle de production d'eau douce extrêmement pure. Les effets sont visibles à l'œil nu : de la surface, on peut distinguer un disque blanc de 30 cm de diamètre situé à 40 m de profondeur.

Les lacs très profonds, toutefois, ont une sorte de défaut de naissance : il faut beaucoup de temps, par le jeu de leurs affluents et de leurs émissaires, pour que leurs eaux se renouvellent en totalité. Pour le bassin nord du Baïkal, par exemple, il faut en moyenne 225 ans, 132 ans pour le bassin moyen et 66 ans pour le bassin sud. Cela signifie que les rejets des habitations et des centres industriels proches séjournent longtemps dans l'eau avant d'être dégradés.

LA MONTAGNE DE FEU

Selon la mythologie grecque, Prométhée, qui avait donné le feu aux hommes, fut enchaîné sur la montagne séparant l'Europe et l'Asie. Des feux couvent toujours dans cette haute montagne isolée dotée d'une faune et d'une flore exceptionnelles. Au-dessus des sommets rocheux, comme ici en Svanétie, tournoient des aigles royaux et dans les forêts luxuriantes du Caucase fleurit l'azalée pontique (petite photo).

Une abondante biodiversité entre deux mers intérieures

Les statistiques sont à la fois impressionnantes et déconcertantes : de toutes les forêts des zones tempérées du globe, les forêts mixtes du Caucase possèdent l'une des plus fortes proportions de plantes et d'animaux endémiques, à savoir des espèces que l'on ne trouve nulle part ailleurs. Un quart environ des plantes vasculaires, c'est-à-dire celles possédant un système vasculaire, et 10 % des espèces d'invertébrés sont uniques à cette chaîne de montagnes reliant la mer Caspienne et la mer Noire. Une telle richesse en espèces endémiques se rencontre habituellement sur les îles éloignées. Or, si l'on observe le Caucase sur une carte, il a

effectivement un aspect insulaire : la montagne est prise entre deux mers intérieures, à l'ouest et à l'est, les basses plaines de Russie au nord et une dépression marquée au sud. Habituellement, les îles ne sont pas des écosystèmes d'une grande biodiversité, surtout si elles ne sont ni tropicales ni subtropicales et si, comme le Caucase, elles comptent des sommets culminant à plus de 2 000 m, c'est-à-dire dans l'étage des neiges et des glaciers. Or la haute montagne considérée comme la frontière entre l'Europe et l'Asie se caractérise par une immense richesse biologique avec plus de 5 000 espèces de plantes vasculaires indigènes, 7 000 de plantes plus primitives et 700 d'invertébrés.

Pour les géologues aussi, le Caucase est varié et unique. Varié, avant tout, du fait de la quasi-absence de lacune géologique dans sa succession de roches, des schistes datant de plus de 500 millions d'années aux couches d'éboulis « jeunes » de 1 million d'années. Comme dans les autres jeunes

chaînes montagneuses d'Eurasie, ces strates se sont fortement plissées ces derniers 60 à 70 millions d'années, puis fragmentées et couronnées de volcans, éteints depuis, tout autour du mont Elbrous et de son sommet de 5 642 m.

Une montagne pas comme les autres

Si continu qu'il paraisse sur une carte, le Caucase ne s'intègre pas réellement dans la ceinture orogénique de type alpin : il fait cavalier seul. Contrairement aux Alpes, dont les masses rocheuses ont été déplacées

Naissance dans une dépression

Lors de la collision entre deux plaques, l'intérieur de ces plaques peut fortement s'amincir et donner naissance à une montagne. Cela se produit essentiellement dans les zones de faiblesse comme les dépressions, sous lesquelles la croûte terrestre est mince et facilement déformable.

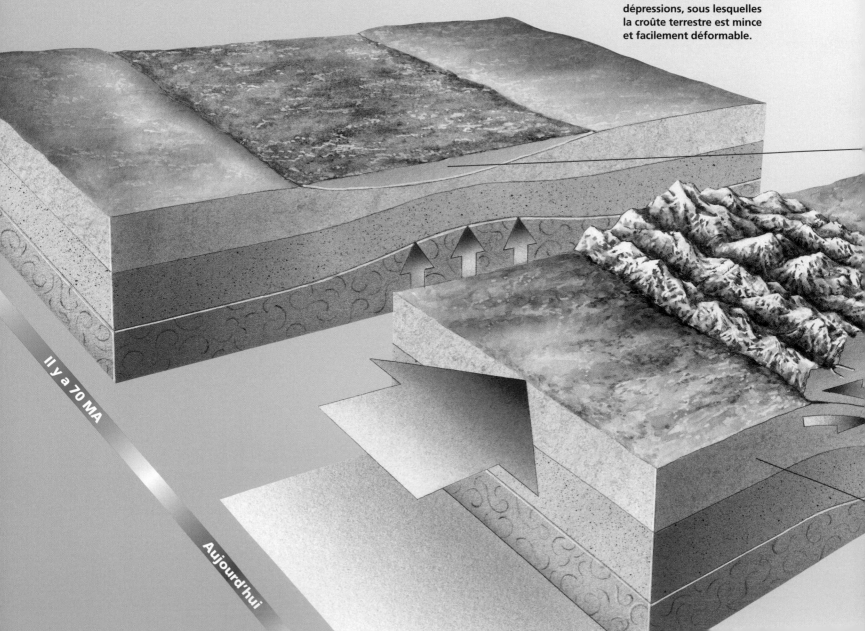

Il y a 70 MA

Aujourd'hui

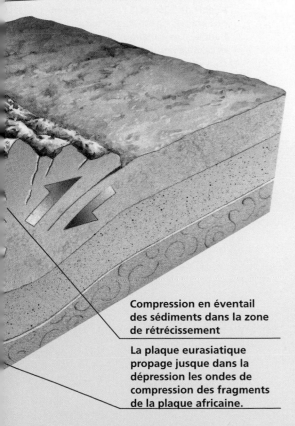

Depuis l'origine de la Terre,
d'épaisses couches de sédiments
se sont accumulées dans la dépression
des basses plaines de Russie.

Compression en éventail
des sédiments dans la zone
de rétrécissement

La plaque eurasiatique
propage jusque dans la
dépression les ondes de
compression des fragments
de la plaque africaine.

sur des centaines de kilomètres vers le nord lors du soulèvement de la montagne, sous l'effet des fragments de la plaque océanique qui se rapprochaient, dans le Caucase, les glissements ont été nettement moindres et essentiellement orientés vers le sud ou dans les deux directions. Si la structure interne des Alpes ressemble à une série de vagues qui se brisent sur la plage puis s'inversent, le Caucase ressemble, lui, à un gigantesque éventail ouvert.

Tout a commencé par une dépression

Les formes géologiques des Alpes sont bien plus variées que celles du Caucase, qui, par ses dimensions – 1 500 km de longueur pour environ 200 km de largeur –, est leur contemporain. Huit de ses sommets dépassent une altitude de 5 000 m et 15 sont plus hauts que le mont Blanc. Les plus hauts sommets du centre du massif, comme l'Elbrous, se composent pour partie de roches volcaniques vieilles de quelques millions d'années et pour partie de granit, de gneiss et d'autres roches métamorphisées sous l'effet de la pression et de la chaleur. Comme le sous-sol des basses plaines de

Russie voisines, celles-ci remontent en majorité au début de l'ère primaire, il y a plus de 540 millions d'années. En marge du massif se succèdent d'épaisses strates plus jeunes, celles de la formation jurassique, datant d'il y a entre 144 et 206 millions d'années, pouvant même atteindre 15 000 m. Cela indique un affaissement de longue durée relativement constant et plutôt lent de la croûte terrestre car on trouve dans les strates des types de roches comme le calcaire récifal, formé dans les mers peu profondes, ou le charbon, formé dans les continents.

Les strates plus jeunes ne contiennent aucun vestige de la croûte océanique, qui, lors de la collision des plaques contre l'écorce terrestre immobile, a été généralement comprimée dans la zone de déformation. De ce fait, on n'a pas la preuve que le Caucase, comme les autres jeunes chaînes montagneuses du globe, est né dans la zone de collision de deux plaques. Ses formations géologiques et ses types de roches suggèrent au contraire que le Caucase doit son existence à la compression d'une zone de faiblesse dans une dépression située à l'intérieur d'une plaque, à une certaine distance de la véritable zone de déformation marquée par les chaînes d'Anatolie, d'Arménie et d'Iran.

Des strates prises en étau par des forces colossales

Depuis plus de 70 millions d'années, des fragments de l'ancien continent austral du Gondwana heurtent la plaque eurasiatique et la compriment fortement. Les ondes de compression se propagent de la marge de la plaque à la plaque voisine et rencontrent une dépression, sous laquelle la croûte continentale solide est mince et plus facilement déformable, puis compriment les strates accumulées dans cette dépression en créant une architecture en éventail. Dans le cas du Caucase, le plissement était, et

demeure, particulièrement intense car la croûte située sous les basses plaines de Russie est très épaisse et, de ce fait, forme une butée. Telles les mâchoires d'un étau, les forces s'exercent sur les strates accumulées dans la dépression.

Une montagne intracontinentale est un îlot accessible pour toutes sortes d'espèces animales et botaniques. Aucune autre montagne d'Eurasie occidentale n'héberge autant de populations différentes que le Caucase – Tchétchènes, Tcherkesses, Abkhases, notamment – et aucune ne compte une flore et une faune venus d'autant d'écosystèmes différents : basses plaines d'Asie centrale, hauts plateaux d'Anatolie et d'Iran, montagnes du centre et du sud de l'Europe.

Une mosaïque d'habitats

Cette région est ouverte à toutes les masses d'air : air froid de l'Arctique de secteur nord, air chaud et humide de l'ouest, qui absorbe beaucoup d'humidité en passant au-dessus de la mer Noire, buran et autres vents des steppes de secteur nord-est chargés de poussière et de neige. Chaque versant de montagne dispose donc d'un climat propre où s'opposent les températures – nord froid et sud chaud – et les précipitations – Caucase occidental très humide, parfois plus de 4 000 litres par an et par mètre carré, et Caucase oriental plus sec, avec 1/10 des précipitations annuelles.

Si l'on considère une troisième dimension, celle des conditions de vie selon l'altitude, on peut ajouter une multiplicité de compartiments montagneux offrant des conditions idéales à des milliers d'espèces. Souvent, le nom des espèces non autochtones indique leur origine : par exemple, le myosotis des Alpes et le chêne de Perse.

Entre 2 000 m d'altitude, à l'ouest, et plus de 3 000 m, à l'est, s'étendent des prairies de montagne très fleuries. Les nombreux fourrés et plantes herbacées atteignent souvent 1 m de hauteur. L'endémisme est élevé, mais on trouve également des plantes originaires des hautes montagnes d'Europe centrale comme les silènes, les séneçons et les épilobes.

Au pays des flammes

« Il y a d'abord eu une forte explosion, puis d'énormes flammes sont sorties des flancs de la montagne... » Ce témoignage semble concerner l'éruption d'un volcan, mais l'éruption qui s'est produite en octobre 2001 en Azerbaïdjan, dans les contreforts sud-est du Caucase, n'a rien à voir avec une éruption de ce genre. Du cratère sommital de la montagne ne s'est écoulée aucune lave, mais un mélange de boue, de blocs de roche, de gaz et d'eau.

Il n'y a plus de volcans actifs en Caucasie, mais des volcans de boue – 400 rien qu'en Azerbaïdjan, dont certains ne font que quelques mètres de hauteur (photographie) et d'autres 1 000 m, comme le Kagatdag. Les gaz soumis à une pression élevée dans les profondeurs se fraient un chemin vers la surface et entraînent avec eux boues et roches. Dans la cheminée, les roches se heurtent et provoquent des étincelles qui enflamment les gaz. On comprend aisément pourquoi Azerbaïdjan signifie « terre de flammes ».

Le bouquetin du Caucase,
ou tur de l'ouest
du Caucase (ci-dessus),
est doté de cornes arquées
et bosselées et vit jusqu'à
4000 m d'altitude.

L'orchis est une orchidée
représentée dans les
montagnes du Caucase
par des espèces
endémiques (ci-contre).

S'ajoutent à cela de nombreuses plantes endémiques comme la trolle du Caucase, le sapin du Caucase et l'orme du Caucase.

Un foyer de l'évolution

Au-dessus de la limite des neiges, qui, de l'Ouest humide à l'Est sec, s'élève entre 2 700 et 4 000 m, le paysage se caractérise par des champs d'éboulis et de neige et de petits glaciers. À l'étage en dessous, la flore est d'une diversité, de formes comme de couleurs, inégalée : gentianes, glaïeuls, primevères, centaurées, fritillaires, orchidées rares et des espèces de campanules, de pieds-d'alouette et d'aconits, qui peuvent atteindre 2 à 3 m de hauteur. Près de 1 000 plantes vasculaires différentes, dont 1/3 est endémique, prospèrent dans l'étage végétal compris entre la forêt et les neiges, un nombre inhabituel pour une haute montagne. Dans les bois et forêts des étages inférieurs poussent quelques milliers d'espèces.

La faune n'a rien à envier à cette diversité. Le Caucase est un foyer de l'évolution, où se

sont développées de nombreuses espèces endémiques, dont la vipère du Caucase, venimeuse, le bruyant tétraogalle du Caucase ou le très agile roi de l'escalade qu'est le bouquetin du Caucase.

Des reliques de l'Europe d'autrefois

Veines d'or dans les pierres les plus anciennes, au cœur de la montagne, gaz naturel et pétrole dans les strates les plus récentes situées en marge : le sol du Caucase regorge de richesses. Or celles-ci attisent les conflits entre les populations caucasiennes et attirent toutes sortes d'aventuriers, à l'instar des Argonautes légendaires partis pour la Colchide – zone autrefois marécageuse faisant aujourd'hui partie de la Géorgie – à la recherche de la Toison d'or. De nos jours, la plaine d'inondation fertile s'étendant à l'ouest du Caucase, ainsi que le versant nord très arrosé de la montagne,

sont réputés pour un tout autre trésor : les forêts de Colchide.

Dans l'ouest de l'Oural, les forêts de feuillus sont les plus variées du monde et abritent des arbres rares comme le zelkova, le faux noyer du Caucase ou le plaqueminier. Ces forêts naturelles, proches des forêts tropicales, sont très représentatives de la flore qui dominait l'Europe avant qu'elle ne soit prise par les glaces et que ses plantes soient décimées, espèce après espèce. On y trouve notamment l'azalée pontique (petite photo p. 276) qui, au début des périodes chaudes, jusqu'il y a 300 000 ans environ, tout comme le plaqueminier, était répandue en Europe occidentale, jusqu'en Irlande. Le zelkova, de la famille des ormes, quant à lui, a disparu d'Europe il y a 3 à 4 millions d'années. Dans le climat subtropical chaud et humide de la Colchide, ces reliques de la flore du tertiaire ont survécu.

DES ÎLES DANS LE CIEL

Il est rare que la couverture nuageuse qui surmonte les gigantesques montagnes tabulaires de la Guyana se déchire et dégage la vue sur les étranges protubérances rocheuses de l'Auyán Tepui. Alors, seulement, les rayons du soleil peuvent atteindre les rares broméliacées (petite photo), dont certaines sont carnivores. Ce paysage archaïque a bien gardé, jusque récemment, le secret de sa naissance.

Le monde hors du temps des tepuis

Le saurien volant qu'était le ptérodactyle est depuis longtemps éteint, tout comme l'iguanodon, qui appartenait aux dinosaures à dents d'iguane et a disparu il y a quelque 100 millions d'années. Pourtant, à en croire le roman de l'écrivain britannique sir Conan Doyle *le Monde perdu*, publié en 1912, ces géants de la faune des montagnes tabulaires du Roraima seraient encore pétulants de vie. Là, au cœur de la montagne de la Guyana, le protagoniste du roman rencontre en effet des animaux dont la « taille était impressionnante. Même les jeunes étaient aussi gros que des éléphants. Mais les deux plus vieux dépassaient tout ce qu'il m'avait été donné de voir. »

Depuis, on n'a plus jamais entendu parler de tels fossiles vivants dans ce coin peu peuplé d'Amérique du Sud, le père de Sherlock Holmes n'ayant rien fait d'autre que laisser libre cours à son imagination. Mais les plantes et animaux primitifs comme le cycas du Japon ou le dauphin

Orénoque, vestiges d'une faune et d'une flore éteintes, ont bien survécu dans les montagnes et leurs contreforts.

Les Indiens Pemón qui habitent la région donnent aux montagnes tabulaires le nom de tepuis, « maisons des dieux ». Un botaniste américain y a recueilli 140 000 végétaux, dont un nombre de plantes carnivores unique au monde. La faune et la flore des montagnes situées entre l'Amazone et l'Orénoque ne sont pas les seules à être énigmatiques. Les nombreux cours d'eau empruntent ici des voies étranges : parfois, ils laissent les fissures des roches les mener où bon leur semble, parfois ils ont l'air de décider eux-mêmes où ils veulent aller.

La montagne guyanienne est une région relativement calme comparée aux

nombreuses zones d'Amérique du Sud perturbées par des éruptions volcaniques et d'importants séismes, catastrophes naturelles qui sont accompagnées de déplacements de la croûte terrestre. Mais ici, dans le cœur géologique le plus ancien du conti-

Les tepuis, reflet de périodes climatiques

Depuis au moins 180 millions d'années, les montagnes de la Guyana ont connu une alternance de périodes humides et sèches. Les formes de paysage reflètent ces cycles contrastés par des plaines d'érosion, d'une part, et des montagnes tabulaires, d'autre part.

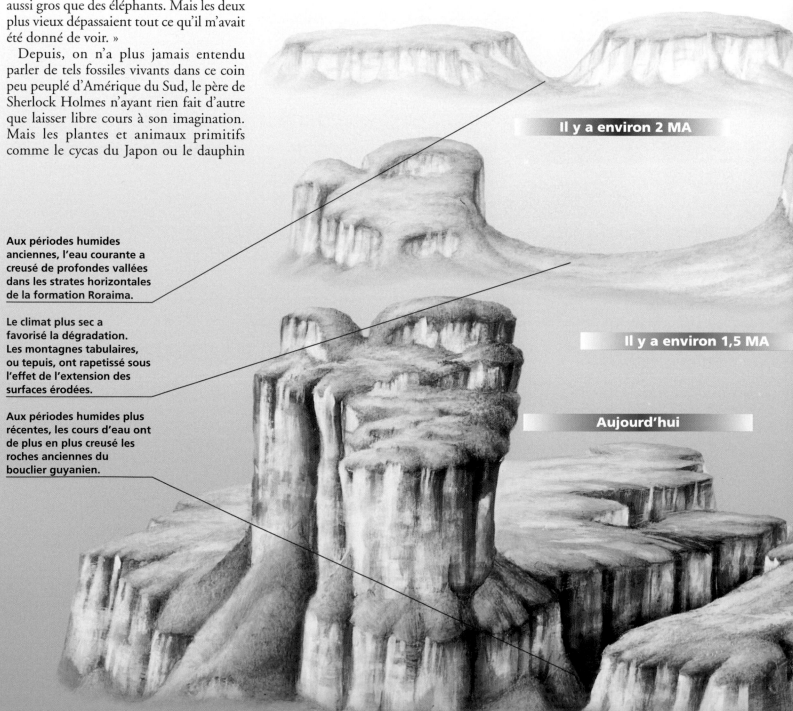

Il y a environ 2 MA

Il y a environ 1,5 MA

Aujourd'hui

Aux périodes humides anciennes, l'eau courante a creusé de profondes vallées dans les strates horizontales de la formation Roraima.

Le climat plus sec a favorisé la dégradation. Les montagnes tabulaires, ou tepuis, ont rapetissé sous l'effet de l'extension des surfaces érodées.

Aux périodes humides plus récentes, les cours d'eau ont de plus en plus creusé les roches anciennes du bouclier guyanien.

Sur le sommet plat et dénudé des tepuis, la végétation colonise de préférence les fissures de roche, où elle trouve de l'eau, des nutriments et un abri contre le vent et les intempéries.

Plus de la moitié de la flore de certaines montagnes tabulaires se compose de belles orchidées (1). Les plantes carnivores (2) sont tout aussi fréquentes mais moins discrètes.

1

2

Une passion dévorante

Un petit insecte s'approche d'une feuille fleurant le bon nectar situé à l'intérieur, dont la couleur rouge est des plus attirantes. Mais ce qui ressemble à une feuille est en réalité un piège sophistiqué qui se referme à la vitesse de l'éclair, retient sa proie, l'enveloppe d'un liquide gluant et la tue.

Voilà ce qui arrive aux insectes qui tombent dans les urnes (ci-dessous) de certaines plantes ou se posent sur les feuilles émaillées de gouttes odorantes et visqueuses d'un droséra : ils sont absorbés par des sucs digestifs ou des micro-organismes. La flore compte de vraies plantes carnivores qui attirent, capturent et tuent de petits animaux comme les mouches, les araignées ou les fourmis. Les plantes dotées de grandes urnes, comme celles du genre *Heliamphora*, très représentées dans les tepuis, peuvent même digérer des grenouilles ou de petits mammifères. Leurs pièges ressemblent à des cornets recueillant les eaux de pluie, où les animaux se noient et sont ensuite décomposés par des bactéries.

Nombre de ces plantes portent des noms évocateurs tels que plante cobra. Elles ne tuent pas par plaisir, mais pour y puiser certains nutriments que leur offrent leurs proies, dont de l'azote, du phosphore et du potassium. Toutes ces plantes s'épanouissent au mieux dans les sols de grès et de quartzite des tepuis, acides et très pauvres, contenant peu de nutriments et très lessivés par l'humidité.

nent, où les roches affleurantes peuvent être vieilles de 3 400 millions d'années, la Terre se repose. Il y a 1 900 millions d'années, les strates de la croûte terrestre se sont pliées et fragmentées pour la dernière fois, déformées par la chaleur et la pression et traversées par du magma. 100 millions d'années plus tard, la montagne était aplanie. Dans les zones aplanies se sont accumulées d'épaisses couches de sable et de cailloux qui constituent aujourd'hui les grès durs, le quartzite et les conglomérats du Cerro Roraima, qui culmine à 2 772 m au centre des montagnes, et des autres montagnes tabulaires.

L'Amérique du Sud primitive : une montagne de l'époque des dinosaures

La présence de roches primitives n'indique pas que le relief soit lui aussi primitif. En règle générale, les paysages se sont modelés longtemps après la formation de leurs roches, à savoir au cours des derniers millions d'années. Les zones montagneuses, vallées et plaines qui ont plus de 60 à 70 millions d'années sont de rares exceptions : la région montagneuse de la Guyana en fait partie.

Lorsqu'on observe son profil, on distingue deux niveaux d'érosion étendues :

l'une court entre 2 000 et 2 900 m d'altitude, sur la ligne de crête des tepuis, et l'autre s'étire jusqu'à 2 000 m plus bas parmi la cinquantaine de montagnes tabulaires. La zone supérieure existe depuis environ 180 millions d'années, les sédiments du jurassique et du crétacé en témoignent, et l'apparition de la zone inférieure remonte à l'époque des dinosaures. Conan Doyle n'a pas manqué d'instinct en choisissant ce décor pour son *Monde perdu*.

Même le tapir des plaines (ci-contre), comme son nom ne l'indique pas, habite les montagnes tabulaires. Comment les gros animaux sont arrivés là demeure une énigme.

Paysage de l'Autana Tepui, au Venezuela (ci-dessous) : sous les montagnes tabulaires, des montagnes arrondies forment un second étage au-dessus des vastes plaines. Elles se composent essentiellement de granit du bouclier guyanien d'origine.

Les vastes écarts d'altitude entre les hauts plateaux des montagnes tabulaires et la zone érodée inférieure indiquent une forte altération par les rivières et les ruisseaux, parallèlement à une élévation lente mais constante de la croûte continentale. Il faut pour cela qu'il ait beaucoup plu, comme dans la bourgade vénézuélienne de Puerto Ayacucho, sur l'Orénoque, où la pluviosité annuelle moyenne est de 2 000 l/m², soit deux fois plus qu'en altitude, sur les tepuis. De nos jours, le climat pluvieux alimente suffisamment les eaux courantes pour qu'elles se fraient facilement un chemin dans le substratum cristallin de ce que l'on appelle la formation Roraima.

Des montagnes grignotées sans relâche

Autrefois, cette partie de l'Amérique du Sud a dû être bien plus sèche, presque aride. Dans les plaines où coule la rivière Meta, aujourd'hui très marécageuses et couvertes d'une végétation plus dense, des dunes témoignent d'une période ancienne de climat plus sec, difficile à dater précisément. Cela n'indique pas nécessairement une pluviosité moyenne annuelle moins importante que de nos jours : la saison humide était sans doute plus courte mais caractérisée par des pluies torrentielles. Le sol, durci par les longues périodes de sécheresse, ne pouvait absorber les masses d'eau, qui formaient des cours d'eau à hauteur de la cheville ou du genou et opéraient une érosion horizontale et non linéaire comme aujourd'hui, l'écoulement empruntant des chemins bien délimités et précis. C'est ainsi que le pied des montagnes tabulaires a été sapé. En période sèche, les surfaces dénudées s'étendaient au détriment des montagnes, jusqu'à usure totale pour certaines.

L'érosion continue de ronger les restes de la formation Roraima, autrefois dominante dans les montagnes de la Guyana, et maintient les versants en pente raide. Nombre d'entre eux se dressent presque à la verticale jusqu'à une altitude de 1 000 m et empêchent tout accès, et pas seulement aux hommes. L'inaccessibilité et l'isolement géographique depuis des millions d'années sont les conditions idéales pour que se développent des espèces endémiques, comme sur une île perdue dans l'océan.

Dans les étages de végétation inférieurs, la savane, la prairie tropicale et la forêt pluviale dominent toujours le paysage. À mesure que l'on monte, la flore typique des hautes montagnes tropicales prend le relais.

Une vie riche sur un sol aride

Au-dessus de 1 500 m d'altitude environ commence la région du Pantepui, une entité biologique unique, remarquable par sa division en zones distinctes de quelques kilomètres carrés. Ses autres caractéristiques sont des températures relativement fraîches pour les tropiques, d'environ 10 °C en moyenne annuelle, des gelées occasionnelles, une masse nuageuse rarement percée par les rayons solaires, l'humidité et, sur les flancs érodés des tepuis, un sol pauvre en nutriments pour la végétation et lui offrant à peine le minimum vital en eau. Dès lors,

Des entailles bien ordonnées

Un entrelacs d'entailles parcourt les montagnes dénudées du Landmannalaugar, en Islande. L'eau y fait un travail d'érosion méticuleux et trace un réseau dans lequel toutes les eaux courantes, du plus petit ru aux grands collecteurs, ont leur place.

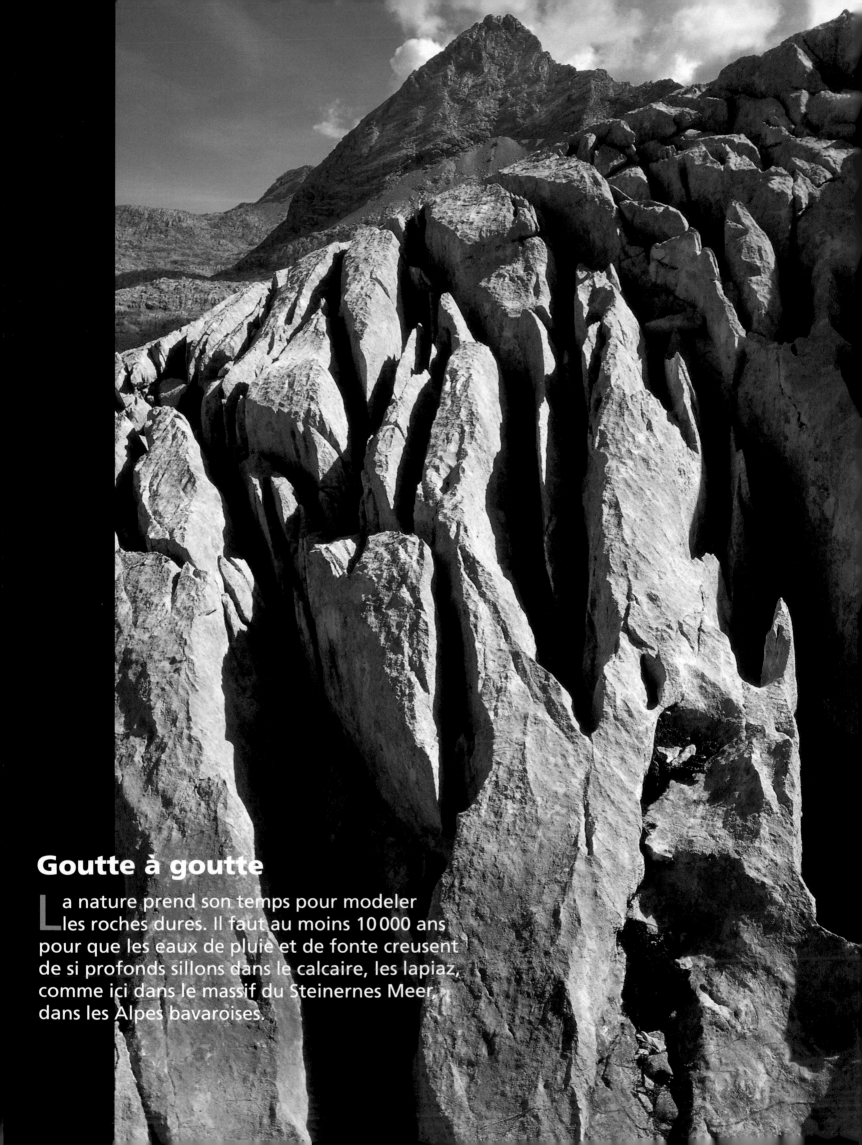

Goutte à goutte

La nature prend son temps pour modeler les roches dures. Il faut au moins 10 000 ans pour que les eaux de pluie et de fonte creusent de si profonds sillons dans le calcaire, les lapiaz, comme ici dans le massif du Steinernes Meer, dans les Alpes bavaroises.

PERLES DES MERS DU SUD

Bora-Bora (ci-contre), île volcanique échancrée d'étroites baies, culmine à 700 m d'altitude. Aratika, en revanche, est un récif corallien qui affleure à peine de la mer. Telle est la diversité des îles de la Polynésie française, qui ont toutefois un point commun : elles s'enfoncent petit à petit dans l'océan. Des habitats sont détruits mais de nouveaux apparaissent, surtout dans les récifs coralliens qui cernent les îles et abritent une faune variée comme ce poisson-perroquet (petite photo).

Des volcans transformés en atolls

La Polynésie, littéralement « îles nombreuses », regroupe les îles et archipels du centre de Pacifique, dont Tahiti qui, de même que 120 autres îles, est française depuis le XIXᵉ siècle. Cette île née de deux grands massifs volcaniques se trouve à l'extrémité sud-est de l'archipel de la Société, l'un des cinq que compte la Polynésie française, et s'élève à plus de 2 000 m au-dessus du niveau de la mer. Comme les îles voisines de Moorea et Bora-Bora, Tahiti fait partie du groupe d'îles traditionnellement appelé « îles hautes » par les navigateurs. À l'extrémité nord-ouest de la chaîne insulaire, quelques îles basses s'intercalent entre ces îles hautes aux contours échancrés. Presque plates, leur

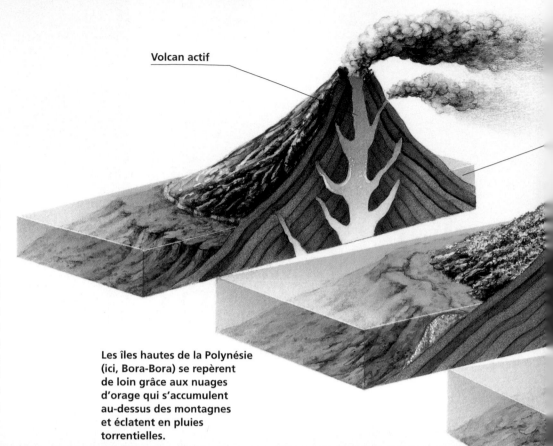

Volcan actif

Les îles hautes de la Polynésie (ici, Bora-Bora) se repèrent de loin grâce aux nuages d'orage qui s'accumulent au-dessus des montagnes et éclatent en pluies torrentielles.

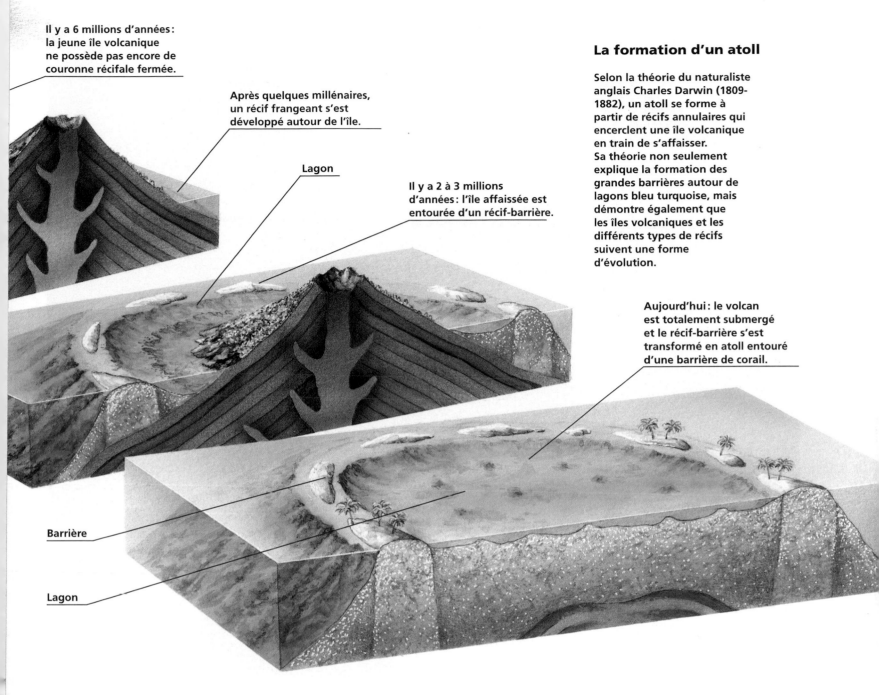

Il y a 6 millions d'années:
la jeune île volcanique
ne possède pas encore de
couronne récifale fermée.

Après quelques millénaires,
un récif frangeant s'est
développé autour de l'île.

Lagon

Il y a 2 à 3 millions
d'années: l'île affaissée est
entourée d'un récif-barrière.

Barrière

Lagon

La formation d'un atoll

Selon la théorie du naturaliste anglais Charles Darwin (1809-1882), un atoll se forme à partir de récifs annulaires qui encerclent une île volcanique en train de s'affaisser. Sa théorie non seulement explique la formation des grandes barrières autour de lagons bleu turquoise, mais démontre également que les îles volcaniques et les différents types de récifs suivent une forme d'évolution.

Aujourd'hui: le volcan
est totalement submergé
et le récif-barrière s'est
transformé en atoll entouré
d'une barrière de corail.

surface se compose de calcaire récifal. Vues du ciel, ce sont d'étroites langues de terre en forme d'arc ou de fer à cheval ou des chaînes de plus petites îles également organisées en arc ou en fer à cheval. Leur contour présente la forme typique des atolls, récifs coralliens circulaires enserrant un lagon et généralement édifiés sur une base de roches volcaniques.

Parmi les différentes théories sur la formation des atolls, celle de Charles Darwin semble la plus plausible, du moins pour les grands récifs annulaires. Selon sa théorie, un atoll se forme à partir d'une île volcanique, de type stratovolcan ou volcan bouclier, qui, par affaissement du sous-sol, plonge lentement dans la mer. Sur le littoral de l'île apparaît d'abord un étroit récif frangeant, qui va du volcan vers l'extérieur et finit par former un récif-barrière encer-

clant un lagon. Il faut toutefois que la croissance des coraux, qui ne peuvent vivre qu'entre quelques décimètres et quelques mètres sous la surface, se fasse au même rythme que l'affaissement. Ce dernier se poursuivant, seul un piton rocheux émerge encore du lagon central. Le stade de pseudo-atoll est alors atteint et, une fois ce dernier vestige de l'île volcanique dis-

paru à son tour dans la mer, ne subsiste que la couronne récifale. Le monde insulaire de la Polynésie française présente ces différents stades de formation: Tahiti-Iti, la

Les pluies étant rares sur les atolls et les îles coralliennes plats (ici, Tetiaroa) et le sol calcaire étant perméable et pauvre en nutriments, peu d'espèces végétales peuvent s'y installer.

UN PARADIS PRÉCAIRE

Telles des rangées de perles, des îles verdoyantes affleurent à peine au-dessus de l'océan. Sous l'eau, des poissons tropicaux paradent dans des jardins de corail aux couleurs éclatantes. Les glaciations et les régions polaires semblent bien loin. Or le sort des Maldives est lié à celui des pôles glacés.

Des fondations invisibles

Maldives, nom d'un État insulaire de l'océan Indien à cheval sur l'équateur, signifie « mille îles ». En réalité, ce sont 1 200 îles, auxquelles s'ajoutent quelques centaines de bancs de sable. Elles sont alignées de façon régulière en une vingtaine d'archipels annulaires, appelés *atolu* dans la langue locale, d'où le nom d'atoll, qui désigne toutes les formations similaires du monde. Composé de calcaire récifal, un atoll est en fait la version annulaire du récif de corail.

De quelques mètres à plus de 50 km de diamètre, les atolls n'ont pas de dimensions prédéfinies et peuvent même être imbriqués les uns dans les autres. Un grand atoll se compose essentiellement de récifs circulaires de taille moyenne, dont les lagons encerclent également des micro-atolls.

Aux Maldives, ces couronnes moyennes appelées faros s'égrènent comme des perles dans la mer. En règle générale, qu'il soit en forme de cercle ou de fer à cheval,

un faro mesure 1 à 2 km de diamètre et sa partie fermée fait face à l'océan. Au centre, le lagon n'est profond que de quelques mètres.

La formation des atolls a été expliquée par le naturaliste anglais Charles Darwin selon l'exemple des atolls de Polynésie, qui résultent de l'affaissement d'îles volcaniques. Les grands atolls des Maldives illustrent parfaitement le lien entre volcanisme et croissance récifale car ils reposent sur un substratum sous-marin de roches volcaniques constituées il y a près de 60 millions d'années. Il est donc hautement probable qu'ils se soient formés de la façon décrite par Darwin. Mais qu'en est-il des faros, ces atolls d'atolls ? Pour expliquer leur formation selon la théorie de Darwin, il faudrait partir du principe que les chapelets d'îles volcaniques se seraient enfoncés dans la mer les uns après les autres. Or, à ce jour, on n'a encore découvert aucun anneau volcanique sous-marin.

Les atolls des Maldives

Les Maldives sont un groupe d'atolls composés de récifs annulaires. Les plus grands reposent essentiellement sur un substratum volcanique. L'intérieur du récif est occupé par un lagon plat, d'où émergent quelques constructions coralliennes isolées. La couronne récifale est généralement divisée en îles individuelles séparées par des passes reliant le lagon à la haute mer.

Faro
Lagon
Passe
Récif
Substratum de roches volcaniques (dorsale des Maldives)

Deux réflexions s'imposent: d'une part, de nombreux récifs portent en eux le germe d'un atoll et, de l'autre, la formation des récifs s'est faite il y a au moins 2 à 3 millions d'années, à une époque géologique très tumultueuse.

Dur à l'extérieur, tendre à l'intérieur

Les coraux durs et autres organismes bâtisseurs de récifs trouvent des conditions de vie idéale à la bordure externe des récifs. À cet endroit, les vagues incessantes apportent des eaux claires et riches en calcaire et en nutriments, très oxygénées dans la zone des brisants. C'est pourquoi les colonies de coraux poussent rapidement et, au fil du temps, constituent des couches de calcaire récifal compactes qui peuvent être renforcées par une croûte d'algues calcaires. À l'intérieur du récif, les conditions de vie sont moins favorables et ne permettent que la formation de pinacles isolés, sorte de piliers coralliens entre lesquels se déposent des sédiments plus meubles comme de fines particules de coquillage et du sable.

Si le ressac parvient à se frayer un passage dans le récif, le centre plus tendre est petit à petit dégradé par les vagues et les courants de marée, puis remplacé par un lagon. C'est ainsi que les récifs en plateforme, qui reposent souvent sur un volcan aplani, se transforment en atolls : non pas par affaissement du support volcanique, mais sous l'effet de l'érosion.

Comme pour presque toutes les formes d'érosion, l'ampleur de la dégradation par

Des îles précaires

Le plus haut sommet des Maldives est une dune haute de 2,40 m. Si ces îles, dont 80 % ne dépassent pas 1 m de hauteur, se trouvaient dans des zones de cyclones, elles seraient souvent submergées. Mais d'autres dangers menacent : le niveau de la mer monte aujourd'hui à une vitesse inquiétante, de 1 à 2 mm par an, soit 10 fois plus vite que la moyenne annuelle depuis le début de notre ère. La cause en est le constant réchauffement de l'atmosphère, qui fait fondre les calottes glaciaires des pôles et les glaciers de haute montagne, contribuant à l'extension des océans. La disparition des îles semble n'être plus qu'une question de temps.

le courant dépend du dénivelé. Dans les mers où l'amplitude des marées est importante, comme l'océan Indien, le flux accélère la sortie des masses d'eau du lagon vers la haute mer et creuse des passes, ou chenaux. Ce phénomène a été particulièrement marqué pendant les glaciations, lorsque le niveau de la mer était 120 m plus bas qu'actuellement. Les constructions récifales affleurant à peine aujourd'hui étaient à l'époque d'imposantes colonnes. La pluie s'est ensuite chargée d'altérer la roche tendre du centre des îles, de creuser des fissures dans le calcaire soluble, puis de modeler les dépressions lagunaires cernées de hautes bordures, que l'eau de mer est venue remplir dans les périodes chaudes qui ont suivi.

Les atolls des Maldives se composent essentiellement de faros (premier plan) en forme de fer à cheval et d'îles de sable corallien ovales.

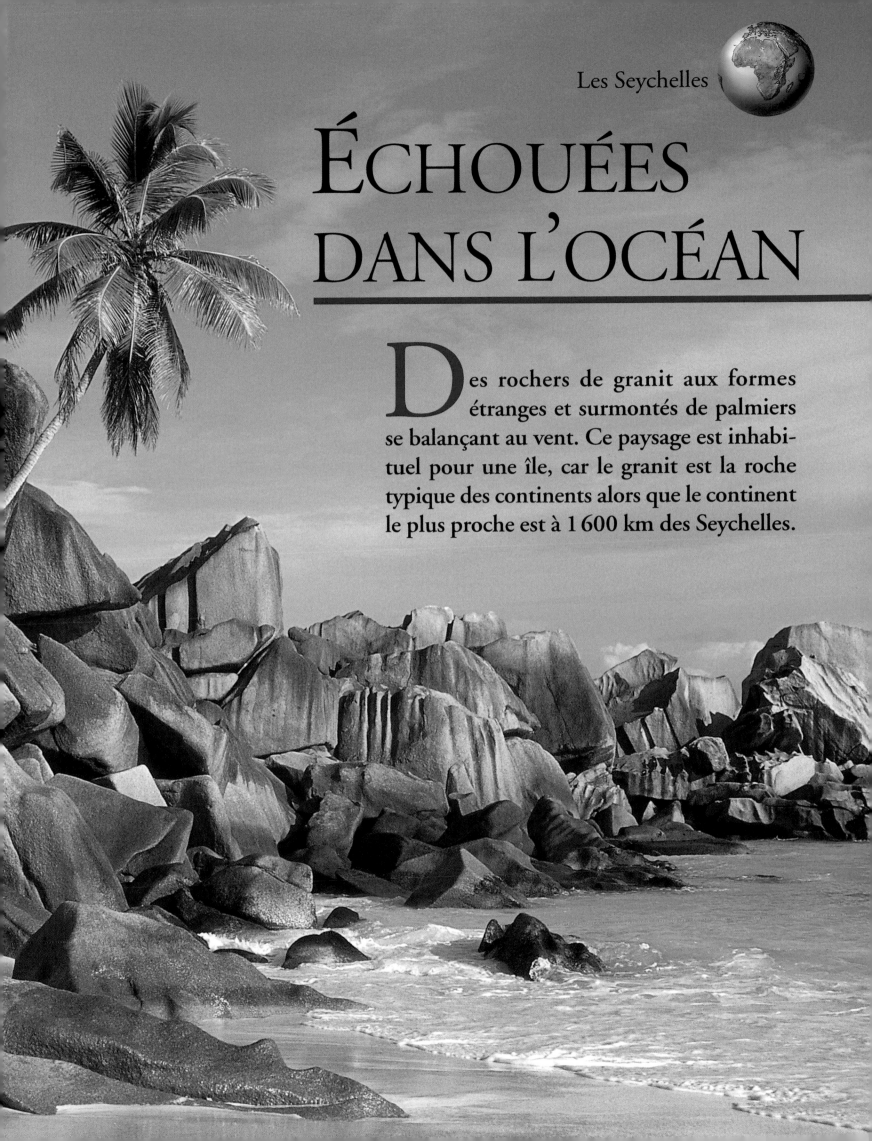

ÉCHOUÉES DANS L'OCÉAN

Des rochers de granit aux formes étranges et surmontés de palmiers se balançant au vent. Ce paysage est inhabituel pour une île, car le granit est la roche typique des continents alors que le continent le plus proche est à 1 600 km des Seychelles.

Des îles sur un support primitif

À première vue, les Seychelles intérieures, dans l'océan Indien, dont l'île principale, Mahé, est à 1 600 km de la côte est de l'Afrique et à 2 800 km de la pointe sud de l'Inde, diffèrent peu des autres îles tropicales. Les 40 grandes îles bordées de récifs coralliens sont tapissées d'une végétation dense qui, en nombre d'endroits, recouvre les versants de sommets atteignant 1 000 m d'altitude, bien arrosés grâce au vent. Sur les 50 îles des Seychelles extérieures, en revanche, règne un climat plus sec. Ces îles coralliennes d'une altitude de quelques mètres n'ont rien à envier à celles du Pacifique.

Les chaos granitiques des Seychelles

Les étranges blocs de granit empilés les uns sur les autres portent le nom de chaos granitiques. Ils résultent d'une érosion chimique en profondeur.

Les roches volcaniques qui caractérisent la plupart des îles du monde, parfois recouvertes d'une épaisse couche de calcaire corallien, sont absentes au centre des Seychelles. Près de 1 000 km à l'est cependant s'étend une chaîne d'îles volcaniques et de volcans sous-marins. Tandis que, au sein de la chaîne volcanique, les éléments en fusion montent jusqu'à la surface, le magma sous le cœur des Seychelles s'est solidifié en granit en profondeur depuis plusieurs centaines de millions d'années. Les îles de Mahé sont les seules îles granitiques de haute mer.

Une roche parcourue de fentes

Comme sur toute île granitique, la côte et l'intérieur des Seychelles présentent des formations étranges, parcourues de sillons, les chaos granitiques. Ces entassements sont constitués d'une roche à grains grossiers, gris clair à rougeâtre, dans laquelle on distingue à l'œil nu du feldspath potassique, du quartz et du mica clair ou sombre, principaux composants du granit. Ces massifs granitiques sont entrecoupés de veines de dolérite érodée de couleur sombre, parfois jaune ou rouge, variante à gros grains du basalte. La surface de cette roche magmatique présente

elle aussi des fissures en V. La dolérite témoigne par ailleurs du volcanisme qui régnait autrefois, dans les contreforts tout au moins, sous les îles du groupe de Mahé.

Un granit touché par la karstification

Les chenaux en forme de V ressemblent jusque dans le moindre détail aux lapiaz des paysages karstiques, ces longues fentes aux bords acérés creusées dans le calcaire et autres roches aisément solubles. Un autre phénomène typique des régions karstiques est la kamenitsa. Ces dépressions circulaires de quelques décimètres de diamètre creusées dans la pierre contiennent de la terre et sont donc colonisées par des végétaux : ceux-ci forment des îlots de verdure dans le granit gris. De telles formes karstiques dues à l'érosion chimique ne devraient pas exister dans le granit ou la dolérite, deux types de roches composées de minéraux peu solubles.

L'explication la plus simple de ce phénomène est que ces lapiaz énigmatiques seraient en fait des pseudo-lapiaz : ils ressemblent à des lapiaz mais ne sont pas apparus à la suite de processus de dissolution. Ils résulteraient de l'érosion méca-

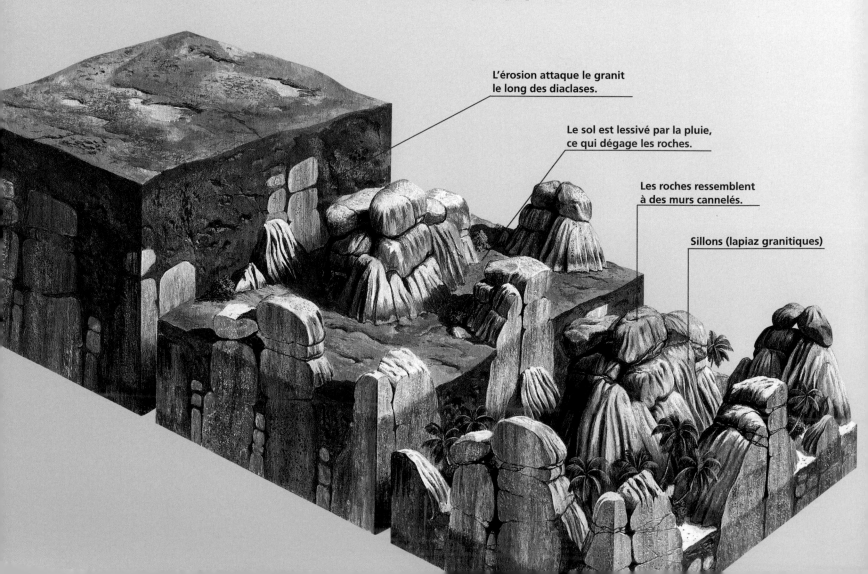

L'érosion attaque le granit le long des diaclases.

Le sol est lessivé par la pluie, ce qui dégage les roches.

Les roches ressemblent à des murs cannelés.

Sillons (lapiaz granitiques)

nique de la roche par les eaux de ruisselle-
ment. Mais cette explication n'est que par-
tiellement satisfaisante.

Le soleil et la pluie altèrent la surface des roches

Lors des pluies tropicales torrentielles, l'eau
s'écoule le long des versants granitiques des
Seychelles du groupe de Mahé. Avant la
pluie, le soleil a chauffé la roche nue à plus
de 50 °C et les précipitations, froides car
sous les tropiques elles sont apportées par
des nuages d'altitude, refroidissent brutalement la roche. Ces chocs thermiques répétés
finissent par altérer le granit et par creuser des
sillons dans cette roche pourtant dure.

Les habitants de l'île
nomment *glacis* ces zones
où affleure le granit nu.
Entre les roches, les plantes
doivent se contenter de peu
d'eau et de nutriments.

Les fruits du cocotier de
mer peuvent peser jusqu'à
18 kg. Ce sont donc les plus
grosses graines du règne
végétal.

Ce que l'on sait sur la solubilité des roches
et des minéraux est fondé sur des essais en
laboratoire, ce qui présente à la fois des
avantages et des inconvénients. Par
exemple, en laboratoire le facteur temps est
une inconnue : par la force des choses, il est
impossible d'effectuer un essai sur des siècles

et encore moins des millénaires. Un autre inconvénient est que l'environnement d'un laboratoire n'a rien à voir avec la nature. Dans la nature, l'eau contient divers acides et sels qui, par une réaction chimique complexe nommée hydrolyse – dissolution par l'eau –, peuvent dissoudre le feldspath potassique, principal composant du granit, pourtant difficilement soluble. Exposé pendant des millénaires à une eau riche en dioxyde de carbone, à l'écume salée et au climat tropical chaud, le granit peut donc se dissoudre et présenter en surface des formations semblables à celles du calcaire.

La faune et la flore soulèvent des questions biologiques…

Dans les petites vasques (kamenitsa), les plantes doivent se contenter de petites quantités de terre, de nutriments et d'eau :

La forme de champignon des roches de calcaire corallien d'Aldabra est due à l'érosion marine, aux coquillages et aux animaux fouisseurs situés au niveau de la mer (ci-dessus).

À marée basse, le lagon de l'atoll d'Aldabra (grande photographie, zone bleu clair) se vide. Le calcaire de la couronne récifale est karstifié.

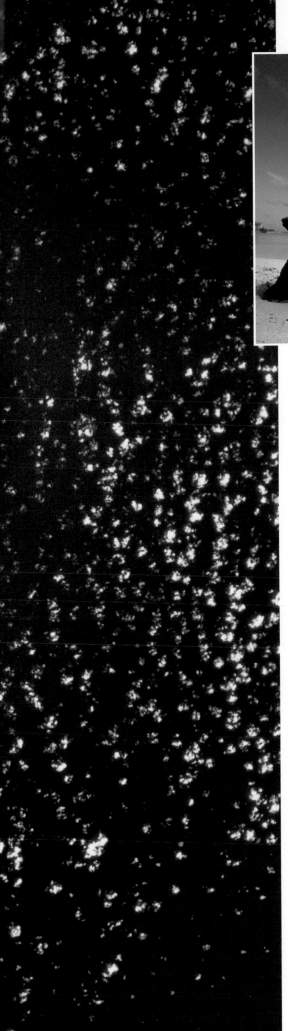

Aldabra est le dernier refuge de la tortue géante dans l'océan Indien. Environ 150 000 de ces reptiles à carapace peuplent aujourd'hui l'atoll.

c'est le cas du bois de natte des Seychelles au parfum musqué, une espèce endémique. Parmi les espèces n'existant qu'aux Seychelles, on compte le cocotier de mer, qui porte des noix de coco gigantesques. Au total, un tiers des espèces botaniques indigènes sont endémiques. La faune, elle aussi, se caractérise par un certain endémisme, par exemple, la tourterelle des Seychelles, le hibou des Seychelles, mais aussi 4 grenouilles endémiques et 7 espèces de cécilies, des amphibiens vermiformes.

Le fait qu'un grand nombre d'espèces endémiques se développent sur des îles éloignées est normal, mais la présence d'amphibiens endémiques aux Seychelles a de quoi étonner. De fait, ils sont absents de la plupart des îles océaniques, probablement parce qu'ils peuvent parcourir tout au plus 1 000 km sur les océans et que ces îles se trouvent ainsi hors de leur portée. De plus, la distance entre les Seychelles et le continent africain, leur voisin le plus proche, riche en amphibiens, est nettement plus grande.

Les liens de parenté entre les espèces animales et végétales acclimatées aux Seychelles et celles d'ailleurs sont une autre énigme. Ainsi, il existe aux Seychelles une espèce de plante du genre *Amaracarpus* que l'on ne trouve autrement que sur l'île de Java, à 5 000 km de là.

... qui trouvent des réponses géologiques

Ces parents « exotiques » constituent un élément primordial pour percer le mystère des Seychelles. Ils révèlent que cet archipel de l'océan Indien est un fragment de terre auquel étaient autrefois soudés l'Afrique, l'Asie, Madagascar, ainsi que d'autres continents et îles : le Gondwana, détaché du supercontinent Pangée il y a 200 millions d'années et qui a continué à se morceler. Tous ces fragments ont été entraînés dans diverses directions par les courants du manteau terrestre, jusque dans l'hémisphère Sud. Celui des Seychelles était alors encore relié au sous-continent indien qui, comme elles, se composait en grande partie de granits primitifs. Il y a quelque 140 millions d'années, des failles se sont ouvertes entre l'Inde et les Seychelles et ces dernières ont commencé à dériver vers le nord-est. 70 millions d'années plus tard, tel un gigantesque iceberg, elles se sont « échouées » sur une zone de fracture placée en travers de leur route. Depuis lors, ce massif granitique est une île géologique au sein de la croûte océanique.

Des îles d'exception

Les Amirantes, Farquhar et Aldabra, sont dépourvues d'affleurements granitiques : elles se composent de calcaire récifal et de sable corallien meuble reposant sur un support basaltique. Les quatre groupes d'îles forment une chaîne s'étirant des îles de Mahé vers le sud-ouest jusqu'à 700 km des côtes africaines, aux îles Aldabra. Ces dernières, petites et plates, sont des atolls en forme d'anneau ou de fer à cheval qui ponctuent l'océan bleu de taches vertes.

L'île principale de ce dernier groupe, Aldabra, n'est habitée que par des chercheurs qui l'ont baptisée les « Galápagos de l'océan Indien » en raison de sa flore et de sa faune uniques d'un endémisme élevé. Outre la plus grande population de tortues géantes du monde, cette île abrite notamment la roussette d'Aldabra, une chauve-souris, et le râle de Cuvier, le dernier oiseau ne volant pas qui ait survécu dans l'océan Indien.

UNE TERRE

ÉCARTELÉE

Dans l'île du Sud, en Nouvelle-Zélande, les oiseaux qui ne volent pas, comme le kiwi (petite photo), passent leur temps au sol, tandis que d'autres utilisent leurs ailes pour nager. Sur cette île alpine du Pacifique, dont les glaciers sont prolongés par une forêt dense sempervirente, les extrêmes se rencontrent. C'est le reflet des déplacements massifs qui ont eu lieu dans le sous-sol.

DES OASIS DANS

UN DÉSERT DE GLACE

Le terme Antarctique évoque un continent inhabité, enfoui sous la glace, et les manchots qui peuplent l'étroite bande côtière non englacée. Or, au beau milieu de ce désert de glace, la terre Victoria est une minuscule oasis de vie libre de glace : vallées modelées par les violentes tempêtes, lacs salés, comme dans les  déserts arides du globe et créatures qui, contre toutes les lois de la nature, se sont acclimatées à l'environnement hostile.

Le mystère des îles libres de glace

Le continent entourant le pôle Sud couvre une superficie de 14 millions de kilomètres carrés. L'Antarctique est donc presque deux fois plus grand que l'Australie, sa cousine géologique, les deux continents étant des fragments du Gondwana d'origine. Les roches de ce continent austral disloqué affleurent en de rares endroits, 98 % des terres étant recouvertes d'une calotte glaciaire épaisse de 4 800 m. Celle-ci pèse tellement sur la croûte terrestre que le socle rocheux s'est enfoncé et se trouve entre quelques centaines et des milliers de mètres en dessous du niveau de la mer.

Sachant que 98 % du territoire sont englacés, on peut se demander pourquoi les glaciers ont épargné les 2 % restants. En effet, ils se prolongent jusque dans les grandes échancrures des mers de Ross et de Weddell et, bien au-delà de la ligne côtière, constituent des plates-formes glaciaires dépassant 800 km de longueur, comme la banquise de Ross. Or, à proximité immédiate de ces gigantesques masses de glace flottantes, d'une superficie égale à celle de la France, quelques vallées de la chaîne Transantarctique offrent des surfaces désenglacées. S'agit-il du même phénomène de régression glaciaire que celui observé actuellement dans les hautes montagnes, partout dans le monde ?

Les stries glaciaires pour témoins

Sur la terre Victoria, partie australe de la chaîne Transantarctique bordée par la mer de Ross, 6 grandes vallées se succèdent du sud au nord : Taylor, Wright, McKelvey, Balham, Victoria et Barwick. Elles mesurent 5 à 10 km de largeur et 15 à 80 km de longueur. À l'ouest, de hautes croupes de montagne les séparent de l'inlandsis antarctique et leur superficie libre de glace couvre un total de 1 500 km² environ. Elles sont également appelées vallées sèches de McMurdo : sèches parce qu'aucun courant de glace ne les parcourt, et McMurdo parce qu'elles sont à portée d'hélicoptère de la station de recherches McMurdo, sur l'île de Ross.

Les langues glaciaires qui s'écoulent à travers les brèches des versants des vallées pour en atteindre le fond, les remplissant souvent à mi-hauteur, montrent que l'inlandsis n'est pas loin. Ces glaciers auraient-ils, il n'y a pas si longtemps, rempli à ras bord les vallées aujourd'hui sèches et seraient-ils contraints à la régression par l'effet de serre ? De fait, les vallées ont été autrefois totalement englacées, en témoignent les roches striées par la glace charriant des débris de roche dure. Mais ce phénomène a dû se produire il y a au moins 4 millions d'années, l'âge des courants de lave qui se sont écoulés dans certaines des vallées.

Les vallées bénéficient-elles d'un climat plus chaud, à l'image de la péninsule antarctique et de son étroite bande côtière dépourvue de glace ? L'été, pendant quelques semaines, la température moyenne de l'air est supérieure au point de congélation dans les vallées mais, en moyenne annuelle,

La formation des vallées sèches

Les hautes crêtes de la chaîne Transarctique barrent l'accès des courants de glace venant de l'intérieur de l'Antarctique aux oasis déglacées de la terre Victoria. Des vents extrêmement secs et souvent violents empêchent la formation de glaciers autonomes dans ces vallées sèches.

celle du fond des vallées oscille entre – 5 et
– 25 °C, bien en dessous des valeurs pré-
valant sur la côte.

Ce sont les croupes de montagne fermant
les vallées du côté ouest qui les protègent
contre la pénétration des glaciers alentour :
elles sont plus élevées que ces derniers, qui
s'écoulent de l'intérieur du continent glacé
jusqu'à la mer de Ross et alimentent la plate-
forme glaciaire. Ces barrières interdisent
l'accès des vallées aux courants de glace.
Ceux-ci étant particulièrement rapides et
s'écoulant parfois dans une cuvette profonde, comme le Byrd – l'un des plus
rapides glaciers de l'Antarctique, avec une
vitesse de fluage de 750 à 800 m par an –,
la surface du glacier est située bien en dessous des crêtes des montagnes. Et, à section de lit et à masse d'écoulement égales,
une vitesse d'écoulement élevée signifie une
hauteur de glace moindre que pour les
glaciers lents.

Une neige dissipée par le vent

Une autre question se pose : pourquoi n'y
a-t-il pas de glacier autonome dans les vallées
sèches de McMurdo alors que le climat y est
suffisamment froid et que, contrairement
à la tendance mondiale, il l'est de plus
depuis deux décennies ? La réponse se trouve

Le sol dépourvu de glace de la vallée de Wright est creusé de remarquables motifs circulaires et polygonaux. L'alternance permanente du gel et du dégel des couches supérieures du sol provoque le phénomène de la gélifraction – une dégradation des roches en pierres grossières et en terre fine – et crée des figures géométriques.

Les croupes montagneuses empêchent l'invasion des vallées par des masses de glace venant de l'intérieur du continent.

Lorsque les vents froids et secs balaient les vallées, l'air se réchauffe et disperse la neige ou la fait évaporer.

Les vallées sèches n'ont pas d'émissaire. Toutes les matières arrachées aux roches sont lessivées par les eaux de fonte vers les lacs extrêmement salés des extrémités.

Le lac Vanda est situé dans la vaste vallée de Wright. Les couches supérieures d'eau douce plus légère ou d'eau saumâtre se figent en une croûte de glace transparente qui peut atteindre 5 m d'épaisseur. Comme les surfaces terrestres attenantes, elles sont parcourues de fissures. Dessous, l'eau salée et lourde reste liquide même en dessous du point de congélation.

dans l'expression vallées sèches : il neige trop peu (à peine 30 cm par an), il n'a pas plu depuis plusieurs millénaires dans certaines vallées et la majeure partie de la neige fraîche est littéralement dissipée par le vent. Par conséquent, les quelques glaciers autonomes des vallées sèches sont sous-alimentés. Les êtres vivants, qui doivent se contenter de peu de nutriments, s'y développent très lentement mais sont souvent très anciens, tout comme les glaciers insuffisamment alimentés. L'âge du glacier Meserve, dans la vallée de Wright, par exemple, est estimé à 3,4 millions d'années au moins.

Les glaciers réagissent vite aux variations climatiques

Au cours de ces derniers millions d'années, les courants de glace de l'inlandsis antarctique ont dû parvenir à plusieurs reprises à surmonter les barrières montagneuses et à envahir les vallées sèches de la terre Victoria, au moins pour partie. Les dépôts de

moraines et les blocs de roche polis par la glace sont là pour en témoigner.

Il convient de chercher la raison de cet englacement passager hors des vallées, et avant tout dans la banquise de Ross et ses principaux glaciers affluents. En dépit de leur taille, les glaciers gigantesques de l'Antarctique réagissent étonnamment vite aux variations climatiques. Lors de ce qu'on appelle la période d'optimum climatique, il y a entre 5 000 et 8 000 ans, épisode jusqu'ici le plus chaud de l'époque récente (holocène), le glacier Byrd a reculé de quelque 500 km en seulement 1 400 ans. Lorsque le climat a de nouveau refroidi, il s'est à nouveau avancé. En règle générale, quand le climat refroidit, les glaciers augmentent de volume, phénomène qui a contribué à l'englacement provisoire des vallées sèches de McMurdo : à mesure que les glaciers s'étendent, le niveau de la mer baisse car des milliers de kilomètres cubes d'eau se retrouvent fixés sur le continent à l'état solide. Lorsqu'il y a régression marine, les plates-formes glaciaires qui, pour la plupart, flottent sur l'eau, descendent au fond de la mer : par frottement des masses de glace sur le sol, l'écoulement des glaciers perd de la vitesse. Il en résulte un entassement au-dessus de la zone de frottement, à savoir une telle accumulation de blocs de glace que les glaciers sont alors en mesure de franchir les barrières les séparant des vallées sèches.

Les tempêtes antarctiques

L'Antarctique connaît les tempêtes les plus fréquentes et fortes du monde : on y a déjà enregistré des vents de 320 km/h. Les ouragans d'une telle violence, capables d'attaquer les roches les plus dures en projetant contre elles des cristaux de neige acérés et des grains de sable, décapent les roches à la façon d'une sableuse et leur donnent les formes les plus étranges, comme au col de Bull, entre les vallées sèches de McKelvey et de Wright. Normalement, les dunes se composent de grains de sable d'un diamètre maximal de 2 mm : dans celles des vallées de Victoria et de Barwick, les particules mesurent jusqu'à 6 cm de diamètre. Pour transporter de telles charges, le vent doit au moins souffler à 200 km/h : on imagine ce que serait la vie des hommes et des animaux dans un tel enfer !

Le caractère changeant des vents est encore plus étonnant que leur violence. Une brise légère dans les vallées sèches peut être suivie, quelques minutes plus tard, par un

Des tafoni comme en Corse :
l'érosion a altéré de l'intérieur
les roches granitiques des flancs
de la vallée de Wright et facilité
le travail de l'érosion éolienne.

ouragan de force 16. Celui-ci balaie la neige fraîche, privant ainsi les glaciers d'une alimentation déjà pauvre, et l'emmène jusqu'à la mer. Puis, aussi rapidement que la tempête a éclaté au-dessus des vallées, le vent peut se calmer brutalement en quelques minutes. Les sources de ces vents étranges se situent loin de là, sur la calotte glaciaire antarctique, où l'air se refroidit fortement et, de ce fait, devient plus dense et lourd. Ici et là, une masse d'air froid et lourd se met en mouvement, suit la déclivité de la surface glacée jusqu'au littoral et s'abat sur les vallées sous la forme d'un vent descendant froid d'une puissance extrême.

Des oasis inhospitalières

Les surfaces non englacées, appelées oasis de l'Antarctique, couvrent un total de 280 000 km², soit à peu près la superficie de la Nouvelle-Zélande. La côte est dépourvue de végétation, mais pas d'animaux : environ 175 millions de manchots vivent là, auxquels s'ajoute le même nombre d'oiseaux aquatiques et 15 millions de phoques.

La situation est très différente dans les oasis de l'intérieur des terres : il n'y a pas de poissons dans les cours d'eau de fonte qui coulent l'été dans les vallées sèches et tarissent presque aussitôt, un oiseau s'aventure de temps en temps dans ces coins perdus et les mammifères terrestres sont complètement absents, par manque de nourriture. Dans les lieux humides, on trouve ici et là l'une des 80 espèces de mousses indigènes et 200 espèces de lichen tapissent les roches à l'abri du vent. Le reste n'est apparemment que roche nue, en fait peuplée par des algues, champignons et bactéries microscopiques, qui ont trouvé une niche écologique confortable dans les minuscules cavités séparant les grains de grès. Transparents, les grains de mica laissent pénétrer un peu de lumière, les pores de la roche emmagasinent de l'eau et les organismes trouvent leurs nutriments dans les parois de leur habitat. Même les champions de la survie comme les lichens ont du mal à s'accommoder des vallées froides, sèches et venteuses et ne poussent parfois que de 1 cm par an. La faune se résume à quelques invertébrés, essentiellement des puces des glaciers, des araignées, des tardigrades et des filaires.

L'énigme des phoques

Le climat froid et sec de la terre Victoria a momifié des cadavres de phoques. Des centaines de ces animaux sont éparpillés dans les vallées sèches et sur les rives du lac Vanda et d'un lac baptisé ironiquement lac Tchad par un chercheur.

Éloignés de 30 à 120 km de la mer, les phoques sont ici aussi peu à leur place que dans la savane africaine. Ces cadavres sont là depuis 2 500 à 3 500 ans, voire 10 000 ans. On sait que ces animaux se nourrissaient de crevettes, alimentation typique des habitants de la banquise. Contrairement aux phoques d'aujourd'hui, ceux-ci n'avaient pas de mal à se déplacer sur la glace et sur la terre ferme. Pouvant atteindre une vitesse de 25 km/h, ils pouvaient parcourir de grandes distances. Pourquoi ont-ils dû s'éloigner de leur habitat d'origine jusque dans les vallées sèches hostiles, à plus de 1 000 m d'altitude ? La question demeure posée.

Un chercheur a qualifié ces vallées sèches d'intemporelles. De fait, le temps semble s'être arrêté dans ces lieux au moment où les premières formes de vie sont apparues sur terre. Loin sous la carapace de glace, le fond des lacs salés est parfois tapissé de plusieurs mètres d'algues, bactéries, champignons et autres micro-organismes. Au fil des millénaires, ils se sont développés dans une eau qui peut être dix fois plus saline que l'eau de mer et empêche ainsi que les lacs gèlent complètement l'hiver. Dans les couches d'eau profondes très salées, la température est plus élevée car le rayonnement solaire pénètre la glace transparente : son énergie est rapidement absorbée par la saumure des fonds. Au fond du lac Vanda, par exemple, l'eau peut atteindre sous la glace une température de 25 °C.

Crédits

Abréviations : h : haut, m : milieu, b : bas, g : gauche, d : droite.

Photographies

Couverture : haut (Bryce Canyon) Olivier Grunewald ; bas (euphorbe des Canaries) BIOS/WILDLIFE PICTURES/H. Verbiesen ; milieu : Ingo Arndt/SAVE BILD ; Berbhard Edmaier/GEOPHOT ; Frans Lanting/SAVE BILD.

1 g : TCL/Bavaria ; h.d : Ingo Arndt/Save-Bild; m.d : Bernhard Edmaier GEOPHOT; b.d : Frans Lanting/Save-Bild. 5 Doug Williams. 2/3 Simon Fraser/SPL/FOCUS. 6 m : Shashin Koubou Co. Ltd./IFA-Bilderteam ; b : Photo Resource/Mauritius. 7 h : Martin Bond/SPL/FOCUS ; m : Stock Image/Premium ; b : Bernhard Edmaier, GEOPHOT. 10 d.h.e.b : Klaus D. Francke/Bilderberg ; E. Kristof/Nat. Geographic/Premium ; RAGA/zefa visual media ; Thomas Peter Widmann. 11 d.h.e.b : Klaus Bossemeyer/Bilderberg ; Hauke Dressler/LOOK, Waltraud Klammet ; Snowdon/Hoyer/FOCUS ; Ph. Bourseiller/FOCUS ; Max Galli/LOOK. 12 h.g : Snowdon/Hoyer/FOCUS ; m.g : Pcholkin/Mauritius ; b.g : Karl-Heinz Bochow ; m : Paul Spierenburg ; b.m : Kay Maeritz/LOOK ; b.d : Ph. Bourseiller/FOCUS. 13 d.h.e.b : P. Arnold/Save-Bild ; George Steinmetz/FOCUS ; Rainer Hackenberg ; Axel Krause/laif ; Sarawak Tourism Board-Deutschland, Veitshöchheim. 14 h : Hanf/Save-Bild ; m : Hauke Dressler/LOOK ; b : C. Emmler/laif. 15 d.h.e.b : Prof. Sepp Friedhuber ; Yann Arthus-Bertrand/Altitude ; Nils Reinhard/Okapia ; Huber/laif ; Tim Zielenbach/Contact/FOCUS. 16 d.h.e.b : Günter Lenz/LaTerraMagica ; Manfred Braunger ; Burkard/Bilderberg ; F. Damm/Bildagentur Huber ; Bernhard Edmaier/FOCUS. 17 d.h.e.b : B. & C. Alexander ; Karl Johaentges/LOOK ; Detlef Möbius/f1 online ; Erich Spiegelhalter/FOCUS ; Erich Spiegelhalter/FOCUS. 18 h : age/Mauritius ; m : Gonzales/laif ; b : Geoffrey Cliffort/FOCUS. 19 d.h.e.b : Volkmar E. Janicke ; Thomas Peter Widmann ; Luiz C. Marigo/P. Arnold/Save-Bild ; Carlos Humberto/Contact/FOCUS. 20 h : D. & E. Parer/Auscape/Save-Bild ; m : Jean-Paul Ferrero/Auscape/Save-Bild ; b : Joel Ducange/agence TOP/FOCUS. 21 d.h.e.b : Thomas Peter Widmann ; Hauke Dressler/LOOK ; C. Emmler/laif ; Colin Monteath/Hedgehog House New Zealand. 22/23 Shashin Koubou Co. Ltd./IFA-Bilderteam. 24/25 Snowdon/Hoyer/FOCUS. 25 Patrick Frilet/FOCUS. 27 Günter Lenz/LaTerraMagica. 28/29 Erich Spiegelhalter/FOCUS. 29 Aibo & Peter Göbel. 30 h : Rolf Hicker Rainbow Productions ; b : Aibo & Peter Göbel. 32 Harald Lange. **Panorama** Titre : Bernhard Edmaier, GEOPHOT ; Double-page : Yann Arthus-Bertrand/Altitude ; Intérieur : Photo Resource/Mauritius, h.g : Bernhard Edmaier/GEOPHOT, b.g : G. Brad Lewis/SPL/FOCUS ; Dos : Philippe Bourseiller/FOCUS. 33 g : Longman Group Limited 1983, reprinted by permission of Pearson Education Limited ; d : Erich Spiegelhalter/FOCUS 35 h : Erich Spiegelhalter/FOCUS ; b : Frieder Blickle/Bilderberg. 36/37 Bernhard Edmaier/FOCUS. 37 Erich Spiegelhalter/FOCUS. 39 h : Erich Spiegelhalter/FOCUS ; m : Rainer Hackenberg. 40 Peter Mathis. 40/41 Rainer Hackenberg. 41 Jay Dickman/Matrix/FOCUS. 42/43 Axel Krause/laif. 43 blickwinkel.de/W. Schmidbauer. 45 h : Catherine Karnow/Woodfin Camp/FOCUS ; b : Aurora/Bilderberg. 46 h : C. M. Bahr/Save-Bild ; b : Brian Kenney/Wildlife. 46/47 Aurora/Bilderberg. 48, 48/49 : George Steinmetz/FOCUS. 50 Bruno Baumann. 50/51, 51 : George Steinmetz/FOCUS. 52 Georg Fischer/Bilderberg. 52/53 Geoffrey Clifford/FOCUS. 55 h : Georg Fischer/Bilderberg ; b : Peter Gebhard/FOCUS. 56 Dr. Michael Baales. 56/57 Waltraud Klammet. 59 G. Krämer/Helga Lade. 60 Dr. Michael Baales. 60/61 Snowdon/Hoyer/FOCUS. 61 Aibo & Peter Göbel. 62 h.g : D. Nill/Save-Bild ; h.m : Jan Jepsen/FOCUS. 62/63 Rainer Hackenberg. 64/65 Ralf Freyer. 65 h : Ralf Freyer ; b : Hans Reinhard/Reinhard-Tierfoto. 66/67 Joel Ducange/Agence TOP/FOCUS. 67 Paul Spierenburg. 68 Stefan Weindl. 69 Klaus-D. Francke/Bilderberg. 70 Gavriel Jecan/Save-Bild. 70/71 Jean-Paul Ferrero/Auscape/Save-Bild. 72/73 Burkard/Bilderberg. 73 Paul Chesley/FOCUS. 74, 75, 77 : Peter Mathis (5). 78/79 Klaus Bossemeyer/Bilderberg. 79 Stefan Weindl. 81 Wilkin Spitta. 82 h : Wilkin Spitta ; b : Stefan Weindl. 83 Erich Spiegelhalter/FOCUS. 84/85 Photo Resource/Mauritius. 86 Vaughan Fleming/SPL/FOCUS. 86/87 Hauke Dressler/LOOK. 88 Bert Wiklund. 89 g. Britt Marie Lindström/Länsstyrelsen, Västernorrlands Län ; d. Länsstyrelsen, Västernorrlands Län. 90/91, 91 : Ralf Freyer. 92/93 Ph. Bourseiller/FOCUS. 93 Wilkin Spitta. 94 Enrico Ferorreli/DOT/FOCUS. 95, 96 : Celentano/laif. **Panorama** Titre : Rainer Kiedrowski ; Double-page : Bernhard Edmaier, GEOPHOT ; Intérieur : Bernhard Edmaier, GEOPHOT, h.d : Rudi Schmidt, b.d : Bernhard Edmaier, GEOPHOT ; Dos : David Parker/SPL/FOCUS. 97 g. J. Warren, April 21, 1990/U.S. Geological Survey/Alaska Volcano Observatory ; d : Günter Lenz/LaTerraMagica.. 98 Doug Williams. 99 dpa. 100 S. Kaufman/Save-Bild. 100/101 Bernhard Edmaier/SPL/FOCUS. 101 h : Rolf Hicker Rainbow Productions ; m : U. Walz/Save-Bild. 102 Hans Sautter/FOCUS. 102/103 Rainer Hackenberg. 105 Rainer Hackenberg (2). 106 Detlef Lämmel/Okapia. 106/107 E. Kristof/Nat. Geographic/Premium. 108/109 Michael Peuckert/FOCUS. 109 Otto Stadler. 110/111 Thomas Peter Widmann. 111 Chuck O'Rear/FOCUS. 113 g : Bernhard Edmaier/FOCUS ; d : Thomas Peter Widmann. 114 M. Kirchgessner/Bilderberg. 114/115 Hauke Dressler/LOOK. 115 Boehnke/zefa visual media. 116/117 Gunter Hartmann. 117 Nigel Dennis/NAS/Okapia. 118/119 The Natural History/IFA-Bilderteam. 119 Michael Martin/LOOK. 120/121 Kay Maeritz/LOOK. 121 C. Boisvieux/Bilderberg. 123 h : Joachim Chwaszcza/LOOK ; b : Craig Lovell/Eagle Visions Photography. 124/125 Aibo & Peter Göbel. 125 g : Mike Andrews/Animals Animals/FOCUS ; d : C.M. Bahr/Save-Bild. 126 Craig Lovell/Eagle Visions Photography. 126/127 K. Wanecek/Okapia. 128/129, 129 : Klaus-D. Francke/Bilderberg. 130 J. Beck/Mauritius. 131 Klaus-D. Francke/Bilderberg. 132 LaTerraMagica. 132/133 Ph. Bourseiller/FOCUS. 134, 135 : LaTerraMagica. 136/137 Tim Zielenbach/Contact/FOCUS. 137 Frans Lanting/Minden/Premium. 138 Paul Spierenburg. 139 h : Michael Peuckert/FOCUS ; b : Paul Spierenburg. 140/141 Gonzales/laif. 141 Vision 21/LaTerraMagica. 143 Prof. Sepp Friedhuber. 144 Vision 21/LaTerraMagica. 144/145 Roda/Premium. 145 dpa. 146 Javier G. Corripio. 147 Prof. Sepp Friedhuber. 148/149 Martin Bond/SPL/FOCUS. 150/151 Jean-Paul Ferrero/Auscape/Save-Bild. 151 B. & L. Cropp/Auscape/Save-Bild. 152 h : M. Cavardine/Bios/Okapia ; b : Thomas Peter Widmann. 154 Parc National de Miguasha. 154/155, 156/157 : Karl Johaentges/LOOK. 158 Rainer Kiedrowski. 158/159 Alfred Vollmer/LaTerraMagica. 159 Thomas Peter Widmann. 160 Rolf Kunz/Save-Bild. **Panorama** Titre : Hans Larsson/Matrix/FOCUS ; Double-page : Bernhard Edmaier, GEOPHOT ; Intérieur : François Gohier/Ardea London, h.g : AFP/National Park Service/dpa, b.g : Paul Sereno/Matrix/FOCUS ; Dos : Louie Psihoyos/Matrix/FOCUS. 161 g : G. Winter ; d : Manfred Braunger. 163 h : Urs Kluyver/FOCUS ; b : G. Winter. 164/165 Max Galli/LOOK. 165 Ulrich Sauerborn. 167 h : Mehlig/Mauritius ; b : E. Kuchling/Save-Bild. 168/169 F. Damm/Bildagentur Huber. 169 Musée national d'histoire naturelle, Stuttgart. 170/171 Delpho/Wildlife. 172 g : Christian Heeb/LOOK ; d : Karl Johaentges/LOOK. 173 g. Wunsch/IFA-Bilderteam ; d : Christian Heeb/LOOK. 174 M. Pforr/Save-Bild. 174/175 RAGA/zefa visuel media. 175 h : Othmar Baumli ; b : I. Arndt/Save-Bild. 179 Klaus Wanecek/Okapia. 180 h : Othmar Baumli ; b : (c) 2001 Gletschergarten, Luzern. 181 Werner Dieterich. 182/183 Detlef Möbius/f1 online. 183 Rainer Martini/LOOK. 184 A. Maywald/Save-Bild. 184/185 Maggi Hallahan. 186/187 B. Fuhrmann/Save-Bild. 187 Christian Heeb/LOOK. 188 John Reader/SPL/FOCUS. 188/189 Yann Arthus-Bertrand/Altitude. 189 Günter Lenz/LaTerraMagica. 190 Michael Martin/LOOK. 192 John Reader/SPL/FOCUS. 192/193 - 197 : Prof. Sepp Friedhuber (7). 198 Ralf Kreuels/Bilderberg. 198/199 Karl-Heinz Bochow. 200 h : Joachim Chwaszcza ; b : M. Kirchgessner/Bilderberg. 201 h : Joachim Chwaszcza ; b : Gerald Buthaud/Cosmos/FOCUS. 202 Chris Martin Bahr/Ardea London. 202/203 age/Mauritius. 203 Jeffrey Jay Foxx. 204/205 age/Mauritius. 205 Paul W.